Listening to Others

SUNY series in Latin American Cinema
———————
Ignacio M. Sánchez Prado and Leslie L. Marsh, editors

Listening to Others
Eduardo Coutinho's Documentary Cinema

Edited by
NATALIA BRIZUELA AND KRISTA BRUNE

Cover image of Eduardo Coutinho (from his 2006 film *O fim e o principio*); used by permission from the Universidade de Sao Paulo.

Published by State University of New York Press, Albany

© 2024 State University of New York

All rights reserved

Printed in the United States of America

No part of this book may be used or reproduced in any manner whatsoever without written permission. No part of this book may be stored in a retrieval system or transmitted in any form or by any means including electronic, electrostatic, magnetic tape, mechanical, photocopying, recording, or otherwise without the prior permission in writing of the publisher.

For information, contact State University of New York Press, Albany, NY
www.sunypress.edu

Library of Congress Cataloging-in-Publication Data

Names: Brizuela, Natalia, editor. | Brune, Krista, editor.
Title: Listening to others : Eduardo Coutinho's documentary cinema / edited by
    Natalia Brizuela and Krista Brune.
Description: Albany : State University of New York Press, [2024] | SUNY series in
    Latin American Cinema | Includes bibliographical references and index.
Identifiers: ISBN 9781438497914 (hardcover : alk. paper) | ISBN 9781438497907
    (ebook) | ISBN 9781438497891 (pbk. : alk. paper)
Further information is available at the Library of Congress.

10 9 8 7 6 5 4 3 2 1

Contents

List of Illustrations — ix

Introduction: Listening to Others in Eduardo Coutinho's Documentary Cinema — 1
Natalia Brizuela

Part I. Media Ecologies

1. Coutinho's Ecology: Space, Place, and the Disappearing Location — 19
   Jens Andermann

2. Returning to the Sertão in the Films of Eduardo Coutinho — 37
   Ashley Brock

3. The Audiovisual Record and the Corporeal Present: Another Dialogue in Eduardo Coutinho's Cinema of Conversation — 65
   Gustavo Procopio Furtado

Part II. Politics and the Documentary Image

4. From CPC to Videofilmes: Eduardo Coutinho's Trajectory as a Political Filmmaker — 89
   Krista Brune

5. Cinema of/as Garbage: Eduardo Coutinho's Politics of Image from *Jogo de cena* to *Boca de lixo* — 111
   Luz Horne

6. Eduardo Coutinho and *Globo Repórter*: Between Social Documentary and the Mass Media in Dictatorship-Era Brazil   135
Rielle Navitski

Part III. Performing the Self and Others

7. *Um dia na vida*: Copy, Enunciation, Chatter   155
Adriana Johnson

8. To Act or to Act: Present, Presence, and Representation in Eduardo Coutinho's *Jogo de cena*   177
Brenno Kenji Kaneyasu

9. Song, Self, and Sound in Eduardo Coutinho's Cinema   197
Fernando Pérez Villalón

Part IV. On Time and Endings

10. Open Futures: On Ends and Endings in the Conversational Documentaries of Eduardo Coutinho and Errol Morris   223
Bruno Carvalho

11. Parting Glances: The Posthumous Coutinho   243
Nilo Fernando Couret

12. The Right Moment: *Kairos* and the Documentary Cinema of Eduardo Coutinho   263
Vinicius Navarro

Part V. Coutinho in His Own Words
(translations by Flora Thomson-DeVeaux)

13. Gaze in Documentary: Statement/Letter to Paulo Paranaguá   289
Eduardo Coutinho

14. The Melancholy of Twilight *Eduardo Coutinho*	295
15. A Latin Hollywood in Search of Markets *Eduardo Coutinho*	301
16. A Chess Match Between Death and the Knight *Eduardo Coutinho*	307

Part VI. Critical Insights from Coutinho's Contemporaries

(translations by Flora Thomson-DeVeaux)

17. On the Film That Never Was *Ferreira Gullar*	321
18. Brazil by Our Own Selves *José Carlos Avellar*	325
19. Mouth Full of Trash *José Carlos Avellar*	335
20. Victory Over the Ash Heap of History *Jean-Claude Bernardet*	341
21. *Jogo de cena* *Jean-Claude Bernardet*	353
Contributors	363
Index	365

Illustrations

Figure 2.1	Leocádio holds forth on the difference between proper words and common words in Eduardo Coutinho's *O fim e o princípio*.	46
Figure 2.2	Coutinho (right) exchanges a look with someone off-screen during the prolonged silence of João Mariano (left) in *Cabra marcado para morrer*.	51
Figure 3.1	Djalma seeing his younger self on the television set in *Peões*.	80
Figure 3.2	A laptop, held by Cícero, shows an image of him holding photographs in *Sobreviventes de Galiléia*.	81
Figure 4.1	Coutinho and Elizabeth Teixeira in the penultimate scene of *Cabra marcado para morrer*.	97
Figure 4.2	Roberto asks Coutinho if he would give him a job in *Edifício Master*.	104
Figure 5.1	Image of Corcovado overshadowed by steam from garbage and by prey birds from *Boca de lixo*.	112
Figure 5.2	Portraits of the garbage collectors in *Boca de lixo*.	123
Figure 5.3	Garbage collectors watching scenes from the documentary that they starred in near the end of *Boca de lixo*.	127
Figure 6.1	A resident of Ouricuri shows Coutinho and his crew roots consumed out of necessity during a devastating drought.	144

x | Illustrations

Figure 6.2	*Theodorico, o imperador do sertão* highlights how media technologies advance the coronel's exercise of power on his estate.	147
Figure 9.1	A girl singing in *Boca de lixo*.	208
Figure 9.2	Affective responses to music in *As canções*.	212
Figure 10.1	Geraldo asking Coutinho "Were you ever a *peão*?" in *Peões*.	236
Figure 11.1	Alessandra, a "true liar," in *Edifício Master*.	250
Figure 12.1	Eduardo Coutinho in the opening sequence of *Last Conversations*.	267
Figure 12.2	Archival material included in a scene from *Twenty Years Later*.	273
Figure 12.3	Archival material included in a scene from *Metalworkers*.	273
Figure 12.4	Singing performance in *The Songs*.	277
Figure 17.1	Participants watching footage of the aborted 1964 film in *Cabra marcado para morrer*.	323
Figure 19.1	The conversation begins with images in *Boca de lixo*.	337

Introduction

Listening to Others in Eduardo Coutinho's Documentary Cinema

Natalia Brizuela

Eduardo Coutinho's entire body of documentary production, with more than twenty works (for television, on video, and on film) spanning half a century, centers on filmed encounters between himself and others and their exchange before a visible camera. Over the years Coutinho slowly removed everything that could distract from this encounter, leaving not much beyond voice and listening. He never hid the modes of production and always acknowledged the construction, mediation, and artificiality of the encounter, with its voices and acts of listening, and of documentary procedures and modes in general. This focus on encounters and exchanges between bodies as filmed by a camera and crew, homing in on voice, listening, and a reflexivity on the mediation of said encounter, is one of the most salient characteristics of Coutinho's oeuvre, as Latin American critics and filmmakers who perceive him as one of the looming figures of documentary in the region have pointed out. Between the early 1960s and 2015, when Coutinho passed away before completing *Últimas conversas* (*Last Conversations*, 2015), his hyper focalization on these three elements—voice, listening, and a reflexive presence of camera and crew—as the essentials of documentary became a minimalist aesthetic and an ethical practice.

Yet an attention to voice and listening, and a desire to film encounters and exchanges in a reflexive way, is not exclusive to Coutinho. These elements, in fact, are at the center of documentary at large, its histories, practices, and changes on a global scale. Documentary has always been at least equally if not overly invested in the audible vis-à-vis the visible. A desire for stories, information, and knowledge has often mobilized the impulse for and production of documentary. Changing vocal conventions and experiments have conveyed these stories, information, and knowledge from the world via film. Whether using titles, voice-over, voice-of-God narration, interviews, or conversations, documentaries have thought they were offering the voice of the world to spectators since the earliest newsreels and silent documentaries. An interest in "giving voice" to those who otherwise have none in the public sphere has motivated many documentary films. Since the 1980s, documentary practitioners and critics have been signaling and reflecting on the impossibilities of authentic representation. As a result, they have created a range of formal devices, including the appearance of camera and crew on-screen, that reveal the means of production and explore the sonic and haptic possibilities of the genre.

"The category of voice has become central to documentary studies," as Pooja Rangan notes (280), and has overtaken discussions on documentary cinema in the United States since the late 1980s to such an extent that is has also affected documentary production. With his 1983 essay "The Voice of Documentary," Bill Nichols helped to spark this attention to the voice by stressing the verbal over the imagistic as the ethical and aesthetic drive of documentary. Yet, while he used the concept occasionally to refer to the actual speech of characters in films, he mostly employed voice as a metaphor for a film's social point of view and the corresponding organization of materials to convey that viewpoint to the public. As Rangan astutely observes, this hyper focalization on voice as metaphor within documentary film studies has in fact paid little attention to voice itself in the context of a growing field of sound studies. This critical discourse also overlooks new frameworks for thinking about documentary that do not rely on the humanitarian and liberal paradigm of "giving voice" that has been key since at least the 1930s. Rangan turns to Trinh T. Minh-Ha's early writings on documentary and authenticity, where the critic and filmmaker argues that "there is no such thing as documentary" (Trinh 29) if documentary is defined by its project of giving voice, since the voices in documentary are the product of mediations and therefore the fictional core of documentary when framed in such a way. In Rangan's reading of the overdetermined centrality of voice to documentary studies and production, which often overlooks "speaking voices in documentary," she proposes the concept of *audibility* as an organizational and theoretical vector for documentary studies. The concept of audibility allows Rangan to offer a clearer definition of voice that remains expansive while also paying attention to what happens between the voices and those who receive them: "voice is the product of sonic forms and auditory practices that render sound meaningful and call into being practices of listening that resonate with those meanings" (282).

Rangan's redefinition of the voice in documentary helps to frame this edited volume on Coutinho's documentary practice. Like Rangan's reconceptualization of voice, which invites a "relation or resonance . . . between these felt but often unspoken forms of speaking and listening" (282), the chapters in this collection examine the shaping of a listening ear that responds to the call of the documentary's voice. Coutinho's films are as much about the voices as about the listening, primarily his own but also ours as the films' spectators, that these voices summon. By building on Minh-Ha's earlier critique of documentary as an immediate and transparent expression of a true self, Rangan also allows us to think further about Coutinho's attention to voice as an investment in the performatic manifestation of embodied acts. His films resist any belief in voice as heralding the emergence of hidden truths or revelations of a self. Coutinho's documentaries never hide the camera, the director, or other crew members, and instead always make the mediated encounter visible to the audience. This reflexivity is coupled with a growing emphasis on long takes that make time and room for the character to take stage, as we see in the last shot in *Cabra marcado para morrer* (1964–1984) when Elizabeth Teixeira gives her last speech, or when the women and men speak to Coutinho in *Edifício Master* (2002).[1]

Critics and scholars in Brazil and other places in Latin America have described Coutinho's documentary practice as a "cinema of conversation" and "a savage anthropology" (Grupo Revbelando Imágenes), as a "cinema of relation" (Saraiva 558) and a body of work "based on the spoken word" (562), as an "intersubjective universe" (Xavier 612) created by a "master of interaction" (622), and as the "the libertarian insurrection of enunciation" (Bezerra 408).[2] These observations all point to one overarching ethical concern and aesthetic choice: an attention to conversation and enunciation by letting the voice run wild. Following these critics, we could state that the encounter, which took place on film between Coutinho and the people he filmed, was a becoming savage of anthropology precisely because the encounters and conversations between Coutinho and "others" took place with no desire to systematize, organize, or understand them, as classic anthropology and its visual counterpart, ethnographic film, have historically done. Instead, the encounters in Coutinho's films took place so that the voice could unfurl, without restrictions and in insurrection. This approach to the voice explains why Coutinho's documentaries are far from ethnographic cinema or news reporting, which closely relate to documentary but are distinct from it. Ethnographic and news reporting strategies and formulae are sometimes extremely close in Coutinho's documentaries, perhaps because of the years he spent working in news reporting before becoming a documentary filmmaker. The attention to the relation between the listener and the voice might raise the specter of a possible ethnographic drive in Coutinho, especially because of the socioeconomic, racial, and at times religious distance between him and the characters in his films, and the scholarly and critical use of the term "others" to refer to his characters. One distinction between documentary—and particularly Coutinho's documentaries—and ethnography and news reporting is that the latter forms operate to offer didactic information on predetermined topics, places, or peoples. Watching an ethnographic film or news coverage is meant to educate and to convey a truth to those watching. Coutinho does not approach the people he speaks to as anthropological subjects of study or as the "others" of a scientific inquiry. His humanism is critical of any belief in objective, scientific, or single truths. Coutinho approaches people for relation, resonance, or dissonance, and to participate, as a listener, in the appearance (or emergence) of fantastic characters in front of the camera.

The presence of the camera, at a close range, foments the performative dimension of the exposure. The camera functions as both a technological apparatus—it records, so that it can be archived and replayed—and a theatrical device that creates the scene of address. The camera's frame delimits a stage. In the setting of such a stage, the "I" lets go and breaks character—the character built over the course of her life given the set of norms and possibilities—and stages a revelation. Coutinho developed a film practice that waited for and listened to these moments of revelation. This is, as this volume suggests, Coutinho's *cinema of listening*.

Initially, Coutinho's filmed encounters were framed by the interview—a go-to strategy in television and beyond from the 1960s well into the 1990s. If we take the six films Coutinho made during the years he worked for *Globo Repórter* (1975–1984) as his first documentaries, the interview emerges as the nodular strategy through which he meets others and their worlds in at least three of those early films—*Seis dias de Ouricuri* (*Six Days in Ouricuri*, 1976), *O pistoleiro da Serra Talhada* (The Gunman of the Serra Talhada, 1976), and *Theodorico, o imperador do sertão* (*Theodorico, the Sertão Emperor*, 1978). Reflecting the emergence of his documentary practice during those years, Coutinho said that "[he] learned how to talk to people and how to film" (qtd. in Lins, *O documentário* 20) when he worked for television—even when television, rightly so, was fiercely criticized as one of the sites of power where dictatorial rule, industrial sectors, and the bourgeoisie became entangled in Brazil at the time. The irony is worth stressing; during the military dictatorship, while working in the belly of the beast in one of the most reactionary and right-wing fields imaginable for a politically engaged artist, Coutinho learned to "talk to people," to engage in conversation, and to listen, as Rielle Navitski and Krista Brune point out in their chapters in this book. Coutinho himself reflected on his years at Globo and the dictatorship in "Gaze in Documentary. Statement/Letter to Paulo Paranaguá," an essay specifically translated into English for this book and included in the section "Coutinho in His Own Words."

During his television years, the encounters occurred as interviews, as dictated by the journalism genre, but he nevertheless practiced the art of listening by allowing others to express themselves unscripted. As a result, the other emerged as a voice situated in the time of the encounter with Coutinho. For instance, in *Seis dias de Ouricuri*, a man from Brazil's drought-stricken Northeast enumerates all the roots that the famished population had been forced to eat. The shot seems to go on for too long since Coutinho chose not to edit it, instead opening the encounter to the unexpected contingency of duration. According to João Moreira Salles, this sequence is the ground zero for all of Coutinho's cinema as it indicates what will unfold in his documentary practice (Salles 368). To engage in conversation and learn to listen, Coutinho needed to abandon the interview so the encounter could be driven by the sensible appearance of the other, which takes time. This approach rejects orienting the other toward a preestablished script about whom they represent.

The interview was still present in Coutinho's first and best-known documentary feature, *Cabra marcado para morrer* (1964–1984). The film was originally conceived during the director's years with the Centro Popular de Cultura (CPC, People's Cultural Center) as a fictionalized reenactment of events leading to northeastern peasant leader João Pedro Teixeira's 1962 murder. Nonprofessional actors would play either themselves, as was the case with his widow, Elizabeth Teixeira, or key figures in these historical events. The 1964 military coup interrupted this initial production, with only about forty percent of the script shot. In 1981, Coutinho returned to northeastern Brazil to locate and interview the people involved in the 1964 fiction film. Coutinho wanted to know what had happened in their lives during the twenty-year hiatus, to listen to them, and to shift the film from fiction to documentary. He was never interested in returning to the halted production of the fictionalized historical event, which he had questioned during the original shooting because of the disconnect between what the script expected in terms of voice and the people's real cadences and modalities of expressing themselves. He had placed the actors in straitjackets where they were meant to stand in for certain rural residents and Brazilian archetypes.

It was the voice of others as themselves—or whomever they wanted to be for the camera and for Coutinho and his minuscule crew—without a script that brought Coutinho's film back to life. His experience with interviews as a television reporter helped him to stage the encounter of the final film's opening sequence, where participants in 1981 watched footage that had survived from the original shoot. Building on his work at Globo, Coutinho included elements of the camera, equipment, and crew in the shooting, thus breaking the fourth wall and any illusion of objectivity. Like in *Seis dias de Ouricuri*, *Cabra marcado para morrer* features encounters that diverge from the interview format as the camera continued to film people while their voices go adrift in an act that destabilizes the implicit hierarchy of interviews. The chapters by Ashley Brock and Krista Brune in this volume offer readings of *Cabra* as, respectively, one of Coutinho's sertão films and a key political film.

By the 1990s, Coutinho's use of the interview as the framing device for encounters was replaced by unscripted and lengthy conversations. An important turning point toward the "cinema de conversa" occurred in *Santo forte* (*The Mighty Spirit*, 1999), which he shot in a Rio de Janeiro favela in the late 1990s. In 1997, he told film critic José Carlos Avellar that he wanted to make a film "baseado prioritariamente na fala de pessoas comuns, sem narração" (focused primarily on common people's speech, without narration). The Portuguese noun *fala*, from the verb *falar* (to speak), is usually translated as speech, but it can also mean utterance. Because utterances as speech acts carry social meanings and offer worlds rather than interiorities, they are always already dialogic. What is expressed in an utterance is traversed by extra-linguistic statements. Coutinho's documentaries attest to an interest, or even a passion, in *fala* as what cannot be contained by linguistic forms of expression. Given the fraying of the spoken and the deep non-linguistic forms of expression in this concept of *falas*, I prefer to translate the term as utterances, which suggests a less logocentric understanding of communication. *Falas* as utterances also signal the deep and often unknown historical layers present in the texture of any voice. Coutinho's films reveal the entire field of gestures and non-linguistic forms of expressions—interruptions, pauses, twitches, repetitions, and so on—as forms of communication and relationality that offer a less scripted form of presence than verbal communication. Avellar supported Coutinho's dream of capturing these *falas* and helped with the production by making video equipment and tapes accessible, which were key for the emergence of his "cinema of conversation." On video, people could continue to talk freely for longer than on film, and Coutinho could record their silences, interruptions, and mistakes without feeling forced to edit because of the expense or film's material limitations. The nonsignifying elements of utterances thus could be more easily depicted.

Almost every documentary Eduardo Coutinho directed between 1976 and 2014 was structured exclusively through different types of encounters, moving from interviews to conversations. The sole exception to this approach was his 2010 *Um dia na vida*, a ninety-six-minute montage from the nineteen hours of uninterrupted recording from eight channels of public television between October 1 and October 2, 2009. Coutinho only exhibited this rare film if he could lead a conversation with the audience immediately following the screening. Even this exception in his corpus kept the kernel of the encounter format—a conversation, an exchange, or a debate expressing opinions and formulating ideas—as integral to its format, albeit in a para-filmic manner. Along these lines, Adriana Johnson's chapter in this book offers an in-depth study of *Um dia na vida* as an exception in Coutinho's body of work and an invitation for para-filmic encounters.

As the personal encounters on film shifted from interviews to the surprising, errant, and erratic unscripted conversations, Coutinho discarded everything that distracted from the voice of the people he listened to while being recorded He moved away from encountering and depicting others as types, examples, or illustrations of preestablished narratives. With this shift, he aimed to distance his work from abstract and didactic modes central to documentary and to move toward concrete singular lives that paid attention to visible and invisible materialities of being. This focus on voice, without décor, objects, and nondiegetic sound, made Coutinho less interested in capturing fascinating life stories and more interested in the expressive capacities of the body to perform and offer worlds. Critics have highlighted this elimination of everything except the voice as the "purification of the superfluous" (Mattos 27), the development of a "minimalist cinema" (Salles 374), and Coutinho himself as "the master listener" (Lins, "*Últimas conversas*" 44).

Coutinho's attention to voice was interested in singularities or, following Adriana Cavarero's theorization of the voice, the manifestation of "the unique being of each human being" from which a "vocal ontology of uniqueness" can be perceived (173). Cavarero contrasts the ontology of uniqueness that voices offer to the "fictitious entities" (177) or universal categories that philosophy has designated as subjects or individuals. To experience the world through voice is to refuse types and forms that designate people as universal categories devoid of the physical presence of sentient bodies. A focus on singularities needs voice as the expansive audibility of a manifestation with its relations and resonances. Coutinho's documentary practice is a cinema of unique singularities because it is a cinema of the voice, a cinema of conversation, and a cinema of listening.

Even when, in many cases, the subjects of Coutinho's documentaries, the people he encounters and whose voices we encounter as spectators, overlap with figures of the "people"—the peasants in *Cabra marcado*, the favela dwellers in *Santo forte*, the steel factory workers in *Peões* (*Metalworkers*, 2004)—they never appear as types or as stand-ins for the opinion of a group they supposedly belong to, or as the voices of the until-then unheard. Coutinho's documentaries do not take on the work of politics in the literal sense as a form of extension, repair, and compensation of the failure of democracy, be it because of authoritarian rule or because of its neoliberal structure. Instead, his films move away from the epic tales of transcendental collective subjects—the people—to forge the space for subjects to find their own voice and perform their own accounts, in their own way, with no preestablished narrative, aim, or purpose.

When Coutinho moves away from the interview format toward conversations as the exclusive technique for his growing documentary practice, he does so during the 1990s interview boom in Brazil and elsewhere. This global trend occurs in the context of a democratically stable moment with no extreme forms of social unrest in Brazil and the rest of Latin America. Instead, it is a period marked by returns to democracy in the region. Coutinho's modification of the technique rehearses a critique of the norms through which the interview became a ready-made staple and an automatic strategy to supposedly include voices of the people in the aftermath of the military dictatorships that ravaged the region. Coutinho's focus on a heterogeneity of voices through interviews became increasingly important in Brazil as a means to repair the social fabric torn apart by twenty-one years of dictatorship. It is also what distinguishes his work from that of Cinema Novo filmmakers such as Glauber Rocha, who, despite their dreams of a cinema for the people, were never able to engage horizontally with the people—or *others* to themselves—as Coutinho did. Theirs was never a *cinema of listening*, but rather a cinema of vertical representation.

As the book's title indicates, listening to others is an overarching concern throughout Coutinho's career, and the chapters in this volume argue for the inseparable relationship of his films to histories of dictatorship and democratization in Brazil, which remain pressing issues today. An interest in everyday life of regular citizens has been particularly evident in Brazilian literature, culture, and arts in recent decades in relation to the promise of political and socioeconomic development and its subsequent crises or pitfalls. Coutinho represents a continuation of the mid-twentieth-century commitment to the "popular" in the projects of the CPC and Cinema Novo in Brazil as he traces the trajectory of the popular classes through his films of conversation. His documentaries illustrate both the promise of development and the failure of these governmental policies and practices to reach all segments and regions of Brazilian society. They also question the fundamental cornerstone of democracy: representation. His films maintain a political commitment, although varied in explicitness, over the decades as his work parallels the trajectory of Brazil: the military dictatorship; the transition to democracy; the segments of the sertão and the favelas often overlooked by forms of social, economic, and political development; the promise of Luiz Inácio Lula da Silva (Lula) and the Workers' Party (Partido dos Trabalhadores, PT); and the deep inequalities and various difficulties that persist in the country. His belief in difference, conversation, self-presentation, and the plurality of voices as the basis for social life makes his work crucially relevant, even urgent. Voice is always a sign of relation. Coutinho's films offer an extended exercise of being in relation.

This attention to voice and listening, especially to the dynamics between those with a voice and those without one, has a complicated history in the context of Brazilian cinema from the 1960s to the 1990s. This thirst for hearing the "voice of the people," which partly explains the interview boom in the post-dictatorship years, dates to the 1960s, a period of Brazilian cinema best known on a global scale as the years of Cinema Novo. The "new" Brazilian cinema espoused what Glauber Rocha, the movement's best-known director and most prolific and brilliant theorist, called an "aesthetics of hunger." Rather than aestheticize Brazilian reality, films would show the hunger, poverty inequality, and "ugliness," as Rocha wrote in his 1962 manifesto, of the structural problems at the intersection of political and aesthetic representation in Brazil. Rocha and his fellow filmmakers strove to depict the reality of Brazil unadorned and without embellishments for international art film audiences. The reality, that is, of the Brazilian "people."

Rocha's *Terra em transe* (*Land in Anguish*, 1967), one of Cinema Novo's most highly acclaimed and frequently written-about films, stages the crisis of this relationship between "the intellectual" and "the subaltern" in a hyperbolic and highly stylized form. The film also reveals the disconnect between populist politicians and the people whom they should represent. With its piercing critique and theatricalization of the political, revolutionary, and cultural failure to listen to others horizontally without paternalism, *Terra em transe* is one of the salient films that attempted to create a popular cinema by portraying popular figures and "real" concerns, such as the critical need for land reform. Nelson Pereira dos Santos's *Vidas secas* (*Barren Lives*, 1963) and Rocha's *Deus e o diabo na terra do sol* (*Black God, White Devil*, 1964) also exemplify this desire to depict problems plaguing the Brazilian people on-screen. Yet these films, with their cinematic language that challenged even cinephiles, were far removed from the audiovisual forms that impoverished and rural populations had access to and consumed at the time. At the level of film language, Coutinho's documentary method offers a way to revise the legacy of Cinema Novo, whose epic and allegorical depictions of the people had troubled its potentially popular and political work.

Within Brazilian documentary production, Leon Hirszman, who served as one of Coutinho's mentors and an executive producer of the interrupted 1964 film, elaborated on this disconnect between the artist and intellectual class and the people whose concerns they aimed to explore in, among other films, *Maioria absoluta* (*Absolute Majority*, 1964). Jean-Claude Bernardet pays attention to this tension in his important 2003 essay on *Cabra marcado*, "Victory Over the Ash Heap of History," translated into English for this book as part of the section "Critical Insights from Coutinho's Contemporaries." The "absolute majority" of the film's title references the illiterate Brazilians who, as the film's voice-of-God narrator explains, make up the majority of the country's population. These illiterate people speak directly about their lives, difficulties, and realities with no audible interview questions, while the middle-class people are shown as being interviewed. While *Maioria absoluta* subverts expectations about who can speak for themselves, the voice-of-God narration still drives the film's structure. This narrator organizes voices and contingencies into a film that wants to make a point by performing the hierarchies between those who make sense of the world and those whose voices appear only to be interpreted or to prove a larger point.

In both documentary and fiction films in the 1960s in Brazil and elsewhere, filmmakers were, for the most part, not listening. There was an agenda, a political point to make, and a utopia to design, but the voices of the people were not there. Coutinho's initial foray into cinema with the CPC began with similar problems of providing nonprofessional actors with a script to play themselves in the historical reenactment of João Pedro Teixeira's life and death. Written by Coutinho, the script created problems because its language did not echo or make audible the ways people in the region expressed themselves. This established both a priori and a posteriori the seemingly inevitable hierarchical relationship between those who made use of and controlled the film technology and those who were filmed.

However, this difficult encounter was not a Brazilian problem or one that emerged during the 1960s. In an essay from 1938 considered part of the foundational bibliography of documentary studies, John Grierson wrote that films such as the British *Housing Problems* (directed by Edgar Anstey and Arthur Elton, 1935) "showed the common man, not in the romance of his calling, but in the more complex and intimate drama of his citizenship" (215). Film made audible and visible the nuanced realities of the "common man" by creating a work where "something speaks within it that touches the conscience . . . 'transforms' and will not let" (216) the spectator forget. Something, rather than someone, speaks, which is speech itself. As with all speech, it is made up of the difficult relationship between its conditions of possibility, the social and historical frames that limit it and precede it, and the self's attempt to tell their own story and to break those frames and limits. "Something speaks" in film that touches and transforms, but how and why does it touch and transform?

Beyond raising the question of true self-representation or of radical authorial renewal, Grierson's text suggests that an experience of touching, affecting, and transforming the spectator occurs with many documentaries *where people speak for themselves*. Touching indicates proximity, even when used as a metaphor. Being touched reinserts the body into all equations and speaks to the interaction between a body and something else, which unfolds in the realm of the sensorial where speech itself does not matter anymore and, thus, where the unexpected emerges. Polls, statistics, measurement, and other symbolic forms of representation—both political and aesthetic—cannot account for this sensorial experience. In cinematic terms, the contingent. Something speaks: the contingency that constitutes life in its unfolding. Coutinho's attention to the moments when a person speaking with him in front of the camera begins to unexpectedly sing, as in *Edifício Master* or *Cabra marcado*, or his interest in the *fala* of children whose use of language has not yet been formatted, as he tells Jordana Berg in *Últimas conversas*, are some of his most salient attempts to allow the contingent to emerge and be filmed. This also sheds light on why Coutinho practiced the long take with such commitment: because the contingent can never be scripted or expected.

The emergence of documentary studies was partly grounded in this question of who speaks and who represents whom. In his 1974 *Documentary: A History of Non-fiction Film*, one of the first books dedicated to this subject, Erik Barnouw argued that documentaries at the time were focused on "talking people" (262). For Barnouw, one of the main differences between earlier documentaries and those of the 1960s and 1970s was that, in the first decades of sound film, the people and voices who were not "elitist spokesmen" (262) either were presented as nonspeaking subjects or, if they were present, were highly manipulated in the editing process. By the 1970s, those people began to take control away from the director and make the film their own. Something similar happens in Brazil. Early documentaries, like *São Paulo, sinfonia da metrópole* (*São Paulo, A Metropolitan Symphony*, 1929), show masses of workers, immigrants, and other "voiceless" or marginalized peoples moving in and about the city, without their own expressions. Hirszman's *Maioria absoluta* and Coutinho's *Cabra marcado*, as I suggested earlier, are attempts to change this.

In Brazil, the use of interviews as the staple for documentaries became pervasive in the decades following the return to democracy in the mid-1980s. Jean-Claude Bernardet, one of Brazil's leading film scholars, diagnosed the overuse of the interview in Brazil by the 1990s as a naturalized habit and expectation. He linked the practice to a certain automation: "one no longer thinks of documentaries without interviews, and more often than not directing a question to the interviewee is like switching the automatic pilot on" (Bernardet 286). If the questioning is automatic, then the responses are also automatic and formulaic, which eliminates the possibility of unexpected expressions or moments of truth emerging from the exchange. The pervasiveness of the interview also points to the eager consumption of first-person accounts speaking directly, albeit mediated through audiovisual forms of video and film. The contradiction is rich: on the one hand, there is a desire for the appearance of real people addressing the camera, and on the other hand, those very images have been emptied out of any reality because they speak to a formulaic repetition. Coutinho's conversations, with their interest in the contingent, offer a corrective to this saturation of the interview. In doing so, they are anything but formulaic.

The past decade has seen a renewed interest in Coutinho's work in the wake of his death on February 2, 2014. There have been colloquia and homages to his work in the United States and Brazil, notably the "Ocupação Eduardo Coutinho" exhibit at the Instituto Moreira Salles in 2020 and 2021. Retrospective series dedicated to Coutinho's films in Brazil and beyond have heightened the visibility and reach of his films. Critics have referenced his work in essays, edited volumes, and scholarly monographs about Brazilian and Latin American film and documentary cinema. Our volume, *Listening to Others: Eduardo Coutinho's Documentary Cinema*, engages with this interest in Coutinho's work by bringing together scholars of film studies, documentary studies, cultural studies, and Brazilian studies from both the United States and Latin America. The resulting edited collection offers the first English-language book dedicated solely to the Brazilian documentarian. *Listening to Others* addresses his early work, the politics of space in his films, the role of performance in his documentaries, his ethics of encounter, and his place within a larger global documentary moment. This plurality of critical voices echoes the multiplicity of Coutinho's work itself. Rather than remain rooted in his birthplace of São Paulo, Coutinho traversed Brazil to explore the quotidian rhythms, worldviews, and livelihoods of common people from different realities of Brazil. In doing so, he engaged in conversations that formed the basis of his practice.

This book presents twelve essays written by a roster of contemporary critics from diverse disciplinary formations. The chapters are divided into four thematically organized subsections. The first section, "Media Ecologies," features chapters by Jens Anderman, Ashley Brock, and Gustavo Procopio Furtado. These pieces explore distinct elements of Coutinho's engagement with place, mediation, and landscapes, whether environmental or audiovisual. The second section, "Politics and the Documentary Image," includes chapters by Krista Brune, Luz Horne, and Rielle Navitski These chapters examine ideas of politics in Coutinho's films and their production circuits, methods, and images. The third section on "Performing the Self and Others," with pieces by Adriana Johnson, Brenno Kenji Kaneyasu, and Fernando Pérez Villalón, addresses questions of performance, enunciation, and the voice. The final section, "On Time and Endings," contains chapters by Bruno Carvalho, Nilo Couret, and Vinicius Navarro that consider concepts of time, beginnings, endings, and the posthumous possibilities of Coutinho's work.

The political dimensions of Coutinho's early work and their echoes in later films are addressed in the chapters by Navitski and Brune. By listening with care and time to the particularities of language of his interlocutors, Coutinho captured daily life in distinct places of Brazil, such as landfills, favelas, the northeastern sertão, and the interior realms of apartments, theaters, and classrooms in Rio de Janeiro, as studied in the contributions by Brock and Andermann. Coutinho's attention to the voice and speech structures is a documentary practice grounded in the kernel of fiction at the naked heart of documentary, as Kenji Kaneyasu, Pérez Villalón, and Johnson analyze in their chapters. The ethical risks of this conversational approach, of this encounter with "the other," is taken up by Horne. Coutinho's distinctive documentary practice raises questions about his relationship with archival materials and temporalities of past and present, as Furtado, Navarro, and Couret examine in their pieces. A focus on ethical concerns and technical features of Coutinho's films invites comparisons between the Brazilian director and other documentarians, which Carvalho explores in his study of Coutinho in conversation with Errol Morris. These critical voices from the United States and Latin America underscore the multiplicity of linguistic expressions and quotidian experiences within the contemporary Brazil that Coutinho listened to and documented throughout his career.

Listening to Others concludes with two sections of translations of Brazilian texts by and about Coutinho written since the 1970s: "Coutinho in His Own Words," which offers a selection of essays and manifestos written by Coutinho himself, showcases his writings as a film critic and theorist; and "Critical Insights from Coutinho's Contemporaries," which features a selection of key early readings of his work by Ferreira Gullar, José Carlos Avellar, and Jean-Claude Bernardet, three of Brazil's most important film scholars, whose work is foundational and formative for current critics and scholars of Brazilian cinema, as the chapters in this book exemplify. These two sections are crucial for this volume's intellectual project, as neither Coutinho's writings nor the Brazilian critics' work have been sufficiently read and discussed by English-language scholarship. Coutinho's writings from the 1970s provide insight into his relationship with Latin American, Hollywood, and European cinema as a viewer, critic, and filmmaker. These pieces reveal his care as a listener and a creative interlocutor when engaging with the works of other directors, a practice that also guides his own filmmaking. The chapter by poet and critic Gullar, who was similarly active in the CPC, reminds readers of the dangerous climate within which Coutinho and others attempted to effect political and social change through their art in Brazil of the 1960s. Avellar analyzes Coutinho's documentaries from the 1990s with an eye toward language, history, and social dynamics. Bernardet, the final critic featured in this section, reads *Cabra marcado* in relation to Brazil's dynamics of power and to contemporaneous Brazilian films and literature. Another piece by Bernardet situates Coutinho's more recent films within a documentary (or "reality") boom in film and literature of the late 1990s and early 2000s.

By pairing contemporary scholarly voices with earlier pieces by Coutinho and film critics, this volume underscores the historic importance and continued relevance of the filmmaker and his documentary cinema. The inclusion of essays and criticism written in Brazil during the first decades of Coutinho's production also recalls Coutinho's own interest in activating the archive in his films. His cinema listens carefully to stories of the past while also looking at that earlier temporality through recovered footage in *Cabra marcado*, newsreels and documentary clips in *Peões*, and photographs and other personal artifacts in *Edifício Master* and other films. For Coutinho and the interlocutors who recount their memories and stories in his films, the past informs the present. Yet fully living in and embodying this present is an urgent and necessary act, one that can allow for the filmic encounters between Coutinho and other people to arrive at greater empathy and understanding. In this current global moment of heightened political strife, racial injustice, and social unrest, watching Coutinho's films and engaging in critical dialogues about them allow for forms of resistance, hope, and perhaps even democratic collaboration. *Listening to Others* invites readers to enter these crucial conversations.

Notes

1. See my discussion of these dynamics in "Conversation and Duration in Eduardo Coutinho's Films."
2. Translations from Spanish and Portuguese are mine.

Works Cited

Barnouw, Erik. *Documentary: A History of Non-fiction Film*. Oxford UP, 1974.
Berg, Jordana. "Diário de montagem." *Últimas conversas*, edited by Eliska Altmann and Tatiana Bacal, 7Letras, 2017, pp. 9–22.

Bernardet, Jean-Claude. *Cineastas e imagens do povo*. Companhia das Letras, 2003.
Bezerra, Cláudio. "Um documentarista a procura de personagens." *Eduardo Coutinho*, edited by Milton Ohata, Cosac Naify, 2013, pp. 400–13.
Brizuela, Natalia. "Conversation and Duration in Eduardo Coutinho's Films." *Film Quarterly*, vol. 69, no. 3, 2016, pp. 19–27.
Cavarero, Adriana. *For More Than One Voice: Toward a Philosophy of Vocal Expression*. Translated by Paul A. Kottman, Stanford UP, 2005.
Grierson, John, "The Battle for Authenticity." *John Grierson on Documentary*, edited by Forsyth Hardy, U of California P, 1966, pp. 215–17.
Grupo Revbelando Imágenes, editor. *Eduardo Coutinho. Cine de conversación y antropología salvaje*. Nulú Bonsai, 2013.
Lins, Consuelo. "*Últimas Conversas*: entre o filme inacabado e o filme possível." *Últimas conversas*, edited by Eliska Altmann and Tatiana Bacal, 7Letras, 2017, pp. 23–45.
———. *O documentário de Eduardo Coutinho: Televisão, cinema e vídeo*. Jorge Zahar, 2004.
Mattos, Carlos Alberto. *Sete faces de Eduardo Coutinho*. Boitempo, 2019.
Nichols, Bill. "The Voice in Documentary." *Film Quarterly*, vol. 36, no. 3, Spring 1983, pp. 17–30.
Rangan, Pooja. "Audibilities: Voice and Listening in the Penumbra of Documentary: An Introduction." *Discourse*, vol. 39, no. 3, 2017, pp. 279–91.
Salles, João Moreira. "Morrer e nascer: Duas passagens na vida de Eduardo Coutinho." *Eduardo Coutinho*, edited by Milton Ohata, Cosac Naify, 2013, pp. 364–74.
Saraiva, Leonardo. "Narrativa e subjetividade em *Edifício Master*." *Eduardo Coutinho*, edited by Milton Ohata, Cosac Naify, 2013, pp. 558–77.
Trinh, T. Minh-Ha. *When the Moon Waxes Red: Representation, Gender, and Cultural Politics*. Routledge, 1991.
Xavier, Ismail. "O jogo de cena e as outras cenas." *Eduardo Coutinho*, edited by Milton Ohata, Cosac Naify, 2013, pp. 604–26.

Part I
Media Ecologies

1

Coutinho's Ecology

Space, Place, and the Disappearing Location

JENS ANDERMANN

The opening shots of *Seis dias em Ouricuri* (*Six Days in Ouricuri*, 1976), the first of six medium-length TV documentaries Coutinho made for the *Globo Repórter* program prior to his return to the big screen with *Cabra marcado para morrer* (1964–1984), are as classic expository documentary as it gets. A map of northeastern Brazil showing the little town's location in the westernmost corner of Pernambuco opens the sequence, followed by an establishing shot from the distance, approaching Ouricuri from the highway, and finally a slow pan across the empty central square while the extradiegetic, voice-of-God narration underlaid with "sertanejo style" guitar chords makes way for the announcements being broadcast from the local cinema's loudspeakers. The town, we learn, is in the midst of yet another of the catastrophic droughts Brazilian viewers at the time of the film's broadcasting would already have associated with the sertão—not least thanks to the films of Cinema Novo, the visual aesthetics of which are duly referenced throughout *Ouricuri*, as in the bottom-up, tilting pans of leafless trees under a burning sun, reminiscent in their deliberate overexposure of the opening sequence of Ruy Guerra's *Os fuzis* (*The Guns*, 1964) or those of a group of *retirantes*—rural migrants—entering a panoramic long shot of the barren landscape from behind camera to walk across the frame in diagonal, just as the protagonists in Nelson Pereira dos Santos's *Vidas secas* (*Barren Lives*, 1963). This image of a retrograde, "primitive," and desolate Northeast is further reinforced by the narrator's quick summary of Ouricuri's main characteristics, citing socioeconomic and demographic data confirming its status as a "typical" provincial backwater.

But if, in this and the other films he made for the *Globo Repórter* series, Coutinho's aesthetic choices were certainly heavily circumscribed by the protocols of mainstream television (Lins 20–21), already in *Ouricuri* these demands for univocal and totalizing truth delivered by and for an instance of visual knowledge that remains external to the object it beholds are also subtly contested. Most notably, this is the case in the more than three-minute-long take of a young *sertanejo* crouching in front of a wall of anonymous bodies (visible only from feet to shoulders) showing to the camera various kinds of roots, twigs, and dry fruits he used to eat in times of extreme need, and explaining in detail the way these need to be prepared to become edible. An interesting transfer takes place here, from the disembodied, omniscient, and all-seeing camera-eye and third-person narrator of the opening sequence to an embodied, emic voice of local knowledge, with the palisade of the other listeners' bodies literally blocking the open view onto the landscape that had been the omniscient narrator's purview and object of knowledge, its condition and foundation. Here, instead, this space of cartography and of landscape, to which the opening shots had introduced us, materializes as a place, that is, as a network of mutual relations and dependencies between human and nonhuman inhabitants (including animals, plants, water, salt). These multiple interrelations are predicated, furthermore, as the blocked view to the back of the speaker intimates, on a kind of knowledge that is distinct from the surveying gaze of the landscaper: a knowledge that calls on taste and touch rather than vision, and is being shared not through observation but storytelling and listening.

In this chapter, I wish to focus on the ways in which Coutinho's "characteristic self-imposed geographical limitation or 'singular location'" (Allen 82) calls forth a mode of engagement with the profilmic that performs a critique of the social documentary's extraction of visual knowledge for the benefit of an external beholder: the "marginalismo" attitude, which, as Jean-Claude Bernardet (47) has pointed out, in Brazilian documentary cinema has often been tantamount to turning the camera on the border spaces of city and nation, the sertão and the favela, thus also implicitly assuming the urban centers of the south and the "cidade-asfalto" to be the audiences to which the camera caters. Yet, against the prevailing reading of Coutinho's work as responding to the epistophilic protocols of the documentary genre by gradually eliminating from his films any kind of reference to time and space outside the singular, epiphanic moment of the encounter between filmmaker and subject, I want to advance the idea of a different attitude to place and dwelling that is still only vaguely sketched out in *Ouricuri* but that, in later films such as *Boca de lixo*, *Babilônia 2000*, or *O fim e o princípio*, adds up to something like an "ecological" attitude to place. Place, I argue, is construed here as a material and social assemblage accessible to documentary through a particular form of visual and verbal "countersignature" that each film must negotiate with its subjects in ways that are particular to the human and nonhuman elements of the location. The vanishing of such communities that are as much forged by the films as they are found in the location, which in Coutinho's oeuvre occurs from *Edifício Master* (2002) onward, would then become readable not just as an auteurial decision but rather as a response to the wider ecological crisis of Brazilian society, in particular the urban agglomerations of the *centro-sul*.

Following Alice Allen's suggestion that the almost exclusive focus on questions of voice and personhood in Coutinho's "cinema of conversation" has "tended to overlook or at least detract from appraisal of [his films'] fundamental visual qualities" (82), I wish to argue that there is in many of these an intricate relationship between verbal and visual rhetorics of locality that move from landscape as "the visual control of space and the human actions that occur within it" (Cosgrove 21) toward what we could call, with Félix Guattari, an "ecology": a both locally specific and irreducibly open assemblage of "the psyche, the socius and the environment" (Guattari 41).[1] This "ecological turn"—not in the sense of a concern with "nature" or environmental conservation but instead a concern with the "processes of heterogenesis" that involve subjectivities, commonalities, and the material world alike in "the very act of [their] constitution, definition and deterritorialization" (Guattari 44, 51)—also allows Coutinho to break out of the self-imposed creative prison of the location. Tempting as it may be to read into Coutinho's films a movement from space to place—or, in Martin Lefebvre's terms, from painterly landscape as the outsider's view of a commodified land-object to cinematic landscape as a critical interruption and opening of the diegetic chronotope onto "space freed from eventhood" (Lefebvre 22)—the place that emerges in these films remains in fact completely tied to the event, the performative encounter, that goes on, indeed "takes place," inside it. It is, I argue, in their critical engagement with, and subversion of, the painterly and cinematic rhetorics of landscape that Coutinho's films conjure up an ecological assemblage, a scenario in which "potential vectors of subjectification and singularization" converge to forge "incorporeal objects, abstract machines and universes of value that make their presence felt as though they had been always 'already there,' although they are entirely dependent on the existential event that brings them into play" (Guattari 45).

"*De fora para dentro*": ethnography and the journey-form

In a first cut of *Babilônia 2000* (2000), Coutinho's frequent collaborator Consuelo Lins tells us, the filmmaker was going to include at the outset of his chronicle of the last hours of the millennium, as experienced in the two favelas overlooking Copacabana beach, a sequence of aerial shots from a helicopter taken after on-location shooting had been completed. In the end, on advice from fellow director Eduardo Escorel, Coutinho re-edited the film without the opening sequence, as the latter would have conflicted with his intention to "make a film from the inside out" [*de dentro para fora*] without offering our gaze the safety of an external vantage point [*de fora para dentro*] (Lins 128). Indeed, the panoramic shots of the city and beachscape at various times of the last day of the twentieth century that create the film's visual baseline, taken from the elevated vantage point of the hilltop shantytown—culminating, at midnight, in an extended long shot of the fireworks illuminating the night sky over the bay—subtly invert the relations of scopic privilege that prevail in classic expository or observational documentary. Instead of the disembodied, detached perspective that underwrites the landscape form as a knowledge-power apparatus, here the recurring shot of Copacabana bay creates a "double frame" (Allen 84). In looking outward, this shot constantly reminds us "of the position from which the image is being constructed" (Cunha 14)—a visual lesson the film also extends to the images taken of, or rather in, the favela itself. Rather than with the vertical, top-down vision of the aerial shots—the "divine gaze" Michel de Certeau famously associated with a modern, scientific "fiction of knowledge" (140) as opposed to a pedestrian's embodied and experience-based relation to her surrounding—*Babilônia* follows up the panoramic shot of Copacabana with images of the film crew itself leaving its "headquarters" in the favela's residents' association at the foot of the hill and starting to climb up toward the higher reaches of the neighborhood, one handheld camera filming another two that, shouldered by their respective cinematographers, advance toward it.[2] *Babilônia* then includes within the narrative its own *making of*—a refractory and self-reflexive procedure that Coutinho had made a hallmark of his films ever since returning to the big screen with *Cabra marcado*—yet this self-reflexive character does not undermine the epistemic quest of the documentary journey but rather reinforces it.

In fact, a great number of Coutinho's films include, usually at the beginning, a similar disavowal and simultaneous rehabilitation of the journey-form of classic documentary narrative and of its concurrent organization of diegetic space as landscape (a relation between the narrative space-time of travel and the visual protocols of landscape that documentary cinema, following the pioneering work of Robert Flaherty and Victor Turin, adopted from natural history and colonial exploration). The crew's arrival at the scene—usually with a voice-over from Coutinho explaining the film's proposition or captions indicating the latter as well as date and location of the shooting—functions as a kind of "autobiographic prologue" before the director and his crew disappear (except for brief interludes) behind the camera and surrender screen space entirely to the subjects being interviewed. In *Peões* (2004) as well as *O fim e o princípio* (2005), this opening sequence is almost identical: first, a lateral pan or dolly shot from the vehicle taking the crew to the location, then, on arrival, a handheld camera following Coutinho in an over-the-shoulder shot on his way to meet the first interviewee. Yet whereas, in *Peões*, the journey's itinerary has already been determined prior to the shooting—the film crew follows the trajectory of then-presidential candidate Lula da Silva from poor northeastern migrant to union leader in São Paulo's industrial ABC belt—things are less clear-cut in *O fim e o princípio*.

Here, over the initial sequence of lateral pans across the arid countryside of Paraíba, shot from the crew bus in movement, Coutinho's crackly voice lays out the purpose of the film—or rather lack of it, as, he says, all they had proposed themselves to do was to head out, once again, into the sertão, in search of a story to tell, with no previous research or scouting of locations and characters. As the crew reaches the small town of São João do Rio do Peixe, we ourselves are thus subtly turned into allies and accomplices, fellow travelers who arrive on the scene together with the filmmakers (quite literally, with the following shot through the windscreen taken from one of the back seats placing us right inside the crew bus, behind Coutinho and the driver occupying the front seats). While the bus navigates the town's narrow streets, we learn how, while checking in at the hotel, the producers obtained contacts through the local church of some rural schoolteachers in the area, and immediately afterward we enter—traveling now on a dirt road—the forecourt of the Batistas' little ranch. Cut to a now-"grounded" camera shooting Coutinho and the family as they assemble plastic chairs on the porch: once again, the filmmaker is seen explaining to the locals his purpose of making a film based on the stories he finds, if indeed he can find any, when suddenly one of the young women—Rosa, the schoolteacher—has an idea. Turning to Zequinha, her nonagenarian grandmother, she asks the old lady to tell something about her life. When Zequinha can't really think of anything to say, Rosa insists: tell us something about 1915, the drought—eventually succeeding in drawing a vivid statement from Zequinha of life in times of hardship and even getting her to perform on camera one of her "rezas," or healing prayers. Suddenly, the film has found its story—and Rosa, as is clear immediately, is a natural in the craft of interviewing. The next we see is Rosa herself on the crew bus on "Day 2 of the shoot," turning into the near-identical forecourt of another nearby farm. As the crew gets off the bus, it is now Rosa who explains to Coutinho why she chose to make the first stop there and how she was thinking to approach the villagers. "Então fala, vai lá" (go ahead, talk to them), Coutinho replies, gently enticing her forward as the camera follows her toward the ranch: right before our eyes, the film has found a subject, a documentary form, and a narrator. Here, as in many other of Coutinho's films, the story in fact splits into two, one about "the subject," the often only vaguely defined common ground that triggers the telling of stories (here, the memories of an older generation of locals all bound to one another by family ties), the other about the very process of "intersubjectivity": the sharing or even gradual transfer of narrative authority "de fora para dentro," from outside to the inside, of the local universe that is being documented.[3]

Importantly, different from a long tradition of first-person social or ethnographic documentaries such as Jean Rouch's *Moi, un noir* (1958), this transfer of narrative authority in Coutinho's films is not a fictionalizing device—attributing to the subjectivity, the first person that manifests itself in the voice-over, the images taken of the subject, the third person, appearing on the image track—but rather a crucial aspect of the "existential event" that brings the film crew and their subjects into each other's purview and transforms the space-object of the documentary journey into a place, a scene of convergence between "vectors of subjectification and singularization." What I call an ecology, following Guattari, is intimately tied to this assembling activity, to the labor of producing not merely an object of knowledge (or even one of empathy or identification) that the documentary makers, like the traveling naturalists of old, bring back from margin to center, but rather the attempt to forge in and from the event of the documentary encounter a new, virtual space-time of commonality that reaches outward, as a deterritorializing vector, to the stage of editing and even to that of screening the film. To a certain extent, my use of the term ecology is thus akin to what Bill Nichols has called the "axiographics" of documentary filmmaking, as "an attempt to explore the implantation of values in the configuration of space, in the constitution of a gaze, and in the relation of observer to observed. [. . .] Axiographics asks us to examine how the documentary camera gaze takes on distinctive qualities and poses concrete issues of politics, ethics and ideology in terms of space" (Nichols 78). But rather than as an "implantation" of values into a space that is both already "out there" and is being configured by a particular form of documentary gaze, I would like to think of Coutinho's ecology as a mode of spatialization and emplacement that is both virtual and real—at once a negotiated experience of commonality and its being witnessed and shared with film audiences. The fact that a "documentary of personhood" (Bezerra 29) such as Coutinho's spends so much time in setting the scene also points to the importance of the latter as the ground on which the singularity of such personhood can occur and be shared: ground not as a material given but as the negotiation of an agreement between individuals, collectives, and materialities—between "the psyche, the socius and the environment"—that is at once the films' precondition and ultimate objective. This "ecological" strand running almost through Coutinho's entire filmography, then, could also be understood as a contribution to Doreen Massey's call for "uproot[ing] 'space' from that constellation of concepts in which it has been so unquestioningly embedded (stasis, closure, representation) and to settle it among another set of ideas (heterogeneity, relationality, coevalness . . . liveliness indeed) where it releases a more challenging political landscape" (Massey 13).

Boca de lixo (*Scavengers*), the medium-length video Coutinho made in 1992 for CECIP (Centro de Criação da Imagem Popular—Center for the Creation of the Popular Image, an NGO focusing on issues of social exclusion and media citizenship) is one of the most interesting as well as disturbing examples of this movement from representation to coevalness and heterogeneity occurring as a spatial uprooting and a temporal bifurcation within the film itself. Just as in *O fim e o princípio*, in *Boca de lixo* this movement is conditional on the forging of a visual ecology involving filmmakers, viewers, and subjects alike in a shared, reflexive reworking of the image and of the relations of showing, seeing, and being seen that the image ushers in. But whereas in *O fim e o princípio* the intergenerational as well as cross-class and country-city transmission of memory and experience appears to be relatively peaceful, the more conflictive aspects come to the fore in *Boca de lixo*. The film's opening shots feature a handheld, downward-tilting camera advancing into the rubbish dump of Iacoca, part of the township of São Gonçalo on the outskirts of Rio de Janeiro, the lens so close to the heap of decomposing matter that it forces onto our gaze a haptic and olfactory experience that is almost nauseating. Only then the horizon opens for a series of "landscape shots" featuring flocks of herons and vultures picking at these dunes of plastic and rot, Rio's landmark statue of Christ on Corcovado mountain hovering in the distance, before we are back at the scene, now in the midst of a crowd of screaming, rag-clothed men, women and children pushing forward with picks and forks as a garbage truck unleashes its load of "fresh" stuff, juices dripping from its cavernous opening. Again the camera pans around the scavengers at ankle height, digging into the freshly delivered rubbish along with them, before a second camera shows us the cameraman and sound engineer moving into the crowd of scavengers, clearly an outside presence in this hellish underworld—and an unwanted one at that, as the following sequence of garbage pickers covering their faces and turning their backs to the camera makes clear. "What do you get outta this . . . holding this thing in our faces," two young boys challenge the crew, the first in a series of more or less confrontational exchanges in which the garbage collectors defend their activity as "honest work," as if to defy the assumed contempt and derision in the beholder's eye.

Things only begin to change when Coutinho starts asking people for their names, eventually also handing his interviewees photocopied screenshots of themselves and other garbage pickers from the previous round of shooting. It is only now, flicking through the pile of images with their hands still covered in dirt, that the people of the dump warm up to Coutinho and his team, naming fellow workers and commenting (mostly good-humoredly) on their own pictures. In sharing his images and asking for their subjects to be recognized, to be named by the garbage collectors, Coutinho "indicates that what is being proposed is no longer an expropriation of the other's image, following the logic of the media, but the creation of a shared image between the one who films and the one being filmed" (Lins 88). Most importantly, this request for the filmed subjects to "countersign" their "own" images (for a countersignature is always an agreement over the transfer or the sharing of ownership and responsibility) does not attempt to deny or plaster over the antagonistic constellation in and from which this image had emerged. Rather, it opens the antagonism that underwrites the very possibility of this image (in terms of both visual conventions and the possession and operating knowledge of the recording devices) to the *potentiality* of coevalness and reciprocity also implied in the "counter" of countersignature: in Jacques Derrida's formulation, "[o]ne can be 'against' [*contre*] the person one opposes (one's 'declared enemy,' for example), and also 'against' [*contre*] the person next to us, the one who is 'right against us,' whom we touch or with whom we are in contact" (Derrida 11). Having literally changed hands and having been countersigned, the image has also traveled the distance from representation (and its ultimate limit: abjection) to heterogeneity and relationality. Offering up the image, and the countersignatory gesture responding to this offering, the naming of the subject in the picture, have turned out to be preconditions for everything that appears on-screen to become likewise subject to negotiation and reevaluation, very much like the discarded objects the garbage collectors pick from the heap of stuff on the dump. Through countersignature, the image itself becomes the site of a visual ecology, which opens our gaze and that of the camera to the ecology of the site.

Antagonism, difference, and conflict have not simply disappeared, then; rather, they have become the subject of a contractual relation, a "pact" that makes possible the emergence of statements, of claims, on behalf of those local to what had previously seemed a non-place, an ob-scene. I am thinking, of course, of the "civil contract of photography" Ariella Azoulay has so memorably theorized, one that "binds together photographers, photographed persons, and spectators," each of whom "knows what is expected of them and what to expect from the others. This shared set of expectations is a civil knowledge" (Azoulay 26) without, and this is crucial, being mediated through a sovereign power external to this relation. This sharing-out, on behalf of the "photographed persons," of a local knowledge—a skill—would have been impossible under the conditions of *Boca de lixo*'s first, exploitative (because not-yet-countersigned) sequence of images, be it the ability to dissect from the apparently formless heap of rotting matter the items that might still serve a purpose as food or recyclable material or, as in the case of Cícera's teenaged daughter, a talent for singing romantic "música sertaneja" hits. In *Boca de lixo*, crucially, the "civil contract" between the image-makers and what is made to feature in their picture involves not just the human subjects, but must also take into account the materiality of the place and the wider relations of production and consumption that connect it with the audience in space and time. As Enock, one of the most experienced garbage pickers, puts it, garbage "is a part of life . . . it's the final stage of the service, it's where everything starts." Subjectivity, community, and materiality intersect, together forming an ecology—and it is into this ecological assemblage into which the film seeks to invite and articulate us through its performative ethics of the image, its visual ecology of which we are enticed to become countersignatories ourselves. The screening of a first cut of the film inside the dump, to an audience of garbage pickers, is therefore different here from the one at the outset of *Cabra marcado para morrer*—not least because, in *Boca de lixo*, it comes at the end rather than at the beginning of the film. Here, these images are not attempting to usher in a memory performance on behalf of its subjects-spectators, but, rather, they are themselves a countersignatory statement on behalf of the filmmakers, an expression performed to internal and external viewers alike of their having honored the contract into which all sides have entered.

"*De dentro para fora*": testimony and the crisis of place

A cinema of body and voice, even "of the corporality of voices, obsessed with the syntax, choice of vocabulary, and accent of its 'actors'" (Sayad 144), Coutinho's oeuvre has often been read as an increasingly radical process of "subtraction" from the filmic sound-image, of everything that might detract from the event of the *depoimento*, the subject's speech-act that enounces and embodies a singular experience. The increasingly ritualized and explicitly staged nature of the interviews from one film to the next also likens these to multiple forms of confession, from religious and cultic ones to psychoanalysis and self-help groups, all of which rely on some kind of spatiotemporal exceptionality, on forging a "safe space" for the production of testimonial truth. The theater stage of *Jogo de cena* (2007), *Moscou* (2009) and *As canções* (2011) would thus be but a logical consequence, a gradual evolution and intensification, of the already stage-like qualities of the diegetic setting in Coutinho's previous films, especially *Edifício Master* (2002), where the compartmentalized lives in a lower-middle-class apartment building are rendered in a theatrical, or musical, structure of successive monologues/recitals divided by "curtains"—shots of the empty corridors that separate and connect the characters' identical apartments.

While such a reading is certainly plausible, this increasing abstraction from the specificity of the location could also be understood in terms of a *crisis of place*—place understood as the common ground that had emerged from the multiplicity of voices and statements to the point of becoming itself a part of the title of many of Coutinho's films, a "common denominator" organizing their meanings (apart from the ones already discussed here, we could also point to *Santa Marta—Duas semanas no morro*, 1987, or *Volta redonda—Memorial da Greve*, 1989). It is this shared horizon of locality, which the films had both registered through verbal statements and reproduced through their own decomposition and recomposition of the documentary journey, creating a space of convergence and reciprocity between the "here and now" of viewers and subjects, that gradually disappears from Coutinho's more recent cinema, thus also relating it to a wider context of "ecological crisis" in contemporary Brazil. By this I do not mean just the escalating extractivist assault on behalf of mining, fossil fuel prospecting, and agro-industrial capitals closing in on the last remaining enclaves of biodiversity (many of which, incidentally, are also Indigenous lands). Although these instances of neocolonial plunder are part and parcel of the process I am trying to grasp, this process is also not restricted to the new frontiers of extraction, but rather occurs wherever the assembling of "the psyche, the socius and the environment"—the forms of heterogenesis that underwrite "the event of place"—have become blocked, be it because a particular site has literally become uninhabitable because of pollution, flooding, or desecration or because, as in *Edifício Master*, it has become incommunicable and therefore ceases to cohere in and as place.

Crucially, this shared horizon of locality, before *Edifício Master*, had been as much the effect of verbal as of visual forms of reference. It is a "prepositional effect," a way of anchoring the narratives of singular experiences in a material universe that is complementary to the performative space of commonality that emerges in and through the communicative situation of the interviews. In *Babilônia 2000*, one of the film crews (led by a male interviewer) at one point stumbles upon two young women on a porch preparing the food for New Year's Eve. After some bantering about the kind of performance the film crew would like them to enact ("Wait, let me put on some make up first—oh, so it's poverty you want? I know, I know: community," one of the sisters, Roseli, teases the interviewer), a long conversation ensues about living atop the hill and below, about religion and the future of Brazil. The question that triggers the exchange is "What are you doing there?" [O que estão fazendo aí?], which leads to the girls' plans for the evening (going "*down to* the beach" and "back up *here*" to party with parents and friends) and on to the family's rootedness in the neighborhood ("We were both born *here*," "Now we live elsewhere but my parents never leave home, they prefer to stay *here*" "We grew up in this neighborhood, we're a product of our surroundings"). Although not always as explicitly emphasized through spatial markers as in this conversation, many of the interviews in *Babilônia* are similarly hinged on people's experiences of place, on local memories of loss and love that invoke and construe place as a "center of value" around which these stories can evolve and relate to one another, as "time made visible," in the words of human geographer Yi-Fu Tuan: "Human places become vividly real through dramatization. Identity of place is achieved by dramatizing the aspirations, needs, and functional rhythms of personal and group life" (178).

In *Boca de lixo*, many of the garbage pickers similarly organize their statements in terms of an opposition between "here" and "there"—including several women who compare the dump to their previous work as housemaids in the city, even though they come to different conclusions as to where life is better. Another one, Lúcia, whom we first see at work, joking and bantering with the other pickers on the dump, suddenly becomes more constrained and inhibited when the crew comes to visit her at home. "Easier to talk there, isn't it?" Coutinho asks. "It's chaos there. Everybody screaming, joking," Lúcia agrees and tells him how much the work on the garbage dump reminds her of the plantation where she and her husband used to work in their home state, Paraná, where "everybody rode to the field together" on the back of the trucks sent by the farmers. "Everybody knew everybody else. At quitting time, at lunch time, we were a gang. It was a party." Weekends, she continues, were sad because there wasn't anyone around to talk to—"same as here," she says, "there on the dump I'm a different person than at home. There, I shout, I talk, I joke . . ." At home, she says, she and her family always arrive too tired to talk, and there's not much to do around there. As if to prove her point, the film cuts back to a shot of Lúcia at work on the dump, now visibly "a different person" than the clean and proper housewife of the previous shot, as evidenced by not just her work attire but also her loud and lively interaction with her coworkers and the film crew, signaling to the camera where to find a food basket with potatoes and a chicken, "for the pig." In Coutinho's later films, this second image, countersigning yet also connecting the subject's speech to the lived interaction with the environment, would increasingly fall victim to what Consuelo Lins and Cláudia Mesquita call "subtraction"—the elimination from Coutinho's documentary vocabulary of every element that does not immediately belong to the event of the interview and of people's "transformation in front of the camera" (18). Yet it might be argued that, rather than a nonessential image that Coutinho gradually learns to purge from his filmic language, this second image is actually key to the place-making in *Boca de lixo* and to its visual ecology of countersignature. By taking us back to the dump into which, like urban expeditioners into the city's heart of darkness, the first shots had introduced us, but now with the other's verbal countersignature overwriting the image and teaching our gaze to see in what had been a scenario of abjection and savagery a space of skill, autonomy, and community—without at any point denying the social emergency that makes such a space possible—*Boca de lixo* is actually teaching us to see a place where it had previously seemed impossible to see one. But this lesson, arguably, depends as much on the image as it does on its verbal countersignature: the filmed and the spoken image enter into a relation here that is not merely illustrative and requires the collaboration of a reflexive spectator.

The anthropologist Tim Ingold, in a classic essay, has suggested the concept of "taskscape" for this kind of environment characterized by an "ecological" interplay between subjectivities, communities, and materialities, which is also a space where "people, in the performance of their tasks, [. . .] *attend to one another*." The taskscape is therefore akin to an orchestral performance in which, by 'watching, listening, perhaps even touching, we continually feel each other's presence in the social environment, at every moment adjusting our movements in response to this ongoing perceptual monitoring" (65). Hardly anything of this happens in *Edifício Master*, where, in spite of living in an environment almost as densely populated as those of their hillside neighbors at the Babilônia and Chapéu Mangueira favelas, residents hardly ever "feel each other's presence" except in moments of emergency (which are also often the ones they choose to tell to Coutinho's camera, the only ones worth telling and sharing): armed robberies, crimes of passion, a neighbor's solitary death next door or in the apartment above. Even then, many of these stories have only been received and passed on by hearsay, "de reportagem," as one of the long-time residents, Maria do Céu, puts it. Here, the space between one enclave of individuality and the next—the elevators and dimly lit landings between apartments—is no longer one where "perceptual monitoring" of one another's movements is necessary or even possible: only the muffled, ghostly traces of such movements resonate though the corridors as the crew advances from one apartment to the next. The mutual awareness of one another's presence that had underwritten the "orchestral" structure of *Babilônia 2000, O fim e o princípio*, or even *Boca de lixo* is being delegated here to the CCTV cameras that also register the film team's arrival and movement through the building.

In fact, whether Edifício Master is a "building" at all is very much open to question—at least if we think of building in the existential sense of Martin Heidegger, as an infinite process of learning to dwell in one's surroundings and to give expression to it in the form of ideas, concepts, and built structures. "Building as dwelling, that is, as being on the earth—says Heidegger—remains for man's everyday experience that which is from the outset 'habitual'—we inhabit it, as our language says so beautifully: it is the *Gewohnte*" (349). People do not "inhabit" Edifício Master as a building, nor—despite the way in which some of the younger residents talk about "the area" in terms that often sound like real estate agent jargon—does their inhabiting connect them to a social space beyond the confines of the "portaria," the doorman's desk: the final sequence of the film is a series of silent shots from different residents' windows onto the apartment building opposite Edifício Master, where bodies and furnished rooms similarly unconnected to one another can be furtively glimpsed through open or half-closed curtains and shutters.

What *Edifício Master* attempts to capture—and what Coutinho's later work, starting with *Jogo de cena*, will develop further in the all-out elimination of a lived-in, everyday diegetic setting—is, I would argue, a form of crisis of place that is both specific to the early twenty-first century Brazilian city and more universal in scope. It is a crisis of social experiences of "heterogenesis"—of conviviality and reciprocity as well as conflict and violence—which only the older residents still recall from the time, they say, when Edifício Master was a "dangerous place." "It is better now," Maria do Céu says, but the melancholy expression on her face following outbursts of laughter when recalling the turbulent old days also betrays a certain nostalgia for the liveliness and adventure of this past. The "cleansing" of this place of danger through a mixture (as Sérgio, the building's superintendent says with a knowing smirk on his mustachioed face) of the tactics of Jean Piaget, the child pedagogist, with those of Pinochet, being applied to convince less desirable residents to either change their ways or leave, resonates with histories of urban cleansing and gentrification everywhere in the world, and also with the new, global forms of segregation bred by a global regime that is morphing from neoliberalism to neofascism under our eyes. Mary Douglas's anthropology of cleanliness as a social imperative to ward off the danger of contagion joins forces here with Roberto Esposito's notion of "immunitas" as a protective shield the biopolitical reason of modernity has erected and perfected over centuries to contain the contingency and potentiality of "communitas" or what, with Félix Guattari, we have been calling an "ecology," a space and time of reciprocity and assemblage between individuals, collectives, and environments. By contrast, the "landscape" the residents of Edifício Master (and, increasingly, all of us) inhabit is the apogee not of the embodied, multisensorial taskscape of Ingold's essay and of Coutinho's earlier films but rather of detached and disembodied visual surveillance: a "scapeland," in Jean-François Lyotard's expression. The scapeland is that which is outside ecology, outside the "crossroads for the mineral, vegetable and animal kingdoms and for homo sapiens" (Lyotard 189), which had constituted a place and could be known as such. The scapeland, on the contrary, is characterized by "an excess of presence" that, like the mass of CCTV footage collected at a data bank, becomes incommensurable at the same time as it allows "a glimpse of the inhuman and the non-world [*l'immonde*]" (189). Coutinho's ecology responds to this crisis of place and to the emergence of the non-world, of *o imundo*, by way of an archaeology, a mode of space-time travel to the margins of contemporary (Brazilian) society to which experiences of place and worldliness have been relegated, and by a gradual "subtraction" of the spatial element, turning his later films into a kind of memory-work of bodies that live on purely in and as voices.

Notes

1. Jane Bennett has questioned Guattari's contradictory use of the plural to distinguish between 'three ecologies" that nonetheless need to be understood "transversally"—a "characteristically modern move" (114) of simultaneously suspending and reinscribing, in one and the same breath, the exceptionality of the human Guattari is allegedly attempting to overcome. Although I take Bennett's point (hence my use of the singular "ecology" instead of Guattari's plural), I nevertheless find his notion of a tripartite assemblage of subject, community, and material setting useful to think about certain formal and political operations in Coutinho's films.

2. Because of the self-imposed temporal limitation of the shoot—the film was to be shot entirely on New Year's Eve—Coutinho had decided to split his collaborators into separate crews, each of which would conduct interviews and shoot external footage in different parts of the favela as well as on Copacabana beach throughout the day.

3. Early on in his career, in *Theodorico, o imperador do sertão* (1978), Coutinho had already experimented with a very different, but no less effective, version of this sharing-out of narrative authority. Here, the "local subject" who takes the reins of the story by assuming—as does Rosa in *O fim e o princípio*—the position of interviewer is the provincial chieftain, the title-giving "Major" Theodorico Bezerra, owner of the vast *fazenda* of Irapuru in the interior of Rio Grande do Norte. Theodorico, who personally oversees voter registration of the farmhands and mill workers who live with their families on the enormous estate, thus securing his own eternal reelection to state office, not so much interviews his underlings as he lectures and

interrogates them, leaving them hardly any choice but to confirm his own opinions and to sing his praise. By contrast with Coutinho's later films, in *Theodorico* the film crew's restraint produces not empathy but estrangement: by letting the camera run and register the often awkward and coercive exchanges between Theodorico and the workers and their families, the film produces a powerful critique of the power relations that govern both the documentary encounter and the rural universe where this encounter takes place. For a more detailed analysis of *Theodorico*, see Esther Hamburger's essay (422–26) in Ohata's edited volume.

Works Cited

Allen, Alice. "Shifting Perspectives on Marginal Bodies and Spaces: Relationality, Power, and Social Difference in the Documentary Films *Babilônia 2000* and *Estamira*." *Bulletin of Latin American Research*, vol. 32, no. 1, 2013, pp. 78–93.

Azoulay, Ariella. *The Civil Contract of Photography*. Zone Books, 2008.

Bennett, Jane. *Vibrant Matter. A Political Ecology of Things*. Duke UP, 2010.

Bernardet, Jean-Claude. *Brasil em tempo de cinema. Ensaio sobre o cinema brasileiro de 1958 a 1966*. Companhia das Letras, 2007.

Bezerra, Cláudio. *A personagem no documentário de Eduardo Coutinho*. Papirus, 2014.

Certeau, Michel de. "Pratiques d'espace." *L'invention du quotidien, tome 1*. Gallimard, 1990, pp. 137–91.

Cosgrove, Denis E. *Social Formation and Symbolic Landscape*. U of Wisconsin P, 1998.

Cunha, Mariana da. "Between Image and Word: Minority Discourses and Community Construction in Eduardo Coutinho's Documentaries." *Visual Synergies in Fiction and Documentary Film from Latin America*, edited by Miriam Haddu and Joanna Page, Palgrave Macmillan, 2009, pp. 113–50.

Derrida, Jacques. "Countersignature." *Paragraph*, vol. 27, no. 2, 2008, pp. 7–42.

Douglas, Mary. *Purity and Danger. An Analysis of Concepts of Pollution and Taboo*. Routledge, 1966.

Esposito, Roberto. *Bíos. Biopolitics and Philosophy*. Translated by Timothy Campbell, U of Minnesota P, 2008.

Guattari, Félix. *The Three Ecologies*. Athlone, 2000.

Heidegger, Martin. "Building Dwelling Thinking." *Basic Writings*. HarperCollins, 1993, pp. 343–64.

Ingold, Tim. "The Temporality of Landscape." *World Archaeology*, vol. 25, no. 2, 1993, pp. 59–76.

Lefebvre, Martin. "Between Setting and Landscape in the Cinema." *Landscape and Film*, edited by Martin Lefebvre, Routledge, 2006, pp. 19–56.

Lins, Consuelo. *O documentário de Eduardo Coutinho: Televisão, cinema e vídeo*. Jorge Zahar, 2004.

Lins, Consuelo, and Cláudia Mesquita. *Filmar o real. Sobre o documentário brasileiro contemporâneo* Jorge Zahar, 2008.
Lyotard. Jean-Françcis. "Scapeland." *The Inhuman. Reflections on Time*. Polity, 1991, pp. 182–90
Massey, Doreen. *For Space*. Sage, 2005.
Nichols, Bill. *Representing Reality. Issues and Concepts in Documentary*. Indiana UP, 1991.
Ohata, Milton, editor. *Eduardo Coutinho*. Cosac Naify, 2013.
Sayad, Cecília. "Flesh for the Author: Filmic Presence in the Documentaries of Eduardo Coutinho." *Framework*, vol. 51, no. 1, 2010, pp. 134–50.
Tuan, Yi-Fu. *Space and Place. The Perspective of Experience*. U of Minnesota P, 1977.

2

Returning to the Sertão in the Films of Eduardo Coutinho

Ashley Brock

Eduardo Coutinho's best-known film, *Cabra marcado para morrer* (1964–1984), begins by looking back to the leftist, nationalist filmmaking culture out of which Cinema Novo emerged in the early 1960s. The film's opening sequence cuts from color footage filmed in 1981, in which Coutinho sets up a projector and a crowd gathers around a flickering rectangle of light, to black-and-white footage filmed in 1962, in which images of peasant labor play to the cheery tune of Carlos Lyra's "Canção do subdesenvolvido." The song's lyrics describe Brazil's legacy of underdevelopment in the wake of European colonialism and North American imperialism. Coutinho's voice-over explains that these were the concerns of his fellow filmmakers at the time: "The image of misery contrasted with the presence of imperialism. This was the typical tendency of the culture of those times."[1] He adds that as a member of the Centro Popular de Cultura (CPC), a socialist organization that aimed to disseminate revolutionary folk art, he too paid his tribute "ao nacionalismo da época" (to the nationalism of the period) by filming the footage we are now watching.[2]

This self-reflexive sequence serves both to locate the origins of Coutinho's project in this moment of radical political commitment and to distance the finished film from this moment. Like the crowd that gathers around Coutinho's projector in the 1981 footage, we are asked to look back on the footage from 1962 as a remnant of a bygone era. In the nearly twenty years that separate these two moments, the military dictatorship had put an end to the CPC and the idealistic culture of popular resistance it embodied.

Even after Brazil's return to democracy, it would have been impossible for Coutinho to return to his original project.³ In fact, one of the principal stories *Cabra* tells is that of the filmmaker's evolution as he moves away from the neorealist aesthetics and overt leftist ideology of Cinema Novo and begins to forge what would become his signature style, the unscripted conversational documentary.⁴

This evolutionary arc can be traced on a larger scale throughout Coutinho's career, beginning with his early apprenticeship under Cinema Novo auteurs and culminating in films like *Edifício Master* (2002), *O fim e o princípio* (2005), and *Jogo de cena* (2007). Such a shift—from a model of scripted storytelling that dramatizes politically charged events to a model of spontaneous and often intimate conversation with members of a local community—may appear to abandon the radical politics of Coutinho's early career. Indeed, the arc of Coutinho's career belies a degree of disillusionment with revolutionary politics, reflective of broader social changes in the decades following the Cuban Revolution. The filmmaker admits in a 2000 interview that "I cannot transform the world with a film, I have known this already for more than twenty years, and even if we could transform the world with a film, I do not know if I would be capable of making that film" (Avellar 54). Nevertheless, as critic Mauro Luciano Souza de Araújo argues, an anti-authoritarian, decolonial stance runs throughout Coutinho's filmography, often shining light on dynamics of cultural and economic dependency in Brazil (37–38). What changes, then, is how Coutinho's political commitment manifests in his films. Counterintuitively, the more he moves away from fictional representation and toward a uniquely performative model of documentary, the less faith he puts in one of the fundamental tenets of politically motivated documentary: that by revealing injustices and atrocities, a filmmaker might inspire action and thus directly impact the world. Instead, the model of commitment that emerges in his mature filmmaking is rooted in a decolonial critique of representation itself.

Distancing himself from the position he held earlier in his career, Coutinho states in a 1985 interview that the realist political cinema of the 1960s tended toward a militancy and an intellectual arrogance that precluded understanding the very people with whom it aimed to express solidarity: "In the 1960s, we made very political films, with a vision like that . . . a bit authoritarian, more authoritarian than what's accepted today, you see [. . .] We judged the common people and, at the same time, omnipotent, we thought we understood the common people. I think that's over, it's changed" (Viany 423).⁵ In the 1981 interviews included in *Cabra*, we can already see the filmmaker beginning to renegotiate this stance in order to hunt out a humbler and more honest mode of engagement with his subjects, one that would ultimately empower their self-representation rather than reduce them to characters in a political drama conceived by intellectuals who presume to understand the plight of the common man. The resulting film, for many viewers, still expresses "um espírito militante" (a militant spirit) (Fagioli 127). Nevertheless, in this film, one can already discern the seeds of the transformation Coutinho's notion of political commitment would undergo in the decades to come.

This shifting notion of the political work of film is particularly salient in Coutinho's depictions of *sertanejos*, the perennially impoverished residents of the sertão, or rural northeastern backlands. Coutinho, a native of São Paulo who spent most of his adult life in Rio de Janeiro, returned to the Northeast periodically throughout his career: in his time with CPC in the early 1960s, he shot documentary footage and began working on *Cabra*; during the dictatorship, he directed several documentary pieces for the television program *Globo Repórter* as well as the fictional film *Faustão* (1971); after the return to democracy, he would return to the sertão to finish *Cabra* and later to make the documentaries *Os romeiros do Pedro Cícero* (1994) and *O fim e o princípio* (2005). Though these films address typical themes associated with the sertão—banditry, violence, drought, poverty, idolatry, and superstition—they resist reducing the *sertanejo* to stereotypes, in large part because through such projects Coutinho develops a profound fascination with the individual voices of his subjects. The voice is, as Mladen Dolar has argued, precisely the part of speech that exceeds the semiotic function of language and thereby resists abstraction; it evidences above all a singular bodily presence. Nowhere is this fascination with the embodied presence of the individual more evident than in *O fim e o princípio*, which I view as the culmination of a career-long quest to offer the *sertanejo* a different place in Brazilian cinema and Brazilian political discourse than that offered by Cinema Novo.

The *sertanejo* in Cinema Novo: *Vidas secas* and *Deus e o diabo na terra do sol*

The sertão has long been an ambivalent cultural signifier in Brazil, both valued as the autochthonous core or Brazilianess and stigmatized as a symptom of intractable backwardness. These two faces of the sertão would come together uneasily in Cinema Novo, which was conceived of as a nationalistic movement to resist the pervasive influence of Hollywood on Brazilian filmmaking. In his 1965 manifesto, "Estética da fome," Glauber Rocha declares the need to combat the scourge of "films about rich people, in nice houses, driving around in luxury cars; happy, funny, fast films with no message, with purely industrial objectives" (Rocha 17).[6] For Rocha, the popularity of such glossy depictions of bourgeois life is symptomatic both of Brazil's continued cultural dependency and of the nation's shame-driven desire to keep the dire poverty of much of its population out of the public light. The auteurs of the first phase of Cinema Novo (1960–1964) would respond with a stark aesthetic—often filming in black and white, using handheld cameras, and overexposing the film to create a harsh, high-contrast image—and by setting their films in blighted rural landscapes. In what follows in this section, I outline the promise as well as the limitations of the political radicalization of the iconic national landscape of the sertão in two of the most celebrated films of the first phase of Cinema Novo: Nelson Pereira dos Santos's *Vidas Secas/Barren Lives* (1963) and Glauber Rocha's *Deus e o diabo na terra do sol/Black God, White Devil* (1964).

There is a historically deep tradition in Brazilian national literature and cinema alike of coding the sertão as a place of backwardness and *barbarie*, a tradition that proves strangely (or not) compatible with the romanticization of the backlands as a mythic site of origins for the nation.[7] What these two seemingly contradictory rhetorical gestures have in common is that both displace the underdevelopment and violence of the sertão into an archaic past: images of the sertão as a vast, de-peopled natural landscape, as an originary source of autochthonous culture, and of the setting of epic battles between civilization and *barbarie* all occlude the contemporaneity, or what Johannes Fabian calls the coevalness of *sertanejos* who coexist with Brazil's urban modernity. As Jens Andermann has argued, the radical politics of Cinema Novo lies largely in the way it insists on the historical presentness of the "rural backlands and the margins of the city"; they become "no longer a primitive origin but the very focal point of contemporariness" (54). In this act of re-historicization, these films aim to denaturalize the poverty and underdevelopment of the sertão. They thus follow the politically committed regionalist novels of the 1930s to demystify the connection between the misery of the *sertanejos* and their exploitation by the landowning classes and to signal the complicity of the government and the church in this exploitation.[8]

Such a critique is particularly trenchant in the early 1960s in the wake of President Juscelino Kubitschek's "Plan of National Development." Beyond critiquing the injustice of the neofeudal socioeconomic structures that continue to govern the sertão well into the twentieth century, Cinema Novo auteurs challenge the image of Brazil as successfully modernized nation, a vision that Kubitschek's progressivist government had worked hard to propagate in the 1950s: "By situating Brazil's underdevelopment at the heart of its filmic ethics and poetics, *Cinema Novo* shattered the legitimacy of Kubitschek's developmentalist spatial fiction of homogenization [. . . and] rejected the symbolic closure of images of Brazil's development and modernity" (Sadek 62). In addition to revealing the unfulfilled promises of the nation's progressivist ideology, an implicit objective of films like *Vidas secas* and *Deus e o diabo* is to question whether the obedient pursuit of the nation's project of "civilization" could ever liberate the *sertanejo* from his misery or if a more violent form of revolution is the only possible means of escape from the cycle of exploitation and poverty in which he is trapped. Echoing language of the Cuban Revolution, Rocha insists on a revolutionary "estética da violência" (aesthetic of violence) anchored in "um amor de ação e transformação" (a love of action and transformation); according to Rocha, the "mais nobre manifestação cultural da fome é a violência" (the noblest manifestation of a culture of hunger is violence) (17). One of the most radical promises of Cinema Novo, then, might be the way it complicates Brazil's long history of coding the violence of the sertão simply as primitivism or *barbarie* and gives it instead a utopian dimension.

What we see in *Vidas secas* and *Deus e o diabo*, however, is that within the diegetic world of the characters, the liberating potential of revolutionary violence is often thwarted or misdirected. Fabiano, the beleaguered patriarch of the peasant family featured in *Vidas secas*, repeatedly fails to stand up to his oppressors: when threatened with the loss of his job, he subserviently backs away from his accusation that the rancher whose land he works has cheated him out of his earnings, and when confronted with the opportunity to kill the soldier who has beaten, imprisoned, and emasculated him, Fabiano finds himself paralyzed in mid-action and eventually lowers his machete. In contrast, early on in *Deus e o diabo*, the protagonist Manoel uses his machete to kill the exploitative rancher who insists Manoel has no legal recourse to claim his share of the herd. Manoel's act of rebellion does not, however, liberate him from the subaltern position of poor *sertanejo*. Forced to flee deeper into the sertão, Manoel becomes a follower of the messianic cult leader São Sebastião, a figure explicitly compared to the leader of the Canudos revolt, Antônio Conselheiro, and later of the bandit Corisco, a *cangaceiro* in the tradition of the folk hero Lampião.[9] Both of these would-be champions of the common *sertanejos* employ violent methods that point back to the *barbarie* for which the sertão is infamous.

While Rocha's depictions of physical violence signal the atavism and barbarity of would-be revolutionary projects born in the sertão, the form of the film, with its frequent jump cuts, fragmented temporal progression, and abrupt shifts in tone, belies a more insidious form of violence that plagues the psyche of the *sertanejo*: a volatility and gullibility born of utter desperation and ignorance. With no hope of attaining any form of economic protection or legal personhood, no education, or even any mooring in the wisdom of a local community (Manoel's mother is killed in the aftermath of his crime, and he persistently ignores the better judgment of his wife), men like Manoel are extremely vulnerable to the radical and ultimately destructive ideologies represented by the figures of São Sebastião and Corisco. Whipped about violently between extremes—God and the devil, love and hate, hope and despair, pious subservience and passionate outbursts—Manoel is represented as the victim rather than the author of his destiny. This effect is underscored by the role of the blind troubadour, Júlio, who narrates the various turns of fate in Manoel's life through the *cordel* folk songs he sings throughout the film. This "soundtrack" hovers somewhere between the diegetic and the extradiegetic, as Júlio appears on-screen as character, but his disembodied voice also provides voice-over–like transitions in scenes in which he is not present. Casting Manoel as a character in a folk ballad serves to underscore the degree to which he appears to be playing a well-known part, one that has not only already been written (about him in the third person) but that appears to be as old as time.

Vidas secas draws even more attention to the unlikelihood of the impoverished and uneducated *sertanejo* being able to conceive of, articulate, and pursue his own vision for the future. In Pereira dos Santos's film, as in the 1938 novel by Graciliano Ramos on which it is based, it is the family's poverty of language, as much as their material poverty, that condemns them to a nearly subhuman level of existence. The paucity of dialogue in the film is pronounced from the opening shot, in which Fabiano's family slowly becomes visible on the horizon of the stark, sun-drenched landscape. The soundtrack overlaid on this scene is the eerie and grating high-pitched noise of a squeaking wagon wheel, which underscores the muteness of the family as they continue to wordlessly walk, rest, and eat for more than five minutes before Fabiano's wife, Vitória, speaks the first lines of the film, justifying her decision to kill the family's parrot for food: "Também não servia para nada, nem sabia falar" (It wasn't good for anything anyway, it couldn't even talk). The parrot's fatal speechlessness is of course a direct reflection of the lack of verbal expressivity of the family with which it lived. In fact, in the film's many dialogue-free, though rarely silent (we hear animals and the sounds of human movements and labor), shots of the parched landscape, its barrenness seems as much a product of lack of speech as of lack of rain.

It is significant that Vitória, the more vocal of the pair, is also the more ambitious. At the end of the film, Vitória will voice her hope that they will reach the city, where their boys will go to school and learn a trade other than that of their father, and they will all cease to live like animals and become "gente." Fabiano, whose interactions with the city and city people have led to nothing but humiliation, resentment, and disillusionment, is less optimistic. In fact, it is precisely his dispossession of language and subsequent lack of social proficiency that leave him feeling cheated, mocked, and disrespected at every turn, suggesting that his stunted verbal capacity is not only an effect of being an abject *sertanejo* but also the handicap that makes this position inescapable. In the contrast between Fabiano and Vitória, it becomes evident that the extreme linguistic poverty of the former corresponds with his lack of hope and stymied imagination: he can envision no future for himself and his sons beyond the cycle of misery, precarity, and exploitation that has defined his life. When, at the end of the film, Vitória asks if they can possibly continue living like they have been, "como bicho escondido no mato" (like an animal hiding in the bush), Fabiano replies simply, "Não, não podemos" (No, we cannot).

Though these films succeed in making visible the rural poverty and underdevelopment that continue to plague modern Brazil as well as the neocolonial systems of oppression that propagate such misery, they do not break free entirely from what Jens Andermann calls the "allegorical overdetermination" of the rural interior, which historically made it "a screen for projecting the nation's mythical origins" (53). The *sertanejo* remains a type rather than an individual. Moreover, the seemingly intractable poverty of language, culture, and spirit of the *sertanejos* depicted makes the form of solidarity solicited from the viewer necessarily impersonal and paternalistic. Otherwise put, the political potential of these films lies in the hope of awakening revolutionary consciousness in the viewer, while the *sertanejos* themselves (especially the men) remain impervious to such consciousness (in the case of Fabiano) or incapable of directly empowering themselves with it (in the case of Manoel).

Coutinho's sertão:
Cabra marcado para morrer and *O fim e o princípio*

In Coutinho's representations of the sertão, by contrast, material poverty is uncoupled from poverty of language and imagination: the *sertanejos* he interviews speak with conviction and idiosyncratic eloquence about topics ranging from the personal to the political. Many critics have, in fact, interpreted Coutinho's signature conversational documentary style as creating the time, space, and conditions for his subjects to performatively represent themselves for the camera.[10] Though the capacity to imagine and perform one's identity, one's values, one's hopes and fears, and one's place in the world does not necessarily mitigate the difficult conditions of life in the sertão or grant *sertanejos* concrete hope for material and political gains, it does allow them a profound sense of human agency and change the terms on which the viewer encounters them. The material poverty of Coutinho's subjects is clearly visible, but it is rarely the focus of the encounter, and there is no attempt to reduce the *sertanejos* interviewed to political symbols or symptoms of underdevelopment: "The characters are not informants about this or that theme—they are singular people who don't represent, typify, or exemplify anything" (Mesquita and Lins 51).[11] Unlike the most iconic *sertanejos* of Cinema Novo, who, in spite of their complexity, remain archetypal and seem to receive their sense of identity from their circumstances, Coutinho's subjects are delightfully individual and unpredictable.

The wealth of language and creative means of self-expression such subjects possess is pronounced in *O fim e o princípio*, which features interviews with more than a dozen elderly residents of the same small town in Paraíba, many of whom are related to one another. Though many of the interviews touch on common themes—marriage, family, death, beliefs about the afterlife, and so forth—each interviewee presents a unique perspective. The singularity of each interview has less to do with a diversity of life experiences than with a diversity of modes of expression: in fact, the consistency of the setup—nearly everyone appears in medium and close shots filmed from a single angle, either in or in front of the home—serves to underscore the unique quality of each speaker's voice, turns of phrase, facial expressions, and body language. As Mesquita and Lins note, Coutinho uses more close-ups in this film than is typical for him, reflecting a literal and metaphorical proximity between filmmaker and subject that is a product of his own advanced age (the septuagenarian filmmaker had to get quite close to hear them) as well as an intensified interest in the individual face (54).

Coutinho has explained in interviews that the content of what his subjects say and the lives they lead matter less than their capacity for storytelling, "that force, it's that thing, charisma" (Avellar 53).

Based on Coutinho's own words, it would seem, in fact, that he gravitates to the Northeast to capture "the extraordinary richness of speech of the illiterate, especially in less industrialized regions [. . .] In the regions where oral, popular culture is still alive, enriched by all the impurities, even the speech of the literate contains all of these expressive resources" (Coutinho, "O olhar no documentário" 20).[12] Coutinho is quick to clarify that he does not mean to glorify poverty, illiteracy, and underdevelopment, much less defend the conditions that perpetuate it in the Northeast. Yet, as a number of critics have observed, the community in Paraíba on which he settles for *O fim* seems to attract him in part because its residents have minimal access to technologies such as television and telephones and thus have not had their speech homogenized by exposure to modern media.[13] This is one of the messier aspects of the politics of this film: the creative use of speech that elevates Coutinho's interviewees from cultural objects to be documented to performers and artists in their own right cannot be separated from the state of underdevelopment and dependency in which their region has been detained (Souza de Araújo 42). I return to this conundrum at the end of this chapter.

A particularly telling example of the creative language and "força fabulatoria dos indivíduos" (the fabulatory power of individuals) that Coutinho is so adept at capturing is Leocádio, a lanky and self-possessed man whose neighbors describe him as stuck-up because he knows how to read (Mesquita and Lins 57). A perfect antithesis to Fabiano from *Vidas secas*, Leocádio shares with Coutinho a fascination with words: they debate the difference between "palavras certas" (proper words) and "palavras comuns" (everyday words) before Leocádio launches into retellings of the story of Pedro Álvares Cabral's discovery of Brazil and the Tower of Babel, weaving his own mythology in which he includes Coutinho as a character. In this conversation, Leocádio becomes Coutinho's interlocutor, his co-theorist of language, rather than merely his interviewee. This shift, note Mesquita and Lins, in many ways epitomizes Coutinho's approach to the sertão if not to his subjects more generally (59).

What gives Leocádio such a distinctive presence on-screen, even more than his erudition, is his idiosyncratic use of words—he explains he is in poor condition to talk because he lacks "pontuação" or "punctuation"—and his mannerisms while speaking—he gesticulates theatrically and uses his hands and props, such as a yellow folder to frame and sometimes obscure his face in front of the camera (see fig. 2.1). It is in this sense that Leocádio becomes a character of his own creation.[14] There can be no doubt that Leocádio performs for the camera and participates actively in crafting the version of himself that will appear on-screen. As Coutinho explains, "Really the common people, who are in the film, who become characters, they are natural actors. They are people who play themselves well" (Coutinho, "Se eu definisse o documentário" 146).[15] Leocádio's erect posture, his tendency in certain moments to pull back away from the window through which he is being filmed, and his unequivocal stance as an authority on language all contribute to the effect that we are witnessing a moment of self-representation, as if it were Leocádio, rather than Coutinho, writing the script, calling the shots, and making the final cuts. In fact, Coutinho considers that his interviewees "stage themselves" (142).

Creating this effect is precisely the objective of Coutinho's signature documentary style, which is governed by a commitment to spontaneity, an ethos of humility and curiosity, and a critical self-reflexivity that entails revealing (rather than editing out) the moments when the profilmic reality challenges the filmmaker's vision for his project. I would like to suggest that, beyond empowering the self-representation of his subjects, this approach

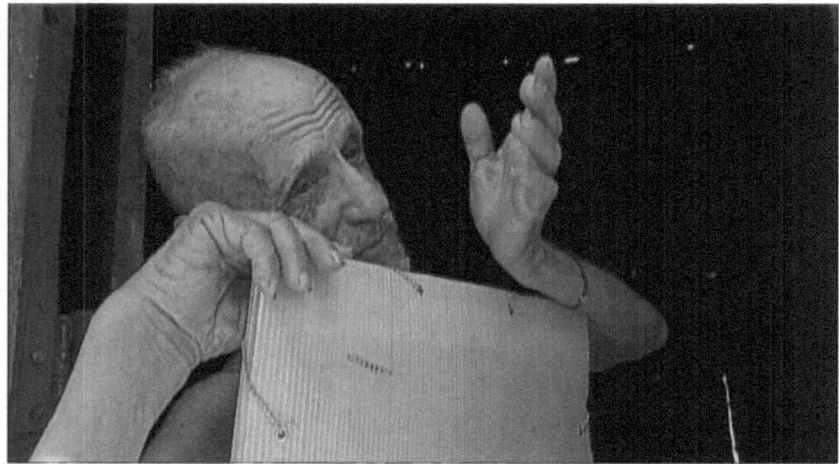

Figure 2.1. Leocádio holds forth on the difference between proper words and common words in Eduardo Coutinho's *O fim e o princípio*. Source: *O fim e o princípio* (*The End and the Beginning*). Directed by Eduardo Coutinho, João Moreira Salles, 2005.

yields a renegotiated notion of authenticity, one that breaks radically both with Cinema Novo and with the ethnographic documentary tradition.[16] Though Cinema Novo incorporated avant-garde technique, it shared with traditional ethnographic filmmaking the conviction that the social value of cinema lies in its ability to hold a mirror up to the world; it sought to reveal the conditions of poverty and exploitation excluded from government propaganda and commercial films alike.

In contrast, as scholars of his films are fond of pointing out, Coutinho does not document a preexisting reality but rather creates a new reality in front of the camera. Cecilia Sayad claims, for example, that Coutinho is not interested in "the reality that preexists the act of shooting" and, in fact, "believes that the only reality the camera can register is that of the shoot (140). What his films document is primarily the impact of the filmmaker and the camera on the subject's behavior" (137). João Moreira Salles, Coutinho's longtime friend and producer of many of his later films, writes: "Everything that happens in Eduardo's films exists only because it's being filmed. The people wouldn't say the beautiful (or sad, moving, terrible, joyful) things they say if it weren't for the presence of Eduardo and his camera in front of them."[17] It is in Coutinho's ability to invite the performance of a new reality that Salles locates the political significance of his colleague's work: "When cinema produces its own reality, making films ceases to be an irrelevant act. Making films—and principally making documentaries—changes the world. Without heroism, very little, subtly, but it changes it."[18] We might thus say, as Ferreira Dias does, that for Coutinho, documentary film ceases to be "o espelho do real" (a mirror of the real) and becomes "transformador do real" (transformatory of the real) (63).

This transformation of the real, I want to argue, depends on Coutinho's own performance of ceding control over his films and embracing contingency. I use the word "performance" not to suggest that Coutinho's films are actually more scripted and manipulated than they appear to be (though this may also be the case), but rather to indicate the way Coutinho self-reflexively draws attention to the spontaneity of his process within his films. My focus, then, is less on how Coutinho coaxes out the performances of his subjects and more on how he himself plays (and transforms) the role of filmmaker for the audience. For example, through a voice-over in *Cabra*, he explains that when he decided to complete the film in 1981, he had no plan beyond finding and interviewing the participants with whom he had worked decades earlier: "There was no previous script, rather the idea was just to try to find the peasants who had worked on *Cabra marcado para morrer*. I wanted to pick up our contact again through statements about the past."[19] *O fim* opens with footage of a van ride into Paraíba and a voice-over that closely echoes Coutinho's statement in *Cabra*: "We came to Paraíba to try to make a film in four weeks with no kind of previous research, no particular theme, no particular location. We wanted to find a rural community we liked and that accepted us [. . .] Maybe we wouldn't find any and then the film would become about the search for a setting, a theme, and above all characters."[20]

In this extremely open-ended plan, one of Coutinho's only parameters is that they settle on a *rural* community that *accepts them*, subtly casting this trip as a recapitulation of the return trip to the sertão in *Cabra*, where the stated objective was first and foremost to reestablish personal connections with the peasants (and thus reconnect with the past). If we are to take Coutinho at his word, *O fim* is to be far more open-ended than *Cabra*, but also more self-reflexive, for this time he and his film crew set off without particular subjects in mind, prepared to make a film about the quest to find an adequate community about which to make a film. Indeed, Mariana Duccini Junqueira da Silva reads *O fim* as the apogee of Coutinho's pursuit of unscriptedness: "a contingência do real é, neste filme, elevada à condição estrutural" (the contingency of the real is, in this film, elevated to a structural condition) (104). Because Coutinho did not know in advance who his subjects would be, he necessarily goes into the film knowing less about his interviewees than in previous films (Mesquita and Lins 51). Early on in the film, he appeals to Rosa, a local schoolteacher, to orient him to the community, thus including in the film the "research" stage that most documentarians complete before the camera ever rolls.

This performance of renouncing the control and foresight typically attributed to film directors reprises a similar gesture in the making of the later parts of *Cabra marcado para morrer*, throwing into relief the degree to which this shift toward a more contingent and necessarily less comfortable mode of filmmaking makes up the primary subject matter of the earlier film. *Cabra* was originally conceived as a dramatic reenactment of the life and death of João Pedro Teixeira, a leader of the peasant movement who was murdered in 1962. Coutinho planned to make the film in Teixeira's town of Sape, hiring local peasants involved in the movement to play themselves. As Coutinho narrates in the film, however, these plans were thwarted early on, as civil unrest and police repression in Sape forced him to change locations. Coutinho and his crew brought Teixeira's widow, Elizabeth, with them to Galiléia to play herself, but they had to find peasants unrelated to the original events to produce the reenactment. This intervention of the politics of the day into the world of the film, changing its course, anticipates the way the filming soon thereafter would be violently interrupted by the 1964 military coup—equipment destroyed, footage confiscated, participants arrested—and put on hold for more than sixteen years.

Coutinho's decision to write these interruptions into the final version of the film—in fact, to make the film about the challenge of revising his original vision in the face of such interruptions—is only the most dramatic way in which the film documents the process of relinquishing directorial control and entering into a dialogic relationship with the profilmic. As part of the original 1964 project, Coutinho had written a script for his actors, but, according to his own admission, the dialogue he had written was "banal," and the best scenes he filmed were those in which the peasant actors improvised their own lines (Ferreira Dias 65). In the finished version of the film, Coutinho narrates over recuperated footage of the scene when Teixeira and the other peasants confront the landowner, informing the audience that the peasant actors had improvised their lines on the set. Paradoxically, then, the heavy-handed intervention of the filmmaker (in the form of this voice-over directing the audience how to understand the footage we are watching) calls attention to his decision to stray from the script and allow for a more spontaneous performance.

The 1981 footage was never scripted, Coutinho insists, and he further highlights its spontaneity by including moments when his subjects do not perform as expected. For example, when Elizabeth says her goodbyes, she follows the crew out to their van and, with the camera still rolling, delivers a final speech on the importance of carrying on the fight her husband started, insisting that the return to democracy is not enough: "The fight that cannot stop. As long as they say that there is hunger and salaries that lead to misery, the people have to fight [. . .] it's necessary to change the regime, it's necessary for people to fight. As long as there is this little regime, this little democracy there . . . democracy without freedom, democracy with salaries that lead to misery and hunger, democracy where the son of the worker and of the peasant doesn't have the right to study, ah . . . there's just no way."[21] By including this highly unscripted moment in the final cut of the film, Coutinho underscores the continuity of the political commitment of the 1981 project with that of the 1964 project: both provide a megaphone of sorts through which to amplify the urgent message of the peasants' struggle for justice. Yet Coutinho's methods in 1981 are radically different than they were in 1964: rather than asking the peasants to re-create a version of events that he finds politically significant, Coutinho now simply keeps the camera rolling, giving them time and space to speak.

These changes reflect Coutinho's *apprentissage* in the world of documentary television in the intervening years.[22] Yet, as fiction gives way to documentary, Coutinho becomes a character and the making of the film an integral part of the plot (Fagioli 124). The statements about the past that Coutinho collects from the film's participants in 1981 reconstruct the story of how they were impacted by the dictatorship; we learn that many of the peasants who acted in the film were persecuted, imprisoned, and tortured because of their participation in the project, which was portrayed in the media as a communist plot to incite a peasant revolution. Elizabeth was forced to go into hiding, breaking ties with her community and her children. The film's title, *Cabra marcado para morrer*, thus takes on new meaning: once reserved for João Pedro Teixeira, a man whose political activism had branded him an enemy of the ruling classes, the phrase "a man marked to die" now described all of those who had associated themselves with the film. As such, the film self-reflexively traces the aftermath of its own intervention into the community where Coutinho filmed in 1964.

It is in this self-reflexivity, combined with Coutinho's commitment to eliciting and airing spontaneous performances, that the ethics of Coutinho's mature filmmaking lies. By including himself and the filmmaking process in the frame (sometimes quite literally), Coutinho submits himself and his projects to the scrutiny of his subjects, thus complicating the ethnographic paradigm in which it is the unidirectional gaze of the intellectual that produces the other as an object of inquiry.[23] This process is sometimes quite uncomfortable, as when Coutinho interviews João Mariano, the man who plays João Pedro Teixeira.

Coutinho introduces João Mariano as the one participant in the *Cabra* who was not political and who had not been involved in the peasant movement; Coutinho explains that he agreed to be in the film because he had been fired by the mill and was unemployed at the time. What makes this interview of particular interest to me is the way Coutinho responds, both on-screen and in the editing room, to João Mariano's evident discomfort at being filmed. The two men sit across from each other at a small street-side table; the camera is trained on João Mariano's face for much of the conversation. Shortly after João Mariano begins to explain that he has always kept out of politics, Coutinho cuts him off, claiming the wind is causing interference with the sound. After this interruption, João Mariano appears reluctant to continue. He looks down in silence. The camera rolls for thirty seconds before he speaks again, in which time Coutinho addresses him four times, encouraging him to continue with his story and asking if everything is all right. During this awkward pause, the camera zooms out to include the side of Coutinho's face in the shot. At one point, Coutinho can be seen exchanging a worried glance with an off-screen crew member, while a young child hovering at the edge of the frame looks on suspiciously (fig. 2.2).

When João Mariano finally speaks, he explains that Coutinho should already know that he never wanted to be involved in revolutionary politics. He claims that he left the mill to avoid being mixed up in such affairs and that when he signed on to do the film, he did not understand the political implications. When Coutinho asks about João Mariano's religion, the latter ambiguously implies that he was thrown out of his church because of his involvement with the film and that this is the reason he is reluctant to carry on with the interview. He adds that he cannot believe that Coutinho is filming what he's saying, making reference to the adage "once bitten,

Figure 2.2. Coutinho (right) exchanges a look with someone off-screen during the prolonged silence of João Mariano (left) in *Cabra marcado para morrer*. Source: *Cabra marcado para morrer (Twenty Years Later)*. Directed by Eduardo Coutinho, 1964–1984. Instituto Moreira Salles, 2014. DVD.

twice shy," but stops short of directly accusing Coutinho of having brought misfortune on him by involving him in the film. When Coutinho asks him point-blank if he was harmed by his participation in the film, João Mariano replies in the negative: "Não fui prejudicado pelo filme" (I wasn't harmed by the film), but then goes on to qualify his statement, claiming that the mill owner wanted to kill him and repeating how disappointed he was to be thrown out of his church. Coutinho's final question in the interview is about whether João Mariano enjoyed watching himself on-screen. João Mariano replies, "Fiquei satisfeito. Porque vi o fruto de meu trabalho" (I was satisfied. Because I saw the fruits of my work).

The inclusion of this scene in the final version of the film, in its full, awkward duration, indicates the filmmaker's openness to critical reflection on the ethics of his project.[24] Whereas some of his subjects, most notably Elizabeth Teixeira, give impassioned performances that support the urgency and value of Coutinho's project, others, such as João Mariano and some of Elizabeth's children, point to the negative consequences the film has had on the individuals and families involved. There are several moments in the interview with João Mariano that could be interpreted as Coutinho trying to avoid what is evidently an uncomfortable subject: when he interrupts João Mariano to check the sound, when he seems to try to change the subject to religion, and when he directs the conversation back to the satisfaction and pride João Mariano felt when watching himself on-screen. It is evident in João Mariano's recalcitrance that he, too, would rather avoid an unpleasant confrontation. By leaving this supremely uncomfortable negotiation in the film, Coutinho not only conveys João Mariano's ambivalence and resentment but also throws into relief the power dynamic that makes it impossible for João Mariano to express these feelings directly on camera: his reticence, ambiguity, and indirection seem to issue from a combination of deference—he is loath to offend Coutinho, who he admits has always been kind to him—and futility—he insists repeatedly that Coutinho should already know how he feels and therefore that he need not spell it out on camera.

This form of self-critical reflection on the encounter between urban, middle-class intellectual and working-class, often uneducated *sertanejo* is central to the ethics and the politics of Coutinho's later films. As Sayad points out, Coutinho prefers to foreground rather than elide the "social, economic and cultural gap between the director and his subjects" (139). Throughout *O fim*, for example, the *sertanejos* interviewed address Coutinho with the formal "O senhor" or "O doutor," and many of them comment on the education and wisdom that he projects by virtue of being an outsider with an urban accent and a camera. Some of them, such as Chico Moisés, who appears skeptical of Coutinho's intentions, even self-deprecatingly ask what he could possibly hope to learn from them. The self-consciousness of the *sertanejos* about the class remove that separates them from Coutinho and his crew is evident in moments such as when Assis reassures them that poverty is not contagious as he invites them into his humble home, or when Antonia refuses to come out and appear on camera until she's changed into her best dress. As Sayad argues, these subjects appear to be highly aware of the possibility of being made an exotic spectacle, an ethnographic exhibit of poverty (139).

Whereas the political work of Cinema Novo was conceived of in terms of revealing poverty and underdevelopment, Coutinho's films subtly underscore the violence of such an act of exposure by capturing how sensitive his subjects are to being reduced to stereotypes in the media. Most importantly, by performing again and again the surrendering of control in which he renounces the idea of script and preconceived objectives for his films, Coutinho draws attention to the extraordinary capacity of his subjects to represent themselves and their visions of the world—which include their impressions, their curiosity, and their suspicion about Coutinho and his crew—on their own terms.

One might object that this renunciation of control is *merely* a performance: after all, Coutinho determines how much of the contingency and spontaneity caught on film to include in the final cut. Moreover, Coutinho's claim at the beginning of *O fim* that he went in with no agenda whatsoever may seem disingenuous given the thematic consistency between the interviews featured. Though we do not always hear the questions Coutinho asks, it is hard to believe that nearly all the subjects arrive at the topics of marriage and mortality without any prompting. It would seem, then, that he curates the thematic content of the film much more than he lets on. Rather than diminishing the authenticity of the spontaneous encounter captured on film, however, the unavoidable presence of the filmmaker and his unmistakable participation in crafting the encounter we witness lay bare the process of mediation that underlies all filmmaking (and ethnography) but that is often effaced in realist film and traditional documentary.

It is for this reason, as Catherine Russell has argued, that experimental techniques of estrangement and self-reflexivity in film can be extremely effective at revising the terms of the ethnographic encounter for the postcolonial moment: "The task of postcolonial ethnography is not only to include the Other within modernity but to revise the terms of realist representation" (6). As we have seen, the performative nature of Coutinho's films, which foreground the intersubjective and spontaneous interaction of filmmaker and subject, shatters the illusion on which traditional ethnographic filmmaking depends: transparent representation of an autochthonous reality unaffected by the presence of the camera.

The political and ethical potency of Coutinho's films, then, cannot be separated from their meta-filmic quality. In other words, what they transform most radically are the terms of representation that govern how common people, like the *sertanejos* featured in *Cabra* and *O fim*, can occupy the screen. It is not that Coutinho alone possesses the power to transform the reality he films, making the reticent talkative, the cash-poor wealthy in wisdom and wit; rather, by performing his own receptivity to unscripted encounters, he stages situations in which his subjects create a new version of their lives, their pasts, their relationships, and their experience of being filmed; and he invites his audience to experience these interviews as instances of what Consuelo Lins has called "self-fabulation" (253). This form of self-possession was always out of reach for the *sertanejos* pictured in Cinema Novo. By making it the focus of his films, Coutinho insists that not only do these marginalized and often forgotten voices form part of our contemporary moment but that they are also perfectly capable of creating their own version of it.

I understand creating the conditions for such versions of reality to be heard and heeded so that the *sertanejo* can become more than a signifier of backwardness and misery to be Coutinho's primary political work in these films. Though this shift away from the revolutionary politics of Cinema Novo may appear to neglect the collective plight of oppressed classes in favor of celebrating individual agency and voice, the composite form of Coutinho's later films generates a new kind of collectivity. By suturing together short interviews with many subjects rather than homing in one or two protagonists, Coutinho foregrounds the question of how *a community* might tell its collective experience. As he states in the opening of *O fim*, "Queremos achar uma comunidade rural" (we want to find a rural community). Beyond giving voice to experiences of repression and disenfranchisement that have been censored and written out of history (Fagioli 125), Coutinho's project entails underscoring the agency and authorship of the *sertanejos* themselves. As we have seen, however, he does so by foregrounding rather than effacing the work of mediation carried out by the film and filmmaker.

Why Return to the sertão?

But the question remains: what is the recurrent appeal of the sertão for Coutinho? Why, as he suggests at the beginning of *O fim*, for example, must his quest for spontaneity, human connection, and acceptance take him to a *rural* community? The answer lies in part in Coutinho's belief that isolated communities that remain outside the influence of mass media and graphocentric culture are founts of "criação verbal, do ponto de vista da sintaxe, do vocabulário, etc." (verbal creation, from the point of view of the syntax, the vocabular, etc.) (Coutinho, "Se eu definisse o documentário" 146). Given his conviction that the sertão is "o lugar no Brasil onde se inventa melhor" (the place in Brazil where people invent best), it would appear that the intentional open-endedness of the project as well as the choice of the sertão as setting serve to set the stage for such creative performances: "he seems to find, in the rich verbal expression of the elderly *sertanejos* that which he intuited when the film was completely open-ended" (Mesquita and Lins 53).[25]

One must ask if Coutinho has completely escaped from the ethnographic paradigm in which, according to Russell, "the primitive Other comes to represent the childhood of civilization" (5), or if he, like so many ethnographers, writers, and artists before him, turns to a more rustic way of life for an authenticity of encounter threatened in modernity.[26] In his writings on ethnographic allegory, James Clifford proposes that the best recourse for modern-day ethnographers seeking to break with "the relentless placement of others in a present-becoming past" is to reveal the cultural other to be "the product of a narrative of discovery, in specific historical circumstances" instead of portraying him or her as "a stable, essential whole" (115). Coutinho remains committed to historicizing the plight of the *sertanejo* and locating his subjects in a "determinado contexto sócio-econômico do país" (determined socioeconomic context of the country), though he does so more subtly in *O fim* than in *Cabra*, thus allowing his subjects to escape being defined by such conditions (Souza de Araújo 40). In this way, he underscores the degree to which the sertão is at once real and mythic, contemporary, and archaic (Souza de Araújo 45). Just as importantly, according to Clifford's model, he also includes in the story the ethnographer's inevitable search for self-understanding and the neo-pastoral desire to recover a more "authentic" mode of being that is lost or obscured in "modern" cultures. This allegorical dimension of ethnography—seeking in the cultural other a kernel of wisdom to illuminate the human condition—contains for Clifford the political and ethical stakes of the ethnographic project and, as such, should be "manifested not hidden" (120). The turn toward intersubjectivity in ethnographic discourse thus requires doing exactly what Coutinho has done: including himself in the frame and making his subject matter the encounter itself. His later films are about the communities he interviews, but they are also about the dialogic and necessarily temporal exchange in which he and his subjects enact the open-ended project of negotiating cultural, regional, and class difference. As Souza de Araújo argues, *O fim* can be read as a film about the encounter between "equipe do Sudeste e povo do Nordeste" (his team from the Southeast and the people of the Northeast) (43).

In other words, the self-reflexivity within and intertextuality between Coutinho's sertão films lay bare the inescapably allegorical nature of the project in which he is engaged: representing the sertão is always also an attempt to give form to something else. I would add, following the Benjaminian and de Manian senses of allegory, that this "something else"—whether it be self-knowledge, linguistic richness tied to oral cultures, or a more authentic mode of connection—is always projected into the (real or imagined) past.[27] It is important here, once again, to distinguish the politics of Coutinho's use of allegory from that of Cinema Novo. I am not proposing reading Coutinho's work as a national or third-world allegory, in which the plight of individuals or communities portrayed would be made to stand in for broader injustices at the national or global scale.[28] Instead, I am interested in the temporality of allegory in the de Manian sense, as a discursive practice of repetition that points to the impossibility of fully recovering a past referent.[29]

The structure of return in Coutinho's sertão films—the physical return of the filmmaker to the sertão both within and between films, as well as the return to the past through storytelling and showing old footage—represents an attempt to recapture the authenticity of an always-anterior moment of spontaneous encounter with the sertão. I do not believe it is coincidental that it is to the sertão specifically that Coutinho repeatedly returns to seek "the contingency of the real" (Duccini Junqueira da Silva 104). The sertão has long been figured in Brazilian letters as a place where the unexpected can and does happen, and this was certainly Coutinho's experience filming in the sertão in the 1960s. In fact, as my reading of *Cabra* suggests, we might even say that it was the sertão that taught Coutinho that embracing the real requires embracing contingency, that seeking an ethical encounter involves exposing oneself to the open-ended form of conversation. In *O fim*, it appears as if Coutinho quite deliberately turns to the sertão once again to re-create the conditions for such spontaneous encounters and spontaneous verbal performances by *sertanejos*.

In self-consciously drawing attention to the gesture of return, however, Coutinho also draws attention to the structural impossibility of re-creating radical spontaneity. As Patrick Dove points out, the structure of allegorical repetition always already marks the dissymmetry between iterations, the impossibility of the return coinciding with the moment of anteriority: "because the postulated return necessarily forecloses the dimensions of chance and surprise that colored the first visit. Memory and calculation precisely get in the way of the recovery they seek to bring about" (177). It is for this reason that Coutinho emphasizes the possibility of failure before the film has even begun: "perhaps we don't find anyone and so the film would become the search for a location, a theme and, above all, characters."[30] In these lines, Coutinho announces that the film is from its inception an ethnographic allegory. The first part of *O fim* is indeed "about the search for a setting, a theme, and above all characters." Even after Coutinho has settled on a community to interview, the film continues to be about the question of whether they will "accept" him and open up to him. Even more fundamentally, it is a film about whether this return journey will yield what Coutinho seeks: to somehow connect "o fim" represented by the last phase of his career and his encroaching mortality (he was seventy-two at the time of making the film and asks his subjects incessantly about death and the afterlife) with "o princípio" represented by his formative first encounters with the sertão in his youth.

Notes

1. "A imagem da miséria contrastada com a presença do imperialismo. Esta era a tendência típica na cultura desses tempos." All translations are my own.

2. This manner of filming screenings of Coutinho's own footage (often focusing on the subjects of the footage as they watch themselves on-screen) becomes a trope in Coutinho's work and contributes to the self-reflexivity of his style.

3. As Natalia Brizuela notes, Coutinho faces an entirely different political moment in 1984: "the farm labor movement had been become the metal workers' movement; and the most pressing question was the turn to democracy" (25).

4. Far from arriving at a finished, static style, however, Coutinho's films continue to evolve, and often to interrogate their own approach, until his death (Mesquita and Lins 50).

5. "Na década de 1960, a gente fazia um cinema muito político, com uma visão assim . . . uma visão um pouco autoritária, mais autoritária do que se pode aceitar hoje, entende? [. . .] A gente julgava o povo e, ao mesmo tempo, onipotente, achava que entendia o povo. Acho que isso acabou, isso aí mudou."

6. "Filmes de gente rica, em casas bonitas, andando em automóveis de luxo; filmes alegres, cómicos, rápidos, sem mensagens, e de objetivos puramente industriais."

7. This tension is perhaps most pronounced in Euclides da Cunha's *Os sertões* (1902), in which the autochthonous culture of the sertão is both condemned for its atavism and eulogized. A similar tension runs throughout nineteenth-century Brazilian romanticism (Süssekind) and into twentieth-century regionalism and the "golden age" Brazilian cinema of the 1930s and 1940s (Andermann).

8. For example, in addition to vilifying the ranch owner Morales, Glauber Rocha's *Deus e o diabo* depicts the local oligarchs and church leaders as conspiring to hire the hit man Antônio dos Mortos to kill São Sebastião and Corisco, thus squelching the possibility of a peasant uprising. In *Vidas secas*, the critique of the church is more ambiguous, as Vitoria appears to draw strength from prayer, but the characters who represent the government—the *soldado amarelo* and the tax official who prohibits Fabiano from selling pork on the street—are depicted as agents of exploitation and oppression on par with the dishonest ranch owner.

9. Antônio Vicente Mendes Maciel, known as Antônio Conselheiro, was a late nineteenth-century religious leader and monarchist who founded a community in the sertão with his followers, who took him to be a messianic figure. When this village, known as Canudos, refused to surrender to government troops, the so-called civil rebellion ended in the brutal annihilation of the town and the loss of more than 15,000 lives, including that of Antônio Conselheiro. The Guerra de Canudos (1896–97) is famously commemorated in Euclides da Cunha's *Os sertões* (1902). Virgulino Ferreira da Silva, known as Lampião, is the most iconic *cangaceiro*, or bandit, of the Brazilian sertão. He and his sizeable band roamed the northeastern backlands throughout the 1920s and 1930s. Though he was infamous for his brutality, his skill at outmaneuvering the police, his charisma, and his surprising piety earned him a reputation as a folk hero.

10. For Cecilia Sayad, it is the bodily presence of the filmmaker that engenders the singular performances of his subjects, whereas for Natalia Brizuela, it is the duration of his long takes. According to Brizuela, the openness of the expanse of time with the camera running creates a theatrical effect, wherein the subjects "play" themselves, creating "performative versions of themselves" (21–22).

11. "Os personagens não são informantes sobre esta ou aquela temática—são pessoas singulares que não representam, tipificam ou exemplificam nada."

12. "A extraordinária riqueza das falas de analfabetos, sobretudo em regiões menos industrializadas [. . .] Nas regiões de cultura oral, popular, ainda viva, enriquecida com todas as impurezas, mesmo o alfabetizado põe na fala todos os seus recursos de expressão."

13. See Mesquita and Lins and Souza de Araújo.

14. Coutinho claims that all his subjects go from being people to being characters once he is in the editing room working with their performances: "I find it essential that the person constructs her self-portrait, with everything she has from the realm of the imaginary" (Avellar 53). This is a far cry from the demand for authenticity often placed on subaltern subjects.

15. "Na verdade a pessoa comum, que tá no filme, que se torna personagem, ela é um ator natural. Ela é uma pessoa que interpreta a si mesmo bem."

16. The authenticity of documentary film has long been linked to the indexicality of the medium, which, like photography, bears witness to the existence of the referent (Bazin, Sontag), yet, as Brian Winston points out, documentarians have taken poetic license with their material since the inception of the genre (11). As such, even "traditional" documentary representations offer something in excess of evidence, complicating how we measure their authenticity. Post-structural critiques of the transparency of representation in ethnographic filmmaking—claiming that the "reality" shown is constructed through memory, imagination, and desire rather than coinciding with a real referent—have further thrown into crisis the notion of authenticity in documentary film. For Catherine Russell, however, this crisis also presents an opportunity to decolonize ethnographic filmmaking by revealing the discursive construction of Otherness: "The failure of realism to present evidence of the real is the radical possibility of experimental ethnography [. . .] Beyond the limits of representation exist other realities of experience, desire, memory, and fantasy. These realities are historical and produce real effects, especially in the institutions and practices of colonial culture. The decolonization of ethnographic film is therefore commensurate with the experimental critique of realist film languages—both narrative and documentary—and the development of new forms of audiovisual representation" (25).

17. "Tudo o que acontece nos filmes do Eduardo existe apenas porque está sendo filmado. As pessoas não diriam as coisas belas (ou tristes, comoventes, terríveis, alegres) que dizem se não fosse pela presença diante delas, do Eduardo e da sua câmera."

18. "Quando o cinema produz sua própria realidade, filmar deixa de ser um ato irrelevante. Filmar—e principalmente, filmar documentários—modifica o mundo. Sem heroísmo, muito pouquinho, sutilmente, mas modifica."

19. "Não havia roteiro prévio mas apenas a ideia era de intentar de encontrar aos camponeses que tinham trabalhado em *Cabra marcado para morrer*. Queria retomar nosso contato através de depoimentos sobre o passado."

20. "Viemos a Paraíba para intentar fazer em quatro semanas um filme sim nenhum tipo de pesquisa previa, nenhum teme particular, nenhuma locação em particular. Queremos achar uma comunidade rural de que a gente goste e que nos acete [. . .] talvez a gente não ache nenhum e ali o filme se tornaria a procuração de uma locação, um tema e sobretudo de personagens.'

21. "A luta que não pode parar. Enquanto se diz que tem fome e salário de miséria, o povo tem que lutar. [. . .] é preciso mudar o regime, é preciso que o povo lute. Enquanto tiver esse regimezinho, essa democraciazinha aí . . . democracia sem liberdade, democracia com salário de miséria, de fome, democracia sem o filho do operário e do camponês ter direito de estudar, ah . . . não pode, ninguém pode."

22. Coutinho credits his years with Globo for giving him a crash course in the documentary genre and thus altering the trajectory of his career as a filmmaker (Avellar 50). See Navitski's chapter in this volume for more on Coutinho's Globo years.

23. As filmmaker Trinh T. Minh-Ha has argued, this paradigm governs much ethnographic documentary film as well, dividing "the world into those "out there" (the subjects of ethnography) and those "in here" (in the theater, looking at them)," thereby objectifying the former as Other (Russell 4).

24. Gauging the ethics of documentary filmmaking has often boiled down to the question of whether the political urgency of the film's denunciatory work or the public's "right to know" outweighs the potential harm done to the participants (conceived of in terms of direct consequences of public exposure such as persecution and blacklisting, as well as in terms of exploitation and voyeurism) (Winston 236–38). Including the costs to participants in the film as Coutinho does represent a move toward putting more ethical weight on the relationship between filmmaker and subjects than on the film's duty to inform the audience.

25. "Ele parece encontrar, na rica expressão verbal dos velhos sertanejos aquilo que intuía quando o filme estava totalmente em aberto."

26. It is worth noting that in his final film, *Últimas conversas*, released posthumously in 2015, Coutinho literally turns to childhood/children seeking a more open and honest form of connection. After the guardedness of high school students sends Coutinho into a crisis about the film, he brings in a five-year-old girl and finally finds what he has been looking for.

27. Paul de Man, like Walter Benjamin, emphasizes that what distinguishes allegory from symbolism is the temporal distance posited by the former: allegory signals a moment of anteriority (Dove).

28. National allegory became a fraught term in Latin American literary criticism in the wake of Frederic Jameson's polemical "Third-World Literature in the Era of Multinational Capitalism" (1986). As Erin Graff Zivin has pointed out, many of the most influential critics of the 1990s, including Doris Sommer, Carlos Alonso, and Roberto González Echevarría, actively distanced themselves from the most reductive use of the term while continuing to disseminate allegorical readings of Latin American fiction, ultimately deepening an aversion to allegorical criticism in many theoretical circles (157–58, 161). A more recent trend has recuperated allegory as a mode of writing and reading that is both inescapable and, following Walter Benjamin's and Paul de Man's elaborations of the term, capable of reflecting critically on the politics and temporality of representation (See Graff Zivin, Dove, and Russell). It is this latter sense of the term that I find helpful in my analysis of Coutinho.

29. De Man writes: "Allegory designates primarily a distance in relation to its own origin, and, renouncing the nostalgia and desire to coincide, it establishes its language in the void of this temporal distance" (207). Though I would not wish to conflate de Manian allegory with Clifford's ethnographic allegory, the latter does echo the former in calling allegory an inescapable condition of representation and in recognizing that allegorical referent is always itself a discursive construction. We can see how the two might coincide in Catherine Russell's description of experimental ethnography in film, which is grounded in Clifford and Benjamin's discussions of allegory but also bears traces of de Manian allegory in its emphasis on distance, negativity, and self-reflexivity: "Allegory is a means of reinscribing "distance" as a discursive practice [. . .] Experimental ethnography is thus an allegorical discourse, one that apprehends otherness as fundamentally uncanny [. . .] Criticism that aims to fracture the edifice of realism apprehends all texts allegorically as traces of a reality that is beyond the text, in history. "The real" conceived as history differs from "the real" of referentiality in that it includes the spectator and the filmmaker in its scope" (24–25). In other words, what becomes legible in experimental ethnography is not the referent of the cultural other, but rather the discursive construction of otherness by the film, the filmmaker, and the spectator.

30. "Talvez a gente não ache nenhum e ali o filme se tornaria a procuração de uma locação, um tema e sobretudo de personagens."

Works Cited

Andermann, Jens. "Exhausted Landscapes: Reframing the Rural in Recent Argentine and Brazilian Films." *Cinema Journal*, vol. 53, no. 2, 2014, pp. 50–70.

Avellar, José Carlos. "The Emptiness of the Backyard: An Interview with Eduardo Coutinho." Translated by Krista Brune. *Film Quarterly*, vol. 69, no. 3, 2016, pp. 44–55.

Bazin, André. "The Ontology of the Photographic Image." Translated by Hugh Gray. *What Is Cinema?*, vol. 1, U of California P, 1967.

Brizuela, Natalia. "Conversation and Duration in Eduardo Coutinho's Films." *Film Quarterly*, vol. 69, no. 3, 2016, pp. 19–27.

Cabra marcado para morrer. Directed by Eduardo Coutinho, 1984.

Child, Benjamin. "The Magical Real and the Rural Modern in Cinema Novo: *Vidas Secas* and *Black God, White Devil*." *South Central Review*, vol. 31, no. 1, 2014, pp. 55–73.

Clifford, James. "On Ethnographic Allegory." *Writing Culture: The Poetics and Politics of Ethnography*, edited by James Clifford and George E. Marcus, U of California P, 1986.

Coutinho, Eduardo. "O olhar no documentário." *Encontros: Eduardo Coutinho*, edited by Felipe Bragança, Beco do Azougue, 2009, pp. 12–21.

———. "Se eu definisse o documentário, não fazia. Por isso não o defino." *Encontros: Eduardo Coutinho*, edited by Felipe Bragança, Beco do Azougue, 2009, pp. 134–57.
Cunha, Euclides da. *Os sertões*. Brasiliense, 1985.
De Man, Paul. "The Rhetoric of Temporality." *Blindness and Insight: Essays in the Rhetoric of Contemporary Criticism*, U of Minnesota P, 1983, pp. 187–228.
Deus e o diabo na terra do sol. Directed by Glauber Rocha. 1964.
Dolar, Mladen. *A Voice and Nothing More*. The MIT Press, 2006.
Dove, Patrick. "The Allegorical Machine: Politics, History, and Memory in Horacio Castellanos Moya's *El sueño del retorno*." *The Yearbook of Comparative Literature*, vol. 61, 2015, pp. 174–201.
Duccini Junqueira da Silva, Mariana. "Estética da subtração: o lugar de autor no documentário de Eduardo Coutinho." *Revista Digital de Cinema Documentário*, vol. 7, 2009, pp. 97–106.
Fabian, Johannes. *Time and the Other: How Anthropology Makes Its Object*. Columbia UP, 2002.
Fagioli, Julia. "Exílio e interrupção: as diferentes condições da retomada dos arquivos nos cinemas de Patrício Guzmán e Eduardo Coutinho." *Aletria*, vol. 30, no. 3, 2020, pp. 107–30.
Ferreira Dias, Verônica. "*Cabra marcado para morrer*: cinema contando História por meio de histórias (e memórias)." *Revista Digital de Cinema Documentário*, vol. 1, 2006, pp. 62–78.
Graff Zivin, Erin. "Beyond Jameson: The Metapolitics of Allegory." *The Yearbook of Comparative Literature*, vol. 61, 2015, pp. 156–73.
Jameson, Frederic. "Third-World Literature in the Era of Multinational Capitalism." *Social Text*, vol. 15, 1986, pp. 65–88.
Lins, Consuelo. "The Art of Encounter and (Self-) Fabulation in Eduardo Coutinho's Cinema of Bodies and Words." *The Global Auteur: The Politics of Authorship in 21st Century Cinema*, edited by Seung-hoon Jeong and Jeremi Szaniawski, Bloomsbury, 2017, pp. 253–67.
Mesquita, Cláudia, and Lins, Consuelo. "O fim e o princípio: Entre o mundo e a cena." *Novos estudos*, vol. 99, 2014, pp. 49–63.
O fim e o princípio. Directed by Eduardo Coutinho, 2006.
Rocha, Glauber. "Estética da fome (1965)." *Arte em Revista*, vol. 1, no. 1, 2014, p. 17.
Russell, Catherine. *Experimental Ethnography: The Work of Film in the Age of Video*. Duke UP, 1999.
Sadek, Isis. "A sertão of Migrants, Flight and Affect: Genealogies of Place and Image in Cinema Novo and Contemporary Brazilian Cinema." *Studies in Hispanic Cinemas*, vol. 7, no. 1, 2010, pp. 59–72.
Salles, João Moreira. "Ao mestre com carinho." *Revista Época*, no. 253, 2002, http://revistaquem.globo.com/Revista/Quem/.
Sayad, Cecilia. "Flesh for the Author: Filmic Presence in the Documentaries of Eduardo Coutinho." *Framework*, vol. 51, no. 1, 2010, pp. 134–50.

Sontag, Susan. *On Photography.* Anchor Books, 1977.
Souza de Araújo, Mauro Luciano. "Subjetivismo e pós-colonização no filme de Eduardo Coutinho: O caso de *O fim e o princípio* (2005)." *Estudios sobre las culturas contemporáneas,* vol. 18, no. 36, 2013, pp. 33–47.
Süssekind, Flora. *O Brasil não é longe daqui.* Cia. das Letras, 1990.
Viany, Alex. *O processo do Cinema Novo.* Aeroplano, 1999.
Vidas secas. Directed by Nelson Pereira dos Santos. 1963.
Winston, Brian. *Claiming the Real II: Documentary: Grierson and Beyond.* Palgrave Macmillan, 2008.

3

The Audiovisual Record and the Corporeal Present

Another Dialogue in Eduardo Coutinho's Cinema of Conversation

Gustavo Procopio Furtado

The work of Eduardo Coutinho (1933–2014) has been variously described as a cinema of conversation, a cinema of listening, and a cinema of the present.[1] It is possible to understand his documentary career, spanning from his work for *Globo Repórter* during the late 1970s to *Últimas conversas*, his posthumous film released in 2015, as a gradual process of purification through which the filmmaker distills cinema to what he considers its essence: the human body in the act of speaking. Through conversation, Coutinho strives to tease out moments of vivid and spontaneous expression from ordinary people. In the process, he reduces cinematic language to its bare bones. The films' soundscapes are made of almost exclusively unaltered diegetic sounds. There is minimal camera movement, and the camera remains within the medium close-up and the close-up range, "the distance from which we can love or kill one another," as Coutinho has stated.[2] The unobtrusive editing style favors long, uninterrupted takes—as if seeking a synchrony between the temporalities of screen time and the living duration of the profilmic present. This Spartan approach appears based on the premise that a reticence in filmic style is necessary to make way for the potential expressiveness of a subject's speech. Coutinho's observations about his own work confirm these ideas. In Carlos Nader's *Eduardo Coutinho, 7 de outubro* (2013), Coutinho notes: "I hate depth, what I want is superficiality," by which he means that his interest lies in the immanent reality of surfaces and gestures rather than in deeper structures of meaning. "The present time of filming is the only thing that matters," he adds, "and the body that speaks is the origin of everything," thereby delineating guiding maxims of his film practice. Despite the apparent simplicity of the intention to record speech acts by ordinary people, Coutinho's approach actually requires great effort and patience because it is rare to find a subject who, standing before a camera, speaks in a manner free of clichés or ready-made phrases that is at once ordinary and arresting and who can emerge as a full-fledged, self-fashioning filmic subject. When this does happen, Coutinho refers to these moments as "the miracle of speech" or the "breaking"—terms that signal that this is a rare and momentous event.[3]

In its investment in the audiovisual rendering of corporeal presence and speech, Coutinho's work is relatable to an undercurrent in film theory that forefronts film's capacity to capture the flow of life and its affinity with the contingent surface of the real. This type of realism, grounded in notions of "medium specificity" and "ontology" rather than in realistic conventions of verisimilitude (Hansen 254), is represented by figures like André Bazin, who argued that "cinema embalms time, rescuing it simply from its proper corruption" (Bazin 14) and Siegfried Kracauer, who claimed that cinema was uniquely able to represent nondramatic moments or the "flow of life" and that it thus had the potential to redeem physical reality for a society that had become alienated from the real and the everyday (Kracauer 71–73). In her remarkable discussion of cinema's aptitude for recording ephemera and the contingent, Mary Ann Doane adds that this quality places cinema in a close relationship not only with the temporality of the unfolding real but also with the temporality of the archive, which preserves and arrests the flow of time in a durable record. The "archive" here is understood not as official institutions that preserve documentary records but as any form of storage that captures the elusive present and preserves it for the future: "Once the present as contingency has been seized and stored, it ineluctably becomes the past," Doane writes. Cinema stores and makes available "the experience of presence. But it is the disjunctiveness of a presence relived, of a presence haunted by historicity" (23). Doane's argument points to a constitutive dialectic that lies at the heart of film, a formative tension between the flow of time and storage, between corporeal duration and archive, between the unique event and its belated accessibility as a record existing independent of the fate of the people involved in the recorded occurrence. While Doane traces this dialectic in the "actualities" of early cinema, I would argue that the documentary is the filmic mode most likely to put on display and consciously explore film's position at the threshold between the flow of life and the fixity of the record, between the fortuitous and the contingent on the one hand and the archive on the other. Bearing in its name a relationship with the notion of the document and having adherence to the historical world, the documentary performs a dual function in relation to the archive. It performs an archival function by producing and preserving lasting records for the future, but it is also the means by which recorded materials are returned to the world and placed in circulation.[4]

Intent on capturing fleeting moments of extraordinary speech by ordinary people, Coutinho's work also engages with this dialectic and makes it an intrinsic component of his filmmaking practice. Born partly from the encounter "between film characters [personagens] and the cinematographic apparatus," particularly the filmmakers himself as interviewer (Pereira 17), his cinema stages and mobilizes the interaction of embodied present in the profilmic and film as a lasting record. This engagement is evinced by his frequent use of reflexive strategies that inflect the flow of time with diachrony, such as by incorporating the image as record in the filming process, even as his primary interest remains the spontaneity of the moment. In a number of his works, Coutinho includes previously recorded materials—materials that are incorporated not only through post-production editing (woven into the fabric of the filmic text and appearing in full screen for the viewer) but also placed in the mise-en-scène of the profilmic during the process of image production itself, a type of incorporation that Phillipe Dubois calls the "mise-en-film" of images. Encounters between bodies and previously recorded images occur in several of Coutinho's major works and throughout all periods of his documentary career. They take place using all manner of technological support—from celluloid film to video to digital—and marshal an eclectic range of images with distinct materialities, including prints that can be held between one's fingers, reel-to-reel films that can be screened for collective viewings, and videos that can be watched on a monitor or TV set, often in the privacy of one's home. The inclusion of the archive of previous images is so essential to Coutinho's practice that his body of work is arguably among the most insistently reflexive in Brazilian cinema, although it is rarely discussed in these terms by critics or by the filmmaker himself.

Paying special attention to *Cabra marcado para morrer* (1964–1984), *Boca de lixo* (1992), *Peões* (2004), and *Sobreviventes de Galiléia* (2014), works that span the director's entire career, this chapter argues that Coutinho's so-called "cinema of conversation" develops another form of dialogue that occurs between the audiovisual record and the corporeal present of the profilmic event. In many examples, images from the archive are brought into contact with subjects in the present so as to help produce a cinematic spark, the hoped-for "breaking" or "miracle of speech." Or, in *Boca*, the images being produced are put on display in the profilmic even as the image-making process occurs. Thus, the understanding of cinema as a form of record and the investment in the fleeting, unfolding real find a symbiotic arrangement. To examine this aspect of Coutinho's work, this chapter first discusses the filmmaker's use of participant-centered reflexivity, which contrasts with predominant forms of reflexivity in documentary, as I argue in relation to *Boca de lixo*. Then the chapter turns to works that deal with image production across extended periods of time, as illustrated by *Cabra, Peões*, and *Sobreviventes*. These films' investment in speech acts is combined with a meditation on cinema as a technology of storage of presence—an unofficial archive that can safeguard from oblivion fragments of the world, particularly the voices and reminiscences of people who inhabit the margins and the background of society—as well as the means of a restitution by which materials can be returned to the light of day. The final part of the chapter extends my reflection on Coutinho's oeuvre beyond these evidently reflexive films to argue that this Janus-faced operation on the threshold between the present and the archive is not a marginal component of a few films but rather structures his entire film practice.

Participant Reflexivity: A First-Person Cinema of the Other

A brief consideration of reflexivity in documentary film can illuminate crucial aspects of Coutinho's work and the mise-en-film of images, which leads to an uncommon form of participant-centered reflexivity and to a sort of first-person cinema of the other. Reflexive films direct attention not only to the worlds they portray but also toward their own processes of filmic mediation, thus bringing into view elements that are typically hidden in finished works. Rooted in grammar, in verbs whose subject and object are the same (Black 56), the term "reflexive" also refers to the reflection in the looking glass. Figuratively speaking, reflexive films hold up a mirror to themselves while showing viewers their reflection. Designating the "reflexive" as one of the major documentary modes, Bill Nichols notes that reflexivity "gives emphasis to the encounter between filmmaker and viewer" and establishes a triangulation between the maker, the text, and the audience (60). As Jay Ruby puts it, "To be reflexive is to reveal that films—all films, whether they are labeled fiction, documentary, or art—are created structured articulations of the filmmaker and not authentic truthful objective records" (10). But who is the addressee of reflexivity as a signifying or revealing procedure? Who is meant to be informed, affected, amused, or provoked by the reflexive gesture? The answer, one could argue, is the viewer—and this is tacitly presumed in the critical bibliography on this topic, in which film is understood as a communicative text whose semantic and affective potentials remain dormant, like messages in a bottle, until they are found by the viewer—much the same way as Jean-Paul Sartre characterized literature, which "can find its fulfillment only in reading" (46).

Though dominant, this viewer-centered reflexivity is not the only form explored by documentary films. Interrogation about the intended addressee of the reflexive gesture reveals that there are two other possible orientations: author-centered and participant-centered. A growing body of films foreground an author-centered reflexivity that bears first on the self-reflecting filmmaker. Here film becomes a means for the exploration of the vicissitudes of the filmmaker's biographical self.[5] Nichols's triangulation takes a different form as viewers of such films look at the filmmaker looking at and crafting their own image. Here the mirror of reflexivity is held by the filmmaker, who gazes at their own image like Narcissus, although this narcissism is also exhibitionistic as it is ultimately performed for the viewing public. Whereas in viewer-centered films reflexivity is primarily a function of editing and postproduction, in author-centered films it is more a function of the mise-en-scène. As Philippe Dubois notes, the mise-en-film use of images of the self is a recurring procedure in this cinema, which casts the filmmaker simultaneously as film author and as subject interacting with their own image. In such filmic constructions, "the subject has no other exteriority than its mise-en-scene, thus exhibiting its own conditions of existence as image" (Dubois 154).

The third and least common form of reflexivity, the participant-centered approach, is addressed first and foremost to the film's participants. The reflexive mirror is held up for those before the camera. Another vertex, one representing the participant, needs to be added to Nichols's triangular geometry involving maker, text, and viewer. Frequent in Coutinho's work, this participant orientation has antecedents in cinema, such as in the work of Jean Rouch and Edgar Morin's paradigmatic work *Chronique d'un été* (1961), in which an eclectic group of Parisians not only participates in the making of a film about themselves but also becomes its first viewers and critics. With potential to unsettle the hierarchy between maker and participant (Rice et al. 223), diffusing the authority of authorship and empowering subjects to participate in the construction of their image, participant reflexivity is most useful in filmic situations fraught with asymmetries of power. Examples abound in films made with or by Indigenous groups, such as Victor Masayesva Jr.'s *Imagining Indians* (1992), Jeff Spitz's *The Return of Navajo Boy* (2000), and the remarkable body of work of the Vídeo nas Aldeias group, which strives to give Indigenous groups in Brazil control over their own image. In these cases, the mise-en-film of images attempts to reverse long-held patterns of both real and symbolic expropriation.[6] As with author-centered reflexive films, participant-centered reflexivity places greater emphases on mise-en-scène than on editing. This kind of cinema is also more invested in film as process than as product. It is a means for interventions in the lived world and has repercussions on participating subjects in advance and even independent of the film's ultimate completion, distribution, and viewership. But it can also incite a qualitatively distinct form of filmic participation and result in works punctuated by multiple points of reflexive inflexion enacted by subjects who engage consciously with their image.

Coutinho's use of participant-centered reflexivity as a filmmaking method is illustrated by *Boca de lixo*. Made in the "Vazadouro de Itaoca," a waste-disposal site on the outskirts of Rio, *Boca* begins with a barrage of negative gestures, corporeal refusals in response to the arrival of the filmmaker and his crew; even children turn their backs to the camera and cover their faces. Others wrap clothes around their faces, giving them the appearance of fugitives or outlaws. In part, the responses reflect the fact that this film was made without advance preparation and the arrival of the camera crew was unannounced. Coutinho was ahead of schedule in finishing another project and decided to use the extra time and resources to film at Itaoca.[7] But the filmmaker's desire meets with the adverse response of the subjects. This is illustrated by the first dialogue included in the film, which takes the form of a challenge by a Black teen: "What do you gain by putting this camera in our faces?" This question could be extended to all ethnographic and journalistic practices—indeed, to all forms of documentary representation of subjects who lack the means to represent themselves in the public sphere. The refusal gestures and the accusative question of the teen reveal a well-formed distrust of the camera, which is implicitly understood to be the extension of an external, hostile power and a tool of extractive violence that expropriates the marginalized subject's image. Perceiving the camera as an accusatory device, another teenager promptly responds: "We are not stealing, we are working." One woman says she feels "outraged with this, you put things on the paper and people think that we are picking garbage to eat it"—thus revealing an awareness of previous misuses of their image. The workers' concern with the particular stigma of eating refuse is recurrent throughout the film—giving its title a double meaning as descriptive both of the site and of the eating taboo. Later, in a lengthier conversation at her home, the same woman clarifies that she eats some of what she finds if it is suitable but cannot accept being indiscriminately represented as and reduced to someone who eats garbage.

It is significant that Coutinho leaves these antagonistic responses in the final cut of the video, exposing rather than hiding the tensions, risks, and conflicts that are part of its condition of production. This is also a form of reflexivity—one that is directed at the viewer, who is made aware of the problematic terrain traversed by the film. These moments could easily have become "the secrets of the film," to borrow João Moreira Salles's phrase for all that is edited out of a finished work and therefore hidden from view, constituting the film's secret archive.[8] But here the conditions of production are openly displayed.

These initial rejections are a major problem for a director whose practice hinges on mutual trust for establishing sincere conversations with his subjects. In *Boca*, the mise-en-film of images is deployed to address this problem and to recast the filmmaker's interactions with Itaoca workers and their relationship with image-making. The decision to incorporate images in the process of filming was somewhat improvised, Coutinho recalls.[9] It just so happened that the video camera they were using had the capability of printing stills, somewhat like a Polaroid, although the stills were of a rough quality. Coutinho asked his cameraperson, Breno Silveira, to print shots of people's faces and then used these prints to initiate conversations. Shortly after the sequence of filmed images of people refusing the camera or speaking defensively to the filmmaker, we see a group of people gathered around the filmmaker as he leafs through the images of Itaoca workers. Those around him identify the people photographed. The effectiveness of this reflexive operation in changing the interaction between Itaoca workers and the filmmaker is in part the result of novelty: although familiar with cameras, these workers are not used to filmmakers who directly hand them images of themselves. Instead, they are used to their images being expropriated to be held and used elsewhere. The act of presenting them with the images being recorded performs a reversal of this pattern and invites their participation in the film under qualitatively different terms.

Folding the filmmaking process back onto itself, as it were, the mise-en-film of images invites the people being filmed to become the first viewers of and commentators on their own images, anticipating all subsequent acts of viewing. Image production thus becomes dialogic. The specific temporality of video technology plays a role in this approach. Celluloid film requires laboratory processing before it can be viewed—in other words, there is a temporal lapse and a physical dislocation that necessarily separate the act of recording from the act of viewing. In contrast, video allows for prompt and even instant playback. Toward the end of the film, we see several sequences of shots of people gathered at the waste disposal site to view images played back on a monitor resting atop the film crew's van. In one sequence, the monitor shows an instant playback of the crowd gathered before it; the scene has the instantaneity of an image reflected in a mirror. Itaoca's workers view themselves viewing themselves in a reflexive situation that is not a gratuitous mise-en-abyme but an almost somatic response to the workers' own initial anxieties about the extraction of their images, reversing, or at least ameliorating, the potential alienating effects through an instantaneous and continuous return of images to the bodies being imaged. At another moment, the crowd watches rough-cut segments of the film with visible excitement, becoming the film's first audience—further illustrating the participant-centered reflexivity of the video. The act of naming the people who appear in these images, which occurs at the moment of their initial inclusion in the film, starts a process of individuation that is essential for this and other Coutinho films. Coutinho does not approach people as illustrations of previously conceived ideas or categories. Instead, they are approached as singular subjects who can articulate their own meaningful narratives about themselves and their place in the world and who have ordinary human lives regardless of their extraordinarily adverse material conditions of existence. According to Coutinho, the motivation for the making of this film came from his earlier visit to Jardim Gramacho, a massive landfill on the outskirts of Rio.[10] What impressed him most there was not the abjection of the site but the ordinariness of social life he observed there. He saw people playing soccer, cooking, dating ("namorando"), and having fun. Note that Coutinho's point here is not at all to romanticize the happiness of the poor but to view their everyday experiences outside the usual framework of "social problems" and other applicable signifying constructs produced outside their sphere of experience. The act of handing people images of themselves that we see in *Boca* is both a formal manifestation of the desire to turn the people filmed into self-fashioning subjects—owners of their own meaning-making discourse rather than objects in the discourse of another—and a practical tool that encourages their speech. Some film critics have noted that this form of collaborative reflexivity amounts to a democratic participation that is much needed in documentary and ethnographic projects made in contexts marked by social marginalization (Everri et al. 74). It is worth noting that Coutinho himself does not place great transformative hopes in cinema—at least not in regard to sociopolitical transformations. His approach, however, involves an ethics of cinematic conversation that grants ample space for his subjects to become the owners of their own discourse about themselves. If we place Coutinho's reflexive method in relation to the author-centered reflexivity of first-person films, we can define his practice as the search for another first-person cinema—a form we could call a first-person cinema of the other. The mise-en-film of images of the (other's) self in *Boca* is significant in this regard. As Dubois argues, the photographic image of the self is a privileged means of autobiographical inscription in first-person films: "The photograph marks the autobiographical inscription of the 'I' by putting into place a particular apparatus—a unique configuration of image and speech, the very thing that articulates psychically the photo-cinema relation as a whole" (154). Speaking of video art rather than documentary film, Rosalind Krauss makes a related point when she notes the danger in that medium's mirrorlike capacity for instantaneous playback. Instant playback enables self-regarding, narcissistic constructions: "Video's real medium is a psychological situation," Krauss writes, "the very terms of which are to withdraw attention from an external object—an Other—and invest it in the Self" (57). The danger Krauss refers to is that of an a-critical form of reflexivity that can lead both the maker and the viewer into a "weightless fall through the suspended space of narcissism" (59). Coutinho's practice bears an oblique relationship to the autobiographical photo-films discussed by Dubois, as well as to the narcissistic possibilities of video noted by Krauss—both of which deal with author-centered forms of reflexivity. In Coutinho's documentaries, participant-centered reflexivity creates the conditions for the emergence of unlikely cinematic selves—ordinary and marginal people who find their self-fashioning voices before the camera, inhabiting momentarily a borrowed space of authorship.

Diachronic Image/Body Encounters and Archival Thresholds

As in *Boca*, *Cabra* and *Peões* also deploy a reflexive mise-en-film of images that functions to broker the relationship between participants and filmmaker and to spur conversations and the kind of speech that interests Coutinho. Dealing with images that cover a broader span of time, however, these films display more complex relationships between the unfolding present and the incorporated images, as well as a more overt, though still subtle consideration of the audiovisual image as an archival record that can be stored away and preserved as well as subsequently retrieved and recirculated. The Janus-faced nature of films vis-à-vis the archive comes to the fore as these films perform a dual operation on the archival threshold: a de-archivization of images from the past and the production of records of the present for the future. Cinema as a mnemonic technology of storage comes into view and, with it, the inevitability of loss—the loss of what leaves no record, or loss that results from the wear-and-tear of time, or even loss that is caused by willful destruction. In fact, it is loss and the fragility of bodies and memory that give meaning to cinema's mnemonic work of preservation.

Cabra is essentially a film about loss and preservation, death and survival. Initially intended as a dramatization of the life of the peasant union leader João Pedro Teixeira, who was assassinated in 1962, the film ultimately became about his widow, Elizabeth Teixeira. The story of this landmark film entangles personal, cinematic, and national histories. Made with a group of peasants in the village of Galiléia, the initial version of *Cabra* was midway through production when it was interrupted by the 1964 military coup. When soldiers arrived in Galiléia, the filmmaker, crew, and Elizabeth barely escaped arrest. Later, certain that her capture would lead to torture or death, Elizabeth went into long-term hiding in a neighboring state under the pseudonym Marta (a name that suggests pain and sacrifice, as in "martírio," Portuguese for "martyrdom") and severed all links with people she knew, including her children. People presumed she was dead, and it was as if she were. The footage of Coutinho's unfinished film was also initially thought to be lost. By sheer luck, the negatives had already been sent to a lab in Rio de Janeiro to be developed, thus escaping confiscation and possible destruction. The rolls of film survived by entering a celluloid version of a clandestine life: they were stored under a decoy title in Rio's Modern Art Museum archive. Both Elizabeth and the film remained hidden until 1981 when, due to the changing political climate of the country, Coutinho was able to return to working on it, though with a different approach. Made on the verge of Brazil's transition to democracy and documenting Coutinho's return to the village where he shot the original footage in 1964, the final *Cabra* performs a de-archivization of that footage, which is presented not just to viewers of the completed film but, before that, to the film's original participants, who interact with those images in the process of the film's 1981 production. Thus, the film establishes a dynamic process that promotes a "plural memorialistic interaction" with the filmic record and the past (Gama and Kluck 2). This return of the images to the participants enables multiple related returns such as the return of fragments of an interrupted past to the present and the return to life of subjects and projects that had been traumatically brought to a halt.

The storage of fragments from the past in the face of loss is a recurring theme in the film. It finds an echo in a story told by Duda, who had participated in the making of the 1964 film. Duda welcomes Coutinho to his home in 1981 and shows him an old copy of Curzio Malaparte's *Kaputt* (1944), which he keeps stashed away in a wooden trunk. Someone from *Cabra*'s crew left Malaparte's book behind when they fled in 1964, Duda notes. The soldiers wanted to confiscate the book, but Duda claimed that it was his and managed to keep it. Though only partially literate, he volunteers to read aloud the prologue of *Kaputt*, in which the history of this text is told. Written clandestinely during World War II, Malaparte's manuscript was saved from destruction by a peasant who hid it from soldiers inside a cavity in the wall of his hut. "The story of this book is a lot like your movie," Duda remarks, providing the first reading of Coutinho's film, which also involves the production of a politicized document, the friendship and collaboration between artist and peasants, a period of unofficial archivization to prevent a text's destruction, and that material's ultimate de-archivization and return to the light of day.

The theme of archival preservation and the return of hidden materials finds its most potent form of articulation in the mise-en-film of images. It is also here that Coutinho's investment in the corporeal present is placed in relation to film understood as a medium that has an inherent affinity with the "flow of time," to evoke Kracauer's phrase, and also with the archive. *Cabra* begins with the setting up of a projector to show the peasants of Galiléia the 1964 footage of the unfinished work—a viewing scene that will itself be shown later in the film and that is rendered in shot-reverse-shot between the projected films and the faces of the Galiléia viewers, underscoring, through this formal construction, the dialogue between images and bodies, between preserved past and unfolding present. Scenes of viewing that include the footage and photographs from 1964 are a leitmotif punctuating *Cabra*; Coutinho often begins conversations by handing his 1981 interlocutors a photo or holding a screening.

Images from the past are not inert records but catalysts capable of affecting people in the present. The return of these images, which the film's participants thought they would never see and that belong to a moment interrupted by the coup, compels acts of remembering. The dialogue between images from the past and bodies in the present gains particular force in the case of Elizabeth Teixeira. By a fortuitous coincidence, Elizabeth's eldest son had located his mother shortly before Coutinho contacted him. After seventeen years of living under a false identity and in complete isolation from her past, Elizabeth publicly reclaims her own name and history through her conversations with Coutinho in the film while viewing images of her younger self. If circumstances had created a fracturing of her life, separating her from her past, her encounter with images is an opportunity for recovery. One of the recurring images of Elizabeth intercut in the film shows her at a political rally in 1963. There, she seems to command the attention of a crowd. The silent footage brings our attention to her corporeal gestures, to Elizabeth's energetic posture and body language at a moment of political enthusiasm: this version of herself is perhaps the one from which she had become the most estranged. Indeed, in the 1981 conversations with Coutinho, she enters the terrain of politics cautiously. With some encouragement from her son, Elizabeth thanks President Figueiredo for the recent political opening. During the process of the two-day conversation, her body appears to gradually return to itself. At the very last moment of the encounter, when the crew is already in the car, ready to leave, Elizabeth's gestures regain an assertiveness only seen in the early footage. Her words, too, no longer imply polite acquiescence. As she lists current examples of political injustice, her gestures resemble those she made at the political rally. These images suggest Elizabeth's transformation during the process of filming, a result of her reclaiming her name and personal history. If the problem of 1981 faced by Elizabeth, and perhaps many others like her, can be characterized as the problem of living in a fragmented present, of having become discontinuous with oneself and one's experience, Coutinho's de-archivization and return of the images from the past to the present can help to return a body to itself. The storehouse of corporeal gestures preserved in the image are, in a sense, repatriated to Elizabeth in the reflexive process of filmmaking. At the same time that *Cabra* performs a restitution of images to the present, the film also reflects on its own archive-like operation of gathering records of the present for the future. Of João Pedro Teixeira, we are told, not even a photograph remains, except for one snapshot of his lifeless body riddled with gunshots, which was published in a newspaper at the time of his death and is included in the film—perhaps because without such inclusion even this meager record is at risk of being lost. We also learn that the remote village of São Rafael, where Elizabeth took refuge and survived for nearly two decades, is about to be flooded for the construction of a water reservoir. The town was scheduled to be evacuated when Coutinho arrived and later it disappeared underwater. If the film's de-archivization of the past is imbued with restorative potential, its work of safeguarding records is undergirded by an awareness of its necessity as well as its limits—so that the film becomes at once "a victory over the wastebasket of history," as Jean-Claude Bernardet puts it (227), and an inventory of losses. The film collects what has been scattered, like the peasants from the earlier project who are brought together in 1981. Elizabeth's children are also dispersed, and she speaks of her wish to be united with them again. Coutinho's film, seemingly more able to accomplish this reunion than Elizabeth, seeks them out, including those who have migrated to Rio and São Paulo, and films conversations with them. It is notable that Coutinho's film ends not with Elizabeth's climactic speech at the door of the van but with another segment that extends the film to note the death of the peasant João Virgínio—a man who, earlier in the film, offers testimony about his extensive torture following his arrest after the coup.[11] At the end of the film we see footage of João Virgínio celebrating his birthday in his backyard and learn that he died shortly after Coutinho filmed him in 1981. Thus, this final segment does not open out to vitalist horizons of recovery but becomes instead a memento mori of a "present" that has irrevocably become the past, surviving only in the afterlife of memory and the record. Given its history of production, spanning from the 1964 coup to the 1981 transition to democracy, and its inimitable imbrication of filmic, national, and personal histories, *Cabra* is a unique film. Yet the film's staging of diachronic dialogues between the present and the past through the reflexive inclusion of audiovisual materials finds echoes in *Peões*. Made on the eve of Lula da Silva's historic election to the presidency, the film opts to produce an unlikely documentary record of the period that is focused on the factory workers who participated in the auto strikes of 1979 and 1980 in São Paulo—the strikes that elevated Lula, then a union leader, to national prominence.[12] Coutinho's film is specifically interested in the factory workers, who did not achieve prominence and went on to live ordinary lives in the background of history. Like *Cabra*, *Peões* incorporates images recorded two decades before, although here they belong to earlier films by other directors: João Batista de Andrade's *Greve* (*Strike*, 1979); Renato Tapajós's *Linha de montagem* (*Assembly Line*, 1982); and Leon Hirszman's *O ABC da Greve* (*The ABC of the Strike*, completed posthumously in 1990). These are relatively obscure works with limited circulation outside circles of cinephiles and leftist intellectuals. Few of the workers involved in the strikes ever saw these films. In one of the most compelling conversations in *Peões*, Zélia, the labor union's cleaning woman, recalls saving the reels of Tapajós's *Linha de montagem*. The police had surrounded the union office and were about to arrest the leaders and confiscate the film, but Zélia, who was only a cleaning woman and thus not under police suspicion, hid the reels in her bag and smuggled them past the police line. She glows with pride when recounting her saving of the film, which she never watched: "It was the only history we had." This story of the film's material survival and later recovery evokes the history of *Cabra*, as well as Duda's comments on Malaparte's *Kaputt*. This history deals in minor acts of archivization—"minor" not necessarily in the sense of "small" but in the sense that they are performed by subjects who lack authority in dominant society and refer to subaltern pasts in danger of complete erasure.[13] Coutinho's interest in such stories reflects the dual procedure of his filmmaking, which preserves records of the present through cinema's archival function while at the same time performing acts of de-archivization that return hidden materials to the world. The differences between the earlier documentaries included in *Peões* and Coutinho's 2004 film are telling. The other directors' films deploy a direct cinema style to register the strikes and are centered on the rising figure of Lula while rendering the autoworkers less as individuals than as a collective social subject: the Worker. In contrast, in Coutinho's *Peões* the central subjects are ordinary individuals whose experiences and memories are explored through intimate conversations. The diachronic combination of images from the past and present in the final film stages a sense of change and loss that pertains both to distinct cinematic approaches and to altered sociohistoric realities. The contrast between approaches defines Coutinho's own method, which favors the singularity of individual speech over the application of analytical or interpretive categories produced elsewhere. It is worth noting that Coutinho is not alone in this preference for the particular over the general. Contemporary documentary in Brazil favors individualized subjects rather than collective ones, as Cláudia Mesquita notes. The "people," the popular collective subject that so preoccupied Cinema Novo and influenced documentarians of the 1960s and 1970s, has given way to a wide array of subjective and individual perspectives.[14] Coutinho's own approach stands out for its skilled emphasis on the speech acts of ordinary people. But the contrast between Coutinho's approach and that of the earlier works he incorporates also reflects a fragmentation of the social body. The same individuals who rallied with some success for worker rights in 1979 and the early 1980s have gone on to endure economic insecurity within the supposed "flexibility" of the neoliberal labor market. Although "peões" continue to exist in the labor force, the possibility of liberation through collective struggle seems to have vanished, or at least greatly diminished, by 2004, despite the imminent election of Lula to the presidency (Lins 185–86). Tinted with melancholy, the film juxtaposes images of worker protests, shot with handheld 16 mm film cameras on the streets, with private scenes set in living rooms and kitchens in which that same footage is viewed on video on TV sets—a change in media formats that reflects a passage from public to private spaces and from collective undertakings to personal experiences. The striking workers portrayed in the earlier films have been dispersed, and Coutinho's film involves the search for them in regions of São Paulo and other parts of Brazil—gathering what has been scattered, akin to *Cabra*'s seeking out of the peasants from the unfinished film or Elizabeth's scattered children. The mise-en-film of images is an instrumental component of this film's participant-centered form of reflexivity. Inviting groups of factory workers and union leaders, Coutinho starts the film by organizing screenings of the earlier footage and showing photographs of the strikes so that the workers can identify individuals in the crowds during the rallies. In this process, participants are picked out from the images by the workers, who point to them and shout their names, evoking the similar procedure of image recognition that occurs in *Boca*. Images from older films are incorporated as indexical records—an indexicality underscored by the workers' gesture of pointing to the images and saying people's names.[15] The mise-en-film of images serves to retrieve anonymous participants from the backdrop of cinematic and national history—participants who will then be sought out by Coutinho and who will articulate a first-person discourse before his camera, inspired in part by the older images that are shown during several of the conversations. The film is peppered with moments in which individuals watch clips of earlier films that show images of their younger selves, thus emphasizing the dialogue between archival images and bodies. At a memorable moment, for example, a worker named Djalma watches his younger self standing next to Lula on the stage during a rally (fig. 3.1). Djalma's body sitting before the monitor is reflected in the glare from the

80 | Gustavo Procopio Furtado

Figure 3.1. Djalma seeing his younger self on the television set in *Peões*. Source: *Peões (Metalworkers)*. Directed by Eduardo Coutinho, Videofilmes, 2004.

screen, as if in a mirror, adding another reflexive image of the participant to this diachronic encounter between past and present, between recorded image and unfolding present.

Operating on the threshold between the filmic record and the embodied present, Coutinho's work often explores the passages between these spheres and temporalities. This logic finds potent expression in a scene from *Sobreviventes de Galiléia* (2014), which records Coutinho's final return to the site of *Cabra marcado para morrer*. Here we encounter Cícero, who participated in the 1964 film. In 1981, when Coutinho returned to the region with the footage of the unfinished film, Cícero was living in São Paulo and working in a factory. Coutinho interviewed him there and included that footage in the final *Cabra*. We also learn that in 2007, the documentary film scholar Cláudio Bezerra had traveled to Galiléia and filmed Cícero and other participants of *Cabra*.[16] Coutinho's conversation with the aged Cícero involves images from all of these periods. We see him at several stages of his life, from his relative youth in 1964 to his frail condition in 2014. As we would expect, Coutinho includes these archival images not just through editing but also in the mise-en-scène of the profilmic. At one point, he uses a laptop to view with Cícero the video of the latter's conversation with Cláudio Bezerra in 2007, when he appeared younger and in better health. In that video, Cícero holds photographs of himself taken in 1981 (fig 3.2). Layers of time and records from the past interadt in a mise-en-abyme of

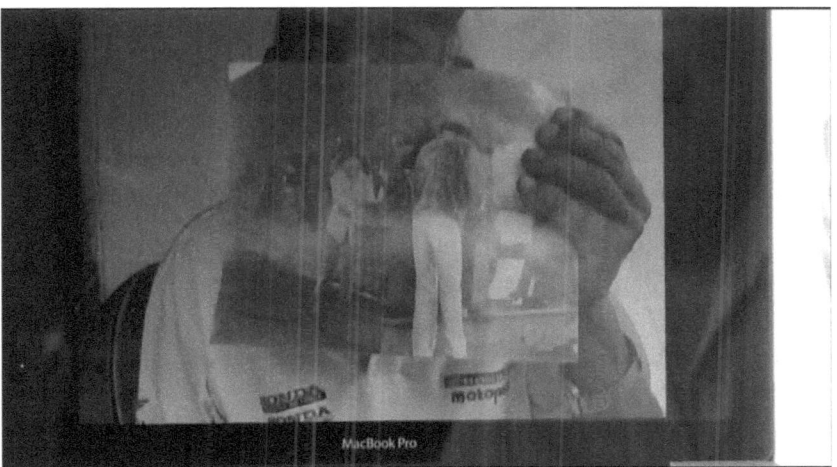

Figure 3.2. A laptop held by Cícero, shows an image of him holding photographs in *Sobreviventes de Galileia*. Source: *Sobreviventes de Galiléia (Galiléia's Survivors)*. Directed by Eduardo Coutinho, Instituto Moreira Salles, 2014.

interactive, multimedia reflexive contacts between recorded images and the imaged body, the fixed record preserved for the future meeting the flow of time unfolding in an ephemeral present. The fragility of the human body rendered in this diachronic juxtaposition of images spanning several decades undergirds the film's own desire to record. In his poetic preface to Consuelo Lins's book on Coutinho's work, Moreira Salles defines this desire in relation to responsibility. "The object of responsibility," he writes, citing Paul Ricoeur, "is the fragile, the perishable that calls to us. Because the fragile is, in some manner, entrusted to our protection." The fragile that finds a place in Coutinho's films includes fleeting moments of expression by people considered to be of only minor importance—people who are rarely listened to by anyone besides their intimates. Their voices, gestures, stories, and memories are in effect given shelter by Coutinho's films.

Conclusion

Appearing in one of Coutinho's final works, the reflexive scene with Cícero epitomizes the dialogue between the archival record and the corporeal present that traverses his entire body of documentary work, although it is not always so plainly visible. One could argue that the reflexive examples discussed in this chapter are the exceptions to Coutinho's work rather than the rule. The arguments presented here, however, bear on his other films as well, even on those that seem to lack a diachronic or reflexive component and appear entirely absorbed by extemporaneous conversations and fleeting speech acts. A present-tense–oriented film like *O fim e o princípio* (*The End and the Beginning*, 2006), which was filmed without advance planning and adheres fully to the "flow of life," generates its own reflexive follow-up, *O fim e o princípio—A volta* (*The End and the Beginning—The Return*, 2007), in which the first film is screened and people's reactions to it are explored through conversations, much as in the examples discussed in this chapter. *Moscou*, his collaboration with the theater group Balcão, which deals with preliminary rehearsals for a production of Anton Chekhov's piece *The Three Sisters*, also includes in its mise-en-scène an array of photographs and images—mainly images of the actors' families that are being used by them to develop their characters' own family-related stories for the play. Though entering a different terrain from most of Coutinho's other documentary work, this film also includes and explores the mise-en-film of images.[17] Sometimes there is an unseen reflexive and archival component to the process of a film's production, which is most evident in *Jogo de cena* (*Playing*, 2007). Here, the filmmaker records a series of conversations with ordinary women and then gives this recorded material to actresses, who are asked to perform the roles in performances that are filmed in exactly the same manner and in the same empty theater. Interspersing the two sets of footage of speech acts (by the original women and the interpreting actresses), the film is generated through an unseen reflexive engagement with images and a dialogue between bodies and the filmic record.

An invisible reflexive process involving performance and its filmed record occurs in his other films as well. Often participants are interviewed and filmed by Coutinho's collaborators in advance of their filmed encounter with him, as is the case with *Edifício Master* (2002). After reviewing this footage, Coutinho determines which of the people will become part of the final work.[18] The filmed encounter with the actual filmmaker is held after this preparatory process so that that encounter will be fresh and feel unrehearsed. Yet through this method, many seemingly spontaneous moments occur under the sign repetition as subjects are speaking before the camera for the second time. Some scenes, such as the one in which Henrique sings the Frank Sinatra song "My Way," appear to have been recorded several times. After he finishes the take we see, Henrique says, "Next time, my voice will be better," suggesting that there were multiple takes. People in Coutinho's films often become aware of the way they are constructing a cinematic image of themselves, as if they were co-authors of their segments, self-archivists who submit their performances to a lasting record. Thus, one of the original women interviewed in *Jogo de cena* asks to be interviewed again because she feels that her previous version was too depressing, too "barra pesada." Each of these examples raises specific issues and invites in-depth analyses of their nuanced deployment of reflexivity, which I cannot undertake here. My point, by way of conclusion, is to indicate that Coutinho's is a cinema of the present as well as a reflexive cinema. His work is keenly aware of film's archival role even as it seeks out spontaneous gestures and expressions. This cinema of the present is always an inherently diachronic practice that seeks to capture the ephemeral and the fragile, giving it filmic shelter and making it available for the future—available for archivizations and de-archivizations to come. Rather than a unique quality of *Cabra* or an incidental feature of some of his films, the awareness of the Janus-faced nature of documentary cinema as a cultural form that operates at the threshold between the embodied present and the preserved record informs Coutinho's entire oeuvre, adding significant complexity to his cinema of conversation.

Notes

1. See, for instance, Consuelo Lins's "O cinema de Eduardo Coutinho: uma arte do presente," Coutinho's "O cinema documentário e a escuta sensível da alteridade," and Natalia Brizuela's "Conversation and Duration in Eduardo Coutinho's Films."

2. The quote is from Carlos Nader's film *Eduardo Coutinho, 7 de outubro* (2013).

3. See Nader's *Eduardo Coutinho, 7 de outubro* (2013). See also Coutinho's interview with Carlos Alberto Mattos in *Eduardo Coutinho: O homem que caiu na real* (2003), where he notes that what guides his filming and editing "is the necessity of the other to constitute himself as a subject, which for me is something absolute" (100).

4. For an in-depth discussion of the relationship between documentary and archive with a focus on Brazilian cinema, see my monograph *Documentary Filmmaking in Contemporary Brazil: Cinematic Archives of the Present*.

5. With roots in the experimental independent cinema of the 1960s and 1970s, most notably the work of Jonas Mekas, first-person films became increasingly common after the advent of video technology—though this subjective turn is not

determined by technology alone. For a landmark study of subjective documentaries, see Michael Renov's *The Subject of Documentary* (2004).

6. For a recent discussion of this strategy in Indigenous cinema in Latin America, see my chapter "The Indigenous 'Contact Film' and its Afterlives in Latin American Cinema" in *A Companion to Latin American Literature and Culture*.

7. Coutinho relates this in "Visões do documentário," a conversation with the filmmaker that occurred in Rio de Janeiro's Casa do Saber. The conversation was filmed and is available on YouTube at https://www.youtube.com/watch?v=ReVHCQ oplro, accessed April 25, 2018.

8. See Moreira Salles's *Santiago* (2007) where the filmmaker elaborates on this in dialogue with a quote by Werner Herzog.

9. "Visões do documentário," https://www.youtube.com/watch?v=hneAOHH CszA.

10. "Visões do documentário," https://www.youtube.com/watch?v=hneAOHH CszA. For a documentary film made in Jardim Gramacho, see Lucy Walker and Vic Muniz's *Wasteland* (2010), which also involves a form of participant reflexivity through which the participants help construct their portraits for Vic Muniz. Though I cannot expand on this here, note that the self-promotion of the artist and the aestheticization of poverty in *Wasteland* sets it far apart from *Boca de lixo*.

11. This testimony, by the way, is the first such documentary testimony of torture suffered by a peasant and constitutes an important historical record (Machado 274–74).

12. Note that this film was made in conjunction with Moreira Salles's *Entreatos* (2004), which follows Lula during the final days of his campaign and, insofar as it focuses on a major figure, remits to a more traditional documentary approach. *Peões* and *Entreatos* were released together in 2004.

13. For this understanding of "minor," see Dipesh Chakrabarty's *Provincializing Europe* (100–01).

14. For some of the implications and cinematic explorations of this disappearance of the "people," see my essay "Where are the People? The Politics of the Virtual and the Ordinary in Contemporary Brazilian Documentaries."

15. In C. S. Pierce's semiology, the indexical sign is not just a trace (like the footprint or the fossil) but also the deictic function of a signifier that is empty without the presence of its referent—like the words "here," "you," "me," etc. The pointing finger is the quintessential indexical gesture. See Doane (69–107) for an excellent discussion of the indexical.

16. At the time, Bezerra was working on a research project that resulted in his book *A personagem no documentário de Eduardo Coutinho* (2014).

17. For an analysis of the film with attention to this inclusion of photographs and in dialogue with Philipe Dubois's theoretical work, see Glaura Cardoso Vale's *A mise-en-film da fotografia no documentário brasileiro* (2016).

18. For Coutinho, this is an anxiety-ridden process as documented in Beth Formagini's *Coutinho.doc, Apartamento 608* (2009), a behind-the-scenes take on the

making of *Edifício Master*. Coutinho is always skeptical, even pessimistic, about the potential of the interviewees to become compelling characters—to "break" before the camera and yield "the miracle of speech." He labors in full awareness of the likelihood of failure.

Works Cited

Bazin, André. "The Ontology of the Photographic Image." *What Is Cinema*. U of California P, 2005, pp. 9–16.
Bernardet, Jean-Claude. *Cineastas e imagens do povo*. Companhia das Letras, 2003.
Bezerra, Cláudio. *A personagem no documentário de Eduardo Coutinho*. Papirus, 2014.
Black, David Alan. *Law in Film: Resonance and Representation*. U of Illinois P, 1999.
Brizuela, Natalia. "Conversation and Duration in Eduardo Coutinho's Films." *Film Quarterly*, vol. 69, no. 3, 2016, pp. 19–27.
Chakrabarty, Dipesh. *Provincializing Europe: Postcolonial Thought and Historical Difference*. Princeton UP, 2000.
Coutinho, Eduardo. "O cinema documentário e a escuta sensível da alteridade." *Projeto História. Revista do Programa de Estudos Pós-Graduados de História*, vol. 15, 1997, pp. 165–71.
Dubois, Phillipe. "Photographic Mise-en-Film: Autobiographical (Hi)stories and Psychic Apparatuses." *Fugitive Images: From Photography to Video*, edited by Patrice Petro, Indiana UP, 1995, pp. 152–72.
Everri, Marina, et al. "Ethical Challenges of Using Video for Qualitative Research and Ethnography." *Challenges and Solutions in Ethnographic Research: Ethnography with a Twist*, edited by Tuuli Lähdesmäki et al., Routledge, 2020, pp. 68–83.
Furtado, Gustavo Procopio. *Documentary Filmmaking in Contemporary Brazil: Cinematic Archives of the Present*. Oxford UP, 2019.
———. "The Indigenous 'Contact Film' and Its Afterlives in Latin American Cinema." *A Companion to Latin American Literature and Culture*, edited by Sara Castro-Klaren, Wiley Publishing, 2022, pp. 634–45.
———. "Where Are the People? The Politics of the Virtual and the Ordinary in Contemporary Brazilian Documentaries." *Latin American Documentary Film in the New Millennium*, edited by María Guadalupe Arenillas and Michael J. Lazzara, Palgrave Macmillan, 2016, pp. 115–31.
Gama, Mônica, and Erick Kluck. "Memória cultural e recordação—Narratividade e espera no documentário *Cabra marcado para morrer*, de Eduardo Coutinho." *Revista Recorte*, vol. 16, no. 1, 2019, pp. 1–17.
Hansen, Miriam Bratu. *Cinema and Experience: Siegfried Kracauer, Walter Benjamin, and Theodor W. Adorno*. U of California P, 2011.
Kracauer, Siegfried. *Theory of Film: The Redemption of Physical Reality*. Princeton UP, 1997.

Krauss, Rosalind, "Video: The Aesthetics of Narcissism." *October*, vol. 1, 1976, pp. 50–64.
Lins, Consuelo. "O cinema de Eduardo Coutinho: uma arte do presente." *Documentário no Brasil: tradição e transformação*, edited by Francisco Elinaldo Teixeira, Summus, 2004, pp. 179–98.
———. *O documentário de Eduardo Coutinho: Televisão, cinema e vídeo*. Jorge Zahar, 2004.
Machado, Patrícia. "Imagens que faltam, imagens que restam: A tortura em *Cabra marcado para morrer*." *Significação*, vol. 42, no. 44, 2015, pp. 271–93.
Mattos, Carlos Alberto. *Eduardo Coutinho: o homem que caiu na real*. Festival de Cinema Luso—brasileiro de Santa Maria da Feira, 2003.
Mesquita, Cláudia. "Retratos em diálogo: notas sobre o documentário brasileiro recente." *Novos estudos*, vol. 86, 2010, pp. 105–18.
Nichols, Bill. *Representing Reality: Issues and Concepts in Documentary*. Indiana UP, 1991.
Pereira, Cilene Margarete. "O cinema documental (político) de Eduardo Coutinho: Narrativa, personagens e memória." *Revista Recorte*, vol. 16, no. 1, 2019, pp. 1–19.
Renov, Michael. *The Subject of Documentary*. U of Minnesota P, 2004.
Rice, Carla, et al. "Making Spaces: Multimedia Storytelling as Reflexive, Creative Praxis." *Qualitative Research in Psychology*, vol. 17, no. 2, Apr. 2020, pp. 222–39.
Ruby, Jay. "The Image Mirrored: Reflexivity and the Documentary Film." *Journal of the University Film Association*, vol. 29, no. 4, 1977, pp. 3–11.
Sartre, Jean-Paul. *What Is Literature?* Philosophical Library, 1949.
Stam, Robert. *Reflexivity in Film and Literature: From Don Quixote to Jean-Luc Godard*. Columbia UP, 1992.
Valle, Glaura Cardoso. *A mise-en-film da fotografia no documentário brasileiro*. Filmes de Quintal e Relicário, 2016.

Part II
Politics and the Documentary Image

4

From CPC to Videofilmes
Eduardo Coutinho's Trajectory as a Political Filmmaker

Krista Brune

Brazilian filmmaker Eduardo Coutinho often claimed, "What differentiates me from many directors is that I don't make films *about* others, but *with* others" (qtd. in Lins, "The Cinema" 200). Throughout his career, he maintained a political and social engagement with the popular that became increasingly grounded in a cinema of conversation and an ethics of listening.[1] Differentiating his specific approach from a more generic one, he clarified that "the formula 'to meet the people' repels me. I do not meet the people, I meet persons" (Gardnier et al. 91).[2] Coutinho's investment in hearing the voices of others became more radical as he stripped down his films to the essence of conversation and positioned himself as a curious interlocutor. As Coutinho moved from the Centro Popular de Cultura (CPC, People's Cultural Center) of the National Students' Union to television's *Globo Repórter* to the Center for the Creation of the Popular Image (Centro de Criação de Imagem Popular or CECIP) to the Videofilmes production company, he embraced new modes of production and corresponding technologies, shifting from 35 mm to 16 mm to video and finally to digital. By examining the production and circulation of his films in dialogue with evolving concepts of the popular, this chapter contends that Coutinho's development as a filmmaker parallels shifts in the political landscape and in the creation, financing, and distribution of films in Brazil over the past fifty years. Approaching Coutinho's career with an interest in modes of production invites us to think about how questions of resources, access, and global capital shape political filmmaking.

Brazilian critic Cláudio Bezerra has identified three phases in Coutinho's work. He defines the first stage as one of experimentation as Coutinho transitioned from fiction film to documentary work during his years at Globo. According to Bezerra, the "gestation of a style" characterizes the director's second phase, spanning from *Cabra marcado para morrer* (1964–1984) to *Boca de lixo* (*The Scavengers*, 1992) ("Um documentarista" 401). The third phase, beginning with *Santo forte* (*The Mighty Spirit*, 1999), represents the consolidation of his documentary style rooted in listening to characters.[3] While these divisions prove useful to understanding the director's overall trajectory, they gloss over shifts in production, distribution, and financial support. Focusing on the infrastructures that made Coutinho's films possible, I conceive of his career in four moments: first, his early work with the leftist CPC, which gave root to his masterwork *Cabra marcado* and his vision of social and political commitment; second, his documentary training ground of *Globo Repórter*; third, his venture into independent and nonprofit documentaries with *Cabra marcado* and the CECIP productions; and, fourth, his ongoing partnership with Videofilmes production company starting with *Santo forte*. Coutinho's evolving relationships with modes of production and material resources impacted the technical specificities, ethics of representation, and perceived politics of his films.

The turn to documentary as a space for political work is not unique to Coutinho's films. Documentary offers a realm to represent reality, to examine truth claims, and to educate viewing publics. During the 1920s in Soviet Russia, documentary filmmaking developed in concert with political beliefs as its construction of reality aligned with revolutionary ideology. Dziga Vertov conceived of documentary as a dialectical phenomenon where life-facts become film-facts that are then combined through montage into film-truth. This concept of film-truth reemerged in the 1950s and 1960s as *cinéma vérité* in French documentaries such as *Chronique d'un été*, the 1961 film by Jean Rouch and Edgar Morin. *Cinéma vérité* envisioned the camera as a participant and the director as a provocateur who aimed to bring hidden truths to the surface. In *The Politics of Documentary*, Michael Chanan astutely links the political to documentary's relationship with its audience, noting that "documentary addresses the viewer primarily as a citizen, member of civil society, putative participant in the public sphere" (vi). Recognizing viewers as citizens who exist in a broader public sphere heightens documentarians' interest in their films' political stakes and repercussions, as Coutinho's trajectory exemplifies.

Coutinho's Early Years: Political Engagement with the CPC

Coutinho's contact with *cinéma vérité* while studying film in Paris in the 1950s informed his vision of what cinema could be as he returned to Brazil and became involved with the CPC's efforts to create politically committed film.[4] In the 1960s, Cinema Novo in Brazil, *tercer cine* in Argentina, and other iterations of New Latin America Cinema prioritized an attention to modes of production in the face of limited resources as a political gesture.[5] Brazilian director Glauber Rocha's concept of an aesthetic of hunger underscores how the lack of financial support and material resources among filmmakers demands an alternative aesthetic, one distinct from the practices of Hollywood or European cinema at the time. According to Rocha: "the hunger of Latin America is not simply an alarming symptom: it is the essence of our society [. . .] Cinema Novo shows that the normal behavior of the starving is violence; and the violence of the starving is not primitive [. . .] From Cinema Novo it should be learned that an esthetic of violence, before being primitive, is revolutionary" (60). Though Rocha theorized Cinema Novo as revolutionary films that would resist colonial forces, his works had limited political potential given their epic allegories and extravagant aesthetic language. In films like *Deus e o diabo na terra do sol* (*Black God, White Devil*, 1964) and *Terra em transe* (*Land in Anguish*, 1967), he engaged with the popular in a mythical language disconnected from the real, which limited his ability to enact political change and to affect lived experiences and socioeconomic conditions.[6]

Rocha articulated his vision for an aesthetic of hunger in 1965, a year after the military coup forced Coutinho and his team to abandon filming *Cabra marcado*. Coutinho shared with Rocha and, more broadly, Third Cinema concerns about how to create films that were aware of and responded to material realities. As Mike Wayne explains, "Third Cinema can work with different forms of documentary and across the range of fictional genres. It challenges both the way cinema is conventionally made [. . .] and the way it is consumed. It refuses to be mere entertainment, yet banishes from your mind a cinema that is worthy but dull or a cinema of simplistic polemics" (5). This description resonates with what Coutinho aimed to create with films that listened to voices often absent from Brazil's cultural imaginary. By viewing these interlocutors as his films' subjects, rather than objects, Coutinho grounded his political commitment in an ethical gesture. He interrogated documentary's relationship to the real, noting that "every documentary is, in essence, precarious, incomplete, imperfect, and it is exactly from this imperfection that its perfection is born. The documentary is always a subjective vision" (Figueirôa et al. 215).[7] In response to technological and financial demands, he adopted new modes of production that would innovate documentary cinema in Brazil.

Indications of Coutinho's contribution to producing and consuming documentary films appear in his earliest work with the CPC, which informed his vision of the popular as tied to the daily lives of ordinary Brazilians and his approach to filmmaking as a collaborative process with nonprofessional actors. Coutinho was a production manager for the CPC's *Cinco vezes favela* (*Five times favela*), a 1962 film consisting of five shorts shot in the favelas in Rio de Janeiro by directors later recognized as leading figures of Cinema Novo, including Carlos Diegues, Joaquim Pedro de Andrade, and Leon Hirszman. The experience of going into the favelas over the three-month shoot helped establish Coutinho's lifelong interest in the favela as a site for filmmaking. He would return to Rio favelas in subsequent documentaries: *Santa Marta: Duas semanas no morro* (*Santa Marta: Two Weeks in the Hillside Slums*, 1987), *Santo forte*, and *Babilônia 2000* (*Babylon 2000*, 2000). After his work on *Cinco vezes favela*, Coutinho went with the Traveling CPC caravan to the Northeast, where he learned about labor leader João Pedro Teixeira, whose life and death served as the basis for *Cabra marcado*. The unique speech and daily struggles of people in the sertão emerge as recurring topics in his work with Globo and in his 2005 film *O fim e o princípio* (*The End and the Beginning*). His interest in the favela and the sertão resonates with a generalized fascination with these spaces in Brazilian cinema, which Ivana Bentes associates with a "cosmetics of hunger" (124) whereby contemporary Brazilian films transform Cinema Novo's aesthetics of hunger into stylized imaginations of impoverished realms.[8] In contrast, Coutinho portrays the favela and the sertão with a realistic minimalism. By focusing on the voices, memories, and hopes of individuals living in these communities, his films depict the popular as belonging to and emanating from people, rather than as commercialized mass media.

Working with the CPC also introduced Coutinho to a model of collaboration that granted a greater degree of agency to all project participants. This cooperative process anticipated the documentary techniques that Coutinho developed as, in the view of Consuelo Lins, a "savage linguist" attuned to the pauses, slips, and silences of language as a personal mode of expression ("Eduardo Coutinho" 30–31). The CPC's use of nonprofessional actors like Elizabeth Teixeira to play characters modeled on their own lives blurred distinctions between documentary and fiction. Coutinho would further question the porous line between the real and the fictional in the final stage of his career, most notably with the intercuts of ordinary women and famous actresses in *Jogo de cena* (*Playing*, 2007). Across his filmography, Coutinho aimed to include people in the process of depicting their lived experiences and personal expressions on-screen. His approach to collaborative filmmaking grew out of the CPC's efforts to represent Brazil's often marginalized peoples in a realistic and respectful manner.

Globo Repórter as Coutinho's Documentary School

After the CPC and its projects abruptly ended with the 1964 military coup, its ethos of social and political commitment continued to inform the work of Coutinho and other filmmakers. While Diegues, Andrade, and Hirszman emerged as prominent names in Brazilian feature films over the next decade, Coutinho followed a different path toward renown as a filmmaker. After writing screenplays including *Lição de amor* (*Love Lesson*, 1975) and *Dona Flor e seus dois maridos* (*Dona Flor and Her Two Husbands*, 1976) and collaborating with Hirszman on fictional films like *ABC do Amor* (*ABC of Love*, 1966), he sought stable employment as a journalist, first with *Jornal do Brasil* in 1972 and then with *Globo Repórter*, starting in 1975. During the dictatorship, artists and intellectuals operated within structures of funding and production that seem to contradict their political views. As Marcelo Ridenti notes, the decision of leftist filmmakers like Coutinho to work at Globo, Brazil's hegemonic television network, has been seen either as "ideological capitulation in the face of the bourgeoisie" or as a "possibility to bring a critical vision to the television spectator, contributing to social changes" (324).[9] In interviews with Ridenti about their Globo years, directors like Coutinho and Renato Tapajós reveal that during the 1970s they enjoyed greater freedom in terms of content and style (324–36). As Brazil began to open politically, they suffered more restrictive censorship due to market demands. According to Igor Sacramento's study of the work of Coutinho, Gustavo Dahl, Paulo Gil Soares, and Walter Lima Júnior, among others, with *Globo-Shell Especial* (1971–1972) and *Globo Repórter* (1973–1983), leftist filmmakers had a complex and often contradictory relationship with the television industry in the 1970s and 1980s. As director of *Globo Repórter*, Soares aimed to develop a specific, cinematographic language on television that would attract an educated public and critical acclaim (Sacramento 106). The program functioned within Globo's network expectations and general parameters of news reporting, even though Soares and the filmmakers he hired strove to challenge conventions with longer takes and more in-depth segments.

For Coutinho, Globo served as a school in documentary techniques where he learned to research, write, film, direct, and edit, all within a strict time frame. Globo granted directors a degree of freedom, as aesthetic norms and content preferences were not as narrowly defined as they are now. Coutinho has lamented that the relative freedom he experienced at Globo during the 1970s no longer exists in the current television landscape, where censorship occurs based on consumer's preferences and market demands (Avellar 49). In *Seis dias de Ouricuri* (*Six Days in Ouricuri*, 1976) and *Theodorico, o imperador do sertão* (*Theodorico, the Sertão Emperor*, 1978), Coutinho challenged television norms with long takes that allowed him to explore lived experiences and expressions of the sertão. These pieces reveal how the less expensive reversible 16 mm film could create more adaptable and portable films that better captured popular voices and images and, in turn, expand the perspectives of Globo's bourgeois viewers. Though the director aimed to subvert expectations, his films still followed a dramatic arc typical of television documentaries. In a 2007 interview, Coutinho underscored the limitations of television work: "In some moments, it was possible to make something that seemed like a documentary, but those moments were rare" (qtd. in Sacramento 128).[10] Conventional techniques of voice in off and nondiegetic music typical of northeastern Brazil served to underscore thematic points and evoke emotional responses. The Globo documentaries preceded the importation from the United States of the newsmagazine model where well-known anchors report on various stories.[11] The format of *Globo Repórter* evolved from three segments of ten to fifteen minutes each to an episode-length film on a sole topic with *Seis dias de Ouricuri*, a forty-one-minute documentary filmed over six days in drought-ridden Ouricuri, a town of 60,000 in the interior of Pernambuco. Coutinho continued this single-subject approach with *Theodorico*, about Theodorico Bezerra, a federal representative and land baron from Rio Grande do Norte. The film exceeded the time span for a normal episode but, to the director's surprise, was aired in its entire forty-nine minutes (Sacramento 137).

While at *Globo Repórter*, Coutinho explored how modes of *cinéma vérité* and direct cinema could function to best render popular voices in documentary form. Two representations of people talking about their own lives anticipate Coutinho's future cinema of conversation: one scene in *Seis dias* with a man recounting strategies to survive drought and another in *Theodorico* with the protagonist reflecting on his life in a small town in the sertão. Using reversible film reduced production costs and limited possibilities for postproduction editing so episodes could be finalized with more autonomy (Hamburger 417). With this technical freedom, Coutinho employed unconventional long takes with direct sound that allowed him to develop a practice of listening to the voices of others. In *Seis dias*, a long take of three minutes and ten seconds captures a man detailing how and when he ate roots and seeds during previous droughts. The camera shifts between focusing on the man and zooming in on the roots with minimal intervention from Coutinho, whose off-screen voice asks the man, "Did you eat that?" The question alerts viewers to the filmmaker's presence and reveals a mode of engaged listening perfected in subsequent films to create what Natalia Brizuela has aptly described as Coutinho's cinema of conversation and duration (20).

Theodorico similarly approaches a cinema of conversation without an additional voice-over narrator. The narration consists entirely of Theodorico's reflections and conversations either as diegetic sound or voice in off. A more conventional soundtrack with nondiegetic music typical of the Northeast opens and closes the film. After the title sequence introducing Theodorico, the camera zooms in on the landowner sitting in front of his home as he describes his life. His narration continues even after the camera cuts away to panoramic shots of the landscape and the town. When asking his tenants about their lives, Theodorico occupies a conversational position analogous to the one held by Coutinho in later films, but the authoritarian landowner maintains power imbalances and a disdain for listening that the director would shun. Working at *Globo Repórter* was foundational for Coutinho as a documentarian interested in representing specific voices, memories, and experiences to transform viewers' perspectives of social and political issues affecting the poor or other people whose lives differ from their own. The television documentaries solidified his fascination with the peoples and modes of speaking in the Brazilian Northeast. A desire to depict the nuances of spoken language and to capture the body that speaks would continue to guide Coutinho's work.

A Masterpiece and Some Experiments: The Years of *Cabra marcado* and CECIP

Coutinho returned to the project of *Cabra marcado para morrer* from 1981 to 1983 while still employed by *Globo Repórter*. He brought the skills gained during his years at Globo to the footage of Elizabeth Teixeira, her children, and other rural laborers that the 1964 coup had forced his team to abandon. Rather than re-create the fictional film as it was first envisioned, Coutinho turned a documentary lens on the story. He found the people involved in the original project, talked with them about their lives, and, in the process, captured the passage of time and the changing visions of political commitment in Brazil. As Carlos Alberto Mattos rightly notes, "In the Brazil of 1964, one tried to build a more just country and a cinema that united creativity and utility. In the Brazil of the 1980s, one sought to break the silence of an oppressive regime and to heal wounds" (117).[12] Coutinho embarked on this task while receiving his Globo salary and having access to their equipment, which allowed him to draft the screenplay, shoot additional scenes on 16 mm film, edit the film, and blow it up from 16 to 35 mm for its debut in Rio de Janeiro. He finalized the film during a six-month unpaid leave, from which he never returned (Avellar 50). *Cabra marcado* was a watershed moment that served as the culmination of experiences and influences from his years at the CPC and Globo. The success of *Cabra marcado* solidified Coutinho's position as one of the preeminent Brazilian documentarians and leftist filmmakers of the twentieth century.[13] Moreover, the film foreshadowed his development as a documentarian invested in conversation and his role as an ethical listener, as the penultimate scene most evidently illustrates (fig. 4.1). Coutinho is in the car, ready to leave, and Elizabeth is in the house, looking out at the director. He rolls down the car window and the two exchange a goodbye that points to the ongoing presence of the other and the power of the encounter. Allowing these encounters between the director, his subject, and the camera to unfold in front of the camera would emerge as an essential trait of Coutinho's conversational films.

After the resounding success of *Cabra marcado*, Coutinho completely dedicated himself to documentary by creating films for nonprofits like the Superior Institute for the Study of Religion (Instituto Superior de Estudos da Religião or ISER) and CECIP. As Brazil transitioned to democracy, the director moved toward the single-location cinema of conversation that would define his style. In 1986, the filmmaker helped to establish CECIP with his friend Claudius Ceccon as a nongovernmental organization committed to collaborating with popular Brazilian subjects to create short videos and documentaries with a pedagogical intent (Mattos 136). By developing projects in areas of education, communication, technology, memory, and culture, CECIP aims "to contribute to the strengthening of citizenship, producing information and methodologies that influence public policies promoting fundamental rights" ("Quem somos" n.p.).[14] Coutinho's work with CECIP

Figure 4.1. Coutinho and Elizabeth Teixeira in the penultimate scene of *Cabra marcado para morrer*. Source: *Cabra marcado para morrer (Twenty Years Later)*. Directed by Eduardo Coutinho, 1964–1984. Instituto Moreira Salles, 2014. DVD.

ranged from educational videos like the 1989 *O jogo da dívida: Quem deve a quem?* [*The Game of Debt: Who Owes Whom?*], which employed animated graphics and a didactic tone, to medium-length documentaries *Santa Marta* and *Boca de lixo*, where he refined the site-specific, conversational mode of filmmaking that characterized the last fifteen years of his career. Like the CPC before it, CECIP focused on popular voices and images, suggesting that explicit depictions of the popular as part of a mission of social and political engagement are more possible in Brazil during periods of democracy.

With CECIP, Coutinho returned to a mode of socially committed filmmaking reminiscent of his work with the CPC that also incorporated techniques and styles learned during his years at Globo.[15] The documentaries with CECIP represented a continuation of his stylistic development, as he used video and incorporated his subjects more fully in his films' conversational process. The director filmed in a single location for a fixed period with *Santa Marta*, where he limited himself spatially to the favela and temporally to two weeks. According to Lins, Coutinho found these restrictions creatively fruitful, as they forced him to work within confines and to examine carefully the words generated in conversation (Lins, *O documentário* 65). By filming in Santa Marta, a slum situated on the hills between Botafogo and Humaitá in Rio's wealthy southern zone, Coutinho returned to the marginal space of the favela, which he had previously explored with CPC's *Cinco vezes favela*. Sequences of Coutinho and his crew walking into Santa Marta render the director as a character who listens attentively to people reflecting on their varied life experiences and, thus, serves as the film's proxy for its viewers. This positionality enables Coutinho to propose a documentary practice foregrounding conversation as essential for listening to the popular and recognizing its political potential.

Though Coutinho does not visibly appear in the documentary after this initial sequence, his voice remains present as he asks residents about where they came from, how long they have lived in Santa Marta, what they think about life in the favela, and how they relate to daily tasks of parenthood and work. This style of questioning forms the basis of Coutinho's cinema of conversation in subsequent films like *Edifício Master* (*Master Building*, 2002), where the director asks questions that everyone could answer based on their own experiences. Consisting of brief encounters with Santa Marta's residents, the film does not reveal the director's later interest in duration. The residents are identified by their jobs rather than by their names, as they will be in subsequent films *Babilônia 2000* and *Edifício Master*. Across these works, a focus on individuals and specific experiences shapes Coutinho's approach. According to the director, "When I film a person, she is a person. When I am going to edit, she becomes a character of the film. I forget that she is a person, she is a character" (Avellar 53). Fascinated with the line between the real person and the fictional character, Coutinho pays attention to how people speak and embody language. An interest, apparent in *Santa Marta*, in language and music becomes fleshed out in later films as Coutinho connects these creative corporeal expressions to the popular as a lived experience, a documentary subject, and a political potential.

From 1988 to 1991, while affiliated with CECIP, Coutinho made *O fio da memória* (*Memory's Thread*, 1991), a feature-length documentary that exists as a relative outlier in his filmic production. Commissioned to commemorate the centennial of abolition in Brazil, the film received financing from, among other sources, the Fundação de Artes do Estado do Rio de Janeiro (State of Rio de Janeiro's Art Foundation, FUNARJ). Distributed by RioFilme, an entity supported by the city government, this longer documentary was filmed on 16 mm rather than the cheaper video to which Coutinho had become accustomed. Unlike Coutinho's other feature-length films, *O fio da memória* was not a project he chose. The director still found his own "fio," or thread, to ground reflections on the history and ongoing legacy of slavery in Brazil. To complement Ferreira Gullar's voice-over narration of key historical dates, the film centers on the memories and experiences of Gabriel Joaquim dos Santos (1892–1985), a descendant of enslaved peoples. Coutinho paired Afro-Brazilian actor Milton Gonçalves's voice-over narration of Gabriel's story with historical footage of slavery and more recent images of Gabriel and other Afro-descendants to craft a narrative of slavery and its repercussions in Brazil focused on the specific. Using individual experiences to tell a broader story became a common practice in Coutinho's documentaries with his increasing interest in the lives and languages of people on the margins of history. By listening with care and insisting on co-presence in front of the camera, the director collaborated to create films as an ethical space of political potential.

Aesthetically, *O fio da memória* has more in common with the explicitly pedagogical impulses of the Globo and CECIP documentaries and, perhaps most relevantly, the earlier project of the CPC. The documentary has two narrators, Gullar and Gonçalves, which recalls the narrative structure of earlier films *Cinco vezes favela* and *Cabra marcado*. Gullar was one of the poets affiliated with the CPC's *Violão da rua* imprint and had previously narrated part of *Cabra marcado*. Coutinho's later films rarely feature narrators, and, when they do, he is the sole narrator. More often, his films aim to capture his encounters with others in front of the camera without a narrator as guide. The educational and moralizing elements of *O fio da memória* betray the pressures from funding sources to explicitly condemn slavery and clearly indicate the film's point of view via narration. Although an exception in the director's career as a commissioned piece, the film also reveals continuities given its use of individual stories to shed light on social and political concerns.

Coutinho's next film, *Boca de lixo*, produced by CECIP and released in 1992, employs similar techniques to those used in *Santa Marta*. Unfolding mostly at the single site of the landfill Itaoca in São Gonçalo, Rio de Janeiro, the documentary features conversations with the garbage pickers. The film retains traces of Coutinho's Globo years in its more conventional use of nondiegetic music and his voice-over narration to heighten emotional responses to images of daily life at the dump. By foregrounding conversations with the scavengers, the film aims to capture on camera encounters between the director, his subjects, and their mediated images. With video, Coutinho could film continuously without a set plan, which allowed his interlocutors to participate more fully in the documentary process. As the director explained in 1998, "Now I only film on video, because on film, you are required to be so economical that it doesn't work for telling a life story" (Macedo 19).[16] Rather than ask pointed questions, Coutinho let people describe their lives, thus establishing more rapport with the community. Some scavengers initially looked down or turned away, a discomfort with being filmed that Coutinho respected by asking for permission to photograph them. He later gave these photographs to the scavengers, granting them ownership over their image and providing them with an indexical reminder of their encounter with the director. In this process, Coutinho examined tensions that exist between imagined, real, and mediated images in the realm of documentary.[17] Reflecting on these mediated interactions in *Boca de lixo*, Lins rightly surmises, "Filming and being filmed, the image of oneself and the image of the other, the media images, these are the questions that will traverse many of Coutinho's films from here on" (*O documentário* 89).[18]

Santo forte marks the gradual transition into the final stage of Coutinho's career as a film funded and produced by CECIP that received supplemental support from other sources. It also inaugurated the director's collaboration with editor Jordana Berg, which continued through his final, posthumously released film, *Últimas conversas* (*Last Conversations*, 2015). To complete *Santo forte*, Coutinho sought additional funding from government sources including RioFilme. With film critic José Carlos Avellar as its director, RioFilme was more likely to support a project like *Santo forte*, which proposed filming in the single location of Vila Parque da Cidade during Pope John Paul II's visit to Rio. Coutinho asked residents about their spiritual beliefs and then used these conversations to make a documentary more generally about religion in Brazil. The film lacks the pedagogical tone and melodrama of his earlier work with Globo and CECIP, but remnants of a more conventional documentary style remain, namely transitional shots filmed separately that link conversations and underscore religious themes. Sequences of Coutinho entering and leaving the favela turn the director into a character whose body appears on-screen occasionally but whose voice is a constant presence as he invites residents to share how Catholicism coexists with Afro-Brazilian religions in their lives.

Returning to a favela to depict popular cultures and knowledges, Coutinho honed the site-specific, conversational format of documentary that he would perfect during the rest of his career. In a 1998 interview,

Coutinho explained that "my vision in the films is anthropological, albeit savage" (Macedo 21).[19] As a participant-observer in the favela, he collaborated with residents in a mode of "savage anthropology" documented via film. Through these interactions, Coutinho realized that representations without excessive mediation could affect how his viewing public understood the daily lives and religious practices of others whose realities differed from their own. Because Coutinho wanted his first encounters with his subjects to be caught on camera, his crew vetted residents and suggested whom he should meet and what questions he should ask. Shooting on video facilitated this process of collecting footage to be edited over four months into the film's final cut. Critics have recognized that this interest in the moment of encounter and the corporeal expressions of language indicate the consolidation of Coutinho's style, which would be fully realized in his productions with Videofilmes.[20] His work on *Santo forte* benefited from his belief that, as he explained in Carlos Nader's documentary, "Only I want to and can make this film." *Santo forte* was a personal project that facilitated his exploration of relevant interests such as faith, language, and creative expression among people living in favelas. By delving into these topics, the film inaugurated what Esther Hamburger describes as "a series of experimental variations about the nature of the interaction between the filmmaker, his crew and the characters that come to life in his films, in front of the camera" (430–31).[21] Capturing these encounters on film emerged as Coutinho's main concern as his cinema of conversation and duration coalesced over his years working with Videofilmes.

The Videofilmes Collaborations and the Maturation of Coutinho's Style

In the final stage of his career, Coutinho refined his role as a savage anthropologist and linguist fascinated by the creative expression of others. He crafted films documenting memories, lived experiences, and daily routines of Brazil's peoples to present a more inclusive portrait of the popular beyond the limited realms of the favela and the sertão. These documentaries illustrate how listening to diverse voices, recognizing their value, and representing them with care could affect social and political change. Embracing a collaborative model of filmmaking that recalled his experiences with the CPC, Coutinho now worked with prominent figures of contemporary Brazilian film, including João Moreira Salles as producer, Lins as researcher and writer, and Berg as editor. These prolific fifteen years at the end of his life coincided with a renewed investment in culture in Brazil as the passage of Lei Rouanet in 1991 allowed companies to make tax-exempt donations to cultural projects, the National Agency of Film (Agência Nacional do Cinema or ANCINE) was established in 2001, and the Brazilian economy expanded.[22] In this period, Coutinho's documentaries received support from RioFilme, ANCINE, and cultural initiatives of corporations like Petrobras. With these funds and his partnership with Videofilmes, Coutinho had access to better equipment, which allowed him to shoot *Edifício Master* and *O fim e o princípio* on 35 mm film and to use digital video starting with *Peões* (*Metalworkers*, 2004).

This investment in Brazilian film contributed to a professionalization of the field of national documentaries, a process that, in Coutinho's case, was enhanced by his personal relationships with Salles as the Videofilmes producer and a fellow documentarian. Coutinho's films achieved a more polished look given the better financing, equipment, and technical support from working with a larger crew. By collaborating with a similar group of people on successive films, Coutinho developed a process of research, filming, and editing that let the spontaneity of the conversational encounter unfold on camera. The films produced with Videofilmes benefited from government incentives and cultural initiatives as they circulated domestically and internationally via film festivals, university and museum circuits, and career retrospectives. With his greater visibility in the documentary scene and as a character in his own films, Coutinho became increasingly recognized as a preeminent documentarian in Brazil and beyond. He was even the subject of documentary films, including *Coutinho Repórter* (*Reporter Coutinho*, 2010) and *Eduardo Coutinho, 7 de outubro* (*Eduardo Coutinho, October 7th*, 2013).

Recent films like *Edifício Master*, *O fim e o princípio*, and *Jogo de cena* reached a relatively widespread audience in Brazil and abroad, but their receptions have paled in comparison to the success of his seminal work *Cabra marcado*. After debuting at the 1984 International Film Festival in Rio, where it received a gold prize, it won best documentary or jury's choice at festivals in Havana, Italy, Paris, and Berlin in 1984 and 1985. In New York, it was featured in the New Directors/New Films series in 1985 and received a favorable review in the *New York Times*, which asserted that "Coutinho's commitment to his characters is all the more effective for being cool, controlled, and unsentimental" (Canby n.p.). This statement holds true over the next three decades as Coutinho stripped down the filmic apparatus to better capture his encounters with his subjects in front of the camera. As the director explained in a 2010 interview, "In my personal trajectory, I discovered that what interested me in film [. . .] was the conversation with the other, the encounter, the conflict with the other always and when there was a camera in the way" (Paiva and Russo 153).²³ Whether talking with people from the favelas of Santa Marta and Babilônia, the sertão of Paraíba, or the middle class, theater groups, and public school students of Rio de Janeiro, Coutinho listened attentively, remained open to their experiences, and strove to capture their distinct forms of speaking and embodying language.

Shifts in film production, distribution, and consumption in recent decades have made Coutinho's documentaries more accessible through the DVDs released by Videofilmes and, informally, YouTube. While his films still circulate at festivals and retrospectives, these new distribution technologies allow people to see his films without having to pay for a ticket or attend a specific screening. The versions posted online, often without the proper rights, tend to lack subtitles; they are intended primarily for a Brazilian public. This comparatively easy access to Coutinho's work was achieved, paradoxically, while his films were produced by Videofilmes, a company run by members of one of the wealthiest families in Brazil, brothers Walter Salles and João Moreira Salles. The production work of elites made it possible for the voices of often-marginalized peoples to reach a broader audience with greater political and social capital. Digital technologies may democratize modes of creation and consumption, but these processes remain embedded in structures of cultural and material capital, especially for leftist artists and intellectuals of an older generation like Coutinho. While their films benefit from more widespread circulation in the digital age, they remain most praised and discussed in social and academic circles where people gain access to popular voices and cultures via artistic mediation.

The expanded distribution now enjoyed by Coutinho's films resonates with earlier efforts by the CPC to share their films with people depicted in them. In both moments, filmmakers mediated the experiences and expressions of poor, working class, or otherwise marginalized peoples primarily for comparatively elite viewers who might be moved to enact political change by hearing these stories. What has changed over the intervening decades are the forms of production and distribution that diminish technical and financial barriers to making films not only about, but also with and for, the people represented in the films. In earlier films, Coutinho created a feedback loop by showing individuals involved in the documentary their photographic or filmic images. For instance, *Cabra marcado* depicts Elizabeth Teixeira, her children, and other film participants gathering in the early 1980s to watch black and white footage salvaged from the original CPC project. The camera uses parallel editing to capture their responses to seeing their younger selves on-screen, which underscores the passage of time and reveals Coutinho's desire to involve his subjects in various levels of the project. Working with film, however, posed technical limitations to integrating his subjects into the filmmaking process and granting them ownership over their images. As the video and digital era made printing photos and showing clips easier, Coutinho could more readily share his in-process film and other visual images with his subjects, as evidenced in *Boca de lixo*. The director presented the scavengers with photographs of themselves and included in the film's final cut a scene of them standing in front of a television, watching video footage of the documentary they were currently creating.

Coutinho's efforts to involve the people he filmed in the creative process and grant them agency over their own images unfolded within an imbalance of power between a director and his subjects. He aimed to minimize this gap by insisting on having conversations, not interviews, with his subjects where he listened carefully without judgment. Despite Coutinho's desires to make films with people, transcending divisions between the director and the lower middle-class residents of *Edifício Master* or the former metalworkers of *Peões* proved difficult. The filmed subjects often referred to Coutinho as "o senhor" (mister) rather than the more egalitarian "você" (you). As Roberto, an older, unemployed man living in the Master building, reminds viewers, Coutinho was a filmmaker with no power to directly change the lives of

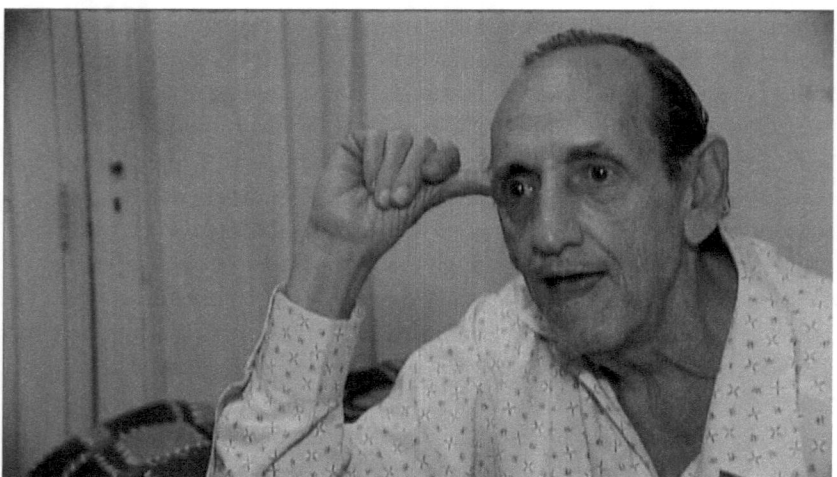

Figure 4.2. Roberto asks Coutinho if he would give him a job in *Edifício Master*. Source: *Edifício Master (Master Building)*. Directed by Eduardo Coutinho, Videofilmes, 2002.

those he filmed (fig. 4.2). Even if they, like Roberto, asked for a job during their conversations, Coutinho could not provide it.[24] The director's political commitment remained confined to the realm of cinema, where he could suggest more ethical models of listening and documenting the popular, not as an idealized, folkloric vision but rather as the experiences and expressions emanating from the diverse peoples of Brazil.

Concluding Thoughts

In the last decades of his career, Coutinho occupied a different landscape as a politically committed filmmaker because of changes in production and distribution that rendered obsolete the explicitly leftist approaches of the CPC in the 1960s or the possibilities of radicalism within the Globo network. Coutinho's concern with underrepresented voices persisted, as his depictions of favelas in *Babilônia 2000* and the sertão in *O fim e o princípio* exemplified. Rather than portray these realms as isolated enclaves of "authentic" popular culture, his films illustrate how these historically marginalized spaces have become less separated from the rest of Brazil given expanded media networks and shifting geopolitical and socioeconomic landscapes. Coutinho's fascination with how people on the margins use language and express themselves in unique ways led him to explore the voices of other forgotten groups like the metalworkers who participated alongside Lula in labor strikes without gaining political renown. With representations of these laborers in *Peões*, middle-class apartment dwellers in Copacabana in *Edifício Master*, and students from public high schools in Rio de Janeiro in *Últimas conversas*, Coutinho's later films reveal the proximity between favela, sertão, cities, and peripheries.

By expanding understandings of the popular and the politically engaged artist, Coutinho's work speaks to the shifting political and cultural landscape of contemporary Brazil. Organizing his career into four distinct phases, as I have outlined in this chapter, helps to highlight the continuities, divergences, and, more importantly, the ways that modes of production and distribution have impacted his approach to filmmaking. Coutinho's documentaries force his audience to rethink the national-popular as a living concept defined not by populist politicians or leftist artists and intellectuals, but rather by ordinary people who embody the words, memories, and rhythms of Brazil in their distinctive use of language and their daily lives. Though Coutinho died tragically in 2014, before the impeachment of Dilma Rousseff and the election of Jair Bolsonaro, one cannot help but wonder what the director's film about these political events testing the state of Brazil's democracy and ignoring the voices of its most marginalized citizens would have looked and sounded like.

Notes

1. In this chapter, the "popular" refers to ideas, expressions, artistic works, cultural traditions, and practices of everyday life among people, including the poor, powerless, or uneducated, historically marginalized by elites. See Flores for more on how ideas of the popular shift with time and the emergence of mass media (17–29). Chauí's essays on the people, popular culture, and politics offer insight into the construction of these concepts in Brazil. See Bernardet for an original study of images of the people in Brazilian documentary films from the 1960s and 1970s.

2. All translations are mine, unless otherwise noted. Coutinho stated in a 2002 interview, "A fórmula 'encontrar o povo' me repele. Não encontro o povo, encontro pessoas."

3. Bezerra's essay in Ohata's edited volume provides an overview of these phases. See his 2014 monograph for a deeper analysis of the phases in relationship to the role of characters and performance in Coutinho's documentaries. See Mattos for another division of Coutinho's trajectory into seven phases: student, fictional creator, reporter, social documentarian, filmmaker of conversation, experimental director, and a character of his own life.

4. The CPC existed from December 1961 to March 1964 as the culture branch of the student union affiliated with the Brazilian Communist Party. Carlos Estevam Martins's manifesto for a popular, revolutionary art guided their artistic and cultural initiatives. See Ridenti, Hollanda, and Garcia for more on the CPC and the 1960s in Brazil.

5. Argentine directors Fernando Solanas and Octavio Getino coined the term *tercer cine* as one form of New Latin American Cinema with "Hacia un tercer cine," originally published in the Cuban journal *Tricontinental* in October 1969. See Taboada for more on the theoretical foundations of *tercer cine* in the manifestos of Solanas and Getino, Rocha, and García Espinosa. For a reconsideration of global Third Cinema, see the volume edited by Guneratne and Dissanayake. Part Four of Schroeder Rodríguez's *Latin American Cinema: A Comparative History* provides an overview of key films and theories of New Latin American Cinema.

6. See Xavier's seminal work on allegory in Brazilian film for more on Cinema Novo's political limitations. Brock's chapter in this volume examines the differences between Rocha's mythical sertão and Coutinho's real sertão.

7. According to Coutinho, "todo documentário, no fundo, é precário, é incompleto, é imperfeito, e é justamente dessa imperfeição que nasce a sua perfeição."

O documentário é uma visão subjetiva sempre."

8. Stam emphasizes the favela and the sertão as central to Brazilian cinema since the 1930s. *Cinco vezes favela, Rio 40 graus* (1955), *Black Orpheus* (1959), *Orfeu* (1999), and *City of God* (2002), among others, are set in favelas. The sertão is key to *Vidas secas* (1963), *Deus e o diabo na terra do sol* (1964), *Bye Bye Brasil* (1979), and *Central do Brasil* (1999). See Bentes for more on the continued iconicity of these spaces in contemporary Brazilian film.

9. Ridenti identifies "capitulação ideológica diante da burguesia" and a "possibilidade de levar uma visão crítica ao telespectador, contribuindo para mudanças sociais."

10. In Coutinho's words, "Em alguns momentos, era possível fazer alguma coisa que parecia documentário, mas eram raros os momentos."

11. See Tardin's 2010 documentary *Coutinho Repórter* for more on Coutinho's experience at *Globo Repórter*.

12. Per Mattos, "No Brasil de 1964, tentava-se construir um país mais justo e um cinema que unisse criatividade e utilidade. No Brasil dos anos 1980, procurava-se romper silêncio de um regime opressor e fechar feridas."

13. At the time of the film's release, Bernardet described *Cabra marcado* as a "divisor de águas" (6). Thirty-five years later, Da-Rin used the same phrase to classify *Cabra marcado* as a watershed for Brazilian cinema and Coutinho's work (64).

14. See its website (http://www.cecip.org.br) for more on its mission: "contribuir para o fortalecimento da cidadania, produzindo informações e metodologias que influenciem políticas públicas promotoras de direitos fundamentais."

15. See Mattos for an astute reevaluation of Coutinho's work as a social documentarian with CECIP (135–77). His analysis includes lesser-studied films *Volta redonda—Memorial da greve* and *Os romeiros de Padre Cícero*. Some films from this period, like *Santa Marta* and *Volta redonda*, were created for ISER. Mesquita and Oliveira offer a thoughtful study of how audiovisual mediation contributes to social and political struggles and engages with ethical questions by examining the alliances between Coutinho, CECIP, and other social organizations and movements in the late 1980s and early 1990s.

16. In a 1998 interview, Coutinho explained that "agora eu só filmo em vídeo, porque em cinema, você é obrigada a ser tão econômico que não dá para contar história de vida."

17. See Furtado for an original study of archival gestures and practices in contemporary Brazilian documentary. He positions *Cabra marcado* as noteworthy for establishing dialogues between archival images and living bodies, exploring a process of remediation that Coutinho would refine in later films like *Boca de lixo* and *Peões* (10–18).

18. "Filmar e ser filmado, a imagem de si e a imagem do outro, as imagens da mídia, estas são questões que irão atravessar muitos filmes de Coutinho dali por diante."

19. In Coutinho's words, "a minha visão nos filmes é antropológica, embora selvagem."

20. For Bezerra, films in this final phase are invested in the image of the body as central to language. Lins recognizes the importance of the encounter in front of the camera for Coutinho's process given his interest in the spontaneity and specificity of language within social contexts (*O documentário* 109). Emphasizing the centrality of these encounters of bodies and voices, Sayad considers Coutinho's work a "cinema of the corporality of voices" (144). Dias associates the absence of an omniscient voice-over and the visibility of the crew in *Santo forte* and *Babilônia 2000* as characteristic of Coutinho's cinema of conversation, where "orality prevails over spectacle" (113).

21. According to Hamburger, Coutinho's films represent "uma série de variações experimentais sobre a natureza da interação entre o cineasta, sua equipe e os personagens que ganham vida em seus filmes, em frente à câmera."

22. See Dennison for a detailed study of the shifts in Brazilian film culture from 2003 to 2019 that stresses the importance of laws promoting cultural investment and the democratization of film production and consumption.

23. Per Coutinho, "En mi trayectoria personal yo descubrí que lo que me interesaba en el cine [. . .] era la conversación con el otro, el encuentro, el conflicto con el otro siempre y cuando hubiese una cámara en el medio."

24. A similarly tense interaction unfolds at the end of *Peões* when Geraldo asks Coutinho if he had ever been a metalworker ("já foi peão?"), to which the director responds no.

Works Cited

Avellar, José Carlos. "The Emptiness of the Backyard: An Interview with Eduardo Coutinho." Translated by Krista Brune. *Film Quarterly*, vol. 69, no. 3, 2016, pp. 44–55.

Bentes, Ivana. "The *sertão* and the *favela* in Contemporary Brazilian Film." *The New Brazilian Cinema*, edited by Lúcia Nagib, I.B. Tauris, 2003, pp. 121–37.

Bernardet, Jean-Claude. *Cineastas e imagens do povo*. Brasiliense, 1985.

Bezerra, Cláudio. "Um documentarista à procura de personagens." *Eduardo Coutinho*, edited by Milton Ohata, Cosac Naify, 2013, pp. 400–13.

———. *A personagem no documentário de Eduardo Coutinho*. Papirus, 2014.

Brizuela, Natalia. "Conversation and Duration in Eduardo Coutinho's Films." *Film Quarterly*, vol. 69, no. 3, 2016, pp. 19–27.

Canby, Vincent. "New Directors/New Films; Brazil Political Drama." *New York Times*, 5 Apr. 1985.

Chanan, Michael. *The Politics of Documentary*. British Film Institute, 2007.

Chauí, Marilena. *Cultura e democracia: O discurso competente e outras falas*. Moderna, 1980.

Da-Rin, Silvio. "Eduardo Coutinho e suas últimas obras.' *A família de Elizabeth Teixeira + Sobreviventes de Galileia*, edited by Eliska Altmann and Tatiana Bacal, 7Letras, 2019, pp. 61–91.
Dennison, Stephanie. *Remapping Brazilian Film Culture in the Twenty-First Century.* Routledge, 2020.
Dias, Verônica Ferreira. "A Cinema of Conversation—Eduardo Coutinho's *Santo forte* and *Babilônia 2000*." *The New Brazilian Cinema*, edited by Lúcia Nagib, I.B. Tauris, 2003, pp. 105–17.
Figueirôa, Alexandre, et al. "O documentário como encontro: entrevista com o cineasta Eduardo Coutinho." *Galáxia*, no. 6, 2003, pp. 213–29.
Flores, Juan. *From Bomba to Hip-Hop: Puerto Rican Culture and Latino Identity.* Columbia UP, 2000.
Furtado, Gustavo Procopio. *Documentary Filmmaking in Contemporary Brazil. Cinematic Archives of the Present.* Oxford UP, 2019.
Garcia, Miliandre. *Do teatro militante à música engajada—A experiência do CPC da UNE (1958–1964).* Fundação Perseu Abramo, 2007.
Gardnier, Ruy, et al. "Não encontro o povo, encontro pessoas." *Encontros: Eduardo Coutinho*, edited by Felipe Bragança, Beco do Azougue, 2008, pp. 80–101.
Guneratne, Anthony R., and Wimal Dissanayake, editors. *Rethinking Third Cinema.* Routledge, 2003.
Hamburger, Esther. "Eduardo Coutinho e a TV." *Eduardo Coutinho*, edited by Milton Ohata, Cosac Naify, 2013, pp. 414–31.
Hollanda, Heloisa Buarque de. *Impressões de viagem: CPC, vanguarda e desbunde.* 3rd ed., Aeroplano, 2004.
Lins, Consuelo. "Eduardo Coutinho, Savage Linguist of Brazilian Documentary." Translated by Natalia Brizuela. *Film Quarterly*, vol. 69, no. 3, 2016, pp. 28–34.
———. *O documentário de Eduardo Coutinho: Televisão, cinema e vídeo.* Jorge Zahar, 2004.
———. "The Cinema of Eduardo Coutinho." *Studies in Documentary Film*, vol. 1, no. 3, 2007, pp. 199–206.
Macedo, Valéria. 'Campo e contracampo: Eduardo Coutinho e a Câmera da Dura Sorte." *Revista Sexta-Feira*, vol. 3, 1998, pp. 10–25.
Mattos, Carlos Alberto. *Sete faces de Eduardo Coutinho.* Boitempo, 2019.
Mesquita, Cláudia, and Vinícius Andrade de Oliveira. "Alianças audiovisuais em tempos sombrios: Eduardo Coutinho, o Centro de Criação de Imagem Popular (CECIP) e os movimentos civis." *Doc On-line*, no. 28, 2020, pp. 78–96.
Nader, Carlos, director. *Eduardo Coutinho, 7 de outubro.* SESC Filmes, 2013.
Paiva, Valeria, and Pablo Russo. " 'Lo que amo en el cine es el acaso, el accidente, el azar'. Entrevista a Eduardo Coutinho." *Eduardo Coutinho: Cine de conversación y antropología salvaje*, edited by Grupo Revbelando Imágenes, Nulú Bonsai, 2013, pp. 151–65.

"Quem somos." *CECIP*, www.cecip.org.br.

Ridenti, Marcelo. *Em busca do povo brasileiro: Artistas da revolução, do CPC à era da TV.* Record, 2000.

Rocha, Glauber. "An Esthetic of Hunger." Translated by Randal Johnson and Burnes Hollyman. *New Latin American Cinema*, edited by Michael T. Martin, vol. 1, Wayne State UP, 1997, pp. 59–61.

Sacramento, Igor. *Depois da revolução, a televisão: cineastas de esquerda no jornalismo televisivo dos anos 1970.* Pedro & João, 2011.

Sayad, Cecilia. "Flesh for the Author: Filmic Presence in the Documentaries of Eduardo Coutinho." *Framework*, vol. 51, no. 1, 2010, pp. 134–50.

Schroeder Rodríguez, Paul A. *Latin American Cinema: A Comparative History.* U of California P, 2016.

Stam, Robert. *Tropical Multiculturalism: A Comparative History of Race in Brazilian Cinema and Culture.* Duke UP, 1997.

Tardin, Rená, director. *Coutinho Repórter.* 2010, curtadoc.tv/curta/artes/coutinho-reporter/.

Taboada, Javier de. "Tercer Cine: Tres Manifiestos." *Revista de crítica literaria latinoamericana*, vol. 37, no. 73, 2011, pp. 37–60.

Wayne, Mike. *Political Film: The Dialectics of Third Cinema.* Pluto, 2001.

Xavier, Ismail. *Allegories of Underdevelopment: Aesthetics and Politics in Modern Brazilian Cinema.* U of Minnesota P, 1997.

5

Cinema of/as Garbage

Eduardo Coutinho's Politics of Image from *Jogo de cena* to *Boca de lixo*[1]

Luz Horne

Boca de lixo (1992), filmed forty kilometers outside Rio de Janeiro at the São Gonçalo landfill, where thousands of people work and live, opens with a close-up shot of the ground covered in garbage. From close up, the camera pans discarded debris with no single recognizable item; no object stands out. All one can see is an undifferentiated mass of detritus that creates an abstract image. If not for the film's title—which situates us—only once the camera's view rises and begins to focus on the various animals foraging for food—a pig, birds of prey, a dog, and a rickety horse—do we begin to understand where we are. The landscape is post-apocalyptic or, as Consuelo Lins states, science fiction (87). The vapors of rot that rise with the camera to the sky betray the organic state of the waste. Behind the fog—as if it were a natural filter—we see a recognizable but opaque image of the Corcovado and, on its summit, Christ the Redeemer. The resulting image is an uncanny postcard of Rio de Janeiro (absent of the bright sun, lush greenery, and blue ocean) whose tranquility is interrupted by an abrupt change of plane and a howl. A close-up of the back of a waste truck coincides with the cry of a man warning that the garbage is about to be dumped. From that moment, thousands of voices overlap and, behind a viscous liquid that falls like sheet of rain from the truck, we see men, women, boys, and girls pushing themselves in an animalistic struggle to get their hands on the fallen debris. Images of partial bodies follow, grabbing for the discarded food scraps (hands grabbing a potato, a head of lettuce, etc.). In the footsteps of Glauber Rocha, hunger is going to be one of the central axes that mark the development of this film. In his seminal essay "Estética da fome," Rocha spoke out against the condescending perspective of those who, looking from the outside, cultivate "the taste of misery," and proposed instead a new aesthetical approach to the subject: the "aesthetics of hunger," technically deprived and poor. In *Boca de lixo*, hunger is recovered not only as a theme, but also in the way the topic is treated in its aesthetic and technical choices that strive for the construction of an austere cinematic image, distanced from the spectacular (fig. 5.1).

Just as Cinema Novo—and Glauber Rocha's cinema in particular—marked a before and after in the reflection on the links between aesthetics and politics in Latin American cinema, in this chapter I propose that Coutinho's filmography should also be read as a turning point in this debate. In what follows, I intend to show that Coutinho's filmography elaborates

Figure 5.1. Image of Corcovado overshadowed by steam from garbage and by prey birds from *Boca de lixo*. Source: *Boca de lixo* (*Scavengers*). Directed by Eduardo Coutinho, CECIP, 1992.

a theory of the cinematographic image that is interdependent of a specific conception of the subject, which, in turn, sustains an ethic. Only based on an analysis of this framework—evidenced through an anthropological and cinematographic practice—is it possible to grasp the innovation that his filmography presents as a matter of theoretical reflection on the link between image and politics.

Throughout his documentaries, Coutinho has explored different poor communities existing in situations of marginality or exclusion, in favelas and places of squalor. However, *Boca de lixo* is perhaps his film with the greatest ethical challenge. Given that it is filmed in a landfill, the degree of marginality of the people living there and, at the same time, the complicity of a capitalist society based on consumption with this marginality become apparent. In viewing the initial images recently described it is almost impossible not to feel shocked, disturbed, and repulsed. What we see and hear borders on the intolerable and the abject, and the comparison that is established between the material remains and the people who live and work there is practically inevitable. In fact, this is one of the first observations made by the film: we are dealing with the functioning of a biopolitical operation; we are faced with residual lives deprived of their formal character and their subjectivity, reduced to simple living matter or *nuda vida*. As Judith Butler and Athena Athanasiou state in *Dispossession: The Performative in the Political*, in the political imaginary that we live in, "being and having are constituted as ontologically akin to each other; being is defined as having; having is constructed as an essential prerequisite of proper human being" (13). Therefore, it is possible to assert that, in this opening scene, we are looking at people who have lost any ontological entity; we stand before bodies stripped of the idea of humanity and of all legal and social protection: a "state of exception."[2]

Given this context, one of the central questions of the film is how to avoid a cinematic image that perpetuates an exotic, stereotypical, and spectacularized vision of poverty; how not to reinforce and naturalize the biopolitical operation just by showing its functioning; how to adopt an ethical—and ultimately political—stance in face of an intolerable situation of injustice. Or, as José Carlos Avellar says, "how do you film the unfilmable?" (537), a problem that entails a discussion about the status and potential of the image that is inserted into a long-standing debate on the relationship between representation and historical trauma or horror. Although—as Susan Sontag says in *Regarding the Pain of Others*—"for a long time some people believed that if the horror could be made vivid enough, most people would finally take in the outrageousness, the insanity of war" (Sontag 14); showing horror has not, by itself, led to the end of horror. In his analysis of this problem, Jacques Rancière also refers to the political limitation of what he calls "the militant use of the intolerable image," in which it is assumed—mistakenly, according to him—that showing these images should produce an awakening in the bourgeois conscience and a reaction. A long tradition leads us to either naively believe in a direct political effect of images or to distrust them and to suspect not only their ability to show or revert an established order, but also their deceptive, reassuring, and manipulative nature. Against this false alternative, Jacques Rancière and Georges Didi-Huberman's theories of image coincide in the need to criticize the critique of the image in which its political potential is recovered: "a critique of images cannot dispense with the use, practice and production of critical images. Images, no matter how terrible the violence that instrumentalises them, are not entirely on the side of the enemy" (Didi-Huberman 28).

Following this line of thought, I propose that in thinking about the image and the devices of representation that Eduardo Coutinho performs in *Boca de lixo*, a critical potential and a politics of images can be found. The comparison between people and garbage—or between people and animals—as seen in the opening sequence, begins to crumble when a subjectivity that seemed to be removed is restored and we start to recognize the same people as subjects with desires, fears, aspirations, shame, and contradictions; as subjects capable of lying, acting, and exaggerating. To achieve this, the documentary uses certain procedures through which it critiques the use of the image as an illustration and proposes a complex and heterogeneous image instead.

This film, in particular, is ideal for thinking about the theory of cinematic image in Coutinho's filmography as a whole because it reveals a key transition/passage: from garbage as a theme to garbage as a metaphor of the cinematic image. Departing from a naturalistic look, this film produces a critical cinematic image that can be thought of as a "garbage-image" because it constitutes itself as something made of layers of temporality and multiple registers and meanings. The militant use of the intolerable image, which, according to Rancière, assumed a specific effect—the shock would produce an insight and, therefore, an action (Rancière 103)—is discarded to propose instead a complex image in its workmanship; an image in which different expressive registers (sound and vision, word, and gestures) and temporalities coexist. In this manner, the image loses its illustrative function to acquire instead a performative, fictional, affective, bodily, or even material entity, whose effect is subject to chance, surprise, and indeterminacy. As a result, the problem is displaced: it is not about whether to show images of poverty or to stop doing it, but about analyzing the mechanisms through which these images are presented.

To understand the operation that the film performs, I start with an analysis of a later film, *Jogo de cena* (2007), which has been considered by various critics (Jean-Claude Bernardet, Ilana Feldman, Consuelo Lins, Isabel Penoni, and Ismail Xavier) as a hinge film in which Coutinho inaugurates a new stage: he stops filming in "real locations" and proceeds to make a more evident reflection on his own work and on the process of representation in documentary film. In line with Feldman and Bernardet's analysis of *Jogo de cena* as a film essay in which the notion of testimony as confession and as an expression of an individual subjectivity is questioned, I would like to propose that this film offers the possibility to think about an ethical relation established from a dispossessed subjectivity—in the sense in which Butler and Athanasiou understand this concept in the recently cited book—which is consistent with a theory of non-illustrative image.

Although I agree with Bernardet that *Jogo de cena* questions the expressive relationship between language and subjectivity, and that it destabilizes the notion of subject, my reading does not agree with his idea that this film calls into question all of Coutinho's prior films—based on an alleged belief in the statement of the interviewed individuals—but, rather, quite the opposite. As I propose, the detachment between individual subject and testimony that occurs so clearly in *Jogo de cena* allows us to read the testimonies of his previous films in a new light. Instead of dismissing the previous films as false or sterile, *Jogo de cena* allows us to contradict the idea that in previous documentaries the interviewee's discourse was proposed as a direct expression of his/her subjectivity.[3] I intend to take the theory of the cinematic image in *Jogo de cena* and apply it to the analysis of *Boca de lixo* to understand the mechanisms of exhibition when they involve an intolerable image and a type of dispossession inflicted from the outside as an injustice. That is to say, I read *Boca de lixo* retrospectively based on the material for reflection offered by *Jogo de cena*. Imagining *Jogo de cena* as the nucleus of a procedure already used in prior films in a latent manner sheds new light on the link between image and politics.

Jogo de cena:
A Non-illustrative Image and a Dispossessed Subjectivity

In response to a newspaper ad shown in the first shot of the film to lay out the rules of the game, ordinary women seated in an empty theater with their backs to the stage tell their life stories on camera. Professional actresses in the same empty theater then repeat these stories. *Jogo de cena* is made of these interspersed narratives of women telling their own stories and the actresses' accounts. However, there are no acted performances or representations but rather repetitions of the same stories. In some cases, we even first hear the actress and then the actual woman. That is, on-screen, the actresses intermingle with the women whose lives are being represented, so that the status of the narratives becomes uncertain: the spectator cannot always discern between the real interview and the performative act as a theatrical practice of actresses following a script, except—of course—in the few cases in which the actress are famous. The central point of the film lies in the uncertainty that it produces and what it offers in terms of material for reflection about documentary film itself (Xavier 620).

The women selected for the documentary tell their stories related to various types of experiences: loss, frustration, family conflicts, and problems related to maternity or to the fulfillment of professional or amorous desires. Although the film suggests a reading in conjunction with other references to help understand gender relations in contemporary social life (Xavier 623), it does not attempt to provide a portrait of the women's situation from a sociological perspective. The power of interpellation of *Jogo de cena* does not reside in the social commentary regarding the situation of women. Coutinho's own reasons for this choice have to do with his desire to film what is "different." In the case of the women, he speaks about a certain capacity for saying things that men don't dare say, for exposing themselves more freely as fragile. What Coutinho seeks through the female presence is a certain capacity for language, a certain "lack of shame" for telling personal stories and expressing emotions, which he understands as a more pronounced trait among women.[4] Leaving aside whether Coutinho's observations about women are right, I want to highlight that his search is not focused on a generalization, or on offering a set of life stories that illustrates certain recurring problems or female-related issues, but rather on forging an intimacy, a bond that makes it possible for the other to speak about herself and produce a narrative, a life story. In this regard, in lieu of trying to force the singularity of each case into a classification, the film aims toward the thinking about each subject as a subversion of the category of woman as a universal.

In considering the effect on the spectator upon seeing two people tell the same story, many things happen. If we take the interspersed images of the woman telling the story of the child who dies after childbirth and the images of the actress who represents her (Andréa Beltrão), it is impossible for their reactions to be identical even though they are telling the same story. So, in the first place, and in a paradoxical way, the emotional impact of the stories when told by the actresses is sometimes greater than the one produced by the same stories when told by the people who really lived them. This displacement of the impact of the story in relation to its authenticity is fundamental, since it implies that the value of testimony does not necessarily reside in this authenticity and that emotion is not a transparent criterion for deciding. On the other hand, if one can leave aside the question of which one is the actress and which is the real woman—that is to say, the question of authenticity—we witness two ways of living the same thing, two ways to react to pain, joy, or loss; in short, two emotional reactions to the same experience. The outcome of this repetition is that the content of the story is placed in parentheses, left in suspense, to highlight a more affective or corporeal aspect of the account, which—in an odd way—we don't know whom it belongs to anymore. A gap emerges between the content of what is being said and its performance. In watching this, it is impossible not to address an aspect related to language, but which transcends meaning because what differentiates one story from the repeated version is not what is said but the gestures, the laughter, the crying, the facial expressions, the temporality with which the story is told, the interruptions, the repetitions, the mistakes, the lapses, and the places where discourse stumbles. Thus, the comparison between the two stories not only underlines the problem of undecidability between reality and fiction and disconnects the value of the testimony from its authenticity, but also brings to the foreground something that is not completely integrated into the account: an excess that the subject cannot master through her speech, and that is independent of biographical narrative, but simultaneously attached to it. Therefore, the performance in the story of the woman's own life and the spectator's inability to discern the authentic story from the acted version signals the loss of a supposed referent and indicates that there is something that goes beyond the mimetic. The word—or the image, in terms of cinematic image—does not represent anything. It ceases to have value because of its adherence to an individual subject, and it acquires it because of its ability to generate an impact on the viewer. The word does not express or illustrate; it loses its primary function of communicating meaning. Stripped of the support of the self, it becomes sustained in its materiality as a performance, a body, a thing. The comparison between the two narratives reveals that there is no sovereignty over the narrative itself, as there is a corporeal or affective remainder that arises despite oneself that is the condition of possibility of narration. Where the word encounters its limit to convey the biographical history and it breaks away, fiction emerges.

I would like to consider this in relation to what Judith Butler proposed in *Giving an Account of Oneself*. She argues that moral philosophy relies on the ability of subjects to give an account of themselves and their actions. However, given that the subject is not transparent to itself, the question that arises is if such an account is possible: "Does the postulation of a subject who is not self-grounding, that is, whose conditions of emergence can never fully be accounted for, undermine the possibility of responsibility and, in particular, of giving an account of oneself? If it is really true that we are, as it were, divided, ungrounded, or incoherent from the start, will it be impossible to ground a notion of personal or social responsibility?" (Butler 19). On the contrary, Butler argues that this ethical failure gives rise to an ethical disposition in the place of a full and satisfying notion of narrative accountability. Since the opacity of the subject may be a consequence of its being conceived as a relational being, a new sense of ethics emerges from such inevitable dispossession of the subject. *Jogo de cena* could be thought of as an example of this kind of ethical relationship proposed by Butler in the sense that the dispossession of the subject with herself not only does not prevent the narrative about oneself from happening, but it is—as she argues, quoting Jacques Lacan—the very condition of its possibility: "The irrecoverability of an original referent does not destroy narrative; 'it produces it in a fictional direction'" (Butler 37). Of course, the concept of fiction understood as such presents some ambiguity. While watching the film, this slip toward performance and acting becomes evident—not only in the actresses' accounts but also in the women telling their real-life stories—yet it is also necessary to recognize that there is a clear "documentary intention" in the film. That is, there is a desire to show real-life stories. On the other hand, the women's theatricality proposes no alternative story to the biographical account; it does not construct a scene that alludes to it representatively. Fiction acquires certain special characteristics because it does not take the form of verisimilar representation, it involves a theatrical performance but not an alternative story with a plot; rather it looks more like a photograph seen through a filter, a story just offset from itself.

A Spectral Presence

There are two moments in the film where the loss of the illustrative function of the cinematic image and its operation as an affective, performative, and material image become palpable through a temporality displacement.

Through a disjunction between the word and the image, the criticism of the representation displayed in the film is reinforced. In the first scene, Fernanda Torres, one of Brazil's most famous actresses, is acting, and suddenly she becomes tongue-tied; she stops and asks if she can run through the scene again. The camera keeps rolling and it becomes part of the film, resulting in a scene in which Torres explains how she felt to the director and as she tries to understand what it feels like to reenact a script based on a real person and not a fictional character:

> I do not separate her from what she says, I find it impossible to separate the two. When I was talking to you and you were looking at me, it seemed that my memory was slower than hers, you know? It's as if the word comes before you've seen it, you know? So that was bothering me. When I practiced it at home that didn't happen, so I don't know if I should slow it down, . . . I was thinking about what to do.

The time lag that Torres perceived between her own memory and that of the other woman—"it seemed that my memory was slower than hers"—and the acceleration of language regarding what memory brings to mind—"It's as if the word comes before you've seen it"—again indicate the subject's lack of mastery in regard to her own narrative and forge the path for performance, for fiction. There is something—an emotion, a feeling, a gesture—that remains outside the discourse, and the delay she feels highlights this failure to represent without distance from the original speech. The gap where the narration of life separates from life and is unable to reach it reveals its inevitable fictional character (in the sense of which we are here understanding fiction: as a replacement of a nonexistent and unattainable referent).

In a scene at the end of the film, something similar happens. The scene is a bit different from the rest because it shows one of the women who has already told her story when she returns to change it because, in her own words, it ended "in a very tragic light." To repair it, she wants to sing a song. While singing, the voice of the actress who represented her recites the lyrics, spoken with almost no melody and offbeat, with a slight delay in relation to the lead voice. In describing this scene, Coutinho says it is as if the actress "were a ghost-like presence."[5] Indeed, the voice of the actress comes late, with a different timing, like a ghost or a shadow of the lead voice, indicating a distance between both performances, as between self-representation and life itself. The biographical referent fades until it becomes apparent that it never existed as such. His fulfillment can only come through a fictional construction.

As a result of this operation, not only is the word—testimony—or the cinematic image denaturalized, but by highlighting its performative or fictional core and detaching it from the concept of authenticity, it also separates it from the individual subject. It is not a story without intimacy but quite the opposite; it is not a story in which the singularity of the experience of that subject is not read, but it produces a subject open to establish a relationship with the other, to make his/her own life available to the other. Through the telling of that story in the mouths of two different people, as well as through the uncanny and offset perspective offered by the cinematic image in this temporal disjunction, we are presented with an affectivity without an owner, a dispossessed subjectivity that marks the limits of self-sufficiency and establishes us as relational, interdependent beings.

Boca de lixo: From the Image *of* Garbage to the Image *as* Garbage

In a film like *Jogo de cena*, in which the centrality of the device and self-reflection are evident, it can be understood that its main objective is not to make a sociological or representative portrait of the problems of the people who appear in the film, women in this case. The film is oriented toward another place and purpose. In *Boca de lixo*, however, given the type of universe represented, it is much more difficult to shift away from a realistic perspective: it is a film that seeks to document life in a landfill, which seeks to reveal a distant reality to the viewer and delves into the way of life of people who are excluded from institutionalized work, in a regime of precarity and disposable labor. However, as in *Jogo de cena*, a detailed analysis of the mechanisms of exhibition is needed to understand how Coutinho reverts the naturalized look on the universe represented and to grasp its political impact.

As said earlier, the value of the image in *Jogo de cena* does not lie in its authenticity but rather in the effect that it produces—affective, performative—and in the ethical bond that this effect makes it possible to generate. Now, I would like to ask how this theory of image operates when facing a shocking and intolerable image, and a dispossessed subject in a different sense as occurs in *Boca de lixo*.

Butler and Athanasiou's theory put into operation two meanings of dispossession. On the one hand, the one already mentioned, from which we can think about a post-structuralist, post-metaphysical subjectivity in which the referent is lost and, as such, manifests itself through a performativity—or, as proposed, through a fiction—making possible a new modality of a collective relationship; on the other hand, a systematic and political dispossession of people through different forms of injustice: forced migration, unemployment, homelessness, occupation, slavery, and so forth. What we first find in the opening sequence of *Boca de lixo* is a group of people in a state of extreme dispossession in this second sense of the concept. However, both meanings are closely tied, and it is through this link that Butler and Athanasiou propose the following challenge: "We take up the question of how to become dispossessed of the sovereign self and enter into forms of collectivity that oppose forms of dispossession that systematically jettison populations from modes of collective belonging and justice" (xi).

If we think about something similar for Coutinho's films, we can ask ourselves how the meaning of dispossession that appears in *Jogo de cena*—which supports a theory of the non-illustrative cinematic image and a new form of ethics—unfolds in *Boca de lixo* and enables a surprising and denaturalized look at dispossession in the second sense. Outside of the liberal logic of possession, the identification of having and being is called into question and opens up the possibility of finding "ethical and political ways of objecting to forcible and coercive dispossession that do not depend upon a valorization of possessive individualism" (Butler and Athanasiou 7).

Portraits and Names

Immediately following the opening scenes of the film in which we see the landfill's inhabitants in their extreme exclusion, equated to garbage and animals, the scene is interrupted by the title sequences, after which we can think there is a new start. What follows are images of people running away from the camera, covering their faces, asking the cameramen why they are filming them, stating—taking a defensive stance, although they have not been accused of anything—that they are not ashamed of doing what they do. In this way, the violence of the process of representation itself and the voyeuristic act that filming poverty implies become evident. As anticipated, the whole film will transform the violence of the camera into a process of recognition of the people who live in the landfill as subjects of rights. To achieve this, the documentary critiques the use of the image as an illustration and proposes a complex and layered image instead.

Following the scenes in which people cover their faces and try to get away from the camera, as the director begins to ask them questions, they let their bandanas slip down from their faces, allowing themselves to be seen and to engage in a conversation. The first thing that Coutinho does is hand out the printed photographs of their faces. As he hands them out, he asks one young boy if he knows everyone who works there. Given the affirmative response of the child and the confirmation that they are all like family because they've been raised all together, he asks him to name everyone he knows from the photographs. The film's structure is built around the individualization provided by the nominal regime, divided into five distinctive chapters titled with the names and life stories of five people. Coutinho follows each of them and establishes a conversation that takes place in the landfill and, with some, in their homes. Based on these conversations, as spectators, we discover different reasons to live and work there. The film develops in an oscillation between these personal stories, on the one hand, and more collective filming in common spaces and with interventions of several people, on the other.

To analyze the complexity of the cinematic image in this film, I would like to take a deeper look at this scene in which the landfill's inhabitants share the names of the people in the photographs. The first child to say the names is joined by other children and adults, in such a way that the voices accumulate as they recite one name after another while passing around the photographs. In the following image, and simultaneously with the singing of the names, the camera shows us, in close-ups, the faces of the people who are being named. The camera stops on each of these faces in a close-up for a few seconds as if it were an animated photo exhibit. In this scene, a desynchronization occurs: the image moves at a slower speed and remains focused on each face longer than the voices take to say each name (fig. 5.2).

The disjunction between the visual and the sound regimes produces a double image: the visuality is not presented as a mere supplement to the word. It does not illustrate what people are saying; it offers an alternative story. The voices are cheerful and challenging and come from their previous affirmation—in the first disorderly group conversation with the director—of the honest work they do, the absence of shame they feel as they look for food in the garbage, and the dignity implied in living without having to beg or steal. By naming their friends and family, they laugh and re-emphasize

Figure 5.2. Portraits of the garbage collectors in *Boca de lixo*. Source: *Boca de lixo* (*Scavengers*). Directed by Eduardo Coutinho, CECIP, 1992.

a certain choice of this life over other options. The visual images of the faces, on the other hand, do not show smiles or happiness but express accusatory, melancholic, serious, sad, and tired looks. The tension between the two representative registers seems to affirm that there is no possibility of offering a unique and clear account of the lives of these people in the landfill. The visual image does not present a truth that the voices deny, nor does the opposite happen, but rather simultaneity is produced. This tension persists throughout the film in different ways, underlining the impossibility of offering a naturalized and monolithic vision of the universe represented and proposing, instead, a contradictory, open, and surprising image.

In this regard, I agree with João Moreira Salles in that one of the great innovations in *Boca de lixo* was to film the poor from a point of view "removed from the alienation, social contradiction or political struggle" (371), and as such, portray the way they live as a choice. However, I think the tension produced between both representative records adds one more layer to the film because it shows that living there is not an entirely free choice.

The film's innovation does not lie only in the absence of a perspective of political struggle or of a pious gaze, but in showing the contradiction present in the represented subjects themselves, in the ambiguity with which they speak of their lives and the indeterminacy that the cinematic image adopts in relation to the universe represented.[6]

Without contradicting the idea that the camera makes a strong statement about the injustice, the inhumanity, and the "environmental suffering" that these people endure, I am interested in thinking that the gaze of the film—and in this sense, Coutinho's—cannot identify directly with the camera (with the visual image), but rather its originality, precisely, consists of maintaining an indeterminate, contradictory, open, and unresolved gaze—its judgment suspended—about life in the landfill and about the subjects that are being filmed.[7] This gaze is possible thanks to the way the cinematographic image is conceived from a point of view that is alien to the notion of illustration, supplement, or expression.

The Pensive Image

To understand how the cinematographic image is conceived in Coutinho's film, I would like to use Jacques Rancière's concept of "pensive image." In his analysis, Rancière argues that in the passage from a representative regime to an aesthetic regime, there is a change in the way an image is conceived; it ceases to have the status of expressive complement and is emancipated in relation to the action. The image is then constituted from a tension that is established between different regimes of expression: "The 'pensativity' of the image is the latent presence of a regime of expression within another" (Rancière 121). In this manner, if we place the analyzed scenes in this light, the different registers that confront each other would not be giving the last word to the visual image but would remain suspended in a state of indetermination, a doubt that offers coexistence between two registers or between joy and sadness or accusation and choice.

To better define this aspect and then relate this way of understanding the cinematic image to what was already said about *Jogo de cena*, I would like to look at two connected scenes from the *Boca de lixo*. The first one takes place in the home of one of the women followed by Coutinho: Cícera. Inside an adobe dwelling, Coutinho speaks with Cícera. She sits next to her teenage daughter and her daughter's boyfriend, who listen quietly. Cícera gives a brief account of her life, and Coutinho praises her ability to speak and everything she has to say. He asks her if she wants to say something else, to which she replies that the only thing she really wants is a future for her daughter. Then Coutinho asks the girl what she wants: she does not hesitate; she says she wants to be a singer. The next scene shows the girl in front of her mud house, standing alone, singing a cappella.

After a few minutes in which the camera films her full-length, it focuses in on her face and gestures: her eyes closed, her voice strong and imposing, her head swaying, revealing her completely engaged in the scene in her role as a singer. The girl's singing continues as the camera moves to focus on her mother going about her daily chores: lighting a fire in what seems to be the preparation of a meal, washing herself with the water from a bucket, and combing her hair in front of a hand mirror. These scenes of extreme—but dignified—poverty contrast with the vocation of being a famous singer. However, the force of the voice and the girl's confidence as she sings, superimposed on the visual image of poverty, generate a certain contradiction and an emotional effect on the spectator. Just like what happened in *Jogo de cena* through the repetition of the same story by different women, the girl's singing presents us with an aspect of the word that has nothing to do with its meaning and that, according to Coutinho himself, establishes a link, a bond with the interviewee, that is essential in his documentaries:

> We tend to think that the discourse is the spoken or written word, and nothing else. However, when a person speaks from her heart, that is, when one speaks from the gut, the typical place imposed by society and its structures is displaced. That is what interests us, because it is there that a person produces original speech. When someone speaks from the gut, it produces, on the one hand, a text that is both oral and verbal, constructed from a grammar and a vocabulary, as well as a paraverbal text, because people digress, lapse, make mistakes, jump from one topic to another, repeat themselves. On the other hand, the person also produces a gestural text in which the body is absolutely essential. Man is an animal that speaks and speaks through his body. (Russo and Paiva n.p.)[8]

In the scene of the girl singing, a bodily aspect of language is rescued, an aspect foreign to the meaning that, far from being extinguished, is emphasized when the visual image disappears and only the voice is conserved. It is a layered image, dense in its heterogeneity of records that, in its constant rebound and change of emphasis between the different representative regimes, incites to detach the emotion of the girl from her individual figure and makes it possible to think about a subjectivity without ownership, without entire mastery of itself, dispossessed of itself and open to collective belonging. Again, the content of the scene is placed in parenthesis, left in suspense to highlight a vital capacity that links us with each one of these people through something that goes beyond the individual but that it is, at the same time, absolutely singular. The opening sequence of the film is denaturalized, and the identification between not having (being dispossessed of property, food, shelter, work, etc.) and not being human is broken.

The second scene associated with the one of the girl singing is the final sequence of the film, in which the device of still photographs and close-ups of the faces from the opening sequence is brought back. This time, the people we have followed throughout the film appear holding up a photo of a relative or a friend in front of the camera: we see two images of superimposed faces on which the camera pauses. The strategy of introducing them in family groups or series emphasizes what was initially given through the gesture of asking them to introduce themselves to each other: the bond that unites them as a community, the belonging to a group, to a family, to a collective. Unlike what happened at the start of the film, now individual names disappear and are presented in series of two or more, which speaks of a different regime of nomination or individuation and emphasizes the collective bond.

To further strengthen the collective matter at hand, a sound image joins the visual image of the portraits of the people holding portraits: the song that the girl who wants to be a singer just sang is now playing on the radio. When the camera reaches the "photo" of the girl's family, the visual and sound image come together because we see the girl holding the radio in her hands. We found the source of the diegetic sound that was hidden from us at the beginning of the scene. After a few minutes, Coutinho asks the girl to sing over the radio. With both voices in the air, the camera shifts to a collective scene in the landfill: on a television screen up on the roof of a van, they all watch the video of the almost-complete film. That is, as spectators, we see everyone together looking at themselves in a game of mirrors that in turn duplicates itself with the sound: the two overlapped voices do nothing but underline a constant lag of representation, a reminder that what we see and what we hear is always performative, fictional (fig. 5.3).

Like what happened in *Jogo de cena*, the duplicity of the voices produces a phantom-like effect that separates the girl's desire to be a singer

Cinema of/as Garbage | 127

Figure 5.3. Garbage collectors watching scenes from the documentary that they starred in near the end of *Boca de lixo*. Source: *Boca de lixo (Scavengers)*. Directed by Eduardo Coutinho, CECIP, 1992.

from her individual self and offers us a dispossessed subjectivity open to relate to others. These others are portrayed in the visual image and group of faces gesticulating in emotion (with laughter and tears). In this final sequence—from the moment we hear the song on the radio and see the portraits of the people holding portraits until the Velazquian and infinite image of people looking at themselves on television—the gap that emerges between the image and a possible lost referent underscores the materiality of the cinematographic image or its performatic, fictional, and affective quality.

Image and Politics: The Image as Garbage

It would be wrong to understand the distance placed between the lost referent and image as a purely formal or aesthetic operation, for it is in this lag that returns as an affective excess that we find the critical and even political impact that this film seeks.

In *Survival of the Fireflies*, George Didi-Huberman takes a metaphor that Pasolini used to refer to certain fleeting moments of friendship, happiness, and sexual desire linked to an artistic desire and resistance against fascism: fireflies dancing in the night illuminating intermittently in a will to form a community (55). In the seventies, Pasolini sentences the death of the fireflies in the face of what he sees as a cultural form in which there is no room for their sparkle. Pasolini's apocalyptic outlook in his statement regarding the death of fireflies is, according to Didi-Huberman, "to give credit to what the [totalitarian] machine would have wanted us to believe. [. . .] it is being convinced that the machine does its job without rest or resistance. It is not seeing the space although it is interstitial, intermittent, nomadic, based on the improbable, on openings, on possibilities, on that which emerges despite everything" (42).

Therefore, thanks to the metaphor of the firefly, Didi-Huberman can condense different matters in relation to the image but, above all, highlight something related to the *pathos* and to the possibility of generating a bond, an empathy, or a feeling of collective belonging in which a politicity transpires: "it is the place where politics embodies in the bodies, in the gestures and the desires of each one" (24–25). The firefly's intermittence offers an alternative to the absolute darkness of not showing anything or the dark times, as well as to the blinding light of the spectacle. In this sense, the metaphor enters into dialogue not only with Aby Warburg's concept of survival, but also with the dialectical image of Walter Benjamin and the symptom of Sigmund Freud, making it possible to think about the image as a thing whose exact borders cannot be drawn, as something porous and overdetermined, as a result of movements that have settled or crystallized in it. In a way that is related to the pensive image as Rancière defines it, we find ourselves before the image and a complex temporality that condenses different speeds, accelerations, and accumulated layers of time. In this regard, the analyzed scenes of *Boca de lixo* could be assessed in relation to this metaphor, like those moments of exception that Didi-Huberman refers to in regard to Pasolini, in which "human beings become fireflies—luminescent beings, dancing, erratic, elusive and resistant as such—under our amazed gaze" (23).

The cinematic image in *Boca de lixo* is born as if it were a firefly or—more attuned to this same conceptual line and perhaps a more appropriate metaphor—as a piece of garbage. From the opening scenes in which garbage is an amorphous and abstract mass of detritus, to the scenes in which we see people using the objects they have found to eat, read, dress, play, and furnish their houses, garbage—just like the people themselves—assumes an affective charge. Garbage, like the image presented by the film, is a multiple, complex object, full of layers of history and uses—an object that survives. Coutinho said that his films were films "built with shards" (Avellar 537), made from "anonymity, from leftovers, from scraps, from what was thrown away, from garbage [. . .] My film is made from fragments!" (Coutinho *apud* Penoni 36).⁹

In *Jogo de cena,* each woman's story functions independently from the authenticity criteria to acquire its value, and it offers us, in exchange, a performance or an affectivity detached from the self. In *Boca de lixo*, the scenes in which the disjunction between the visual image and the word of the people filmed—or in which we face layered images in their multiplicity of representative registers and their temporalities—offer an open, indeterminate, and pensive gaze on the space and the people filmed.

The cinematic image in *Boca de lixo* can then be thought of as what remains, what survives, what is left after losing its primary referent, and it stands as a subjectivity detached from an individual self. It can then be thought of as a "garbage-image" because it constitutes itself as something made of layers of temporality and multiple meanings. The film confronts us with an image that is presented as a material, corporal, affective, empathetic, and politicized fragment. It is an image that illuminates what emerges despite the subject itself; as if it were a firefly, a spectral voice, or a piece of garbage.

Notes

1. The argument I make in this chapter is further developed in the third chapter of my recent book *Futuros menores. Filosofías del tiempo y arquitecturas del mundo desde Brasil.*

2. I have worked on this topic in relation to contemporary Argentine and Brazilian literature and based on a link between literature and image and on the materiality of the text in the last chapter of my 2011 book *Literaturas reales: Transformaciones del realismo en la narrativa latinoamericana contemporánea*. Gisela Heffes has worked extensively on the problem, and she points out an essential aspect regarding the meanings given to the figure of the waste collector. From her perspective, while in the United States and Europe recycling reflects a commitment to the environment, in Latin America it is a practice motivated more by economic survival. Heffes seeks to synthesize these two issues through the figure of the cartonero: "To a certain extent, the cartoneros emerge as a possible example of how to re-imagine environmental politics and justice as a set of evolving community relations, personalizing the process of recycling through a more communal and less

individualistic effort, one more akin to labor practices" (Heffes, "Trash Matters" 2). On the other hand, Valeria de los Ríos explores the spectral reappearances of waste in some Latin American documentaries, from its ecological impact to its transformation into a means of sustenance, and analyzes various documentary films in which garbage is used. Also interesting in this regard is the article by Daniela Dorfman in which she precisely relates *Ilha das Flores* by Jorge Furtado and *Boca de lixo* from a "spatial justice" perspective and Marcela Romero Rivera's doctoral thesis *The Image of the Reminder in Latin American Literature and Visual Arts*.

3. Bernardet asks, "Como fica quem acreditava que a fala dos entrevistados nos filmes do Coutinho era a expressão de uma subjetividade?" (626, What does this mean for those who believed that the words of interviewees in Coutinho's films were the expression of their subjectivity?) and states: "*Jogo de cena* põe em dúvida toda a filmografia de Coutinho desde *Santo forte* (uma coragem excepcional). *Jogo de cena* põe em dúvida todos os filmes documentários baseados na fala como discurso da subjetividade e no relato de histórias de vida" (628–29, *Jogo de cena* casts doubt [with exceptional courage] on all of Coutinho's films since *Santo forte*. *Jogo de cena* casts doubt on all documentary films based on speech as the discourse of subjectivity and on accounts of life stories).

4. "Filmo lo diferente a mí, me interesa lo que no soy. Por eso las favelas, los obreros, las mujeres. No es sólo una diferencia de clase, sino diferencia de mí. Mis mejores personajes son mujeres. Mis mejores espectadores son mujeres, incluso jóvenes. ¿Por qué? Porque la mujer habla de cosas de las que los hombres aún no hablan. Tiene que ver con la fragilidad, el hombre no llora. El hombre es como una persona pública, como el gran político, y a mí lo que me interesa es la fragilidad, aunque aparezca a veces detrás de la arrogancia" (Russo n.p.; I film what's different from me, I'm interested in what I'm not. That's why [I film] the favelas, workers, women. It's not just a class difference, it's different from me. My best characters are women. My best viewers are women, even young ones. Why? Because women talk about things that men still do not talk about. It has to do with fragility; men do not cry. Man is like a public person, like a great politician, and what interests me is the fragility, although it sometimes appears behind the arrogance). See Russo and Paiva for another interview with Coutinho.

5. "Y en verdad es la voz de un fantasma, porque Marília Pêra es como un fantasma del personaje, ¿no es cierto? Así que cuando ella vino por segunda vez, le pedí que cantara esa canción y que la cantara casi hablando, lo que ella hizo extraordinariamente bien. Me parece que hay algo genial allí, que es el fantasma que aparece de repente y canta junto a ella, pero atrasado en relación a su voz" (Russo and Paiva n.p.; And it's really the voice of a ghost, because Marília Pêra is like a ghost of the character, is she not? When she came the second time, I asked her to sing that song and to sing it almost as if she were reciting it, which she did extraordinarily well. It seems to me that there is something great there, that it is the ghost that appears suddenly and sings next to her, but with a delay in relation to her voice).

6. Gisela Heffes also notes the contradiction between the visual regime and the discursive one. She highlights two moments when the characters' stories and the camera contradict one another. The first time is when one of the women tells Coutinho that life at the landfill isn't so bad, that she has raised her children there and they are all healthy at the same time that the camera shows images of hospital waste in the trash. Then, in response to a question from Coutinho, the same woman begins to show a wound on her foot, which was the result of a syringe. Another similar moment in the film occurs when a woman says she is taking a shower as she pours a jug of water over her head, in a clear contradiction—at least for the spectator—to what one could define as "taking a shower." Although Heffes's interpretation does not contradict what I am saying here, she goes on to highlight a different aspect than the one I choose to focus on because her interpretation of the film is from the perspective of an ecological critique, and, as such, she emphasizes the view offered by the camera and associates that vision with the director's own view: "But these subjects' interpretation of the experience of living in the landfill on occasion will be confronted with Coutinho's own view, who grants the camera the capacity to narrate a different, alternative version to the one offered by the interviewed subjects" (Heffes, *Políticas de la destrucción* 142).

7. This unresolved gaze, dependent on a particular way of conceiving the cinematic image, could be also thought in relation to a broader ethics of non-judgment in Coutinho's films, as often discussed in relationship to his conversational style and as stated by himself.

8. "Se tiende a pensar que la palabra es la palabra dicha o escrita, y que eso es todo. Sin embargo, cuando una persona habla desde el fondo de sí misma, o sea, cuando habla con sus vísceras, sale del lugar común impuesto por la sociedad y sus estructuras. Eso es lo que nos interesa, porque ahí la persona produce un habla original. Cuando alguien habla visceralmente produce, por un lado, un texto que es al mismo tiempo oral y verbal, es decir, construido a partir de una gramática y de un vocabulario, y un texto para-verbal, porque las personas tienen digresiones, lapsos, equivocaciones, saltos de un tema a otro, repeticiones. Por otro lado, la persona también produce un texto gestual en el que el cuerpo es absolutamente esencial. El hombre es un animal que habla y que habla a través de su cuerpo" (Russo and Paiva n.p.).

9. "feito de cacos" (Avellar 537); made "do anônimo, do resto, da sobra, daquilo que foi jogado fora, do lixo [. . .] Meu cinema é feito de fragmentos" (Coutinho *apud* Penoni 36).

Works Cited

Avellar, José Carlos. "O lixo na boca." *Eduardo Coutinho*, edited by Milton Ohata, Cosac Naify, 2013, pp. 537–42.

Bernardet, Jean-Claude. "Jogo de cena" and "Moscou." *Eduardo Coutinho*, edited by Milton Ohata, Cosac Naify, 2013, pp. 626–28.
Butler, Judith, and Athena Athanasiou. *Dispossession: The Performative in the Political.* Polity, 2013.
Butler, Judith. *Giving an Account of Oneself.* Fordham UP, 2005.
De los Ríos, Valeria. "Restos espectrales: materialidades residuales y representación del territorio en documentales latinoamericanos." *Estudios de Teoría Literaria. Revista Digital. Artes, letras y humanidades,* vol. 10, no. 21, 2021, pp. 55–67.
Didi-Huberman, Georges. *Harun Farocki. Desconfiar de las imágenes.* Translated by Julia Giser, Caja Negra, 2013.
———. *Supervivencia de las luciérnagas.* Abada Editores, 2012.
Dorfman, Daniela. "Restos globales: basureros y derecho a la ciudad en Brasil a Propósito de *Ilha das flores* (Isla de las flores, Jorge Furtado, 1989) y *Boca de lixo* (Boca de basura, Eduardo Coutinho, 1992)." *Mitologías Hoy,* vol. 17, 2018, pp. 225–43.
Feldman, Ilana. *Jogos de cena. Ensaios sobre o documentário brasileiro contemporâneo.* 2012. Universidade de São Paulo, PhD dissertation.
Heffes, Gisela. *Políticas de la destrucción. Poéticas de la preservación. Apuntes para una eco(crítica) del medio ambiente en América Latina.* Beatriz Viterbo, 2013.
———. "Redefining Garbage in Contemporary Buenos Aires: The Imagination of Crisis and Its Aesthetic Responses." *Brújula,* vol. 11, 2017.
———. "Trash Matters: Residual Culture in Latin America." *Humanities Futures.* John Hope Franklin Humanities Institute, Duke University, 2017.
Horne, Luz. *Literaturas reales: transformaciones del realismo en la narrativa latinoamericana contemporánea.* Beatriz Viterbo, 2011.
———. *Futuros menores. Filosofías del tiempo y arquitecturas del mundo desde Brasil.* Ediciones Universidad Alberto Hurtado, 2021.
Lins, Consuelo. *O documentário de Eduardo Coutinho: Televisão, cinema e vídeo.* Jorge Zahar, 2004.
———. "O cinema de Eduardo Coutinho: entre o personagem fabulador e o espectador montador." *Eduardo Coutinho*, edited by Milton Ohata, Cosac Naify, 2013, pp. 375–87.
Moreira Salles, João. "Morrer e nascer. Duas passagens na vida de Eduardo Coutinho." *Eduardo Coutinho*, edited by Milton Ohata, Cosac Naify, 2013, pp. 364–74.
Rancière, Jacques. *El espectador emancipado.* Manantial, 2010.
Rocha, Glauber. "Uma estética da fome." *Revista Civilização Brasileira,* no. 3, 1965, pp. 165–70.
Romero Rivera, Marcela. *The Image of the Remainder in Latin American Literature and Visual Arts.* 2012. Cornell University, PhD dissertation.
Russo, Pablo. "Master Class Eduardo Coutinho." *El ángel exterminador,* vol. 2, no. 10, 2008, http://elangelexterminador.com.ar/articulosnro.10/masterclasscoutinho.html. Accessed 19 Apr. 2018.

Russo, Pablo, and Valeria Paiva. "Lo que amo en el cine es el acaso, el accidente, el azar. Entrevista a Eduardo Coutinho." *Tierra en Trance. Reflexiones sobre Cine Latinoamericano*. Julio/Agosto 2010. http://tierraentrance.miradas.net/2010/07/entrevistas/entrevista-a-eduardo-coutinho-lo-que-amo-en-el-cine-es-el-acaso-el-accidente-el-azar.html, Accessed 19 Apr. 2018.

Sontag, Susan. *Regarding the Pain of Others*. Picador, 2003.

6

Eduardo Coutinho and *Globo Repórter*
Between Social Documentary
and the Mass Media in Dictatorship-Era Brazil

RIELLE NAVITSKI

Eduardo Coutinho's documentaries for the *Globo Repórter* news program embody an unlikely confluence between two of Brazil's most iconic producers of moving images—the leftist filmmakers of the Cinema Novo movement and the powerful Globo television network. Cinema Novo's approach was famously defined by Glauber Rocha as an *estética da fome* (aesthetic of hunger), in which the populace's poverty of means and the filmmaker's poverty of resources acted as catalysts for aesthetic experimentation and social transformation. Conversely, Rede Globo is distinguished by its *padrão de qualidade* (standard of quality), forged during the network's rapid expansion in the late 1960s and early 1970s. The network's glossy production values and technological sophistication have facilitated its long-standing domination of the domestic television market (which continues despite challenges in recent years from the rival Record network) and its transnational and transmedia expansion. By contrast, although Cinema Novo films circulated widely at international festivals and became a key point of reference for the politicized filmmaking movements that unfolded on a global scale in the 1960s and 1970s, in Brazil their audience was largely limited to intellectual elites despite the investment in the popular manifest in the works themselves.[1]

Beyond these divergent publics, aesthetics, and modes of production, the presence of leftist filmmakers on the *Globo Repórter* program may seem particularly incongruous given the network's close ties to the repressive military dictatorship that came to power in 1964, the year prior to Globo's launch. At a moment of economic instability, President João Goulart's leftist policies—land reform, the nationalization of some industries, the expansion of voting rights—and direct appeal to the masses had generated opposition among the middle and upper classes and the Catholic Church, facilitating the armed forces' seizure of power. Declared in 1968 in response to widespread political protest, the Ato Institucional 5 (AI-5, Institutional Act Number 5)—often referred to as "the coup within the coup"—marked a turn toward even greater repression that prompted an exodus of intellectuals from Brazil.[2] Allowing a wide-ranging suspension of political rights, the decree was linked to a crackdown on cultural production and allowed for direct media censorship that remained in place until 1979. Beyond its largely favorable coverage of the military regime, Globo's push to create a nationwide network dovetailed with the government's investment in national integration and economic modernization instituted from above. In particular, the broadcaster capitalized on the strategic expansion of Brazil's telecommunications infrastructure through the public-private corporation Embratel, which made long-distance broadcast possible through the use of microwave transmitters and, later, satellites (Herz 84–86, Dos Santos and Capparelli 78–79). Vénecio A. de Lima observes a "double identification between the RGTV [Rede Globo de Televisão] and the military regime," given that Globo "represented the model of a modern, efficient corporation, adjusted to an exclusionary, concentrated and transnational economic policy" and "served as a 'legitimizing agent' through the creation, maintenance and reproduction of a climate of euphoria, made possible by the construction of a distorted representation of life in the country" (121–22).[3]

As Globo expanded its reach through nationally syndicated programming with the launch of the *Jornal Nacional* news program in 1969, the network sought to gain traction with affluent, educated viewers—a previously elusive demographic—by emphasizing journalistic programming and hiring well-regarded leftist filmmakers (Kehl 247–50). Paradoxically, as Roberto Schwarz notes, despite the political repressive climate, "the cultural hegemony of the left [was] virtually complete" in the period, though radical cultural production was targeted to a politically committed audience and absent from mainstream media (127). Nevertheless, many cinéastes associated with Cinema Novo—a movement informed by the efforts of the Centro Popular de Cultura da União Nacional dos Estudantes (CPC) aligned with the Partido Comunista Brasileiro—saw their professional opportunities dry up under the military regime (Ridenti 89–95).[4] According to *Globo Repórter* collaborator João Batista de Andrade, Globo's executives viewed Cinema Novo filmmakers as "a readily available labor force with an acceptable level of modernity" (qtd. in Sacramento 165). Under the circumstances, leftist cinéastes were willing to overlook their peers' disapproval of Globo's close relationship with the military regime, as well as the cultural hierarchies that granted cinema a status superior to that of television. The resulting telefilms were restrained in comparison to perhaps the most radical incursion of Cinema Novo into Brazilian television: *Abertura*, an idiosyncratic free-form program hosted by Glauber Rocha for TV Tupi beginning in February 1979 (Mota 143). *Abertura*'s title referenced the gathering momentum of democratic opening under President Ernesto Geisel, which resulted in a decree of amnesty for dissidents—but also human rights violators—later that year. The program also enacted openness in its relative frankness about political matters and its foregrounding of contingency in production through the use of available light, spontaneous interactions in public spaces, and free-ranging camera movement, verbally directed by Rocha on the fly. The filmmakers who worked on *Globo Repórter* earlier in the decade were constrained by more stringent censorship as well as the logic of the market, even as the network leveraged their formal and narrative innovations and established reputations as auteurs to boost its own cultural capital.

Yet cinéaste Walter Lima Júnior stressed that the *Globo Repórter* program did not simply translate filmic aesthetics to television: "We didn't come to make Cinema Novo on television. But, probably, we came to make a new form of television" (qtd. in Sacramento 145). Bringing elements of the social denunciation associated with Cinema Novo to a mass audience, *Globo Repórter* telefilms are marked by a fusion of cinematic and televisual aesthetics and working methods, a hybrid style shaped by budgetary and censorship constraints. Production teams made use of the lightweight 16 mm cameras and portable sound recorders characteristic of *cinéma vérité* and direct cinema (Silva 61, Bragança, n.p.) while assembling episodes on tight timelines determined by the broadcast schedule and with expectations of high audience numbers (Sacramento 158). Furthermore, *Globo Repórter* segments directed by leftist filmmakers often articulate their social critique through a creative and potentially subversive use of voice-over narration, linked to the program's uneasy position between feature documentary and broadcasting conventions. The program's director, Paulo Gil Soares, sought to distance it from television and link it more closely to the documentary feature film by avoiding the figure of an on-screen host (Sacramento 131–32;

Silva 166). However, all of its installments were initially required to have narration—most often read by Sérgio Chapelin, an anchor for Globo's *Jornal Nacional*—to give continuity across episodes and with the network's other programming (Sacramento 130; Silva 116).[5] This directive would have complex effects on *Globo Repórter*'s aesthetics.

The strategic use of voice-over commentary in Eduardo Coutinho's work for *Globo Repórter* exemplifies how the program worked to open a space of social critique within the confines of an incipient mass medium. In Coutinho's 1976 telefilm *Seis dias de Ouricuri/Six Days in Ouricuri*, which documents the government's inadequate response to catastrophic drought in the northeastern state of Pernambuco, and his 1978 *Theodorico, o imperador do sertão/Theodorico, the Sertão Emperor*, a portrait of a northeastern coronel (political boss), searing images of poverty and deprivation are paired with narration spoken from a position of power. Conventionally, voice-over has been read as a device that imposes a singular, definitive interpretation on the images shown, working to eliminate ambiguity and close off alternative readings. Such uses of voice-over were predominant in Brazilian documentary in the 1960s despite leftist filmmakers' efforts to "give voice" to the marginalized (Bernardet 11–14, 33–34, 42–44, 59–63). By contrast, both *Seis dias de Ouricuri* and *Theodorico, o imperador do sertão* minimize or entirely suppress the customary narration in favor of allowing the documentary's subjects to speak for themselves, and undercut the perceived authority of voice-over through tensions between sound and image. In *Seis dias de Ouricuri*, "voice of God" narration by Cid Moreira offers a matter-of-fact account of humanitarian crisis, even as the audiovisual vocabulary of *cinéma vérité*—long takes and direct sound—elaborates a powerful counter-discourse. Socially marginalized victims of drought directly address the camera and microphone in shots of extended duration that reject television's tendency to commodify viewer attention—that is, its efforts to attract and hold the spectator's gaze through rapid editing or other eye-catching techniques in order to deliver audiences to advertisers. In *Theodorico, o imperador do sertão*, the documentary's subject, Theodorico Bezerra, offers a first-person defense of his benevolent paternalism belied by the image track, which lays bare the substandard living conditions of workers on his rural estate. In this sense, the strategies of Coutinho's telefilms at once signal the institutional and ideological constraints that shaped the *Globo Repórter* program and chart the contestatory possibilities of a markedly experimental moment for Brazilian broadcasting.

Globo Repórter:
Institutional Origins, Opportunities, and Constraints

The roots of *Globo Repórter* can be traced to both institutional and individual ambitions to boost its network's cultural capital in the early 1970s. Following a period of consolidation and professionalization in the 1960s that helped Globo outpace its existing competitors (Goulart Ribeiro and Sacramento 109), the network shifted its focus toward in-depth reporting and prerecorded programming. This move shifted the network's focus away from hugely popular but widely maligned variety programs like *Buzina do Chacrinha*, which suffered government censorship due to risqué humor and displays of popular religion (Kehl 147–50; Sacramento 76–79). The presence of leftist filmmakers on the *Globo Repórter* program helped lend legitimacy to these efforts, and Globo executive Walter Clark's ambitions to work as a film producer also fueled efforts to infuse the network's programming with a more cinematic style (Sacramento 110–11; Muniz n.p.). At the same time, *Globo Repórter* was shaped by existing commercial partnerships with transnational corporations. Globo's relationship with the US Time-Life Corporation, which provided the incipient network with technical expertise and loans totaling $6 million in defiance of Brazilian law prohibiting foreign investment in media companies (Porto 61), offered a precedent for nurturing documentary experiments within a corporate media structure. In the early 1960s, Time-Life financed photographer Robert Drew's development of the lightweight camera equipment he used in innovative direct cinema documentaries like *Primary* (1960) and backed the creation of his production company, Drew Associates. A more immediate antecedent of *Globo Repórter* was the *Globo-Shell Especial* program that aired in 1971 and 1972. This series of documentary telefilms on Brazilian topics was sponsored by the Dutch oil company in an effort to link its brand with national concerns, an initiative credited to João Carlos Magaldi of the Standard Propaganda agency (Borgerth 107–8; Wallach 159).

Globo Repórter was created in 1973 in the face of Shell's waning interest in the program and the renewed push for journalistic rigor at the channel. Initially conceived as a newsmagazine composed of multiple segments in the model of *60 Minutes*, *Globo Repórter*'s format ultimately gravitated toward original telefilms that occupied a full time slot. These programs were broadcast alongside imported documentaries repackaged for a Brazilian public, which outnumbered domestically produced segments in *Globo Repórter*'s early years (Silva 116). During the 1970s, the program employed two in-house production teams (one based in Rio de Janeiro and the other in São Paulo, a coveted advertising market), as well as an independent São Paulo producer of publicity films, Blimp Filmes (Silva 125–34). Cinema Novo filmmakers Walter Lima Júnior and João Batista de Andrade worked directly for *Globo Repórter*, while other cinéastes linked with the movement, such as Gustavo Dahl, directed individual episodes. Broadcast in national syndication beginning in 1975 (Resende 107), *Globo Repórter* offered filmmakers a mass audience far beyond that offered by theatrical film exhibition, with ratings frequently reaching as high as 50% of the viewing public. Initially broadcast at 11:00 p.m., *Globo Repórter*'s significant success with audiences prompted a move to prime time; the show aired at 9:00 pm once weekly between September 1974 and March 1982 (Sacramento 137–42).

Building on the approach of *Globo-Shell Especial*, original *Globo Repórter* telefilms focused on a wide range of uniquely Brazilian subjects, ranging from the recuperation of marginalized forms of folklore to the dilemmas posed by rapid urbanization, including traffic accidents, violent crime, and air, water, and noise pollution. Environmental topics offered an indirect means of addressing military repression; Paulo Gil Soares noted in an interview with Sonia Gama, "We discovered that when you talk about the mistreatment of animals, when you talk about the mistreatment of nature, you can talk about repression, about horror itself, about prison, the imprisonment of people, torture, people's suffering" (qtd. in Silva 148). Furthermore, *Globo Repórter* highlighted the regions and populations left behind by the military dictatorship's conservative modernization projects. Like key works of the Cinema Novo movement, such as *Vidas secas/Barren Lives* (Nelson Pereira dos Santos, 1963) and *Deus e o diabo na terra do sol/ Black God, White Devil* (Glauber Rocha, 1964), *Globo Repórter* telefilms often focused on Brazil's arid Northeast. The region was framed both as an object of popular fascination (as in Maurice Capovilla's 1975 *O último dia de Lampião/Lampião's Last Day*, for example) and as a region left behind by development initiatives and plagued by authoritarian modes of social organization. Coutinho's *Globo Repórter* segments explored this latter vein, addressing the topics of catastrophic drought, *coronelismo*,[6] and deadly vendettas between families that raged unchecked in rural locales, the subject of his telefilms *O pistoleiro de Serra Talhada/The Gunfighter of Serra Talhada* (1977) and *Exu, uma tragédia sertaneja/Exu, a Backlands Tragedy* (1979).

Cinéastes' approaches to social issues were shaped by *Globo Repórter*'s unique mode of production and by financial and censorship constraints.

Several filmmakers who worked for the program commented on its climate of experimentation, which allowed them to test strategies for engaging a mass public (Silva 51; Bragança n.p). Unconventional techniques used range from reenactments of real-life events in the crime-themed telefilms of João Batista de Andrade to extended stretches of complete silence in several segments (Resende 124–25, 162–69). However, the program's artistic director, Paulo Gil Soares, was obliged to contend with government censorship—exercised on both scripts and completed segments—as well as expectations that *Globo Repórter* would maintain high audience ratings (Sacramento 143, 158). Indeed, Coutinho commented that "the most violent internal censorship [exercised on *Globo Repórter*] was that of the market" (qtd. in Resende 127). In this context, filmmakers' attentiveness to visual language impacted *Globo Repórter*'s aesthetics and its political potential. Program veteran Luiz Carlos Maciel credited his fellow cinéastes for introducing "a concern with framing, with narrative film language; we had a constant concern with lighting, cinematic editing, and outdoor shooting" (Muniz n.p.). Highlighting a broader tendency in television of the period to focus on aural elements, an inheritance from radio, Lima Júnior stressed his investment in visuals, whose political thrust often eluded censors: "censorship was much more concerned with text. It didn't notice that the image existed" (qtd. in Sacramento 145). Government intervention thus spurred the adoption of specifically cinematic strategies on the program.

Furthermore, close oversight of *Globo Repórter* was hampered by the fact that the Rio de Janeiro production team worked in a facility separate from the main newsroom. Until 1982, the cost-saving measure of using 16 mm reversal film—a special film stock impregnated with the chemicals needed for developing, which produces a single positive copy rather than a negative that can be used to strike multiple prints—also reduced monitoring of the editing process, as repeated viewings risked damage to the film before it could be transferred to videotape for broadcast (Lins 19). At the same time, the resulting visual imperfections established a distance from Globo's *padrão de qualidade* (Coutinho 17–18). In this sense, cinematic working methods offered a bulwark against attempts to control and standardize *Globo Repórter*'s content and form. The intersection of censorship and budget limitations gave rise to a socially committed documentary language productively shaped by constraint. Neither strictly cinematic nor fully televisual, this documentary language was perhaps most provocatively explored in the telefilms of Eduardo Coutinho. In the following section, I turn to Coutinho's trajectory on the program and the aesthetics of his telefilms before briefly examining their extended reception from their broadcast through the present.

Eduardo Coutinho at *Globo Repórter*

After collaborating with Cinema Novo filmmakers on a series of projects in the 1960s—most notably as producer of the pioneering omnibus film *Cinco vezes favela/Five Times Favela* (1962) produced by the CPC—Eduardo Coutinho joined the *Globo Repórter* team in 1975 after a five-year hiatus from filmmaking. Also undertaken with the CPC's involvement, the production of *Cabra marcado para morrer* (1964–1984), Coutinho's biopic of assassinated labor activist João Pedro Teixeira, was interrupted by the military authorities in 1964. After directing the science-fiction comedy *O homem que comprou o mundo/The Man Who Bought the World* (1968) and the *cangaceiro* [bandit]-themed *Faustão* (1971), Coutinho found himself in need of a stable income after the birth of his first child. A position at the *Jornal do Brasil*, where he wrote film criticism and worked as a copyeditor, led indirectly to employment with *Globo Repórter* at double his previous salary (Resende 97–98). The filmmaker later stressed the role of the financial stability offered by his position at Globo and his renewed contact with Brazil's Northeast during his time there to the reworking of *Cabra marcada para morrer* completed in 1984; he edited the film, in part, in Globo's facilities outside work hours (Avellar 49–50; Sacramento 205).

Suggesting the role of filmmakers' prestige in determining their value to the program, Coutinho recalled in an interview that he enjoyed less creative autonomy than his better-known colleagues Walter Lima Júnior and João Batista de Andrade, who worked only on the direction and the editing of their segments. By contrast, Coutinho participated actively in a broader range of the program's activities, which surpassed the role of film auteur on which it sought to capitalize. He described himself as a "a real employee; I did everything they asked, Portuguese-language versions, scripts, adaptations of foreign documentaries, editing. When they let me make my films . . . , I did everything, production, direction, from beginning to end. . . . In my case, at some moments, it was possible to do something that resembled documentary, but those moments were rare" (qtd. in Sacramento 159). Coutinho's comments signal how the variety of working methods used within the *Globo Repórter* program both reinforced and transformed cinematic models of authorship, as well as the perceived distinction between documentary and the televisual blurred by his telefilms.

In *Seis dias de Ouricuri*, the first *Globo Repórter* telefilm directed by Coutinho, tensions between sound and image undercut both the pretense of documentary authority and the push for televisual standardization characteristic of the program. Portraying a small city in the interior of the state of Pernambuco, the telefilm acts as a sustained exploration of Ouricuri's human geography. Coutinho successfully lobbied Paulo Gil Soares to devote the entire *Globo Repórter* slot to *Seis dias de Ouricuri* rather than the shorter ten-minute report originally planned; it thus became the program's first single-subject telefilm (Avellar 50; Sacramento 201). *Seis dias de Ouricuri* begins by situating the viewer; the narration indicates the city's location 620 kilometers from Recife, paired with an animated zoom into its location on a map. The documentary's opening moments establish the town's remoteness and lack of communication infrastructure as factors that exacerbate the effects of the drought, thus refuting the military dictatorship's rhetoric of national integration and development. As the voice-over explains, the populace can be reached only through announcements made over loudspeakers belonging to a local movie theater, simultaneously displayed through a zoom out and a series of pans. Throughout the documentary, the difficulty of coordinating relief efforts under these conditions is stressed, as exemplified in a scene that shows local relief workers trying to clarify when government officials will arrive via shortwave radio.

Multiple facets of the crisis are explored through a series of encounters with locals suffering the drought's effects or seeking to mitigate it; none of these individuals is identified by name, a choice that stresses their social position over personal identities. Interviews with officials who note the shortcomings of government relief efforts in measured terms are juxtaposed with wrenching firsthand accounts of life on the verge of starvation. The documentary's off-screen discourse also enters into tension with direct-sound testimony from those affected by the drought; significantly, Coutinho described writing a "light" text to balance our "heavy" images (Sacramento 201). For example, early in the telefilm, narration read by *Jornal Nacional* anchor Cid Moreira describes the organization of work brigades over long shots that pan over groups of undifferentiated laborers. Enumerating the state and federal agencies involved, Moreira's narration stresses that "government aid arrived at the right time" while tepidly pointing out the initiative's inadequacies: namely, failure to predict high demand for work and inadequate distribution of the water and food promised to workers. By contrast, the documentary crew's direct encounters with Ouricuri's residents not only attest to the severity of the 1976 crisis, but also allow alternative forms of popular knowledge and historical memory deeply rooted in the spaces of the Northeast to emerge.

In an extended long take of three minutes and ten seconds—one of the most commented-on of Coutinho's career, and often highlighted by the filmmaker in interviews—sufferers testify to survival strategies born of extreme necessity and repeating cycles of drought (Avellar 52; Brizuela 19–20; Coutinho 18; Ehlert Maia and Neto 16, 56–58; Sacramento 202). The take begins as an unidentified man framed in medium shot displays a series of tubers that he and others have been forced to consume by hunger, as Coutinho sporadically poses questions from off-screen. As the man speaks, a handheld camera operated by Edson Santos repeatedly zooms and pans to frame his hand and the roots in close-up before zooming out again to frame him in the context of the surrounding crowd. Through these shifts, the shot alternately emphasizes the concrete particularities of near-starvation and the broader social and historical context, as other members of the crowd chime in with their own experiences of hunger, not only during the present crisis, but also in the previous droughts of 1958 and 1969 (fig. 6.1).

The shot embodies an ethics of filmmaking that resists the eye-catching, rapid-fire editing characteristic of televisual language while foregrounding

Figure 6.1. A resident of Ouricuri shows Coutinho and his crew roots consumed out of necessity during a devastating drought. Source: *Seis dias de Ouricuri* (*Six Days in Ouricuri*). Directed by Eduardo Coutinho, Rede Globo, 1976.

the real's stubborn resistance to the narrativization that shapes conventional documentary as well as fiction film. Coutinho has stressed that "The long take is the essential take, it's the one that incorporates chance, dead time, which is much more interesting than live [eventful] time" (qtd. In Lins 21). Natalia Brizuela argues that the shot's extended duration defies the imperatives of eventfulness and the economical transmission of meaning, pushing it to "the edge of its own structural abyss, [to] the verge of dissolution" (19). At the same time, the shot does not stage a complete breakdown of sense, but rather a sustained, dialogic transmission of socially situated knowledges. The arguably excessive detail of the man's instructions for preparing the variety of roots underlines the simultaneous banality and life-and-death urgency of the information. At one point, Coutinho (still off-screen) apparently becomes engrossed in these details, prompting the speaker to insist, "We don't eat all these things because we find them good and like them. We're obliged to eat them out of need." In this sense, the shot stages an active exchange between filmmakers and subjects—embodying what Sacramento calls a "documentary of coexistence"—for the televisual audience (217). Although *Seis dias de Ouricuri* at times romanticizes popular forms of religious belief that offer local residents faith that the drought will end, it proceeds largely from a position of respect for the other's autonomy, a position that is curtailed in later telefilms directed by Coutinho such as *Exu, uma tragédia sertaneja*, which devotes much less screen time to the voices of the populace (Sacramento 238).

The move from omniscient voice-over toward first-person testimony in *Seis dias de Ouricuri* is extended in *Theodorico, o imperador do sertão*, produced two years later, which avoids an unseen narrator entirely in favor of extended commentary by its subject—at times synchronized with the image, at times functioning as off-screen sound. According to Coutinho, he managed to skirt the narration typically required by *Globo Repórter* by asking Bezerra to record comments that introduced and concluded the telefilm (Sacramento 169–70). This strategy extends a troubling if generative sense of complicity between documentary crew and subject, the sole member of the elite whom Coutinho engaged in his dialogic documentary practice, the "cinema of conversation" he states he discovered at the *Globo Repórter* program (Lins 23; Hamburger 414). Coutinho and his crew allowed Bezerra to take control of interviews with the tenants on his estate, to the obvious discomfort of the latter. Demonstrating Bezerra's unchallenged power over the physical territory of his estate, *Theodorico, o imperador do sertão* also foregrounds his orchestration of his own image and his control of discourse.

Beyond its inclusion of Bezerra's voice-over commentary on the soundtrack, *Theodorico, o imperador do sertão* stresses his dominance and regulation of speech. While repeatedly demanding that his tenants "speak little so as not to waste time," Bezerra amplifies his own voice using loudspeakers around his property to address them as a group. In one particularly telling sequence, he announces that all the residents of his estate must be photographed for their voter registration card and offer Bezerra his vote, an open reference to the clientelist politics that characterize *coronelismo*. The film implicates both sound and photographic technologies in the regime of power established by Bezerra while pointedly subverting this authoritative voice and the authoritarian reality it organizes through dynamic confrontations between sound and image.

The disconnect between Bezerra's narration and the image is most striking in a sequence where Bezerra extols the virtues of hard work and country living, surrounded by tenants whose bare-bones clothing and somber demeanor make the coronel's words ring hollow. In the opening shot of the sequence, a zoom lens is used to shift from a handheld medium close-up on Bezerra to a wide shot of a ramshackle dwelling, flanked by residents whose blank, pained expressions belie his description. Bezerra's commentary then continues off-screen as the camera tracks slowly back and forth over the pained faces of a sharecropping family lined up for a group portrait before cutting back to Bezerra's speech. Detaching the temporality of the soundtrack from that of the image, the sequence lays bare how Bezerra obliges the residents of his estate to participate in the staging of spectacles for the camera (Werneck 17), prompting reflection on the documentary crew's parallel role in placing human misery on display. This moment of self-reflexivity calls attention not only to the relations of domination between coronel and worker, but also to the labor—and the latent violence—of the documentary image's creation (fig. 6.2).

Television critic Paulo Moreira Leite offers a compelling reading of this strategy's effects in a 1978 review, noting that the use of Bezerra's verbal commentary eliminated a "tone of illusory neutrality, of someone not caught up in the events he is narrating—a task that *Globo Repórter* usually delegates to Sérgio Chapelin's narration" (qtd. in Silva 150). Instead, Moreira Leite notes the active labor of interpretation demanded of a viewer who "confronted with a major [a reference to his status as a political boss] who openly took on the defense of his ideas and commandments, could simply believe in his words—or confront them with the images the camera was showing" (qtd. in Silva 150). In this sense, sound-image relations in *Theodorico, o imperador do*

Eduardo Coutinho and *Globo Repórter* | 147

Figure 6.2. *Theodorico, o imperador do sertão* highlights how media technologies advance the coronel's exercise of power on his estate. Source: *Theodorico, o imperador do sertão* (*Theodorico, the Sertão Emperor*). Directed by Eduardo Coutinho, Rede Globo, 1978.

sertão embed social critique within a critique of conventional documentary form. The telefilm highlights Bezerra's staging of his own power and control through visual and aural means, an action at once paralleled and subverted by the documentary crew's framing of his social world for the camera. In the process, clear contradictions between sound and image foreground the stark inequalities concealed by these spectacles. Interrogating the didactic effects of voice-over narration, the strategies of *Theodorico, o imperador do sertão* invite the viewer to oscillate between complicity and critique.

Coutinho's Telefilms: Circulation, Reception, Afterlives

Signaling how Coutinho's telefilms pushed the limits of ideological acceptability on air, the broadcast of both *Seis dias de Ouricuri* and *Theodorico, o imperador do sertão* was limited by political concerns. According to *Globo*

Repórter editor-in-chief Washington Novaes, concerns about *Seis dias de Ouricuri*'s less-than-enthusiastic endorsement of government policy resulted in its broadcast at the 11:00 p.m. rather than the customary 9:00 p.m. slot (Silva 159). However, Coutinho recalled the delayed broadcast as a consequence of a compressed production schedule, noting that final postproduction tasks were not completed by the usual broadcast time (Sacramento 161–62). Such logistical problems were not uncommon as a consequence of the rivalry between the *Globo Repórter* team and the network's newsroom staff, who sometimes hampered the completion of program segments by offering highly unfavorable hours for videotape transfer and editing (Muniz n.p.). In the case of *Theodorico, o imperador do sertão*, Bezerra was able to block the broadcast of Coutinho's telefilm in his home state of Rio Grande do Norte on the grounds that he was running for political office at the time (Silva 159). Despite this restriction, *Theodorico, o imperador do sertão* captured an impressive 43.7% of Brazil's TV audience, a testament to Globo's audience reach as well as the episode's appeal (Sacramento 170).

Ironically, given these attempts to limit their audiences, both of the telefilms circulated beyond their initial broadcast in alternate exhibition contexts. The year following its television debut, *Seis dias de Ouricuri* screened at the Cinemateca do Museu de Arte Moderna do Rio de Janeiro, at a Rio de Janeiro cineclub with Coutinho present at the screening, and at the Universidade Federal Fluminense in nearby Niterói ("Extra" 1977a, 6; "Extra" 1977b, 3; "Extra" 1977c, 3). The film was also shown as part of a slate of cultural activities organized during a student strike at Rio de Janeiro's Pontifícia Universidade Católica (PUC) ("Oito mil alunos em greve na PUC," 2; "Alunos da PUC entram em greve por 3 reivindicações," 13). *Theodorico, o imperador do sertão* was screened during the second Week of Northeastern Culture sponsored by the Universidade Federal do Rio Grande do Norte, followed by a panel discussion on "Coronelismo in Northeastern Politics" ("II Semana de Cultura Nordestina," 11). The post-broadcast circulation of *Seis dias de Ouricuri* and *Theodorico, o imperador do sertão* suggests how Coutinho's telefilms were ripe to be reclaimed as cinema within institutions dedicated to education, political activism, and cinephilia, which attracted the intellectual audiences Globo had been so keen to reach.

Although *Globo Repórter* telefilms captured significant audiences both within and beyond the televisual sphere, garnering a sense of cultural legitimacy from which the network benefited, shifts in the network's production practices led to the growing standardization of the program's style and content. The shift to shooting on videotape in 1982 and the incorporation of the Rio-based *Globo Repórter* team into the main Globo newsroom led to a break with the quasi-cinematic working methods and aesthetics developed within the program in previous years. Shot duration diminished (Resende 316), and the figure of the on-screen reporter gained greater importance, approximating the program to Globo's other journalistic offerings (Batista de Andrade 116). As cinéastes left *Globo Repórter*—Batista de Andrade resigned in 1978 and Coutinho departed in 1984—their telefilms were increasingly forgotten, a product of the ephemeral character of broadcast television. The participation of leftist filmmakers on the program largely receded from popular memory, gaining renewed attention only in 2002, when fourteen telefilms produced for *Globo-Shell Especial* and *Globo Repórter* by Coutinho, Lima Júnior, and Batista de Andrade, among others, were exhibited during the São Paulo documentary film festival É Tudo Verdade. The retrospective worked to reinscribe the telefilms within the history of Brazilian documentary, sparking renewed interest in the texts, although many remain precariously preserved and difficult to access.

The production, aesthetics, and dissemination of Coutinho's *Seis dias de Ouricuri* and *Theodorico, o imperador do sertão* register the complex intersections between the material infrastructures and ideological orientations of Brazilian film and television under dictatorship. Structured by aesthetic and censorship limitations specific to *Globo Repórter*, whose production practices and aesthetics approximated the cinematic even as the network strived for standardization across programming, *Seis dias de Ouricuri* and *Theodorico, o imperador do sertão* engage and defy these constraints. By emphasizing the disjuncture between voice-over narration aligned with a discourse of power and the direct visual records and aural testimony captured by portable 16 mm cameras and sound recorders, Coutinho's telefilms interrogate both Brazilian social reality and standard documentary form, transforming broadcasting into a site for denunciation precariously positioned between leftist cinema and the mass media.

Notes

1. Links of solidarity between intellectuals and the working classes were directly targeted by Brazil's military regime (Schwarz 127).

2. The expression is credited to Maria Celina D'Araújo, Celso Castro, and Gláucio Ary Dillon Soares in their 1994 collection *Visões do golpe: A memória militar sobre 1964*, a characterization critiqued by historians who stress the decree's continuity, rather than radical break, with earlier tendencies in the regime (Fico 34, 57).

3. All translations from Portuguese are the author's.

4. It should be noted that the creation of the state film Embrafilme agency in 1969 led to a counterintuitive rapprochement between leftist cinéastes and the state, particularly after filmmaker/producer Roberto Farias's appointment as director in 1974 (Amancio 176).

5. Suggesting his close and enduring association with the program and the Globo brand, Chapelin retained his role as the public face of the program until his retirement in 2019.

6. *Coronelismo* refers to a mode of clientelism in which powerful landowners linked to national-level politics dominate rural communities. The classic study is Victor Nunes Leal's 1948 *Coronelismo, enxada e voto: O município e o regime representativo no Brasil*, translated into English as *Coronelismo: The Municipality and Representative Government in Brazil*.

Works Cited

"Alunos da PUC entram em greve por 3 reivindicações." *Jornal do Brasil*, 30 Mar. 1977, p. 13.

Amancio, Tunico. "Pacto cinema-Estado: os anos Embrafilme." *Revista Alceu*, vol. 8, no. 15, 2007, pp. 173–84.

Avellar, José Carlos. "The Emptiness of the Backyard: An Interview with Eduardo Coutinho." Translated by Krista Brune. *Film Quarterly*, vol. 69, no. 3, 2017, pp. 44–55.

Batista de Andrade, João. *O povo fala: um cineasta na área de jornalismo da TV brasileira*. Senac, 2002.

Bernardet, Jean-Claude. *Cineastas e imagens do povo*. Brasilense, 2003 [1985].

Borgerth, Luiz Eduardo. *Quem e como fizemos a TV Globo*. A Girafa, 2003.

Bragança, Felipe. "A TV desconhecida: Globo Repórter/Globo Shell Especial." *Contracampo*, vols. 39/40, May 2002, n.p., http://www.contracampo.com.br/39/frames.htm. Accessed 12 July 2016.

Brizuela, Natalia. "Conversation and Duration in Eduardo Coutinho's Films." *Film Quarterly*, vol. 69, no. 3, pp. 19–27.

Coutinho, Eduardo. "O olhar no documentário: Carta-depoimento para Paulo Paranaguá." *Eduardo Coutinho*, edited by Milton Ohata, Cosac Naify, 2013, pp. 14–20.

Coutinho, Eduardo, director. *Seis dias de Ouricuri*. Cinematography by Edson Santos; sound by Jair Vieira, Globo, 1976.

Coutinho, Eduardo, director. *Theodorico, o imperador do sertão*. Cinematography by Dib Lufti; sound by Jair Duarte, Globo, 1978.

Dos Santos, Suzy, and Sérdio Capparelli. "Coronelismo, radiodifusão e voto: A nova face de um velho conceito." *Rede Globo: 40 anos de poder e hegemonia*,

edited by Valério Cruz Brittos and César Ricardo Siqueira Bolaño, Paulus, 2005, pp. 77–101.
Ehlert Maia, João Marcelo, and Simplício Neto. *Seis dias de Ouricuri*. 7Letras, 2017.
"Extra." *Jornal do Brasil*, 22 May 1977, p. 6.
"Extra." *Jornal do Brasil*, 3 June 1977, p. 3.
"Extra." *Jornal do Brasil*, 23 Sept. 1977, p. 3.
Fico, Carlos. "Versões e controvérsias sobre 1964 e a ditadura militar." *Revista Brasileira de História*, vol. 24, no. 47, pp. 29–60.
Goulart Ribeiro, Ana Paula, and Igor Sacramento, "A renovação estética da TV." *História da televisão no Brasil: do início aos dias de hoje*, edited by Ana Paula Goulart et al. Contexto, 2010, pp. 109–35.
Hamburger, Esther. "Eduardo Coutinho e a TV." *Eduardo Coutinho*, edited by Milton Ohata, Cosac Naify, 2013, pp. 414–31.
Herz, Daniel. *A história secreta da Rede Globo*. Tchê, 1987.
Kehl, Maria Rita. "Eu vi um Brasil na TV." *Um país no ar: História da TV brasileira em três canais*, edited by Inimá F. Simões et al., Brasiliense, 1986, pp. 167–276.
Lima, Venécio A. de. "Globo e política: 'Tudo a ver.'" *Rede Globo: 40 anos de poder e hegemonia*, edited by Valério Cruz Brittos and César Ricardo Siqueira Bolaño, Paulus, 2005, pp. 103–29.
Lins, Consuelo. *O documentário de Eduardo Coutinho: Televisão, cinema e vídeo*. Jorge Zahar, 2004.
Mota, Regina. "A programa 'Abertura' e a épica de Glauber Rocha." *História da televisão no Brasil*, edited by Ana Paula Goulart Ribeiro et al., Contexto, 2010, pp. 137–55.
Muniz, Paula. "Globo Repórter: Os cineastas na televisão." *Aruanda*, 13 Aug. 2001.
"Oito mil alunos em greve na PUC," *A Luta Democrática* [Rio de Janeiro], 30 Mar. 1977, p. 2.
"II Semana da Cultura Nordestina," *O Poti*, [Natal], 22–21 Apr. 1979, p. 11.
Porto, Mauro P. *Media Power and Democratization in Brazil: TV Globo and the Dilemmas of Political Accountability*. Routledge, 2012.
Resende, Ana Claúdia de Freitas. *Globo Repórter: Um encontro entre os cineastas e a televisão*. 2005. Universidade Federal de Minas Gerais, Master's thesis.
Ridenti, Marcelo. *Em busca do povo brasileiro: artistas da revolução, do CPC à era da tv*. Record, 2000.
Sacramento, Igor Pinto. *Depois da revolução, a televisão: cineastas de esquerda no jornalismo televisivo dos anos 1970*. 2008. Universidade Federal do Rio de Janeiro, Master's thesis
Schwarz, Roberto. "Culture and Politics in Brazil, 1964–1969." *Misplaced Ideas*, edited and translated by John Gledson, Verso, 1992, pp. 126–59.
Silva, Heidy Vargas. *Globo-Shell Especial e Globo Repórter: as imagens documentárias na televisão brasileira*. 2009. Universidade Estadual de Campinas, Master's thesis.
Wallach, Joe. *Meu capítulo na TV Globo*. Top Books, 2011.

Werneck, Alexandre. "Fala e escuta: *Theodorico, o imperador do sertão*, os personagens e a '*Verstehen*' de Eduardo Coutinho." *Theodorico, o imperador do sertão*, edited by Eliska Altmann and Tatiana Bacal, 7Letras, 2017, pp. 7–41.

Part III
Performing the Self and Others

7

Um dia na vida

Copy, Enunciation, Chatter

ADRIANA JOHNSON

The television viewer cannot write anything on the screen of his set. He has been dislodged from the product; he plays no role in its apparition. He loses his author's rights and becomes, or so it seems, a pure receive, the mirror of a multiform and narcissistic actor. Pushed to the limit, he would be the image of appliances that no longer need him in order to produce themselves, the reproduction of a "celibate machine.

—Michel de Certeau, *The Practice of Everyday Life*

Nobody is as poor as those who see their own relation to the presence of others, that is to say, their own communicative faculty, their own possession of a language, reduced to wage labor.

—Paolo Virno, *The Grammar of the Multitude*

In her analysis of Eduardo Coutinho's posthumously completed film *Últimas conversas* (2015), Consuelo Lins comments on the director's apparent frustration with the process of interviewing teenagers from public high schools in Rio de Janeiro in contrast to his delight at an interview he conducts with a child, one that was included in the final cut after his death. Coutinho had wanted to pursue a film with children but, because of numerous legal issues involved in filming children, had reluctantly decided to interview adolescents instead. According to Lins, what the interview with the child offers is an instantiation of the "infancy of language" when "meanings are not yet given, when ways of speaking are still not grounded, when the relationship between sounds, words, and things is still not defined" (Lins, "Eduardo Coutinho" 28). In contrast, his interviews with the adolescents—in particular the first two interviews—are marked by the presence of the "generic": "Coutinho intervened too much and did something of which he had always been critical: generic affirmations that, according to him, don't lead anywhere and intimidate the two young girls: 'all adolescence is cruel,' 'life is suffering,' 'a young person is complicated because he lives, but has no memories because no one has yet died.' He offers few 'why?' or 'explain that to me' responses of the kind that he so often used in his prior films" (31). While Lins offers the word "generic" to describe Coutinho's interventions, I would argue that the word might also apply to many of the adolescents who come across as entangled in scores derived from mass media. They have neither the ungrounding of children nor a sufficient store of lived experience, of the accumulated details of bodily living, that might provide a counterweight. If so, then the filmic project of *Últimas conversas* finds its limits in the gravitational pull of the generic, which stalls the emergence of the kind of word Coutinho pursues and which leads to the sense of disconnection Coutinho expresses in a dialogue with Jordana Berg (also included in the final cut): "I don't really know," says Coutinho. "Momentarily or forever I have lost the connection with the world that I had, or that I could have had, and that is the end" (29).

I want to argue that a similar limit is reached in another film of his late phase, *Um dia na vida* (2010), and that it also involves something like the pull of the generic. The critical reception of Coutinho emphasizes his pursuit of a spoken word event, a collision between speaker, filmmaker, and technical apparatus that "brings speech to the center" (Xavier 38). Not just any speech, but a particular kind of speech in which a certain infancy of language—which is not in fact limited to young children—is allowed to take place. Crucially, this depends on what Natalia Brizuela has identified as duration: "[I]t is not just the accumulation of words, their sheer quantity nearing the nonsensical, the limit after which whatever form is still holding together the work of art would become undone. It is also, crucially, the duration through which the word—and through it, thought itself—is allowed to emerge and inhabit its own multiple, nonsynchronic temporality" (21). Thus, someone is speaking on camera and the shot is allowed to extend itself, sometimes to a breaking point. In and through this temporality, dilated through the camera, thought emerges, or a new kind of subject who narrates his/her life at this moment of encounter. *Um dia na vida* both radicalizes and stretches that project to its limit. What I want to argue here is that the effect of the film—and the tensions it unleashes—opens up a relation to what the Italian Marxist tradition has theorized as the "general intellect" insofar as this term holds together both potentiality of language as a kind of standing reserve as well as a flatness and generality (the use semiautomatized repetitions and clichés) that enables it to function precisely as a kind of social infrastructure or ligament that is put to work. It is this relation that I intend to trace.

A Cinema of the Spoken Word

Um dia na vida consists of nineteen hours of recorded footage from eight television channels on January 10, 2009, "concentrated" into a one-and-a-half-hour compilation. It was not meant to be a fully finished film in itself, but the first part of a longer project: the opening titles identify it as "material gravado como pesquisa para um filme futuro" (material recorded as research for a future film). Based on commentaries made by Coutinho in a Q&A session after a screening of the film on April 26, 2014, it seems as if this future film would have involved a reenactment or "copy" of the material ("Fragmentos da História"). This was dropped, according to Coutinho, because it would have been too expensive (it would have required too many actors) and because he came to the conclusion that there was no point in parodying the material. The film didn't even have a title until the Mostra Internacional de Cinema em São Paulo demanded one to be able to screen it.

For this experiment, Coutinho chose only open/public channels (Bandeirantes, CNT, Globo, MTV, Record, Rede TV, SBT, and TV Brasil), which were thus those that were potentially available to a widespread swatch of Brazilians. He also chose what he called a "neutral day," one on which nothing in particular was happening, one without an important soccer game, for example ("Fragmentos da História"). Given these indications, one might suggest then that Coutinho was pursuing a distillation of television as a sort of "commons" in its everydayness. The final cut includes, among other fragments, the following: two English lessons; a Tom and Jerry scene; news reporting on the looming decision in Copenhagen as to where to hold the 2016 Olympics and on the earthquake in Indonesia; various news reports on crimes; snippets of both Brazilian and Mexican soap operas; ads for refrigerators, mattresses, camcorders, jewels, calcium supplements, and a doll that urinates; various religious programs; two ads for political parties (the PPS [Partido Popular Socialista] and PCB [Partido Comunista do Brasil]); a show on women's makeovers; gossip about famous people; an interview with a plastic surgeon; and a show that features two bikini and boot-clad women out in the mud learning how to catch crabs.

The fact that this is essentially pirated material is important and has marked its conditions of circulation and contributed to its scant presence within the critical reception of Coutinho: it was only shown a few times in public exhibition, "clandestinely" and free of charge, and with Coutinho present (Sayad 16). For some time, it was available on YouTube.com (something to which Coutinho was stridently opposed), but this has since been blocked for reasons of copyright.

The film's marginal place within Coutinho's corpus is also due to its apparent deviations from many of the characteristics that mark his work. As noted above, Coutinho's filmography has been characterized as a cinema of the "spoken word" in which a conversation takes place on-screen, without any preparation, between the director and the various subjects of his films. The presence of Coutinho within the film's frame—either bodily or simply through his voice—is thus a recurring structure in his films and one that functions as "the motor for the production of testimonies" (Sayad 13). The visible and aural indices of Coutinho's body in most of his films serves as a platform for the "space of listening" (Lins, "El cine" n.p.) that is constructed in his films as an analytical and ethical mode. A particular kind of structure of reception is created—one that is simultaneously "empty" (without preconceived notions) and "attentive" (Russo 52)—to allow the unscripted word to emerge. As many critics have suggested, his documentary poetics is thus never about a claim to present a reality or world "as it exists" through a finished representation that would hide its own conditions of production. Neither is it about self-expression. His films are instead a "savage anthropology" (in his own words) generated by the field of forces that emerges—in real time—in the encounter or interaction between Coutinho, the camera, and his subjects (Paiva 72).

If Coutinho practiced a cinema of the word rather than the image, then, it is insofar as his films are not composed by stringing together images so much as by tracking human orality in the process of formation. Coutinho tries to create the conditions of possibility for those moments in which something new, unexpected, and different emerges from within the grammar of the social. In Coutinho's own words: "When a person speaks from the depths of him or herself, when they speak with their entrails, they get away from the commonplaces imposed by society and its structures. That is what interests us, because that is when the person produces an original speech" (160). His films try to allow for the passage from langue (a system, a stock of materials) to parole (its transactions and uses) or from musical score to performance or improvisation. Coutinho's project might be understood as a traveling companion to Michel de Certeau's *The Practice of Everyday Life* where the linguistic concept of "enunciation" ("the *construction* of individual sentences with an *established* vocabulary and syntax" [xiii]) becomes key to conceptualizing the practices of micro-antidiscipline that counterpose the structures and techniques of power as elaborated by Foucault. Critics will frame this operation in Coutinho's documentaries as precisely similar to de Certeau's interest in the reappropriation of a language by its speakers, as "the gestures by which a subject appropriates his or her condition" (Xavier 42).

The subjects—or the bodies that can become the subjects that interest Coutinho—are—not "the other" but "an other"—someone, anyone, who is unlike him and who might range from popular subjects, middle class, inhabitants of rural spaces or favelas, trash collectors, urban workers, and women but always insofar as they are singular people and never as representatives of a social category. Indeed, in interviews he specifies that he rejects a position in which a person would be approached as exemplary of something (a social class, for example), as part of a statistic, or as a support for a "generalizing idea" or theoretical proposal: "I have a profound hatred for general ideas," he affirms in an interview ("A linguagem é mais que o autor"). His approach is instead to respect the singularity of the other, "understanding the other's reasons without giving him reason" (Avellar 53). Such a position follows precisely from the unflinching focus on the process of enunciation, on the moment of a speaker's individuation or differentiation from what Paolo Virno will describe as the anonymous, almost zoological, environment of a *langue* that belongs to everyone and no one and a generic *faculty* for speaking: "the passage from the pure and simple ability to say something to a particular and contingent utterance determines the space of an individual's notion of 'my own'" (77). It is this moment of differentiation from the generic that Coutinho's films seek to track.

A Mosaic of Infinite Facts

One might say that a collage of television fragments, where all verbal interactions, if not fully scripted, are at least subject to their condition as work of the culture industry, represents the vanishing point of such a project. Coutinho himself is nowhere to be seen or heard in *Um dia na vida*. The only authorial presence is the compilation itself and the time stamps that note when the material was broadcast and the title cards that precede the images and state when the images were recorded, which channels were used, and that they were recorded as research for a future film. Still, one might say that in *Um dia na vida*, Coutinho turns his savage anthropology on television, and I'd like first to sketch out how we might approach the film in these terms, as an extension of the poetics evident in his other work, where the same practice of making do with whatever is at hand, the same openness to contingency, the same practice of listening, is now trained on televisual phenomena.

Coutinho's interest in respecting the "temporal dimension of things" (qtd. in Brizuela 19) carries over in the fact that the only apparent organizational logic of *Um dia na vida*, as indexed in the title, is chronology: with the first show recorded at 6:50 a.m. and the last at 1:30 a.m. There is a disjunction we shouldn't miss, however, between this chronology and the title: on the one hand, a human-derived temporality is proposed as the film's frame—*one day in life,* where life (a vida) is not one person's particular life but nonetheless an aggregate derived from living bodies—and, on the other hand, what I would call the 24/7 temporality of television where repeatable 24-hour segments are filled with programming. While both "one day" and 24/7 are legible as units in a larger sequence, "one day" still holds onto a sense of singularity within that larger sequence, so that it is not completely subsumed by it. On the other hand, 24/7 signals precisely a temporality that is undifferentiated and tied to unceasing repetition. As Jonathan Crary suggests, "24/7 is a static redundancy that disavows its relation to the rhythmic and periodic textures of human life. It connotes an arbitrary, uninflected schema of a week, extracted from any unfolding of variegated or cumulative experience" (9). The film's title thus acts, perhaps inadvertently, as a frame that is also a membrane, bringing two different forms of temporality into contact. Insofar as it is a membrane, however, the two temporalities do not coalesce or mix but remain disjunctive along the surface.

Where perhaps Coutinho followed a more deliberate effort to interface with an alien logic and allow it to show itself is his refusal of montage. In a Q&A following a screening at São Paulo's Pontifícia Universidade Católica (PUC) in 2012, Coutinho specified that he "avoided deploying montage in expressive ways, stating that the idea was to respect the real chronology of the broadcast, even if this were to lead to difficult choices" (Sayad 16).

Why would montage be, as he says in another Q&A session, "too easy"? It is not only that the images and words would be rearranged to draw out the relations of conflict, juxtaposition, or continuity the filmmaker might want to emphasize, turned thus into mere examples of a theoretical impulse that Coutinho so consistently refused. It is also what such a process would hide. The relations—the discontinuities, echoes, parallels, and incoherencies—could too easily be read, and dismissed, as derivative of the montage process itself, as an effect of the film. Montage would set up the possibility that the relations would exist "only on the screen" (Bazin 45). It is in this sense, I believe, that Coutinho laughingly asserts in the Q&A session that, had he produced a dramatized version of the film as originally planned, the incompatibilities and incoherencies would have led people to think he was crazy. He would have created an opening for the claim that such relations were authored by him, or existed only in function of him. Instead of cutting, jumping, and rearranging, Coutinho's films are organized around duration, where something *else* is allowed to play itself out and where the camera simply follows.

Coutinho's experiment thus tries to hew as close as possible to respecting what André Bazin called the spatial (and we might add, *temporal*) unity of an event (50). The experiment can't, of course, completely avoid montage insofar as it jumps between TV channels and condenses 24 hours of footage into an hour and a half. There is also a deliberate selection of what to leave on-screen and what to cut out; Coutinho notes that there were certain things he chose not to show, such as a woman whose back was covered in scars after plastic surgery, and a pastor in São Paulo who dressed up as a *caipira* and who treated a woman "like a dog" ("Era de vomitar," Coutinho says ["Fragmentos da História"]). But respecting the actually existing chronology keeps the film experience closer to that of a viewer who may switch channels but can't otherwise rearrange the images. It also allows the montage that stitches together the images within the television programs as well as between the programs, through the sequence of advertisements for example, to show itself. Respecting the spatial and temporal unity of television is thus to respect this primary montage and foreground the actually existing relations of television.

One of the long fragments of television material whose duration is pronounced is a sequence that follows an interview with a plastic surgeon. The sequence begins with an announcement that the interview will be coming up. We then cut to the point of view of a camera that follows the interviewer walking down the corridor to a luxurious presidential suite. As she reaches the door and before she knocks, she remarks, in a hushed voice, that she hopes that they are not interrupting him. The very next shot is taken from the other side of the door, where the surgeon in question opens the door and greets her warmly. The existence of a camera on the other side of the door (as well as the preceding announcement of the interview) reveals the suspense set up with the scene in the corridor—as if he might not be there or might not deign to speak with the interviewer—as obviously false. Commenting on this editing sequence, Coutinho says: "É absolutamente extraordinário. . . . A primeira regra do cinema, o que o cara aprende é o seguinte . . . quando você chega de surpresa, não pode ter uma câmera dentro da casa!" ("Íntegra da conversa com Eduardo Coutinho na PUC-SP 4/27/2012"; It's absolutely extraordinary . . . The first rule of cinema, what someone learns is the following . . . when you arrive by surprise, you cannot have a camera within the house!). But this is television and not cinema. The ultimate function of staged or campy suspense is not to actually induce suspense but may be first simply to follow a televisual grammar where direct live transmission is absolutely central and, second, to set up a relationship of reverence with the supposed authority of the plastic surgeon.

Another montage to which Coutinho draws the audience's attention in Q&A sessions comes up in a program featured at the end of the film that sells rings. The focused attention on the commodity for sale generates a bizarre (and for Coutinho, fascinating) succession of images of a woman's hands. The hands are not meant to be seen in and of themselves (they are not beautiful hands, he says) but to act only as the support or structure holding up the rings. The logic where the woman—and more specifically her hands—is made to function only as a carrier chops off her hand, so to speak, from the rest of the body. The woman does not exist on-screen; only her hands, and voice, do. This lopsided emphasis on the presence of the rings over the hands also leads to a situation in which the hands are sometimes made to carry up to six rings. Where rings are intended to be ornamental, a supplement to a woman's hands, the selling of rings turns the woman's hand into the supplement or into an invisible infrastructure bearing the weight of rings ("Íntegra da conversa").

By turning on Brazilian television practices developed through encounters with subjects, and which produce subject-effects as a result of the encounter, Coutinho's project draws out a ghostly subjectivity from Brazilian television in which a collective, multiform, schizophrenic subject seems to be speaking to us: on the one hand, an "infinity of facts—a mosaic that no one understands" ("Fragmentos da História")—and, on the other, patterns of relations that emerge from the heterogeneous mosaic. The catalogue Coutinho himself offers of the detectable patterns includes the following: the large number of Protestant churches that dominate public television, the exploitation of women, the constant presence of English words, a sustained attention to violence and insecurity, the self-referentiality of television, and the thorough saturation of all television with its function as a marketplace ("Íntegra da conversa"). I would also add the performance of authoritative statements per se. Let me elaborate briefly on these patterns with examples from Coutinho's film.

First, perhaps the single most present and recurring pattern is the reduction of women to objects to be visually consumed, with the concomitant preoccupations with body shape and youthfulness (and the products that will guarantee such transformation), where the ideal is the whitest vector of whiteness possible (the blonde). A brief clip from *Tom and Jerry*, with a catfight over a feline femme fatale, both gives us an older iteration of this pattern as well as shows us its presence even in programming directed at children. Such objectification is articulated not only by men (like the plastic surgeon selling wearable prosthetics to prevent the sagging of buttocks and breasts), but also by women themselves, as in the *Programa Marcia, Espelho, Espelho Meu*. In the clip we are shown the self-proclaimed "ugliest woman in the world" undergoes not only a makeover but also plastic surgery to turn herself into an aesthetically pleasing object she can herself consume as she kisses her own image in a mirror. In the process, she becomes a mirror for an audience that is alternatively rapt and bored but that claps obediently as Marcia asserts that "Vamos ficar mais bonita só de ver a convidada" (We'll become prettier just by seeing the invited one).

Second is the thorough saturation of television images with their status as the medium through which commodities circulate. This bleeds over even into programs that are not, at first glance, commercials, so that the aggregate effect is that television generally speaks the language of publicity, where the act of acquiring, as John Berger asserts, "has taken the place of all other actions" (153). While the above-mentioned representation of women is a perfect example, another one that is interesting for seeming slightly forced is a news program on the earthquake in Indonesia that quickly devolves into a show-and-tell of the items in the earthquake kits in Japan (helmet, whistle, lantern). While these objects in the kit are not technically for sale, what is noticeable is the deliberate rerouting of whatever story one might want to tell about the catastrophic event in Indonesia and its effects on individual lives and social life through a catalogue of objects. Berger makes the point that ultimately, however, the language of publicity is not about objects so much as about "social relations," or, to put it otherwise, it is the rerouting of social relations through exchange value. What he means by this is that the action of acquiring objects is not directed to use-value in any sense, to the actual enjoyment of the objects, but to generating envy in others. The personal self-transformation that is a feature of the discourse of publicity (and echoed in the televangelists) is thus about acquiring exchange value.

Third is the self-referentiality or closed circuit through which television constantly refers to itself and sells itself as co-extensive with the only meaningful world. This pattern shows up in the branded images of each television channel, the use of actors to sell products, a show that is essentially gossip about the plotlines of soap operas (where our host reads a gossip magazine in front of the camera) and the ubiquitous presence of screens of various sorts within the diegetic world on screen. Perhaps the most telling example, however, (because it seems so unnecessary) is an English-lesson scene that features a staged dialogue in which the English teacher asks his friend, who was sick the day before, if he had stayed home (yes, he replies) and then if he had watched television. To this his "friend" replies, in a mixture of Portuguese and English, "Yes, I did. E o senhor estava ótimo naquele programa de entrevistas" (Yes, I did. And you were great in that interview program). Pleased, the teacher smiles: "Ah, você gostou mesmo?" (Ah, did you really like it?).

Fourth is a widespread discourse on violence and crime, which projects the image of a society drowning in a war with a shadowy army of delinquents. It is not only a discourse on violence but a bellicose discourse itself, taking a side in that war and exhorting the audience to do so as well by sending in crime videos or with the detailed demonstrations of one newscaster on how to stop a robbery by killing the thief as he screens the security camera footage (Coutinho laughingly suggests that the dependence of certain shows on crime could lead the shows to commit the crimes themselves so they could keep producing the shows). The question of violence is of notable concern in the religious programing, which alternately carries forward the bellicose discourse or positions itself against it (even as it is dependent on it):

> Pense nisso. O submarino, ele está dentro d'água, mas a água não está nele. Nós podemos viver nesse mundo ao presente que nós vivemos, nós estamos vivendo num mundo cheio de violência, mas não precisamos ser violentos. Nós podemos viver num mundo cheio de idolatria, cheio de falta de perdão, pessoas

querendo matar pai, querendo matar filho, aquela corrupção generalizada, mas nós não precisamos corromper junto com o mundo. Nós podemos ser como um submarino.

(Think about this. The submarine, it is in water, but water is not in it. We can live in this world to the present that we live, we are living in a world full of violence, but we don't need to be violent. We can live in a world full of idolatry, full of a lack of forgiveness, people wanting to kill fathers, wanting to kill children, all that generalized corruption, but we don't need to be corrupted along with the world. We can be like a submarine.)

Fifth, there is marked obsession with the English language. Coutinho's decision to start off the film with an early-morning English-language program alerts us to the consistent presence of words in English as a value-formation, where using words in English is deemed to automatically add value to whatever is being said or sold: this includes a corset called "Lift and Shape," a doll that urinates called "Little Mommy," and the heavy metal band Massacration performing "The Mummy."

Finally, I would add the continued exhibition of deeply authoritarian and hierarchical structures that manifest not only in the servile reproduction of the valorization of whiteness, wealth, the English language, and the masculine gaze, but also in pronunciations where the content of what is being expressed takes second place to the simple performance of authority and the reproduction of hierarchy as a principle, where television becomes the platform for the one that is supposed to know, the one that can tell the viewer what's what in the world and what one should or should not do: "use fio dental, não perca tempo com inveja, passe filtro solar" (use dental floss, don't waste time with envy, wear sunblock). The exhibition of authority per se is especially marked the more absurd or empty the pronouncements. For example, on a program on nutrition and health, we hear that the best blood type is B and that most millionaires are type B. Also, the Brazilian plastic surgeon (who lived in Los Angeles for thirty-four years) measures the distance between ears and forehead and nose of a blond model—his measurements are overlaid on momentarily frozen images—and declares authoritatively, "uma pessoa bonita tem pelo menos sete crânios e meio de altura" (someone who is pretty measures at least seven and a half craniums in height).

This confrontation with the multiform subject of Brazilian television does not, however, simply lead to its condemnation. Coutinho contrasts what he calls the infinite mosaic of facts that is Brazilian television with Cuban television, which he describes by saying that "quase não há fatos e só uma versão" (there almost aren't facts and only one version, "Fragmentos da História"). Coutinho resolutely refuses a Frankfurt School posture of condemnation of the culture industries even as he stresses the need to recognize the immense power and money in television (and the ties binding politicians and networks). In response to the perplexed questioning of students who want to know if he's offering a critique or what the movie is meant to accomplish, he distances himself from what he describes as a certain paranoid and elitist leftist position that would categorize the world according to abstract but impoverishing categories and according to which the television spectator is a bestialized passive receptor under media control, the mirror image of "appliances that no longer need him in order to produce themselves" (Certeau 31). So the film is not meant to be a simple critique of television. While he will qualify some of the segments as grotesque and frightful in the Q&A sessions, he also describes others as marvelous.

In particular, his comments about the sequence of hands selling rings—a reference he returns to several times in the Q&A with obvious delight—contains the outlines of a structure of reception that would match the one practiced in so many of his other films. The woman who is implied by the hands but never seen as such generates an effect such that she is, he says in the Q&A session, "more mysterious to him than the Mona Lisa" ("Fragmentos da História"). I want to stay for a moment with this statement. One could certainly read the bodiless hands as a further sign of the repeated and brutal reduction of women's bodies to objects to be studied, measured, fixed, and sold, a pattern Coutinho readily verbalizes and condemns. Nonetheless, what Coutinho might be perceiving instead is an opacity that is inadvertently generated as a side effect of the drive-to-be-a-marketplace that traverses television. The single-minded focus of the program on the rings to be sold frees the rest of the woman's body from televisual capture. She is implied by the program—there must be a body behind the hands—but not subject to the same kind of scrutiny and measurement of the other female bodies. She acquires thus a curious impersonality and inaccessibility. To posit television as a subject, one to be approached with the same open-ended listening lent to all of Coutinho's other subjects, to perceive its incoherencies and the strange effects that are inadvertently generated, is to see and hear it such that something new surfaces, something that is not contained in pre-established categories through which we process or critique television. Coutinho stresses the multiplicity of television in his contrast between a "mosaic of infinite facts" (Brazilian television) and the single version, without facts, that is Cuban television to him. If, in the second case, unity is what predominates over and organizes all the fragments (which cease to be facts insofar as they are subordinated to the central perspective becoming instead *examples*), in the case of Brazilian television, what he perceives is something like a heterogeneous assemblage, in which new and unexpected relations can emerge from the arrangement of the fragments, the primary montage that holds together the stream of televisual voices and images.

There is finally another angle to the question of duration that Coutinho brings to television, which refers back to the 24/7 temporality of television. As the product of the extension of the working day to and past the limit of human potential, 24/7 is the chronotope of nonstop production, circulation, and consumption where, like a machine, one is supposed to always be "engaged, interfacing, interacting, communicating, responding or processing" (Crary 15). What this means for television is a logic organized by the stretching of human practices to fit this temporal conveyor belt and fill the time slot so that there is no significant pause. In particular, as Coutinho observes, there is never silence on television: "A regra do jogo da televisão [é que] . . . o silêncio não existe. Se vê neste filme, não tem um segundo que tenha silêncio. Ou tem música ou tem alguém falando" ("Íntegra da conversa"; The ground rule of television [is that] . . . silence doesn't exist. It's seen in this film, there isn't a second with silence. Either there is music or there is someone talking). As many critics have argued, in contrast to cinema, what fills the space of television is language and voice; it is primarily an acoustic rather than visual medium where the main narrative thread is given by constant chatter and the image largely plays a supplementary or supporting role to the soundtrack (Birdsall and Enns). One might even speculate that it was the primary nature of voice on television that drew Coutinho to the project, particularly in the form of the various talk shows that Coutinho underscores, including news shows, preachers, language lessons, and even advertisements. This might also explain one recurring feature of television that seems emphasized in Coutinho's film, which is the visual presentation of written words on-screen, where the visual image is auxiliary to the voice: this ranges from names of products being sold or of the programs being promoted, lyrics of a song being sung, excerpts from the Bible, the transcription of the Communist Party's statement that "o capitalismo é incapaz de solucionar problemas" (capitalism is incapable of solving problems), and, finally, in perhaps the strangest scene, a moment in a celebrity show in which a journalist fakes a swoon over a young, handsome celebrity and begins to talk in heavily accented English where her words are emphasized through their transcription on-screen as English spelled in Portuguese phonetics. The necessity to generate verbal production leads to what I'd call a communicative overgrowth or overproduction where talk is generated for the sake of talk as opposed to the need to communicate something in particular: this leads alternately to speculative, improvised moments on-screen, to empty idle chatter, or simply, as noted before, to authoritative statements meant to transmit a performance of authority. One notable overproduction of talk of this type concerns a news program about a man who has been shot in the streets of São Paulo. We can't see much as we watch the scene from a helicopter hovering overhead as the newscaster at first simply tries to tell the viewer what he/she is seeing (the squad of firemen is working, trying to resuscitate him), but as the scene prolongs itself and the commentator has already repeated himself a few times, he then breaks into a speculative commentary discouraging urban migration:

> Por enquanto não reestabelecido o batimento cardíaco. . . . Dá para perceber de longe que . . . quando os pés continuam abertos ali . . . não houve . . . a tentativa de ressuscitação mecânica . . . tiro em São Paulo, provavelmente por causa de uma briga . . . Briga no trânsito! . . . Tiro provoca parada cardíaca . . . cardiorrespiratória numa vítima . . . Estão tentando de todo jeito . . . Você está vendo o que é viver numa grande cidade, não é? Isso é viver numa grande cidade. Ah, eu tenho um sonho, morar na cidade grande. É o caminho mais perto do céu. Primeiro porque pode morar em prédio alto ou então levar um tiro por uma briga. Eu já falei: não briguem em trânsito. . . . Também não sabemos se foi uma briga em trânsito. Pode ter sido um assalto.

(The heartbeat not yet reestablished . . . You can realize from afar that . . . when the feet continue open there . . . there wasn't . . . the attempt of mechanical resuscitation . . . shots in São Paulo, probably due to a fight . . . A fight in traffic! . . . Gunfire provokes cardiac arrest . . . cardiorespiratory in a victim . . . They are trying by all means . . . You are seeing what it is to live in the big city, aren't you? This is what it is to live in a big city. Ah, I have a dream, living in the big city. It is the path closest to heaven. First because you can live in a tall building or then get shot in a fight. I already said: don't fight in traffic . . . We also don't know if it was a fight in traffic. It could have been a holdup.)

This scene brings to the fore one of the consequences of direct live recording according to Eliseo Verón, which is that while in cinema an image can't be unintentional, on television, in contrast, not only is it possible but a fundamental principle (Carlos 83). The voice in this segment runs precisely after an unpredictable, unplanned image, and the need to provide a stream of discourse to accompany an image that doesn't essentially convey very much in itself leads to both to the incomplete and run-on sentences as well as abrupt changes in affect: from exclamation (A fight in traffic!) to a simultaneously melancholic and ironic mood (skyscrapers and bullets both take you to the heavens) to an imperative (don't fight in traffic). It is also clear how much pure chatter is taking place where the narrator doesn't actually know anything very concretely when he admits in the end that, rather than a fight in traffic, it could have been a holdup. In the duration or extension of these scenes, what acquires more density is less the particular content being transmitted and more the simple capacity to generate utterances out of language. But what kind of language is language-on-television? And what kind of enunciation is possible?

Language, Potential

Cecilia Sayad uses *Um dia na vida*, and the seeming absence of authorship in the film, to offer a theorization of Coutinho's particular way of performing authorship, which "relocates the textual markers of authorial intervention" away from self-expression and toward the author's exterior gestures; his films show not the author's world but the author *in* the world, she argues (14). *Um dia na vida* takes this to the extreme by removing, as mentioned, the visible and aural indices of the documentarian's body that had functioned as his "authorial signature" (12). In *Um dia na vida*, Coutinho is an "orchestrator," a "spectator," and a "consumer" but not a producer or creator of images, she argues (17).

We might take a distinction offered by Michel de Certeau to suggest how Coutinho's position as a consumer of images is also a form of creation in *Um dia na vida*. Certeau describes television as having not one, but two kinds of production: the second kind of production is consumption, a kind of "poaching" marked by "its clandestine nature, its tireless but quiet activity, in short by its quasi-invisibility, since it shows itself not in its own products (where would it place them?) but in an art of using those imposed on it" (31). The quasi-invisibility of the authorial function in *Um dia na vida* might be understood therefore as a function of its status as precisely an exercise in poaching or piracy, in its use of that which is not and cannot be "proper" to it. The project also turns, for that same reason, on the radicalization of the enunciative moment.

In this sense, one might suggest that the material presented in *Um dia na vida* be understood as an experiment along the lines of Borges's Pierre Menard, who, in copying the Quixote word for word three centuries later, nonetheless generated something completely different. What matters is the way in which a copy is its own enunciative act. While many of Coutinho's documentaries probe for that breakaway moment when a subject says something new with the same-old grammar that binds us all, some of his later movies seem to press for or isolate that liminal moment where score and performance are indistinguishable, and where all that distinguishes them is the enunciative moment itself. It is not that they collapse into each other, but that there is a probing of the place of maximum contact between them and an effort to discern the thin membrane of what is *unlike* in the place of maximum likeness. In *Jogo de cena*, for example, Coutinho brings together women from Rio de Janeiro who tell their stories on-screen and then actresses who reenact the very same scenes. The film jumps back and forth between the series of doubled women narrating their lives such that it is not always clear who is the "original" and who is the "copy." What the movie also shows, however, is that the reenactments—even when they are almost word-for-word—are never simply a copy of the other woman's words and that they unfold in often surprising ways. It is, for example, the actress, and not the original narrator, who breaks down in a scene in which she tells the story of "her" baby's death as a result of the network of connections and memories activated by the words of the other woman, words that become hers in a different way.

Um dia na vida experiments with a kind of poaching, one that takes place not solely through consumption but through the process of creating a different kind of enunciative act, an event that is quasi-invisible insofar as it also does not use its own products. Part of the question posed by this experiment might be phrased in the following way: what changes in our experience of these audiovisual images when that which is produced for one media, according to the grammar of that media for one kind of circulation and audience (Coutinho specifies that he deliberately did not include fragments of films that were shown on TV because he was looking for material that was specifically made for television ["Íntegra da conversa"]), is dislocated into a different circulatory stream and context of reception?¹ What happens when a concentrated drop of Brazilian television in placed in a context—the movie theater—in which, as Coutinho says, one is subjected to the material without being able to change the channel? ("É uma tortura!" [It's torture!] he affirms) ("Íntegra da conversa"). The encounter that previously took place on-screen in Coutinho's other films is now shifted off-screen into the movie theater with the audience: hence, I think, an additional reason for his presence at the few screenings of the film and his engagement in a Q&A with the audience. Hence, also, why I think it is interesting to read those scenes as I've been doing here as an extension of the filmic experiment. The happening—if it happens—would now take place between his body present in the screening room, the filmed material, and the audience.

Might it, however, also not take place? This is the question that arises with what one might call the "misencounter" that is captured in the Q&A session after a screening of the film on April 26, 2014, where many of the students seem to puzzle at the film and return periodically to the question of how the film might offer a critique, prompting Coutinho at one point to note that he would have liked to screen the movie to a more heterogeneous, popular audience: "Só terei leituras novas se um dia eu fizer uma exhibição para um público popular que é o público que vê televisão . . . aí pode ser que eu aprenda alguma coisa" ("Fragmentos da História" 1:25; I'll only have new readings if one day I hold a screening for a popular public that is the public that watches television . . . then I might learn something). What might be the limits to trying to bring out a new enunciative act from televisual material?

The first is a legal limit to this kind of poaching. The experiment trips up against the issue of copyright, which declares the enunciative act Coutinho wants to stage as illegal. Branded an act of piracy, the film becomes ephemeral, and the possibility of its repeated circulation is barred. Coutinho confronts this limit in his comments on the movie. The experiment, he admits, was motivated in part by his interest in working with material that would be composed entirely of citations: "Ainda me interessa essa coisa . . . como tudo é aproveitado . . . em todo livro há tanto do alheio quanto do próprio. Isto daí é um troço que me interessa. . . . Essa coisa da originalidade é um mito . . . isso não existe . . . nada é puramente cópia" (This thing still interests me . . . like everything it's used . . . in every book there is as much of the foreign as of the personal. This here is a thing that interests me . . . This thing of originality is a myth . . . it doesn't exist . . . nothing is purely a copy). Literature and film are terrains that should "lack private property." The copyright regime threatens such intertextual flow, however. He notes that "o direito da imagem tornou-se uma mercadoria . . . na França . . . você pode fotografar pessoas andando na rua, [mas] um casal se beijando perto da Tour Eiffel não pode. Tem que pedir autorização. . . . Acabou o cinema! Acabou" ("Fragmentos da História"; the right of images became a commodity . . . in France . . . you can photograph people walking on the street, [but] a couple kissing near the Eiffel Tower you can't. You must ask for authorization . . . Cinema is over! It's done).

Another limit emerges if we approach the film as situated not only in the tension between the original and copy, but as caught up in the historical pressure on language and linguistic capabilities that Paolo Virno stages as a problem insofar as "the sharing of linguistic and cognitive habits" is a constituent element of contemporary processes of labor. Humans are capable of working—of teaching, cooking, transporting, performing, serving, working in data entry—inasmuch as we are speaking-thinking beings and can minimally communicate and cooperate with others (65). It is insofar as these intellectual capacities are distributed and shared across human bodies that they are general and also, therefore, generic: not specialized but common to all human animals as linguistic animals. Like a skeletal structure that supports linguistic communication at its most basic level, these capacities include the faculty of language; the disposition to learn, to ask questions, and to scan faces for information; memory; imagination; the power of abstraction and relation; the tendency toward; self-reflexivity; and formal and informal knowledge.

While these faculties are generic, the extent to which they are embodied in the human animal for Virno also means that there is necessarily an element of virtuosity in them. What he means by this is that they are not preprogrammed or automatic; there must be a conversion of langue into parole for every utterance that takes place: "In order to represent the relationship between general intellect and living labour in Postfordism we need to refer to the act through which every speaker draws on the inexhaustible potential of language to execute contingent and unrepeatable statements" (Virno, "General"). Like the pianist who delivers a memorable performance, where the performance exceeds the score but exists only in the performance, in the activity itself, the airline steward does not just mechanically follow a preestablished text in his/her labor (although there is also a script to be followed) but also draws on linguistic and cognitive capacities to check in with fellow stewards, assesses what needs to be done, and attend to the needs of particular passengers if they arise. The metaphor or image of the *score* is brought in to describe this relationship between a skeletal or generic potential and its instantiation. The score is a kind of infrastructure that underwrites human linguistic and cognitive capacities and exists in function of the musical performance to which it can give rise. It is both that which is not yet performance as well as the promise or the projection of that performance: "The pianist performs a Chopin waltz, the actor is more or less faithful to a preliminary script, the orator has at least some notes to refer to; all performing artists can count on a score. But when virtuosity applies to the total of social labor, which one is the proper score? From my perspective, I maintain without too many reservations that the score performed by the multitude in the post-Ford era is the Intellect, intellect as generic human faculty" (63). The difference between the pianist, actor, or dancer from which the metaphor is taken, however, and the communicative performance of all speakers in a society is that the score of the artistic performers is an "end product in its own proper and restricted sense" and as such also a determined script (which may be more loosely or strictly followed). The "score" in the case of the general intellect, however, is simply the faculty of language and doesn't produce an end product apart from the performance of its own communicative activity; it is a script only insofar as it coincides with "pure and simple *dynamis,* with pure and simple potential" (66). General intellect is not a book or an algebra formula—not the work produced by thought—but the faculty to think and to communicate. This potentiality—this capacity to exceed a script—is in Virno's analysis not taken as a source of rupture or freedom, as in de Certeau's analysis of enunciation, however, but understood precisely as a resource that is put to work as the primary force of production.

Within this configuration, the culture industry occupies a special place for Virno. While on the one hand spectacle is the specific product of the so-called culture industry, what is delivered in the spectacle is human communication (the reigning productive force of society). The televisual spectacle is therefore both a particular product of a particular industry as well as the "quintessence of the mode of production in its entirety" (60). In this sense, the culture industry is the industry of the means of production (communication). According to Virno, what the Frankfurt school critics miss as they focus on the "factories of the soul" (publishing, cinema, radio) as subjected to the same processes of standardization and serialization as the factories of material goods are the fact that the spaces that remain open to informality, to communicative and creative improvisation, and to the unforeseen spark are not simply residues of a pre-factory past but anticipatory of the increasing subsumption of labor: "the informality of communicative behavior, the competitive interaction typical of a meeting, the abrupt diversion that can enliven a television program (in general, everything which it would have been dysfunctional to rigidify and regulate beyond a certain threshold) has become, in the post-Ford era, a typical trait of the *entire* realm of social production" (63). An analogy that might clarify this point is given by James Scott, who notes that in a work-to-rule strike, employees begin doing their jobs by meticulously observing every one of the rules, regulations, and procedures outlined by the company, and performing only the duties stated in the job descriptions, with the result that the work grinds to a halt. The action illustrates how "actual work processes depend more heavily on informal understandings and improvisations than upon formal work rules" (Scott 310). The flip side of this moment of the strike is that such improvisations are what make everything run; "virtuosic activity shows itself as universal *servile work*" (Virno 69).

If we turn back to Coutinho's documentary project, Virno's analysis asks us to pay attention to the conditions under which linguistic and performative acts take place on television. What does it mean that they are characterized not only as private property, subject to copyright law, but also as a form of labor? Or, if we want to take television as a multiform subject, might the vacuity of so much of its speaking result from its staging (its poaching) of a human communicative capacity as such? Might this putting to work of enunciation itself—the very spectacle of television as a medium—pose a limit to the kind of word-event Coutinho pursues in his other documentaries, just as he notes the logic of copyright poses a limit to cinema? Like *Últimas conversas*, *Um dia na vida* runs up against the fundamental ambivalence of what is necessarily generic in the common. Further, while it may abstract out the moment of enunciation like his previous films, the differentiation between the potential of language and particular and contingent utterances no longer carries the kind of political valence that someone like de Certeau might have assigned to it. Instead, the capacity to utter sound and words is folded back into itself and stretched out into an overproduction of language like a television oriented fundamentally to 24/7 transmission.

Note

1. "A ironia é justamente que este filme pirata, sem um único plano dotado de qualquer valor estético, se revele um dos filmes que mais pedem pela força da projeção de cinema. O grande gesto de *Um dia na vida* é justamente pegar todas estas imagens sem valor e transferi-las para uma sala de cinema e, no processo, emprestar a elas uma força que não apresentam por si mesmas. Algo como Ana Maria Braga jogando Guitar Hero pode parecer grotesco na TV ou no computador, mas sua função muda quando apresentada no contexto de uma projeção. A grande vitória de *Um dia na vida* é a de, partindo de imagens de televisão, recuperar o valor da função social de exibição em cinema. Os sentidos do filme são inseparáveis dela" (Filipe Furtado; The irony is that this pirated film, without a single frame imbued with any aesthetic value, is one of the films that most asks for the force of cinema projection. The big gesture of *Um dia na vida* is precisely in taking all these images without value and transferring them for a movie theater and, in the process, lend to them a force that they don't present by themselves. Something like Ana Maria Braga playing Guitar Hero can seem grotesque on TV or the computer, but its function changes when presented in the context of a screening. The great victory of *Um dia na vida* is that of, departing from television images, recuperating the value of the social function of theatrical screening. The film's meanings are inseparable from it).

Works Cited

Avellar, José Carlos. "The Emptiness of the Backyard: An Interview with Eduardo Coutinho." Translated by Krista Brune. *Film Quarterly*, vol. 69, no. 3, 2016, pp. 44–55.

Bazin, André. *What Is Cinema?* Vol. 1. U of California P, 1967.

Berger, John. *Ways of Seeing*. Penguin, 1990.

Birdsall, Carolyn, and Anthony Enns. "Introduction: Rethinking Theories of Television Sound." *Journal of Sonic Studies,* vol. 3, no. 1, 2012, n.p., https://www.researchcatalogue.net/view/262391/262392. Accessed 8 June 2022.

Brizuela, Natalia. "Conversation and Duration in Eduardo Coutinho's Films." *Film Quarterly*, vol. 69, no. 3, 2016, pp. 19–27.

Carlo, Mario. *De lo cinematografico a lo televisivo: Metatelevisión, language y temporalidad*. La Crujía, 2006.

Coutinho, Eduardo. "A linguagem é mais que o autor." Interview with Eduardo Coutinho given to Mariano Blejman, http://www.fndc.org.br/clipping/a-linguagem-e-mais-que-o-autor-entrevista-com-eduardo-coutinho-248757/. Accessed 8 June 2018.

Coutinho, Eduardo. "Íntegra da conversa com Eduardo Coutinho na PUC-SP." 27 Apr. 2012, https://www.youtube.com/watch?v=eLSMA4qZm34. Accessed 6 June 2018.

Crary, Jonathan. *Late Capitalism and the Ends of Sleep*. Verso, 2013.

De Certeau, Michel. *The Practice of Everyday Life*. U of California P, 2011.

Furtado, Filipe. "Um Dia na Vida, de Eduardo Coutinho (Brasil, 2010); e Aquilo que Fazemos com as nossas Desgraças, de Arthur Tuoto (Brasil, 2014)." *Revista Cinética: Cinema e Crítica*. 11 Feb. 2014, revistacinetica.com.br.

"Fragmentos da História: O filme de compilação: Debate com o Eduardo Coutinho sobre *Um dia na vida*." 26 Apr. 2012. *CINUSP Paulo Emílio*, https://www.youtube.com/watch?v=JtR4lspJo8I. Accessed 2 June 2018.

Lins, Consuelo. "Eduardo Coutinho, Savage Linguist of Brazilian Documentary." Translated by Natalia Brizuela. *Film Quarterly*, vol. 69, no. 3, 2016, pp. 28–34.

———. "El cine de Eduardo Coutinho: un arte del presente." *Tierra en Trance: Reflexiones sobre cine latinoamericano*, tierraentrance.miradas.net

Sayad, Cecilia. "Variations on the Author." *Film Quarterly*, vol. 69, no. 3, 2016, pp. 12–18.

Scott, James. *Seeing Like a State: How Certain Schemes to Improve the Human Condition Have Failed*. Yale UP, 1998.

Virno, Paolo. *The Grammar of the Multitude: For an Analysis of Contemporary Forms of Life*. Semiotexte, 2004.

Xavier, Ismail. "Inquiries into Eduardo Coutinho and his Dialogue with Modern Tradition." Translated by Krista Brune. *Film Quarterly*, vol. 69, no. 3, 2016, pp. 35–43.

8

To Act or to Act

Present, Presence, and Representation in Eduardo Coutinho's *Jogo de cena*

Brenno Kenji Kaneyasu

> Eu trabalho com palavra, eu edito a palavra primeiro; na verdade, a palavra me gera a vontade de imagem. A diferença é: a imagem existe, mas a palavra é que provoca a imagem. Você tem anteriormente a palavra.
>
> (I work with words, I edit the word first; really, the word generates in me the will of the image. The difference is: the image exists but the word it what provokes the image. You have the word prior.)
>
> —Eduardo Coutinho, "O vazio do quintal"

> In the beginning there was the Act.
>
> —Goethe, *Faust* Part I, Scene I

This chapter originated from an invitation I received to introduce Eduardo Coutinho's *Jogo de cena* (English title: *Playing*) before a screening of the movie at the University of California, Berkeley, in the spring of 2016. When preparing the introduction to the film, I debated between reading a prewritten version of it, or bringing with me just a few talking points, and elaborating from them as it were in real time. The choice, it occurred to me, related on a deep level with the movie we were about to see. It was a choice that concerned the nature of representation. Preparing a text in advance and reading from it meant, first of all, that my engagement would be primarily with the text, and only secondarily with the audience. Second, it meant, to paraphrase one of the actresses in the film, that the speech, the voice, and the script would come first, and only then would the feeling and the thought—the affective and intellectual engagement with what is said—arrive, if at all. This second-hand performance, this reenactment of ideas and insights thought beforehand, sometime in the past, and now merely repeated, blurred the lines, I thought to myself, between presentation and re-presentation, between a presentation that is past and a present that can only be re-presented. Was I presenting the film to the audience? Was I, in some deeply mediated way, representing it?

Coutinho's *Jogo de cena* reflects on these questions while at the same time performing them. It does so by presenting us with what I would like to call, in broad lines, the three paradoxes of representation. First, there is the paradox of presence: how do presentation and representation relate? What kind of *presence* does *re-presentation* postulate, foreclose, and make possible? Second, the paradox of temporality: how does representation, the performative and/or conceptual reenactment of a present, relate to a presentation that is always past and, conversely, to a present that, itself no longer present, can only be re-presented? Last, the paradox of acting, a verbal noun whose very name denounces its ambiguous performative status as both deed and representation of the deed. To act or to act: this predicament, at once Hamletian and anti-Hamletian, seems to be the performative question per excellence, embodying, enacting, and problematizing in one multifaceted gesture the distinction between action and discourse, body and word, whose complications lie at the origin of theater and configure the multibranched root of representation.

Who's There?

No fundo, está tudo contido na primeira fala do primeiro ato de *Hamlet*: Quem está aí?

(At the end, it's all told in the first speech from the first act of *Hamlet*: Who's there?)

—Fernanda Torres, "No dorso instável de um tigre"

Vladimir: So there you are again.

Estragon: Am I?

—Samuel Beckett, *Waiting for Godot*, Act I

The opening line of Shakespeare's *Hamlet*—the prototypical play about plays within a play, that mirroring vertigo of mise-en-scènes-en-abyme in which acting indefinitely defers action—marks, on a fundamental level, the starting point of all mise-en-scènes, and could be taken as the premise and ongoing inquiry of Coutinho's own *jogo de cena*: "Who's there?" Such is Bernardo's question addressing the stranger who approaches him in the silent night. From its beginning, theater raises and stages the question of presence. Yet the question that opens Shakespeare's self-reflective masterpiece—"Who's there?"—is followed by a rejoinder that is not so much an answer as an invitation—it does not provide closure but rather offers itself as an opening for the dialogical space of drama, a call to action. "Nay, answer me: stand and unfold yourself" is Francisco's response to Bernardo's interpellation. With this response, the unified *logos* is split in two, giving way to dialogue. The dual *logos*. Two voices and two bodies meet, asking of each other, each in its own way, the same fundamental question: who are you? Yet this question, ontological as it may seem, is a theatrical, not a theoretical, one. Although the two Greek inventions—theater and theory—partake of the same root (θέα-, *théa-*: sight, view, contemplation), announcing the necessary distance that binds together spectacle and spectator, in theory that distance is one between subject and object, the establishment of a difference that is also a subordination, a categorical hierarchy. In theater, on the other hand, that distance is one between subject and subject, the establishment of a difference grounded on a radical equality. Moreover, this binding distance between subject and subject that we find in theater is twofold: it takes place between actor and actor, on the one hand, and between actors and audience, on the other. In both cases, it is a distance that constitutively acknowledges the presence of the beholder: the second actor without whom no dialogue would be possible; the audience to whom the performance as performance is directed, who is constituted by the spectacle as an audience, and who, therefore, is an integral element of the theatrical situation. It is in this twofold awareness of the beholder, coming to the surface the moment the interaction between subject and subject is acknowledged, that its theatricality resides.[1] The theatrical question posed by the "Who's there" is, then, a question that, resisting the temptation of postulating the abstraction of a view from nowhere,[2] embraces the constitutive role of context in the shaping of identity, aware that the "there" in its formulation is as important as and as inseparable from the "who," who, when addressed, is always already *there*, always already inserted in a context, always already situated.[3] It is this constitutive role of situation in the shaping of identity—"um espaço, uma cenografia, um enquadramento, um 'clima,' uma disposição dos corpos que condiciona o registro da fala" (Xavier 181; a space, a scenography, a framing, a "climate," a disposition of bodies that condition the register of speech)—that will render mere repetition impossible, introducing difference into identity, thus complicating the relation between presentation and *re*-presentation, act and reenactment. Like in Borges's Pierre Menard's rewriting of the Quixote, the reenactment of an act at a different time and place, inserted in a different network of relationships, becomes, in the same gesture whereby it is performed, both itself and other, tearing apart the monological fabric of identity with which theory has traditionally draped itself.

This emphasis on the situation of the intersubjective encounter, on the there-ness where the "who" stands and unfolds itself in response to the voice that breaks the silence, is of seminal importance in Coutinho's films. Since at least *Cabra marcado para morrer* (1964–1984), this emphasis has taken the shape of a displacement, a dislocation, a movement toward the space of the other. In his films, the "there" of the interlocutor has as a rule taken precedence over the "here" of Coutinho himself. Coutinho has noted that his interests lay in those who were other than he was: his interlocutors were his "others" regarding gender, class, age, and geography. As he put it in the interview that appeared in *Revista Cinemais*:

> O que acho fundamental é o seguinte: não pode ser nem de baixo para cima, nem de cima para baixo, entende? O grande problema é a relação que você tem com o outro na filmagem. A primeira coisa é estabelecer que somos diferentes . . . O que quero dizer é o seguinte: só a partir de uma diferença clara é que você consegue uma igualdade provisória e utópica nas entrevistas. Quando me dizem: "as pessoas falam para você . . ." Sim, falam, e eu acho que é por isso: porque sou o curioso que vem de fora, de outro mundo, e aceita, não julga.

(What I find fundamental is the following: it can neither be from bottom up, nor from top down, right? The big problem is the relationship with the other that you have with the other in the filming. The first thing is establishing that we are different . . . What I mean is this: it is only from a clear difference that you can reach a provisional and utopic equality in interviews. When they tell me: "people talk for you . . ." Yes, they talk, and I think that it is due to this: because I am a curious person who comes from outside, from another world, and accepts without judgement.) (Coutinho 65)

In Coutinho's films, to use Jean-Claude Bernardet's words, "o entrevistador procura o entrevistado" ("Jogo de cena" 632; the interviewer seeks out the interviewee). In *Santo forte* (1999) and *Babilônia 2000* (2000), the favelas are the meeting place for the conversations that unfold; in *Boca de lixo* (1992), the dialogue takes place in the dumping ground alluded to in the title of the film; in *O fim e o princípio* (2005), the backlands of Paraíba are the background against which the stories unfold; in *Edifício Master* (2002), it is in the homonymous apartment block in Rio de Janeiro's Copacabana that the encounters and the intersubjective displacements they entail take place. If it is true that "a entrevista privilegia o entrevistador, que tem uma posição central mesmo que ele não esteja presente na tela, como em geral não está, mas é ele que estimula a fala do entrevistado e é a ele que se dirigem as respostas e o olhar do entrevistado" (Bernardet, "Ismail Xavier e Jean-Claude Bernardet" n.p; the interview privileges the interviewer, who has a central position even if not present on the screen, as in general he isn't, but he is the one who stimulates the interviewee's speech and to whom the responses and gaze of the interviewee are directed); if, in Coutinho's own words, the encounters he seeks consist of "uma câmera e dois lados. Diferenciados, porque o lado que tem a câmera tem poder e o outro não tem" (274; a camera and two sides. Differentiated, because the side with the camera has power and the other has none), we could perhaps say that the movement toward the space of the other, together with the acknowledgement of the difference that underlies this very displacement restitute in however minimal a degree, not through the pretense of eliminating asymmetry but rather through its doubling up—the camera on the one hand, the dislocation on the other—some of the power back to the side who does not have control over the camera.

Coutinho's *Jogo de cena*, however, complicates this movement. Its displacement is of a different order, its dislocation no longer toward the space of the other. Its space—a theater stage—is, properly speaking, neither "here" nor "there," while being at the same time *both* here *and* there. It is not so much the space of the other, but rather, to the degree that it is possible to do justice to the irreducible dialectics of the concept and with full awareness of the oxymoronic structure of the expression—tautological in form, antithetical in substance—the space of *otherness itself*. It is not simply that the theatrical stage is a *heterotopia* in the Foucauldian sense of the word. Foucault will indeed tell us that the theater stage, like the cinema, is an other-space to the degree that it juxtaposes several spaces in a single real space: "thus it is that the theater brings onto the rectangle of the stage a whole series of spaces that are foreign to each other; thus it is that the cinema is a very odd rectangular room, at the end of which, on a two-dimensional screen, one sees the projection of a three-dimensional space" (Foucault 25). This may perhaps suffice to characterize the stage theater as an "other space." However, the claim that the stage theater is the space of "otherness itself" is, I believe, of a different kind. "Otherness" (centrifugal, differential, and non-identical) seems to be precisely that which cannot be "itself" (centripetal, stable, and self-identical). Rather, I want to suggest, the theatrical stage is a space of *otherness itself* to the extent that, once placed on it—once *mise-en-scène*—, everything, and everyone, is both always already itself (a prop, scenery, a piece of equipment, an actor) and an other (an object, nature, an effect, a character), both matter and meaning, it and "it," presence and representation, person and persona, subject to a doubling that is at the same time a split, a *both/and* that is—to the extent that it is irreducible to the affirmation of a stable identity—at the same time a *neither/nor*. It is this non-identical duplicity—already inscribed in the name the Greeks gave to the stage actor, the *hypokrites*—that permeates the relationship between presentation and representation, utterance and citation, event and repetition, act and act, the complications of which Coutinho's *Jogo de cena* goes on to explore.

Person, Persona

Thirteen women speak about their lives;[4] their stories provide the scripts for actresses who then play them. The actresses—three of whom are widely known to a Brazilian audience, and therefore readily recognizable—themselves women among the women they play, in turn speak about their own lives. The lines separating person and persona are, as in the inaugural scene of theater, blurred, complicated. The film's very title already contains a provocation that is also an invitation to us, its would-be spectators. The words in the title play with their own meaning, in a way that the English rendition—*Playing*—playful in its own way, fails, at least in part, to capture. The Portuguese *jogo de cena* is an almost-too-literal translation of the French "mise-en-scène," and precisely owing to its literalness it is able to problematize its French counterpart, turn it on its head, and go beyond it. It does not simply "place it in scene," as "mise-en-scène" would imply; it does not simply stage it; rather—the Portuguese word "jogo" meaning not only to "throw" or to "place" ("joga ali"; "throw it there"), but also the noun "game"—it plays with its own dynamics, its own premises, its own no-longer-implicit pact with the audience, the characters, the actresses. The fact that we are presented—or should one say re-presented?—with life stories also insists on the link between a past that has been lived and a present that is a reenactment. But this apparent contradiction is more, or perhaps less, than a contradiction: it is a complication. Because the present of reenactment is, of course, also its own present, at once act and reenactment. A representation is, at the same time, its own presentation, inhabiting its own present and embodying its own presence, presenting itself in the same gesture whereby it represents something else. Like the actor who embodies it, representation is from its inception double, dialogical, dialectical: it splits (and multiplies) the *logos*—the logic, the word, the sense, the senses—into self and other. (It is no wonder then that, since Plato, *theater* has been both the mirror and the horror of *theory*: reflection finds itself frozen with terror when it catches, Medusa-like, its own reflection in the objectifying mirror of theory.) The actresses who play the women are, themselves, women. Their act is also action. The women, in turn, play themselves in front of the camera. Coutinho's film stages the ambiguity at the root of the very word "act": the deed and its representation.

This complication is presented to us within the first minute of the documentary. Having been shown the newspaper ad inviting "women older than 18 years old, living in Rio de Janeiro, with stories to tell" to take part in an audition for a documentary film—seemingly the one piece of information in the film to inhabit a space other than the theater stage on which the shooting is carried out, a token of the outside that vouches for the trustworthiness of that which takes place inside the screen—we follow the first woman as she ascends the stairwell onto the stage of the Teatro Glauce Rocha, in Rio de Janeiro, where the conversation with director Eduardo Coutinho will take place. We do so, however, from the point of view of the camera that follows her, watching her ascension from behind, listening to the sound of her footsteps. The candid "behind the scenes" impression that we are afforded by being able to see her before she arrives on-stage is only made possible by a displacement of the boundaries of the stage, the boundaries that mark where the behind-the-scene ends and the scene itself begins. As she comes out of the stairwell onto the stage, she crosses a boundary that at the same time is no longer there. The camera that follows her gives us a glimpse of the material conditions of possibility of the scene, which as a rule remain external to the frame, the outside that renders the inside possible: lighting equipment, cameras and their operators, audio equipment, scattered cables, the seats of the audience, the circumstances of the mise-en-scène. The microphone, which up to this point had deliberately and fastidiously recorded the sounds of her footsteps, now captures as if by accident fragments of a conversation caught in progress, *in media res*. The conversation gradually dies out as she reaches the stage, as though the arrival of the first character had interrupted something, and, in doing so, had marked the beginning of something else. Action stops in order to give way to action. Cut. Play.

Her name is Mary Sheyla, but we do not know it. Nor will we in fact know it until the credits appear at the end of the film: her name is neither mentioned, nor is it displayed on the screen as she begins to speak, as is common practice in documentaries, including those by Coutinho himself (*Santo forte* and *Edifício Master* being two examples). All we are presented with are her words, her face, her gestures; all we hear is her story, intimate, personal. It is as though that other Shakespearean question—what's in a name?—were here given a different, hyper-nominalist twist. The proper name, that token of irreducible individuality, ceases to be necessary, becomes indeed almost improper, when confronted with the singularity of a personal story. To name is to fictionalize. To follow the convention of displaying her name on the screen, to the extent that it would be following a convention, would almost seem to detract from the raw truth revealed to us by the frame: let the words speak for themselves; or rather—since that is never quite possible—let a particular (some)body at a particular time and place articulate them, in a gesture that is simultaneously one of owning and one of sharing. Those of us familiar with Coutinho's other films have learned to trust the revealing power of words articulated in situations like these and—to borrow a phrase from Ismail Xavier's insightful analysis of Coutinho's goals and methods—the "emergence of the singular" that they make possible (Xavier 186). Reassuringly, we remember just a minute earlier having been shown the cameras, the filming crew, the scattered cables, all the material circumstances of the mise-en-scène. We remember, with regained trust, that Coutinho's game of staging is a transparent one: it shows rather than conceals. Its visual rhetoric is one of frankness. Its pact with the audience is one based on a straightforward kind of trust: what you see is what you get. There is no need for us to willingly suspend our disbelief, for, as the first image in the film, the silent still of the newspaper ad, insists on reminding us, what we are watching is a "documentary film"—a "filme documentário," in Coutinho's exacting phrase—not a work of fiction. Real persons were invited to audition for it; they called in response to the invitation, were selected on the basis of the stories they had to share, and were now revealing themselves to Coutinho (and, vicariously, to us) in front of the camera.

As soon as the conversation between Mary Sheyla and Eduardo Coutinho starts, we learn that she, the first character, is herself an actress. The distinction between "actress" and "non-actress" on which the film allegedly turns appears to be more complex than it seems. As in the inaugural scene of the theater, Mary Sheyla, too, reacts to the question "Who's there?," a question that is here posed tacitly, by the mere fact that she *is* there to share her life story with us. And she, too, reacts to it not with an answer that settles the question and brings closure to the dramatic conflict, but with another question, rhetorical in appearance, which nonetheless unsettles the appearance of rhetoric and emphasizes the constitutive situationality of the "who" being addressed: "Como é que eu, negra, sem estrutura nenhuma, vou entrar numa de ser atriz?" The intimation is clear: being "Black" (and a woman, as the gendered adjective in Portuguese reminds us) and "lacking [social and economic] structure" stand in the way of acting. She, Black, woman, poor, "who didn't even finish the fourth grade" and as a kid, owing to the logic of a drunken system ("é a embriaguez, né, do sistema"), desired to become one of the (white, blond, and blue-eyed) Paquitas on Rede Globo's *Show da Xuxa* despite not having "pele clara, olho azul, e nem cabelo bom" (light skin, blue eyes, or good hair)—she *acted* against all odds. The hurdles against acting on the theatrical stage mimic the hurdles that stood in the way of acting on the broader social stage.

Despite the obstacles, Mary Sheyla, as we learn, was eventually able to join the theatrical group *Nós do Morro* run by Guti Fraga at the favela of Vidigal, in Rio de Janeiro, where she had now been acting for ten years. There, in the theater, she tells Coutinho, she had learned to read, to interpret, to become a woman, to become a person.[5] When asked about her current role on the stage, she reveals that she plays Joana, the protagonist of Chico Buarque and Paulo Fontes's *Gota d'água*, an adaptation to the context of a twentieth-century Brazilian favela of Euripides's ancient tragedy *Medea*. Once again, it seems, the social and the theatrical stages reveal their shifting boundaries. Talking about her role, Mary Sheyla emphasizes Joana's strength in face of adversity at the same time that she identifies with her—'Ela é forte, né, eu gosto da Joana porque ela é forte. Eu empresto a minha força pra ela. Ela foi traída, né, coisa e tal. E ela mata os filhos" (She's strong, you know, I like Joana because she's strong. I lend her my force. She was betrayed, you know that thing. And she kills her kids). In doing so, she anticipates many of the themes—motherhood, strength, resignation, betrayal, courage—that will run through the stories that the remaining twelve women in Coutinho's *Jogo de cena* will share. As João Moreira Salles remarked in the commented track of the film's DVD, she becomes a synthesis of the entire film. Interestingly enough, if Mary Sheyla's story, to the extent that it focuses solely on her relationship to acting and the theater, approximated her, in the economy of the film, to the well-known actresses who would soon appear on-screen, it was by means of the citation of a fictional role written for the theatrical stage that she would come closer to the anonymous women, the non-actresses who, agreeing to come before the camera to share fragments of their own lives, would enact their own stories of motherhood, strength, resignation, and courage on the stage of Teatro Glauce Rocha to an audience that was both there and not there.

"Who's there?" As we continue to watch the film, we are led to ask the question again and again. After the cut that takes Mary Sheyla off the screen, a second woman comes to the stage. This time, however, we do not follow her ascension from the stairwell; no moving camera shows us her arrival before she arrives, complicating through the moving image of the present the relationship between before and after. The frame is now fixed, and we see an empty seat waiting for her. She enters the frame and takes her seat as she greets Coutinho, who is outside the frame, to our side of the picture plane. She then begins to share her story: her dreams, a pregnancy, the interruption of her dreams, a complicated relationship. Then, following a straight cut, another face fills the frame, repeats her last sentence—a sentence that, perhaps coincidentally, emphasizes both a coupling (through the figure of marriage) and a blurring of focus: "Então eu saí um pouco do foco do casamento" (Then I stepped out of the marriage's focus a bit)—and continues where she left off, in the first person, as though the story were her own, as though two were one. To a Brazilian audience, that second face would be promptly recognizable, that of well-known actress Andréa Beltrão. To an audience less familiar with the Brazilian Rede Globo star-system (the same system, incidentally, that kindled Mary Sheyla's impossible dream of becoming a Paquita), the fact that two different people seemed to share the same story, telling it in the first person with no solution of continuity, would itself be enough reason to pause.

Several minutes later, after five other women—actresses and non-actresses, singular and double—had made their appearance in front of the camera to share their stories, a sixth woman comes to the stage to tell a story fragment that we have heard before. A straight cut separates her from—and connects her to—the woman who came before her. This time, no ascension from the stairwell to the stage; no empty seat waiting for her arrival. The straight cut takes us from one face to the other, with minimal change in the way they are framed. When she makes her appearance, the sixth woman—her name is Jeckie Brown, but we do not know it yet, nor will Coutinho be the one to tell it to us—is in the middle of a gesture, one hand on her face, pensive, the other hand in midair, her conversation with Coutinho already in progress. He has asked her a question we do not hear, the content of which we can only surmise by her response. She talks about the adversities she has faced and the conviction that all she went through made her, in the end, stronger. After another straight cut, Coutinho refers to the rap group of which she is a part, asking her to sing to the camera some lyrics of her own, to which she agrees.[6] As we listen to the lyrics, we catch fragments of a story already familiar to us:

> Jaqueline Ferreira Gonçalves
> Neguinha pequenininha do cabelo de Canecalon
> E tinha o sonho de ser Paquita do Show da Xuxa, mas que ilusão:
> Não tinha pele clara, olho azul, e nem cabelo bom . . .
> Eu, Jeckie Brown, tinha um estilo muito louco . . .
> Mesmo assim na minha época eu era discriminada
> Agora, em 2006, eu tô na moda, tô no *Nós do Morro*
> Cresci, venci, sobrevivi. Tenho 27, tenho *dread*
> E me chamam de Jeckie.
>
> (Jaqueline Ferreira Gonçalves/ Little Black girl with Kanekalon hair / And I dreamed of being Paquita on the *Show da Xuxa*, but what an illusion:/ I didn't have light skin, blue eyes, nor good hair . . . / I, Jeckie Brown, had a very crazy style . . . / Even so in my day I was discriminated / Now, in 2006, I'm in vogue, I'm in *Nós do Morro* / I grew up, I won, I survived. Now I'm 27, I have dreads/ And they call me Jeckie)

The spectator will recognize some of the references from a previous conversation: the dream of becoming "Paquita do Show da Xuxa," the obstacles that stood in its way, the reference to the theatrical group *Nós do Morro*.

We have heard those references in the story that Mary Sheyla, the first unnamed woman to appear in *Jogo de cena*, shared with Coutinho in the beginning of the film. Once again, the film invites us to ask its inaugural question: Who's there? Who is speaking, and in the name of whom? Yet more interesting perhaps than engaging in detective work to ascertain the ownership of the words uttered,[7] and more illuminating of the dynamics of *Jogo de cena* as a film, is to call attention to the circumstances in which the story has been told, the context of its utterance. The revealing bits of information—Jeckie Brown's name, the fragments of her story that overlap with that of Mary Sheyla—were delivered as lyrics in a song. As such, they are pieces in a language game whose rules we cannot be certain and whose subscription to factual veracity is, at best, facultative.

These series of duplicity—two voices and two bodies sharing the same discursive "I," seemingly factual statements uttered in a context (a song, a theater stage, a film that presents itself as a game) whose relationship to factual statements is noncommitted and ambivalent—threaten to unsettle the foundation of trust on which our relationship to Coutinho's documentary was initially built, the pact to which we had tacitly subscribed, our willingness to believe. We then remember the game and its circumstances: it is a staging game, *um jogo de cena*. It takes place on the stage, that space of *otherness itself*, we will recall, where everything and everyone is always already both self and other, subject to a radical duplicity. Whenever an actor enters the stage and says "I," or acts in her own name, the grammatical first person is both split and multiplied: it becomes, through its very performance, original utterance, and citation, I and "I," act and act. By choosing to juxtapose two faces in one I, two voices in one story—and doing so again and again, as these are not the only instances of such duplicity in *Jogo de cena*—Coutinho gives, through the literality of his operation—a literal doubling up: literally two persons, literally two voices, literally two faces[8]—a visual, narrative, and performative articulation to what is, no more or less (which in this case means *both* more *and* less) the logic—dialectical, dialogical, paralogical—of representation.

Fiction's Back Door

Ter fé é difícil. Recuperar a fé é muito difícil.

(Having faith is difficult. Recovering faith is very difficult.)

—Eduardo Coutinho, *Últimas conversas*

Faced with this uncertainty, we grope for reassurance: we want to hold onto our initial assumptions, to that straightforward kind of trust that we had learned to expect from Coutinho's films and the transparency of his method. We remember, hopeful, the first image of the film, the silent still of the newspaper. But was it really silent, that still image? Was it really still? Did not the open audio channel that accompanied it, and the white noise that ensued, insert in the very core of that stillness a reminder and a remainder of the passing of time, an opening that took us from a singular here-and-now to a shareable, citable, and repeatable there-and-then? The newspaper ad, we insist, reassured us that what we were watching was a "documentary film," not a work of fiction. Real persons were invited to audition for it; they called in response to the invitation, were selected for the stories they had to share and were now opening themselves up to Coutinho in front of the camera. But what kind of documentary requires that its participants *audition* for it? What can indeed be believed? What can indeed be doubted?

It is this state of uncertainty that is the birthplace of the scene of fiction that Coutinho's film offers us, the matrix of his *jogo de cena*. Fiction takes place at the intersection of belief and disbelief, the offspring of their irreducible dialectics. The mise-en-scène, all mise-en-scènes, are made of this duplicity, of this explosion of the one into the many: things and people are what they are: props, actors, elements of scenography, words uttered right there and then; yet, at the same time, in the same gesture, they are something else: a present that is past and can only be re-presented, that can *only*—and can *never*—be repeated.

This dialectic is embodied with striking clarity in Fernanda Torres's performance in *Jogo de cena*, one of the three well-known actresses in the film, as it relates to that of Aleta, the non-actress of whom she plays, as it were, the double. It could be said that both Fernanda's and Aleta's appearances are reenactments of all the other appearances in *Jogo de cena* to this point. In the economy of the film, their performances play the role, as it were, of a play within a play.⁹

As with Mary Sheyla, the film's first character, we too follow Aleta's ascension from the stairwell to the stage of Teatro Glauce Rocha, where the conversation with Coutinho will take place. Once again, we do so from the point of view of the camera that follows her, watching her from behind, listening to her footsteps. This time, however, Aleta acknowledges the camera and speaks to it. Through her remarks as she climbs the stairs, we learn that the pace of her ascension is dictated by the pace of the camera ("Tá rápido"); we hear, as the stairs seem to go on indefinitely ("Ai, que nunca acaba isso!"), her own representation in dramatic fashion of her spectacular arrival on the stage ("Tchan-ram!"); and as she arrives on the stage, she acknowledges, for the first time in the film, the presence of other people on stage ("Quanta gente!"), the filming crew that, outside the frame and therefore unacknowledged by the camera, makes up an integral part of the circumstances of the mise-en-scène, and is as such fundamental to the existence of *Jogo de cena* the film itself. As Aleta takes her seat and repeats, with visible surprise, her last interjection ("Muita gente!"), Coutinho greets her and acknowledges her reaction. He does so, however, in a telling way. Instead of acknowledging it as that which it seemed to represent (her surprise, her nervousness), he approaches it as if it were a line in a script, referring to it as a nice "phrase" that had not yet been used in the film (" 'Muita gente,' boa, ninguém disse essa frase ainda"). His reaction is followed by a straight cut, and what follows is the same interaction reenacted again, this time with Fernanda Torres in the role of Aleta. Once again, Fernanda Torres remarks on the human circumstances of the mise-en-scène ("Nossa, quanta gente, hein!"); once again, Coutinho addresses the remarks as though they were precisely what they were: lines in a script. He then goes on to greet Fernanda not as Aleta, but as Fernanda herself, emphasizing however what she did "exactly like her" ("Fernanda, você fez igualzinho como ela, que começou do começo . . ."), to which Fernanda, with a nervous smile and pointing to one of the cruxes of the film, replies: "É mentira, né?" (It's a lie, isn't it?).

We arrive here at the core of the film, its moment of unconcealed truth. Yet we note with perplexity that what the unconcealed truth of the film seems to reveal to us is its status as a lie. Like the Liar Paradox—the sentence that asserts its own falsehood, and in doing so breaks with the logic that allows us to understand it as either true or false—*Jogo de cena* breaks with the logic that clearly distinguishes fiction from nonfiction, representation from presentation, act from act. In the film, this leads Fernanda Torres into the articulation, to Coutinho and to the camera, of her own crisis of representation. She seems at times to hesitate, at times to forget her lines, at times to address Coutinho as Aleta and at times as Fernanda, at times to represent and at times to present to us her own thoughts regarding her representation and its failure. We witness Fernanda Torres the actress breaking character, reflecting on the obstacles that stand between her person and her persona, as well as between her persona and Aleta's person. She remarks on the temporal gap that splits representation from the present—now past—which it attempts to re-present ("Parecia que a minha memória estava mais lenta que a dela . . . Parece que a fala vem antes de você ter visto") (It seemed like my memory was slower than hers . . . It seems like the speech comes before you have seen it). Interestingly, as she contrasts the difficulties involving the representation of a real character (who, being fully realized, reminds the actress of the degree to which she falls short) with those of a fictional character (who, being a work in progress, is given its own reality by the actress' performance and exists as such), she seems to present us with the reversal of what Coutinho had once said regarding his own practice of documentary making. At the time of the production of *Babilônia 2000*, Coutinho had contrasted the freedom that dealing with real people allowed him with the restrictions involved in the adaptation of a fictional work to the cinema:

> Fazer uma adaptação de um livro . . . Hoje eu não quero nem ouvir falar disso, porque eu já entro culpado, eu já entro vencido, eu tenho que corresponder ao parâmetro . . . Vou fazer *Angústia*, do Graciliano Ramos: eu já entro vencido, tenho de corresponder no cinema à grandeza do livro do Graciliano. Agora, um filme sobre a passagem do século numa favela. Bom de fazer porque nesse caso o ponto de partida é um zero. Eu não tenho que esperar nada, eu vou conversar com os caras, vamos ver o que vai dar.
>
> (Making an adaptation of a book . . . Today I don't want even to hear talk of this, because I already begin blamed, defeated, I must compare closely to the text . . . I am going to make *Angústia*, by Graciliano Ramos: I already begin defeated, I must compare closely in film to the greatness of Graciliano's book. Now, a film about the transition of centuries in a favela. It's good to make because in this case the point of departure is zero. I don't have to wait for anything, I am going to talk with the guys, we'll see what comes out of it.) (Coutinho 59)

It seems that we have entered the territory of fiction unexpectedly and through an unusual route. Instead of arriving at it through the front door—clearly marked, highly ornamented, tirelessly guarded by the vigilant eye of nonfiction—we have reached it, inadvertently, as it were through the back door. This unannounced, unspectacular entrance into the territory of fiction demands of us a painful revision of our horizon of expectations, instituting, as we go, different conditions of engagement to the work at hand. It requires a rewriting of the customary pact, a radical revision of its parameters. What is asked of us is no longer the Coleridgean "willing suspension of disbelief" that allows us to accept temporarily—and in the comfort of the certainty that it is so—the implausibility of a world of make-believe that we know not to be our own. Rather, more demandingly, it is the *unwilling suspension of our belief* that is required of us, unsettling that which we take for granted, taking from us both the comfort that comes with our certainties and the comfort of knowing that we have momentarily escaped from them. Entering fiction through its back door, subject to an unwilling suspension of belief, we are allowed neither full acceptance nor full rejection, but an attitude that, including neither, to some degree includes both.

At the risk of reading too much into it—but is that not the risk involved in all acts of interpretation, Fernanda's in her interpretation of Aleta, my own in the writing of this chapter, the reader's in the reading of it?—I want to point out last what is possibly a remarkable coincidence between Aleta's appearance, Fernanda's performance, and the questions put forth by Coutinho's *Jogo de cena*. It pertains to the story of Aleta's name, which we hear not from Aleta herself, but (perhaps significantly) from Fernanda Torres as she plays Aleta. The story of her name is itself the story of a double origin. On the one hand, we learn it comes from Hal Foster's *Prince Valiant*, an adaptation to the comic strip format of the fantastic Arthurian England, where Aleta, Queen of the Misty Islands, is Prince Valiant's sweetheart. On the other hand, we are told that Aleta comes from *aletheia*, the Greek word for truth in the sense of revelation or unveiling.[10] That *Jogo de cena*'s moment of unconcealed truth—the honest revelation of its status as a lie—should have come about as we listened to *Aleta*'s story—and that her name should partake of a double origin not unlike the duplicity at the center of *Jogo de cena*'s staging game—should perhaps give us pause. What is, after all, in a name?

༄

Jogo de cena. Mise-en-scène. A game of staging. *Playing*. The provocation contained in the title of Coutinho's *Jogo de cena*, its invitation to us, is carried on to the setting on which the film is staged. Inside an empty theater, the women speaking turn their backs to the vacant seats of a spectral audience and face instead Coutinho, to whom they tell their stories, and that other eye, as attentive as it is indifferent: the camera. The presence of the camera, always acknowledged in Coutinho's films, and the presence of Coutinho himself, remind us of the performative paradox at the root of his own brand of *cinéma vérité* and indeed, perhaps, of all acting (in all senses of the word): that which, borrowing the term from the social sciences (or, why not, from physics) we could call the "observer's paradox": to which extent does the awareness of the camera, or the awareness of the other who observes us and listens to us as we speak, influence, affect, render impossible, *or make possible* a certain kind of spontaneity? Rather than merely blurring the lines between acting and non-acting, between playing and doing, between acting and *acting*, Coutinho's *Jogo de cena*, I hope to have suggested, instead displays the knot that binds them together.

Let us not forget, to conclude, something that is so obvious that it runs the risk of being overlooked. The women inside the empty theater who share or represent, or share *and* represent, their stories with Coutinho and the camera are also sharing them with us, the audience. But we have access to their performance, to their exploration of the ambiguities of representation and reality, through shadows projected on a screen. We, the audience in the theater room—literally embodying the seats in the room, filling them with our bodies—we are faced, as the film begins, with women facing us as they face the empty lens of a camera while turning their backs to the empty seats of a symbolic audience. *Jogo de cena*. Mise-en-scène. A game of scene, a game of staging. As the inversion of point of view the end of the film suggests—for the first time we see the stage, for the first time we, the beholders, occupy our own seats—we, too, perhaps, are already implicated in the game to which the title of the film refers.

Notes

1. I borrow this definition of "theatricality" from Michael Fried, who developed it both in his 1967 essay "Art and Objecthood" and subsequently in the 1980 book *Absorption and Theatricality*. However, I diverge from Fried in that he sees theatricality's dependence on the circumstances of the work of art—its situation or context—as a threat to its internal integrity, whereas I see that dependence as inseparable from and to a significant degree constitutive of it.

2. Such has long been the aspiration of theory, whose purportedly removed point of view betrays a desire for a neutrality and objectivity that fails to take into account the dialectical role of the observing subject in the constitution of the observed object. Only relatively recently has contemporary science begun to problematize this assumption and embrace the relative situationality of observer

and observed, outside and inside, as in Kurt Gödel's Incompleteness Theorem or Werner Heisenberg's Uncertainty Principle. Or, to mention a more recent example, this time from the social sciences, and alluded to by Coutinho himself in one of his interviews, that of Pierre Bourdieu's critique of the positivist belief in epistemological purity: "The positivist dream of an epistemological state of perfect innocence has the consequence of masking the fact that the crucial difference is not between a science which effects a construction and one which does not, but between a science which does this without knowing it and one which, being aware of this, attempts to discover and master as completely as possible the nature of its inevitable acts of construction and the equally inevitable effects which they produce" (Bourdieu 18). Along similar lines, Samuel Weber, in his analysis of Plato's allegory of the cave in *Republic*, highlights the importance of the spectator's relativity of point of view: "The cave dwellers do not understand what they see, not because they are blind . . . but because they are bound—unable to get up and move about, and thereby to experience the *relativity* of their point of view. Their positions are fixed and stable, but the very stability of their point of view prevents them from seeing it as *situationally conditioned*. They have never known any other position, or situation, and therefore are not aware of the relations that frame the situation from which they see. Lack of alternative experience and force of habit make what they see and hear seem entirely natural" (5). On theory as a "view from nowhere," see Thomas Nagel's classic work *The View from Nowhere*.

3. Cf. Michael Fried's characterization of a theatrical sensibility as one concerned "with the actual circumstances in which the beholder encounters [the] work," the experience of "an object in a *situation*—one that, virtually by definition, *includes the beholder*" (Fried, "Art" 153). Later Fried will connect *theatricality* with "the awareness of an audience, of being beheld"—an awareness that plays an important role in Coutinho's *Jogo de cena* (Fried, *Absorption* 99).

4. Although production notes state that of a total of eighty-three women who responded to the ad, twenty-three were selected and filmed—and Coutinho himself repeats the same information in the commented track of the DVD—in the final documentary, only thirteen women (including the actresses) appear.

5. "Lá eu aprendi muitas coisas. Lá eu aprendi a ser gente, aprendi a ser mulher, aprendi a ler. A ler um texto. A interpretar."

6. Incidentally, as Coutinho asks her for a song, a somewhat comic moment in the film takes place. He inadvertently asks her, as it were, to become two in one, singing live to the camera while at the same time performing the accompanying vocal percussion.

7. With some research one can find out that Mary Sheyla was actually born in the community of Vidigal, whereas Jeckie Brown was not, and therefore the evidence points, at least partly, to Mary Sheyla's appropriating and reenacting Jeckie Brown's story. See Ursula de Almeida Rösele's *O Jogo com a cena documentária* (83).

8. My insistence throughout this essay in referring to "voice," "face," and "person" as related concepts, and often enumerating them in the same sentence, is

not completely arbitrary. I am thinking of their common origin in the theatrical notion of *persona*. "Persona" comes from the Latin and refers to "mask" or the "character played by an actor." The origin of the Latin "persona," in its turn, is itself subject of a double narrative. The nineteenth-century traditional explanation traced it back to the Latin *per sonare* (to "sound through") in reference to the fact that it was through the holes in the actor's mask that his voice sounded through. More recent scholarship, however, traces it back to the Greek "prósōpon" (face, appearance, mask), from which words such as prosopopoeia have its origins.

9. Like all reenactments, however, they are reenactments with a difference. One could think here of the words we use to speak of repetition in our ordinary language: the Portuguese expressions "de novo" and "novamente," pointing to what is new (novo) and unprecedented in the act of repetition, or the English "again," inscribing in its body the mark of a constitutive difference (it shares its root with the preposition "against"), while at the same time indicating a surplus ("a-gain," "at a gain") vis-à-vis the original it iterates. As Derrida reminds us in "Signature, Event, Context," referring to the etymology of *iterability*: "*iter*, again, probably comes *itara*, *other* in Sanskrit, and everything that follows can be read as the working out of the logic that ties repetition to alterity" (7).

10. In contemporary philosophy, Martin Heidegger is responsible for the renewed interest in the concept of *aletheia*, which plays a central role in his *Being and Time*. Heidegger made a distinction between truth as *aletheia* (which he translated from the Greek as *Unverborgenheit*, usually rendered into English as "unconcealment") and other conceptions of truth such as that of truth as *adequatio* or "correspondence."

Works Cited

Bernardet, Jean-Claude. "Jogo de cena." *Eduardo Coutinho*, edited by Milton Ohata, Cosac Naify, 2013, pp. 627–36.

———. "Ismail Xavier e Jean-Claude Bernardet," transcribed by Cleber Eduardo. *Contracampo,* http://www.contracampo.com.br/53/ismailbernardet.htm

Bourdieu, Pierre. "Understanding." *Theory, Culture and Society*, vol. 13, no. 2, 1996, pp. 17–37.

Coutinho, Eduardo, and José Carlos Avellar. "O vazio do quintal." *Eduardo Coutinho*, edited by Milton Ohata, Cosac Naify, 2013, pp. 251–83.

Derrida, Jacques. "Signature, Event, Context." *Limited Inc*. Translated by Samuel Weber and Jeffrey Mehlman, Northwestern UP, 1988, pp. 1–24.

Foucault, Michel. "Of Other Spaces, Heterotopias." *Diacritics*, vol. 16, no. 1, 1986, pp. 22–27.

Fried, Michael. *Absorption and Theatricality*. U of Chicago P, 1980.

———. *Art and Objecthood*. U of Chicago P, 1998.

Rösele, Ursula de Almeida. *O Jogo com a cena documentária: um estudo do filme Jogo de Cena, de Eduardo Coutinho*. 2011. Universidade Federal de Minas Gerais, Master's thesis.

Torres, Fernanda. "No dorso instável de um tigre." *Revista Piauí*, vol. 3, December 2006.

Weber, Samuel. *Theatricality as Medium*. Fordham UP, 2004.

Xavier, Ismail. "Indagações em torno de Eduardo Coutinho e seu diálogo com a tradição moderna." *Comunicação e Informação*, vol. 7, no. 2, 2004, pp. 180–87.

9

Song, Self, and Sound in Eduardo Coutinho's Cinema

FERNANDO PÉREZ VILLALÓN

This chapter argues for the centrality of sound and music in Eduardo Coutinho's films, focusing on the importance of the acts of speaking, singing, and listening in his documentary work, from *Cabra marcado para morrer* (1964–1984) to the posthumous *Últimas conversas* (2015). Seen retrospectively, Coutinho's output throughout fifty years of filming seems remarkably coherent in spite of the many topics and the wide variety of social and geographical landscapes it explores. His films are focused on a particular kind of inquiry into people's everyday lives through conversation, strongly characterized by an ethical refusal to situate himself above those he calls his "characters" ("*personagens*") and sustained by a set of rigorous and remarkably stable procedures. As is well-known, these generally include the absence of some of the usual features of documentary filmmaking: voice-over commentary or interpretation, nondiegetic music, and archival footage. Coutinho's films normally lack a script and are structured instead by what the director calls an "apparatus" ("*dispositivo*"), best understood as a set of rules and constraints (typically a time and space framework within which to choose the people who will participate in his films and a very wide topic that serves as a starting point for conversations that often wander in unexpected directions). His work usually involves extended nondirective interviews conducted by the director himself, who is very much aware of the paradox of a directing style that consists mostly of asking very general questions and then listening with open ears and a nonjudgmental attitude to what people have to say. His voice and his constant off-screen presence (entering the frame at times) are a central part of his authorial signature, as is the verbal vitality of subjects who are allowed to speak their minds freely in front of a camera that is interested in understanding who they are rather than using them as examples of a predefined thesis, as sources of information about a given problem, or as defenders of certain opinions about the world. In fact, Coutinho almost always consciously avoided encouraging people to express their opinions, convinced that such an approach would only give them a chance to restate worn clichés and preconceived notions, as well as offering what they thought the "TV reporters" (as Coutinho's team is often referred to) would want to hear.

This is one of many possible examples that suggest that Coutinho's nondirective method is not at all merely passive, and it involves a kind of listening that is far from interested in just anything, and in fact is searching for a very peculiar kind of testimony, one that reveals the characters' identity in a way that goes beyond socially or self-constructed stereotypes, or rather one that pushes stereotypes to the point where the reality underlying them becomes apparent. His interviewing style was thus carefully honed over time to achieve the epiphanic moments that constitute the core of his films. A central aspect of his procedure is the fact that he does not meet the subjects that he will interview on camera before shooting, so what we see on the screen is a unique event (although the characters have been interviewed, and often recorded, by Coutinho's team, without the director's presence, as part of the preparation for every film). Coutinho's listening has been compared with that of a therapist, and even with that of a secular confessor, and indeed his characters will sometimes reveal intensely private secrets, intimate feelings, and shameful or painful family dramas, but this does not seem to be what Coutinho is looking for, or at least not exclusively. Drama, or melodrama, is only one of the aspects of life that Coutinho's movies explore. They are equally interested in so-called normality, uneventfulness, and all the little nothings that most people's lives consist of (because when looked at closely they appear to be far stranger and much more unique or complicated than they seem at first sight). Unlike a therapist's or a confessor's, however, Coutinho's listening does not attempt to provide any kind of absolution or resolution of conflicts, although perhaps it does offer a kind of cinematic redemption, an on-screen afterlife for his characters where they are endowed with a dignity that may have been denied to them in their everyday surroundings. The price they pay for obtaining such "immortality" is being laid bare before the cinematic apparatus, which registers their performance with an attention that no human eye could provide; and which preserves, reproduces, and amplifies it until it becomes something that no longer belongs to them.

Over the years, Coutinho's interviewing method increasingly focused not so much on what people say, on the information they deliver before the camera, but rather on the way they say it, in what Roland Barthes called "the grain of the voice," and on the many ways that an audiovisual register captures tiny bodily and vocal expressive gestures that are symptomatic of aspects of their identity that the characters or the director may not even be aware of (a sort of optical and acoustic unconscious). Thus, the vacillations, reticence, stutters, changes in tone, rhetorical outbursts, and moments of silence become of paramount importance. Coutinho's ear is attentive not only to the semantic, but also to the sonic and performative properties of people's voices as a fundamental area of inquiry. As Consuelo Lins puts it, often the force or the truth stated by the characters in Coutinho's documentaries does not lie in what they are telling, but "in the act of telling it, in the way they express themselves, in the gestures, looks, silences in a conversation, in the sentences' construction, in the words chosen" (Lins, "O cinema" 193, my translation). This approach may be related to a rejection of what Walter Benjamin, one of Coutinho's constant intellectual referents, famously called the "bourgeois conception of language," for which language is only a means of communicating certain pre-given contents, whereas, actually, in any statement it is language that expresses itself through us.[1]

I believe that the mode of listening is deeply rooted in Coutinho's documentary ethics, in a documentary style that does not propose theses or opinions about the world or compile information about certain topics, but rather seeks to provide a context where a revelation of the self in dialogue is possible. This revelation of the self is not at all purely individual: the fact that it happens only in the context of conversation shows that it is profoundly social and political, an instance of dialogism in the Bakhtinian sense.[2]

In *The Voice in Cinema*, Michel Chion argues that film sound has always been vococentric; this is particularly true of Coutinho's films, which rarely feature any actions except talking. His films show people engaged in an act of telling, and in this act a lot more than the specific content of what they tell is revealed, as the camera captures facial, bodily, and linguistic gestures that are often more eloquent than the narrators realize, gestures that make visible several layers of unconscious affective states, ideological and moral convictions, and zones of reticence that become symptomatic of unspoken layers of memory.[3] We, as spectators, are invited to witness these intimate revelations that do not take place solely or mainly at the level of the Said, but rather in the act of Saying, in a performance of the self that ruthlessly exposes it while at the same time carefully protects it.[4] The intensity of these revelations is not only registered and rendered visible by the camera, but also made possible by the tension its presence creates, as Coutinho repeatedly stressed. We might add that the presence of the camera and crew in the set functions also as a reminder of the fact that the performances recorded by Coutinho are potentially public, are destined to be screened, a fact of which his characters often seem very aware.

Coutinho's films dwell on the minute manifestations of this bodily, vocal, and political eloquence, seeking a truth that lies beyond the scope of what he asks his subjects and beyond what they intend to say, a truth that has more to do with the relation between those characters and us, their spectators, than with their merely personal affairs. In that sense, Coutinho's films can be said to be extremely impersonal, regardless of their exploration of people's intimate feelings and personal life stories, since they are looking for the point where those stories are about humanity at a supra—or infra-individual—level. Coutinho's films carry out a sustained anthropological investigation of how human beings experience and tell their lives, of the complex net of forces, affects, gestures, and reflexes that lies beneath the constitution of a human individual, and of the ways in which that net intersects with and is transformed through contact with others, mainly through dialogue. This explains the centrality for his project of the speaking and singing voice, as a site of access to these questions, and as a place of encounter between the private and the public, the individual and the political, the extraordinary and the everyday. These contrasting pairs are perhaps for Coutinho not so much opposites as complementary aspects of the phenomena his cinema is setting out to comprehend, as we discuss in more detail below.

The Search of a Voice: *Cabra marcado para morrer*

As I wrote earlier, *retrospectively* considered, Coutinho's filmography seems of an almost single-minded coherence, but when considered in its chronological evolution (as Consuelo Lins's excellent *O documentário de Eduardo Coutinho* does), a different picture emerges, more dialectical and dynamic, including tentative experiences and procedures that do not always work, several partial failures and successes, and a very gradual discovery of his authorial voice. Only the director's untimely death could interrupt his search for new ways to achieve his goals, rather than resting on his laurels. As we can see in the footage of *Últimas conversas* where we hear Coutinho complaining that the film won't work, that he has lost his touch, that it's no good, this constant search was not without anguish, creative blockages, and moments of hopelessness. His collaborators attest that these fits of discouragement occurred during all his projects, and perhaps part of the thrill of watching a Coutinho documentary, of the paradoxical suspense that it produces, has to do with the fact that we feel that we are witnessing stages of a process whose outcome is not defined from the start. Most of Coutinho's films include surprises, unexpected detours, changes of direction, and most importantly improvisation, unplanned responses to what emerges during the shooting.

Cabra marcado para morrer (1964–1984), the film that established Coutinho's reputation as an innovative documentary filmmaker, is built around the tension between an earlier, unfinished fiction film, shot in 1964 with local workers as actors, about the assassination of farm labor organizer João Pedro Teixeira, and the return to that material nearly twenty years later. Coutinho made a different film structured around the testimonies of the people involved in the original film, in particular João Pedro's widow, Elizabeth Teixeira, who comes out of hiding to give her testimony and becomes the movie's central figure.

From the perspective of sound, it is in many ways a rather conventional film. It features incidental music that contributes to the film's geographical and emotional atmosphere, including a score by Rogério Rossini and songs by Carlos Lyra,[5] among others, devices that Coutinho's later films would strictly avoid (together with any nondiegetic sound). Watching *Cabra marcado* in contrast with those later films, it is clear why: the music artificially underlines the film's most intensely emotional moments.[6] A very clear instance of this happens when, while the camera shows us an image of João Pedro's grave, the off-screen narrator declares, "Not ever a photo is left of João Pedro alive" ("De João Pedro vivo não sobrou sequer uma fotografia"). We are then shown a photograph of his dead body, and after a moment of highly charged silence, we hear dissonant music played by a keyboard, flute, and guitar, leading us to a sequence of images of João Pedro's abandoned former house. The flute flows freely, in a melody lacking a clear tonality, over a sustained chord played by the keyboard (including what seem to be sampled voices), clashing with the tense harmonies of the guitar's metallic strings, played in a percussive style. Meanwhile, the handheld camera circles the house, walking on its veranda. It meets a dog's friendly, puzzled stare and approaches the closed shutters, while a voice-over comments on the house's aspect. If the lack of commentary about the photograph seems to suggest that the image should speak for itself, the music interrupts the image's silence, intensifying the spectator's emotional response, an effect that Coutinho would later consider manipulative and artificial (while, in opposition to the idea that images might speak for themselves, he would concentrate almost exclusively on images of people speaking). Throughout the film, music often enhances visual materials by "commenting" on them: Rossini's music is not seductive or easily pleasant, but rather harsh-sounding and dissonant. It does not easily merge with the images but rather distances itself from them, while at the same time effectively underlining their dramatic qualities.

In addition to Rossini's score, the film's sound features three voice-over narrators whose voices provide contextual information (also something that Coutinho would later avoid): Eduardo Coutinho himself, the poet Ferreira Gullar, and the journalist and writer Tite de Lemos. His later films would normally feature only the director's voice in dialogue with his interviewees, providing very minimal introductions, and no voice-over commentary at all. The use of voice-over narrators may have been inevitable in this film, given the interplay of historical times that lies at its center, the distance between the original footage and the very different film that Coutinho would end up making. The voice-over narrators bridge this gap between the two films, providing information about the first film and its context that does not appear in the interviews with the earlier film's original cast. Coutinho's later films, in contrast, would mostly focus on the present image of the telling of past events, making no effort to bridge the gap between both times. Unlike *Cabra marcado*, his other films often do not seem interested in the past itself but in the retelling of past events as a mise-en-scène of the present self.

The director's voice would continue to be at the center of his films, only not as a disembodied off-screen presence but as a character inhabiting the same temporality and space as the other characters in the film. Thus, Coutinho would retain only one of the modalities of his presence in *Cabra marcado*: the interviewer who converses with characters without a script, following the thread of their responses and reactions. He would not appear anymore (or only marginally) as the authoritative voice of the filmmaker giving unity to the filmed events a posteriori, but as a character, as a body with whom they can relate, a face they can look at, a presence hovering on the edges of the frame, and sometimes entering it.

Even though much in this film's use of sound is conventional, there are nevertheless a couple of remarkable things about it. The first one is the

Song, Self, and Sound in Eduardo Coutinho's Cinema | 203

fact that most of the footage of the 1964 fiction film included in the 1984 film and shown to people who participated in it as nonprofessional actors (and who are filmed watching their younger selves projected on the screen) is featured as silent except for a couple of scenes (not incidentally, one of them focuses on the Teixeira family singing a song together). This introduces a strong dialectical tension between image and sound along the lines of what Sergei Eisenstein called audiovisual counterpoint, as the voiceless images are confronted with a verbal commentary that inscribes them in a different temporality.[7] Coutinho would later avoid this temporal anachronism between sound and image, characteristic of documentaries that deal with past events (most of his films have direct, synchronic sound, and show exclusively images of the present, often even respecting their chronological order in the editing process).

A good example of this happens near the beginning of the film. Right after the titles, we see a night scene of people setting up a film projector and then some images, supposedly from the projected film. As we watch people going about their business in a village of rudimentary huts on a lake, a song's lyrics tell us what we are seeing: "É um país subdesenvolvido, subdesenvolvido, subdesenvolvido" (It is an underdeveloped country, underdeveloped, underdeveloped). The music's humorous and playful tone creates a kind of Brechtian distance, but we are nevertheless being given very little room to look at the images by themselves or to assign them a meaning of our own. They become inevitably instances of underdevelopment. While the music (Carlos Lyra and Francisco de Assis's "Canção do subdesenvolvido"[8]) continues in a parody of *fado* that didactically explains underdevelopment's origins in the colonial period, a voice tells us:

> Abril de 1962. Essas imagens foram filmadas durante a UNE volante, uma caravana da união nacional dos estudantes que percorreu o país para promover a discussão da reforma universitária. Com os estudantes viajavam membros do CPC, Centro Popular de Cultura da UNE, que pretendiam estimular a formação de outros centros de cultura nos estados. A imagem da miséria contrastada com a presença do imperialismo, essa era uma tendência típica na cultura daqueles tempos. Como demostra esta música, a "Canção do subdesenvolvido," um clássico do CPC.
>
> (April 1962. These images were filmed during the traveling National Student Union, a caravan that traversed the country to

> promote the discussion of university reform. With the students traveled members of the union's People's Cultural Center, whose aim was to encourage the formation of other cultural centers in the states. The image of misery contrasted with the presence of imperialism—this was a typical tendency in culture of those times. "Song of Underdevelopment," a CPC classic, is a good example.)

If, on the one hand, the voice-over here is telling us what the images are, and thus in a sense explaining them away, anchoring them in an authoritative text that fixes their meaning, it is also positioning itself in a critical distance from the eye that recorded those images (an epochal cliché), as well as situating Lyra's song in a status of historical symptom rather than didactic truth. The whole sequence is laden with bitter irony and self-criticism. Coutinho's voice comes next, narrating how while on that students' union convoy he accidentally stumbled upon what would become the theme of his film: farm labor organizer João Pedro Teixeira's assassination. In this film, the voice-over narration and commentary serve as a frame to anchor the images we are seeing,[9] calling into question their self-explanatory evidence in a self-aware critical attitude, but also depriving them of some of their visual force by turning them into illustrations of verbal discourse.

The second remarkable feature of this film's treatment of sound is the way in which its capture is highlighted, by showing the recording team's devices, to remind us that this is a film, a constructed technical device, rather than a window that would allow us to see reality directly. This would also become a characteristic feature of many of Coutinho's films, which often at some point or another will show the film crew, the camera, or the microphones that mediate our and the director's relation with the movie's characters. This is not merely a device for reminding us that we are not being shown truths but only representations: it can actually be better characterized as a gesture that underlines the fact that the truth can only be arrived at, if at all, through such self-reflective mediations.

Around the middle of the film, we watch Coutinho interviewing João Mariano, the actor who in the original film had played the assassinated labor leader. This interview provides an interesting contrast with Coutinho's later methods, but it also highlights in a fascinating way the film's relation with sound recording. First we see an establishing shot (of a kind the director would later completely suppress), while Coutinho explains in voice-over that João Mariano has become the leader of a Baptist congregation and that he was taken by surprise by the interview (also something that Coutinho would later avoid, as in his subsequent movies interviewees are selected through a casting process and given the opportunity to prepare themselves before the interviews, which do not attempt to catch them "off guard"). Coutinho and João Mariano are sitting around a table on a village street, and the first is holding a large microphone in his hands. João Mariano, visibly uncomfortable, looks away, avoiding the gaze of both the camera and the director, as he explains that he has distanced himself from any kind of revolutionary movements, covering, in what seems a protective reflex, part of his face with his hand. The microphone captures his vacillating voice while also recording the street's noises, including static caused by a strong wind on the microphone. At that point Coutinho rudely interrupts him to tell him that there is too much wind to record the sound ("momentinho, senhor, tá com som, tá com vento" [Just a minute. There's too much wind.]), orders the crew to cut, fixes the problem, and then tells him that he can now go on. João Mariano falls silent, and Coutinho insists, "You can continue saying what you were saying, it's perfect, you can speak without any trouble, don't be afraid." Before his interviewee's persistent silence, Coutinho looks uncomfortably toward the cameraman, and then insists again. João Mariano resumes his testimony; visibly intimidated by the fact that he is being recorded and by the possible political consequences of what he is saying, he continues to distance himself clearly from any revolutionary movements that he might have been involved with in his youth.

The inclusion of this "failed" interview (both from a technical point of view, because of the low quality of sound, and from an ethical and even cinematic point of view, since the subject feels threatened by the film and speaks very guardedly, thus giving a clearly "inauthentic" testimony) signals an increasing interest on Coutinho's part in how the film apparatus affects its subjects. As he would later figure out, one cannot interrupt a subject to fix a technical problem and then just tell him to resume where he left off. An important characteristic of his interviews is that they are recorded continuously, something that was very costly when the director used analogue film and that became more feasible with the advent of video[10] and later digital technology, since normally the few minutes of intense testimony that we see on Coutinho's films are carefully chosen from a much longer dialogue that is required for those moments to emerge. Finally, it is also interesting to note how in this case for Coutinho ambient sound functions as an obstacle for the proper recording of the human voice, since throughout his filmography, he shows little interest in recording social or natural soundscapes (or visual landscapes, for that matter). Coutinho's listening is, as we said, *vococentric* in Chion's terms, in that it consciously zeroes in on voices and characters' verbal expression, disregarding most other sounds as irrelevant or merely interesting in their impact on his characters' declarations or on the recording process. It is thus not surprising that in his later films he would shoot in closed sets where there is no environmental sound interference. This attitude suggests that the kind of truths or epiphanic moments that Coutinho is seeking require a careful setup, a highly constructed and artificial situation, and even perhaps an isolation of subjects from their usual environment. Coutinho's subsequent filmography often explores the tension between a search for a kind of authenticity and the complex devices through which this authenticity is produced.

Song and Self: From *Boca de lixo* to *As canções*

Coutinho did not completely abandon the use of incidental, nondiegetic music in his following films, but he tended to look for a more seamless integration of the music in the filmed environment, sometimes collaborating with members of the community in the composition and recording of the music, sometimes using music derived from a place's ambient sound.[11] In addition, in many of his later films music is explored as a topic, in and of itself, as a social activity and as a cultural phenomenon that is deeply rooted in individual and collective identities.

Already in *Santa Marta*, the different places and functions of music in everyday life occupied an important place in the film, which shows dancing parties with live music, religious rituals in which music plays a prominent role (be they Catholic, Evangelical, or Candomblé), a *batucada* improvised by a group of children, and several professional musicians interpreting their compositions in front of the camera. *O fio da memória* plays tribute to the enormous importance of Afro-Brazilian heritage for Brazilian popular music, samba in particular but also in social rites in which celebration and worship intermingle closely (Carnival, processions, Candomblé rituals, and various religious ceremonies marked by syncretism). In *O fim e o princípio*, we witness the importance of music in the community's everyday life in the form of collective singing in a religious procession.

Music is also examined as a mass culture phenomenon, something that characters listen to, on the radio, TV, or various reproduction devices. The limit between music as an object of passive consumption, a commodity, and music as a self-fashioning practice is fluid. Composers or professional performers obviously express themselves through music, but Coutinho's films will become increasingly interested in the ways in which subjects can identify with a well-known song up to the point that it becomes an essential part of their identity. This idea is the thesis of *As canções*, which we discuss in more detail below, but it is also a motif that runs through many of Coutinho's films. The music we listen to defines us, but perhaps it also shapes us; the music we perform reveals us, but perhaps it also constitutes us. These are the dialectical tensions that Coutinho's subsequent work would masterfully explore.

The dynamic of identification becomes evident in a scene in *Santo forte* where we see a family absorbed on the TV showing the image of Roberto Carlos, while one of them softly sings along to himself. In the next scene a girl sings Roberto Carlos's hit "Jesus Cristo," also in front of the TV, in a very clear example of how personal identity is often formed through mimicry of the images, attitudes, and structures of feeling offered by mass media, a relevant theme for a movie exploring religious beliefs in the context of a papal visit to Brazil.[12]

If this case seems a clear instance of alienation (although Coutinho is careful not to judge and to avoid the condescending attitude toward religious belief characteristic of the classical left in Latin America), other instances are more ambivalent. When interviewing the family of one of the scavengers in *Boca de lixo*, Coutinho asks, "What do you want to be in life?" "A singer," the girl replies without hesitation. "What do you like to sing?" "Música sertaneja,"[13] the girl answers with a smile. The next image is a long take of the girl with her hands in her pockets, singing "Sonho por sonho," a very sentimental song by Chico Roque and Carlos Colla. The camera frames her in a long shot during the song's first stanza, then advances to a medium close-up on the second stanza, in which the girl sings with her eyes closed, and next juxtaposes the song's refrain with scenes of the everyday routines of her family (fig. 9.1).

The performance is far from perfect in technical terms, but it transmits a genuine intensity. Coutinho here is dangerously close to the territory of TV shows that play with the spectacle of amateurs who dream of becoming stars, and the stark contrast between the girl's dream and her reality of extreme misery is very blatant. The scene, however, is fascinating, in part because it shows that marginal citizens' lives are also constituted by their dreams, which have a reality of their own and can function as survival strategies as well as compensatory fantasies. We are won over by the sheer intensity of

Figure 9.1. A girl singing in *Boca de lixo*. Source: *Boca de lixo (Scavengers)*. Directed by Eduardo Coutinho, CECIP, 1992.

the performance, by the way in which the girl gives herself completely to the music, appropriates it, and becomes a different person when singing it, herself and at the same time an ego-ideal. Performances like this one, with its provocative rawness, can often say more about a subject's identity and self-image than verbal declarations. The tension between the imitation of a model, identifying with it as completely as possible, and the difference that necessarily emerges between the model and its reenactment, is enormously revealing of the way in which subjectivity is constituted, but it also speaks volumes about what sociologist Erving Goffman called the "presentation of Self in everyday life," characterized by him as an elaborate performance that negotiates the tensions between who I think I am and the ways in which I would like others to perceive me and treat me. The notion that our most authentic self does not fully appear when we are alone in our rooms, but when we play a role before others, in a necessarily imperfect performance, is at the core of Coutinho's cinematic aesthetic, and it implies a complex awareness of the interaction between personal identity, role-playing, and spectatorship, a set of paradoxical tensions that his film *Jogo de cena* would focus on. The performance of music seems to be particularly well suited for the exploration of these questions, since it combines affective intensity, exposure through the vulnerability of the voice, and a focus on sound over meaning, on performativity over intentions. A song is also a cultural artifact that works at the hinge point between the social and the singular, the affective and the codified emotions, and the mass-culture clichés and the uniquely creative ways to appropriate them.

Near the end of the movie, we hear the song again, in José Augusto's version, while several of the films' characters stand in front of the camera, as if posing for a portrait. The girl stands next to her parents with a portable speaker in her hands. Coutinho encourages her to sing over the recording, and so we hear her interpretation again, now following more closely the famous singer's version, and backed by his band. It is interesting that we hear the girl singing first by herself and then over the recording. Coutinho's films have registered both situations, but they would eventually choose to focus on the first one, probably because the a cappella voice is exposed in a way that an accompanied one is not. An instrument or a recorded track functions as a guide for the voice's pitch, rhythm, and even emotional inflections, but also as a protective shield that hides the voice's vulnerability by integrating into a larger sound field where its singularity is dissimulated, producing the opposite of what Coutinho is after.

Coutinho's subsequent films include several unforgettable performances, among them that of Fátima, a Janis Joplin impersonator in *Babilônia 2000* who sings a version of "Me and Bobby McGee" with invented lyrics in a nonexistent language that mimics English phonetics.[14] Unlike in *Boca de lixo*, in this case the camera stays with Fátima, singing in the open air on a hill near the Morro da Babilônia at the Pedra do Urubú, the same location, Coutinho observes, where Marcel Camus's *Black Orpheus* was filmed. The singer does indeed seem endowed with a supernatural power that goes well beyond her own personal identity. If songs are a way for subjectivity to manifest itself, they are also a connection between it and other subjects. Those who have sung the song before, those who are listening to it, those who may sing it in the future. Songs are a pattern, a field of forces with which we connect, and through which we become part of a larger temporal and affective flow. Instead of taking the music as background to show other images, or using it as a "sound bridge," to provide continuity between shots, the film lingers on the image of the singing body, recording its gestures with an attention that seems almost obscene at times (one cannot help feeling like a voyeur) but also does justice to the intensity of the performance and to Fátima's obvious pleasure in staging and sharing it with the world.

This famous scene in *Babilônia 2000* functions to a large extent because of the great effectiveness of the performance, its theatricality, and the rather high degree of skill it implies. One of the ways in which recorded musical performances work in Coutinho's films is as a source of pride for marginal individuals who do not usually get any chance of public exposure and obviously relish the opportunity to be "on TV." But not all performances recorded by Coutinho are equally successful or spectacular, and in fact the key to some is precisely their imperfection, as opposed to the standardized polish of professional musicians. *As canções* explores the question of amateur musical performances by deliberately choosing characters who, per Coutinho, sung neither too well not too badly. As he explained, "As pessoas deviam entoar a canção bem, com emoção, exprimir o sentimento com um mínimo de melodia e ritmo. Se elas cantavam bem demais, ou mal demais, não entravam" (qtd. in Maia 116; people were supposed to sing the song well, with feeling, and express emotion with a minimum of melody and rhythm. If they sang too well or too badly, they weren't included). Clearly Coutinho is trying to avoid the pitfalls of what Mladen Dolar has called the "voice as fetish object," as a sublime object of aesthetic perception and enhanced pleasure,[15] and the other extreme of the voice as unmusical failure, as displeasing spectacle at the expense of the singer's ridicule. The film's mise-en-scène is far from naturalistic: just like *Jogo de cena*, it takes place in an empty theater where the subjects are alone with the film crew. They enter through a curtain, walk toward the camera, sit on a chair, and start singing and telling their story. The fact that they are seated is not a minor detail, since it prevents them from dancing, reducing bodily expression to a minimum. In many cases, bodily expression is concentrated on the face, which becomes a fascinating affective landscape, filmed mostly in medium close-ups. Some shots do film the whole body, registering for instance the way in which a character marks the rhythm by tapping his fingers and then his palms on one knee.

Dolar has insisted on the fact that any voice (and more so the cinematic voice) is acousmatic by nature: even when we can see its source clearly, there remains a gap "which can never be quite bridged" between that source and its auditory result, the visible and the visual never really match the acoustic, and the voice remains as elusive an object as the gaze. This observation is very pertinent for *As canções*, in which the characters' voices always emerge as a surprise, a revelation, one that does not necessarily coincide with the expectations produced by the body. At the same time, as Brandon Labelle has usefully pointed out, even if the voice stems from an inaccessible interior and never fully matches its bodily origin, it also "does not move away from my body, but rather it carries it forward—the voice *stretches* me; it drags me along, as a body bound to its politics and poetics, its accents and dialectics, its grammars, as well as its handicaps" (5). The voices filmed by Coutinho emerge from his characters' bodies, but they are far from disembodied. On the contrary, they bring with them the traces of the body's interior, its resonance, its rhythms, its materiality. Thus, more in line with Adriana Cavarero's theorization, the voice functions as a manifestation of each subject's uniqueness, but it also, by bringing it out into the open, reinforces the fact that uniqueness necessarily exists in political relationality. The voice gives us information (even if equivocal) about the subject's age, gender, race, class, regional origins, suggesting that the subject is not simply the intersection of all these variables, but a more singular and elusive entity. It is thus through the voice that our bodies and subjectivities are projected into a common space, or rather come into being when being exposed to that outside. This may help to explain why Coutinho is so interested in the possibility of song as a site of intersection between the subjective and the social, sometimes even more so than in spoken language.[16] Songs, in Coutinho's film, serve as a pretext for a conversation about important events in people's lives, but they are also the film's theme, perhaps even more centrally than its human characters, as the title suggests. The movie quietly explores songs as complex cultural, affective, aesthetic objects, but also as secular rituals, mourning rites, therapeutic reenactment of traumatic events.

As canções shows us how music can effectively serve to evoke emotions (as a character remarks, in a very Proustian observation, the sense of smell and music have the power to evoke events and feelings more intensely than language, in their activation of involuntary memory), but also produce them and reproduce them in the subjects that sing them and in those that listen to them. Musical affect is by nature contagious, and spectators of Coutinho's films often find themselves with a knot in their throats or unexpected tears welling up in their eyes. The affective states evoked by a song can be very intense, but also very indeterminate: one character who suddenly breaks into tears in the middle of his performance keeps repeating, "I do not know why I am crying; this song brings up good memories of my mother, it isn't a sad song for me." We do not know if the tears come from affection toward his mother, from an association with a failed love story or the alienation from his church that he has just talked about, or simply from the affective intensity that the song brings up. Many other characters tell far sadder stories with complete serenity, which suggests that the expression of emotions is not directly related in a simple way to their content: a similar problem appears in *Jogo de cena*, when an actress cannot help crying as she reenacts someone else's story, which the woman to whom it happened tells in a very calm and collected manner (fig. 9.2).

The film does not state it, but the power of songs that it explores may be related to the fact that they not only evoke and produce emotion, but they also may be the place where many of us learned what emotions are, a place where indeterminate affective states took on a socially acceptable character, became rhetorically articulated in a series of recognizable tropes. As Irene Depetris-Chauvin puts it, some songs "become bearers or repositories of our unique and incomparable passions, in spite of the fact that they are also inscribed in the circulation of a generalized exchange of clichés" (n.p.).[17] That paradox is possible because the way that we experience our "unique and incomparable passions" has also been modeled on songs that have taught us how a "unique" passion feels, how it sounds and unfolds. The very structure of passions could, in a sense, be described as musical in its dramatic alternation of intensities, in its inexorable rhythmic flow forward

Figure 9.2. Affective responses to music in *As canções*. Source: *As canções* (*The Songs*). Directed by Eduardo Coutinho, Videofilmes, 2011.

that never reaches its goal, in its harmonic tensions that find peaceful but transitory resolutions, and particularly in its unique timbre, derived from the materiality of the bodies that produce its constitutive vibrations.

The close relation between songs and affect has to do with their equally intimate relation with memory: melodies and lyrics are often memorized, willingly or because they become unforgettable and return to haunt us (it is often remarked that music, metrical rhythm, and rhyme can serve as mnemonic devices, but also that musical hits are designed to be instantly memorable[18]), and thus they are part of our individual and collective, cultural memory (this becomes evident when Coutinho corrects one character's version of the lyrics of a Noel Rosa song). This produces another fascinating paradox: the revelation of the uniqueness of the characters in Coutinho's films through their songs and narrations is what makes possible our empathy and even identification with them: their voices resonate with us in their uniqueness, but also by adopting shapes that we recognize as our own, and by which we feel addressed in our uniqueness.

Songs are obviously a kind of music that is closely interwoven with language. Melodies are designed to follow the inflections of colloquial language, and of a specific language's distinctive features (that is why the translation of lyrics often fails spectacularly, for instance in the case of bossa nova in English). In fact, Brazilian popular music of the twentieth century is particularly characterized by its relationship with colloquial, spoken Brazilian Portuguese, starting with samba (Noel Rosa, one of the composers included in the film with his "Último desejo," is a master of composing songs that sound like spoken monologues or dialogues) and continuing with bossa nova and MPB. If some musical styles are based on marking the distance between spoken and musical language (lyrical operatic singing is the most obvious example), others (from operatic recitative to rap) attempt to give us the illusion that the singer is speaking. For instance, the power of João Gilberto's vocal style has been explained by this, and a recent tendency in Brazilian music is called "canto falado" (spoken singing).[19]

Coutinho has been described as a director who films speech (*filma a fala*). *As canções* explores the continuity between speech and song, their complementarity, their contrast but also their many shared features. The fact that we spend so much time listening to people singing on-screen makes us more acutely aware of the timbre of their voices, the characteristic rhythms of their prosody (the speed with which they speak, their pitch variations, the many non-semantic expressions with which they pepper their narrations), but in addition they allow us to take pleasure in the specific music of the

Portuguese language, which for a non-native speaker is perhaps even more musical. Everything that is said in the film becomes musically inflected because it is heard with the kind of attention that we normally reserve for music.

Listening to Images: The Echo of the Subject and the Acoustic Unconscious

In an essay titled "The Echo of the Subject," Philippe Lacoue-Labarthe attempted to understand subjectivity not as an instance of narcissism emanating from the experience of contemplating one's reflection in a mirror, but as a reverberation, a resonance, an echo chamber. His meditation starts from the realization of a persistent link between autobiographical compulsion and the phenomenon of the "haunting melody" as studied by Theodor Reik in a book of the same title. In this essay, Lacoue-Labarthe advances the possibility of using musical obsessions as a key to the rhythmic constitution of the self, in a mimetic gesture that combines typographic repetition with the singularity of a unique enunciation. Without attempting to elucidate all the philosophical implications of this argument, I would like to suggest that it provides a very productive entry point into the cinematic apparatus' production of subjectivities that are torn between the screen's magic, liquid mirror, and the acoustic mirror around us. We as spectators occupy the place where voice and body, and sound and sight, never fully coincide. If classical narrative film attempts to bridge or overcome this gap, Coutinho's documentaries explore it as the zone where affective states, bodies, subjectivities, speech acts, and social interactions can emerge, brought forth and recorded by the camera's presence. His movies often function like a truthful mirror in that they do not attempt to give us back our image (or anybody's), but rather function as an echo chamber where voices are allowed to resonate, reverberate, vibrate, and move us in unexpected ways that do not depend on the truth of what is said, but on the revelatory potential of the tone with which it is said.

Coutinho films the musicality of voices that reveal the materiality of bodies, but also the multiple layers of their history, and subjectivity's constitution through multiple resonances and echoes of affective vibrations, tones, and rhythms. Starting with *Cabra marcado* and slowly but steadily advancing to an extreme depuration of his resources, his work opens up our notions about what a movie can be, while it also interrogates the ways in which our world, our selves, and our societies are constituted by intricate speech acts, by infinitely complex constellations of gestures, hesitations, rhythmic structures, and subtle interactions that in our everyday experience remain invisible, inaudible to us, and that his films explore, reveal, but also produce before our eyes and ears. Coutinho does not simply register or reveal what is already there, his films produce events that would never take place without them, they do not record reality but modify it to make the invisible appear before our eyes. The invisible domain that the austere visual style of Coutinho's late films manages to make apparent includes the past (apprehended through its traces in the characters' bodies and in their narrations' reenactments of it), the complexity of social structures (condensed in the relations established between the director and his interviewees), the density and weight of material bodies (lost in the two-dimensional image but brought back by sound), and, most of all, the affective intensity of watching and listening, two acts that take place outside the filmic space and are thus not visible within it but nevertheless orient and determine it.

A central aspect of Coutinho's films is that their sparseness teaches us to look and to listen in a different way, with an enhanced attention. Walter Benjamin famously proposed that "through the camera [. . .] we first discover the optical unconscious just as we discover the instinctual unconscious through psychoanalysis" (117). In Coutinho's cinema, the unconscious is optical but also acoustic. Sound recording registers and amplifies everything that a voice says beyond or beneath the words that it forms. His active, extremely receptive, attentive, but also highly selective mode of listening opens for us a new world of unsuspected sensorial and affective richness that cannot leave us untouched. His films expose and explore their characters' subjectivity through the deceptively simple act of inviting them to talk and listening to them, but they also lay bare the structure of the subject as an echo chamber, a receptive and resonating space that corresponds not only to the director's subjective position, but also to our position as spectators, as attentive auditors of his films, subjected to the radical experience of listening to an image.

Notes

1. For a fuller development of Coutinho's relation to Benjamin's essay, see Carlos Nader's "No princípio era o verbo." Laécio Ricardo de Aquino Rodrigues has also explored the relation of Coutinho's word to Benjamin's thought in his "Coutinho, leitor de Benjamin."

2. Consuelo Lins discusses Coutinho's relation to this notion in her book *O documentário* (108–10).

3. I owe this insight to Gonzalo Aguilar's astute remark about the tension between testimony as content in films about the Argentinean dictatorship and gestures captured by the camera that become more telling than any statement, revealing various layers of memory beyond voluntary evocation of the past (*Más allá del pueblo* 143–51).

4. The distinction between the Said and Saying comes from the work of Emmanuel Lévinas. I am taking it from Adriana Cavarero's thoughtful critique of the way in which this opposition privileges the visual presence of the other's face, while not paying attention to the role of the voice in a verbal exchange. She wonders, "why, in order to tell us what he wanted to tell us, did Levinas not take recourse instead in the theme of the voice? It is certainly not a stretch to indicate in the voice a communication of oneself, a physical proximity of the one to the other, as such prior to any consideration of what is said. In the voice both uniqueness and relation—indeed, uniqueness as relation—manifest themselves acoustically without even taking account of what is Said" (Cavarero 30).

5. Rogério Rossini (1949–1989) was a composer known mainly for his work in film music. Carlos Lyra (1939–) is a popular singer and composer, famous for his participation in the bossa nova movement, who later became more politically committed and participated in the organization of the CPC.

6. Guilherme Maia points out: "Utilizando a noção de valor acrescentado de Michel Chion (2011), podemos dizer que a música de Rossini, atuando sempre no plano extradiegético, agrega ao filme signos sonoros que remetem à região do Brasil onde as histórias são tecidas, na função que Gorbman (1987) classificaria com *referencial narrativa*, e signos de tensão e tristeza que operam aderidos ao intenso sentimento de nostalgia e aos conflitos que emergem da história que nos é contada pelas imagens, narrações e depoimentos" (100; Utilizing the notion of added from Michel Chion (2011), we can say that Rossini's music, always acting in the extradiegetic plane, adds to film sonorous signs that reference the region of Brazil where stories are woven, in the function that Gorbman (1987) would classify as *narrative referential*, and signs of tension and sadness that operate adhered to intense feeling of nostalgia and to the conflicts that emerge from the story that is told to us by images, narrations, and testimonies).

7. For his notions on audiovisual counterpoint, see Eisenstein's *Film Form* (passim).

8. The song was initially part of the music for the 1961 play "Um americano em Brasília" (An American in Brasília) by Francisco de Assis and Nelson Lins e Barros. It was later included on the LP *O povo canta* (1963), released to gather funds for the CPC, with which Carlos Lyra was very involved at the time. The CPC was an organization associated with the National Students' Union and committed to the creation and dissemination of popular, politically committed art. It existed from 1962 to 1964, when it was suppressed by the military coup.

9. I am thinking here of Roland Barthes's famous notion of "anchorage," developed in his "Rhetoric of the Image": "a verbal message that directs my gaze to some of the many possible meanings of a visual image ("the text *directs* the reader through the signifieds of the image, causing him to avoid some and receive others; by means of an often subtle *dispatching*, it remote-controls him towards a meaning chosen in advance" (*Image Music Text* 40)).

10. Coutinho explains, "Filmando em película eu nāc poderia ter feito *Santo forte*, nem *Babilônia*, nem *Edifício Master*. Se a fita dura 11 minutos, e o som 15, não dá. É só imaginar o número de pessoas que, no meio de um raciocínio de uma exposição, iriam ser cortadas. É só imaginar as coisas fortes e que valem a pena em um filme, cortadas por causa da técnica. [. . .] Essa descoberta de que o meu dispositivo só funciona com esse material que é o vídeo, foi essencial" (qtd. in Lins, *O documentário* 101; Filming on film I could not have made *Santo forte* nor *Babilônia*, nor *Edifício Master*. If a tape lasts eleven minutes and the sound fifteen, it doesn't work. It's just imaging the number of people that, in the middle of a thought, of an explanation, would be cut. It's just imagining the strong things, and that are worthwhile in a film, cut because of tech [. . .]. This discovery that my apparatus only functions with this material that is video was essential).

11. For instance, in *Santa Marta: duas semanas no morro* (1987), the music is credited to composers from the community where the documentary was filmed, and therefore it functions less as an external commentary on the images than as an expression of the place that the film is trying to portray. The musical score of *Boca de lixo* (1992) by Tim Rescala is a concrete composition constructed through the amplification and modification of the place's ambient noise, which may be understood as a way to ground the music in the film's location.

12. The question of the influence of TV in popular religious attitude has only become more acute since in Brazil, with the rise of a highly mediated evangelical culture.

13. "Música sertaneja" is a style originating in the Brazilian countryside that has become hugely popular throughout the whole country. It is sometimes viewed with condescension by middle-class listeners who tend to prefer more sophisticated styles of bossa nova, MPB, or tropicalismo to this overly tacky and highly sentimental music.

14. Consuelo Lins considers Fátima an example of the ways in which Coutinho's cinema finds characters who respond to social violence, vulnerability, and marginality with vigorous and irreverent verbal creativity: "O inglês é enteramente inventado, da primeira à última palavra, mas a convicção com que as palavras são ditas nos faz quase acreditar que esse, sim, é o verdadeiro inglês, o mais antigo, o mais original, a língua primeira da qual surgiram todas as outras" ("O cinema" 179; The English is entirely invented, from the first word to the last, but the conviction with which the words are said makes us almost believe that this, yes, is the real English, the oldest, the most original, the first language from which all others emerged). This observation aims at the constant presence of the issue of a pre-babelic language in

Coutinho's cinema (developed by Carlos Nader in "No princípio era o verbo"), but it also touches on the power of music and song to function as a supra-language, as a language that precedes the consolidation of linguistic structures with their fixed ideologies, power relations, and fossilized meanings.

15. According to Dolar, singing "brings the voice intensely to the forefront, on purpose, at the expense of meaning," and thus "by focusing on the voice, [singing] actually runs the risk of losing the very thing it tries to worship and revere: it turns it into a fetish object—we could say the highest rampart, the most formidable wall against the voice" (30).

16. As Cavarero puts it, when commenting on Italo Calvino's short story "A King Listens," "The phonic emission exalted by the song, the voice that sends itself into the air and makes the throat vibrate, has a revelatory function. Or better, more than revealing, it communicates. What it communicates is precisely the true, vital, and perceptible uniqueness of the one who emits it" (5). For Cavarero, however, this uniqueness is not something that can be apprehended independently from the sphere of political action: "all human beings are unique, but only when and while they interact with words and deeds can they communicate to one another this uniqueness. Without such communication, without action in a shared space of reciprocal exhibition, uniqueness remains a mere ontological given—the given of an ontology that is not able to make itself political" (196).

17. I am very indebted to Depetris-Chauvin's insightful reading of *As canções* from an affective perspective, both in the essay quoted and in her "*Ter saudade até que é bom. Música y afectividad en dos documentales brasileños recientes.*"

18. See Peter Szendy's *Hits. Philosophy in the Jukebox*.

19. A practitioner and theorist of "canto falado" is semiologist Luiz Tatit, who has proposed that twentieth-century Brazilian music is characterized by it.

Works Cited

Aguilar, Gonzalo. *Más allá del pueblo. Imágenes, indicios y políticas del cine*. FCE, 2015.

Barthes, Roland. "Rhetoric of the Image." *Image—Music—Text*, edited and translated by Stephen Heath, Hill and Wang, 1977, pp. 32–51.

Benjamin, Walter. "The Work of Art in the Age of Its Technological Reproducibility." 2nd ed. *Selected Writings. Vol. 3 1935–1938*. Harvard UP, 2002.

Cavarero, Adriana. *For More Than One Voice. Toward a Philosophy of Vocal Expression*. Translated by Paul A. Kottman, Stanford UP, 2005.

Depetris-Chauvin, Irene. "Los cuerpos de la música" *Informe Escaleno*, marzo 2015.

———. "*Ter saudade até que é bom*. Música y afectividad en dos documentales brasileños recientes." *452ºf* 14, 2016, pp. 45–68.

Dolar, Mladen. *A Voice and Nothing More*. MIT Press, 2006.

Eisenstein, Sergei. *Film Form. Essays in Film Theory.* Translated by Jay Leyda, Harcourt Brace, 1949.
Lacoue-Labarthe, Philippe. "L'écho du sujet." *Le sujet de la philosophie.* Aubier-Flammarion, 1979, pp. 217–303.
Lins, Consuelo. *O documentário de Eduardo Coutinho: Televisão, cinema e vídeo.* Jorge Zahar, 2004.
———. "O cinema de Eduardo Coutinho: uma arte do presente." *Documentário no Brasil. Tradição e transformação,* edited by Francisco Elinaldo Teixeira, Summus, 2004, pp. 179–98.
———. "*Últimas conversas*: entre o filme inacabado e o filme possível." *Últimas conversas,* edited by Eliska Altmann and Tatiana Bacal, 7Letras, 2017, pp. 23–48.
Maia de Jesus, Guilherme. "Um cabra marcado pelas canções: ensaio sobre a poética musical dos documentários de Eduardo Coutinho." *Ouvir o documentário: vozes, músicas, ruídos,* edited by Guilherme Maia de Jesus and José Francisco Serafim, EDUFBA, 2015, pp. 95–119.
Nader, Carlos. "No princípio era o verbo." *Últimas conversas,* edited by Eliska Altmann and Tatiana Bacal, 7Letras, 2017, pp. 49–116.
Rodrigues, Laécio Ricardo de Aquino. "Coutinho, leitor de Benjamin." *Devires,* vol. 8, no. 2, 2011, pp. 118–37.

Part IV
On Time and Endings

10

Open Futures

On Ends and Endings in the Conversational Documentaries of Eduardo Coutinho and Errol Morris

BRUNO CARVALHO

I

And the film said:
'I want to be a poem.'

—"Cinema Novo," Gilberto Gil / Caetano Veloso

In "The End of the Poem," Giorgio Agamben writes about the "poetic institution" named in the title of his essay. Although the elements dealt with by the Italian critic—the tensions "between sound and sense, between the semiotic sphere and the semantic sphere" (Agamben 109)—do not have precise parallels in cinema, the thrust of the piece might inspire a conversation about an equally essential, hitherto little-studied "institution" of cinematographic production: the end of the film.[1]

Beyond a taxonomy of the many variants, conventions, formulas or experimentations by which a film arrives at the end credits, the final photogram, or a blank screen, "The End of the Poem" can provide an analytical touchstone for a different approach to reflecting on the porous, exhaustively debated frontier between fiction films and documentaries.[2] In the essay, Agamben aligns himself with those for whom "the possibility of enjambment constitutes the only criterion for distinguishing poetry from prose" (109).

Without doing the complexity of the argument justice, we might sum it up as follows, adopting the critic's terms: in poetic discourse, *the opposition between a metrical limit and a syntactical limit is at least virtually possible.* To define enjambment, we will echo the author, quoting Nicolò Tibino, who had observed, in the fourteenth century: "It often happens that the rhyme ends, without the meaning of the sentence having been completed" (qtd. in Agamben 110).

Without going so far as to suggest an equivalence between fictional film and prose, or between documentary and poetry, we might argue that something not too distant from the concept of enjambment is what distinguishes one from another. To purposely force the comparison: documentary cinema is that which allows for enjambment, where an opposition between metrical and syntactical limits remains at least virtually possible. To move along with this line of reasoning, we must adjust the formal parameters on which Agamben's analysis rests—here, the characters are to the film more or less as sentences are to the poem.

Let us take the film itself as the counterpart to what is designated as the metrical limit in poetry, which encompasses all of the aspects of production but is ultimately hemmed in by the bounds of the film. In what we refer to as fiction film, this limit generally coincides with the "syntactical limit," "semantic sphere," or with meaning. In documentary, however—and, once again, if a character is to the film as a sentence to the poem—meaning spills over beyond the limits of the production, or those *of the film itself.* Save an array of exceptional cases,[3] we may affirm, while fictional characters exist in the service of the film, documentary characters already existed and continue to exist after the film, even as they are transformed by it.[4] In documentary, to again paraphrase Tibino on enjambment, it often happens that the film ends without the meaning of the character coming to an end.

II.

In an earlier version, published in Brazil, this chapter was titled "Filmes sem futuro," or *films without a future.*[5] Having begun with Agamben's title, it may be worthwhile to parse this other title. The phrase "without a future" might well evoke the film industry's view of the sorts of films we will examine here, even if they continue to captivate our imaginations long after more commercially successful movies fall into oblivion. Given the often myopic logic of a profit-driven market, we can imagine an executive declaring that the eccentric documentaries of a young, unknown Errol Morris or a forgotten Eduardo Coutinho "have no future." This absence of future may also denote something about the very structure of certain films that challenges the expectations for closure of more mainstream narratives. In the fiction features that leave us with characters "living happily ever after," setting off on a new adventure, or dealing with the aftermath of a tragedy, some sort of future is sketched out, suggested, or laid before us. To an extent, documentaries—in making possible the opposition that characterizes enjambment—are inclined toward open-ended futures. Unlike in fiction, the temporalities of a documentary, after all, are not restricted to *the film itself*, or contained within its structures. In this context, what is a film that, besides providing an open-ended future, has no future whatsoever? Beyond the ethical considerations revolving around the fact that the life of a subject exists outside a documentary, what other ethical dimensions do cinematic open futures introduce to contemporary landscapes of foreclosed futures, marked by ecological anxieties and socioeconomic precariousness? Before heading down this path, it may be helpful to examine how the categories of "end" and "endings" may frame reflections on various genres of cinema, as well as documentaries in particular.

There are, as we know, many possible ways to end a movie: uplifting, surprising, tragic, abrupt, and, among them, of course, "The End." But what of the ending that is not *the* defined end, but rather just *an* end? How can we refer to the ending that dispenses adjectives, the ending that simply happens, since the film must arrive at an end somehow? Those that elude formulas and resolutions might simply be called endings, which, unlike the more familiar happy ending, do not cater to expectations of closure or resolution. The English language allows for a distinction here: *the end* is an institution that, while it does not belong exclusively to cinema, and rarely ever appears (spelled out, as an image) in it anymore, still frames the lion's share of classic and mainstream productions. On the other hand, the gerund *ending* signals an ongoing, interrupted process—or perhaps a reticent end, one that resists being assigned meaning, or a delimited and defined temporality.

It is a daring move, in a market-driven environment, to make a film without an end, frustrating viewers' expectations for a digestible message or some sort of conclusion: *what's the point?* In the realm of documentaries, which is our object of consideration from here on out, the distinction between endings and ends relates to another system of classification. Discourse on the practice of documentary sometimes distinguishes between two schools of directing. In one, when the director begins a film, he or she is following a previously mapped itinerary. In another, there is no preconceived point of arrival, and often no guiding map. Although most projects include elements of both approaches, the documentaries preferred by the production and distribution industry belong to the former group; they are more predictable, less experimental, and thus less susceptible to chance, being blown off course, or failing altogether. In his documentaries, Michael Moore, for example, knows where he is headed. He has a point to make and a narrative to follow. Even if his movies contain biting critiques of the status quo, the conservative bent of their formal structure allows the market to assimilate them as cinematographic dossiers, as protest, or as activist productions. It is not surprising that a significant number of documentaries in this genre have circulated widely in the United States and globally in this century.[6]

This chapter focuses on the second group of documentaries, placing Errol Morris's first two films—*Gates of Heaven* (1978) and *Vernon, Florida* (1981)—in dialogue with what we might call Eduardo Coutinho's mid-career works: *Santo forte* (1999), *Babilônia 2000* (2000), *Edifício Master* (2002), *Peões* (2004), and *O fim e o princípio* (2005). After that, beginning with *Jogo de cena* (2007), Coutinho delves into another experimental vein that exceeds the scope of this chapter—his films become more austere, opting for controlled settings. We will also discuss the posthumous *Últimas conversas* (2015), in which Coutinho himself becomes a character.

It is sometimes said that Coutinho's documentaries do not necessarily "travel" well. His films never quite received the recognition abroad that they earned in Brazil. Indeed, his work might not translate as well as other filmmakers' because so much of its appeal is rooted in spoken language.[7] In that sense, the approximation to Errol Morris hopes to offer a useful counterpoint for Anglophone audiences. Despite different styles, aesthetics, and themes, the films in question similarly lack a commitment to an end goal, avoiding the didactic practices common in commercial documentaries. At the same time, Coutinho and Morris achieved some relative measure of mainstream status, with movies circulating outside cinephile circles. The choice of these two directors may be best justified by affinities in the ways they interact with and film the people who take part in their films, a relationship shaped by a conversational approach—as opposed to the logic of an interview. In this set of works, both Morris and Coutinho privilege a conversational (or "rhizomatic") mode of interacting with subjects, where it is unclear where the film will lead, in contradistinction to an interview, which usually has a preset itinerary. This is a defining characteristic of the formal structure of these documentaries, as well as the place that characters occupy within them.

Because the contrasts between the two are greater than the similarities, it is important to note that after his first two films, Errol Morris's career evolved in a direction very different from Coutinho's. Morris's films have adopted a more ornate style—including special effects and musical scores, for example—and often engage in the pursuit of objective or verifiable truths, even if they remain interested in mysteries, ambivalences, and uncertainty. Errol Morris's later movies are still conversational, and sometimes meandering, but they have also tended to privilege high-profile individuals, from Stephen Hawking to Donald Rumsfeld, rather than "everyday life" subjects. Coutinho's films, on the other hand, often conferred visibility on the downtrodden, the illiterate, favela residents, peasants, prostitutes, widows, weirdos, "ordinary" people. While focus on these types of characters is not unusual in Brazilian documentary, Coutinho's films stand apart in that they refrain from making overarching claims on social realities. On-screen, his characters are never reduced to social types: they appear to us as storytellers, performers, bodies harboring thoughts, often proud and dignified, sometimes manipulative or pathetic—almost always inspiringly or disconcertingly human. Coutinho's films evince stories that "needed to be told" (Lins 161), and he became a master of questions that did not lead to set opinions, as interviews might, but that took chances, foregrounding open dialogues, encounters, exchanges. As we will see, his work sometimes reveals and even temporarily inverts the power asymmetries that often mark the relationships between a documentary filmmaker and his or her subjects.

III.

The documentaries of Morris and Coutinho resist easy classification under categories adopted in film scholarship. In his *Introduction to Documentary*, Bill Nichols suggests six subgenres or modes of representation: poetic, expository, participatory, observational, reflexive, and performative (99). Nichols, of course, recognizes that films may move between modes, and although that applies to the documentaries in question here, they would perhaps best fit the "participatory" subgenre. According to the author, in this mode of representation we find "the encounter between one who wields a movie camera and one who does not," giving rise to questions such as "How do filmmakers and social actors respond to each other? How do they negotiate control and share responsibility? How much can the filmmaker insist on testimony when it is painful to provide it? What responsibility does the filmmaker have for the emotional aftermath of appearing on camera? What ties join filmmaker and subject and what needs divide them?" (116).

Nichols draws parallels between this mode and what Jean Rouch and Edgar Morin called *cinéma vérité*, the French translation of Dziga Vertov's *kinopravda*, an idea that, as "film truth," "emphasizes that this is the truth of an encounter rather than absolute or untampered truth" (117). The screened "truth" consists of manipulated documents of relationships between filmmakers and people/characters—as captured by cameras. Documentaries in this mode therefore *document* interactions between those who film and those who are filmed and do not presume an investment in the potential for objective observation or a belief in the camera as a "fly on the wall." Both Morris and Coutinho, in interviews, distanced themselves from that sort of approach (Bloom; Bragança). The narrative arc common to participatory documentaries, however, is absent from the works of these two directors. The participatory mode tends to involve journeys with the director-character at their heart, where the very experience of the film "plays a cathartic, redemptive role in their own lives" (Nichols 118). These documentaries generally lead to some sort of contingent end: they are films that point to a future divergent from the past, through a change that is quite often wrought by the film itself.

Coutinho's attitudes toward cinema may be too modest and skeptical for this mode. While the participatory documentary, according to Nichols, has the interview "as one of the most common forms of encounter between filmmaker and subject" (121), I would argue that films like *Edifício Master* and *Vernon, Florida* are rather structured around conversations. In works such as *Chronique d'un été* by Edgar Morin and Jean Rouch (1961) or *Not a Love Story* by Bonnie Klein (1981), we might say that dialogues "differ from ordinary conversation and the more coercive process of interrogation by dint of the institutional framework in which they occur and the specific protocols or guidelines that structure them" (122). The films by Errol Morris and Eduardo Coutinho that interest us here seem to diverge from this model, in part because they do not accept the premise that "ordinary conversations" are ordinary at all—at least not necessarily. One of the characteristics that approximates Morris and Coutinho is the fact that they are directors marked by an attention to language and by films that have language as their object.

What is *Gates of Heaven* ultimately about? It is a documentary about pet cemeteries in the state of California. Although that may be the most straightforward answer, it is obviously insufficient. We hear from cemetery owners, people who have buried their beloved pets, and even the owner of a rendering plant specialized in "recycling" deceased animals. As the film goes on, however, it ceases to be a documentary primarily about pet cemeteries. The fixed shots, with interview subjects apparently looking straight into the camera, privilege that which is being said.[8] There is no voice-over, no explanatory text, no nondiegetic soundtrack. As the film moves between relatively long takes of different characters (their footage is intermingled, although the narrative begins with one group and ends with another), there are almost no elements that might lead viewers to any single conclusion. According to Roger Ebert, "every time I show this, it plays differently [. . .] People think it's funny or sad or deadpan or satirical. They think that Errol Morris loved the people in the film, or that he was being very cruel to them" (qtd. in Singer 378). It is a documentary, then, that does not guide the viewer's reaction and is open to multiple interpretations. Similarly, the gamut of topics covered in the conversations only widens, ranging from business to love, from autobiographical details to religious theories. Now, to return to our earlier question: what is *Gates of Heaven* about? Of all the potential answers, the most precise may be the following: it is an edited document of a series of conversations with eccentric figures, where a documentary about pet cemeteries serves as pretext. Like *Vernon, Florida* and the films of Coutinho, it is a narrative made up of acts of narration, and it is also fundamentally about ways of telling stories.

Even when they recognize or introduce a historical framework, the documentaries in question privilege storytelling over history. In the first part of *Gates of Heaven*, for example, the images of newspaper headlines announcing the bankruptcy of a given cemetery seem only to contextualize a few of the stories told therein. In Coutinho's *Peões*, which introduces us to a variety of figures involved in the industrial strikes of 1979 and 1980 in greater São Paulo, another historical landmark is key: the footage was recorded in the final days of the 2002 presidential elections, led by Lula, who had been involved in the strikes. The director nonetheless privileges the subjects' personal lives, asking about relationships, jobs, marriages, childhood, origins. Though many workers speak of the soon-to-be president, the film does not seek to justify itself out of a notion of historical value.

IV.

What we referred to earlier as a conversational mode, in this context, relates both to *metrical* and *syntactical limits*, to return to our initial premise.

We are dealing with works that record encounters and take on meaning through them, but also through narratives of spoken language that, to an extent, reproduce what we might call the spatial logic—or cartography—of the practice of conversation. In an interview originally published in 2003, Eduardo Coutinho draws a distinction between testimonies, interviews, and conversations: "I never thought of what I do as interviewing people. I try to build this thing that's different, because it's conversation. First off, in interviews you're more clearly directing, you know?" (Bragança 105). We might then draw an analogy between documentaries that stick to some sort of script (or a preset itinerary) and interviews, the type of dialogue that implies some kind of preconceived direction or goal, with imagined points of departure and arrival. Open futures condition a conversation; we cannot know, with a reasonable degree of certainty, what directions a conversation will take, or where the dialogue might lead.

If the cartography of an interview—as in the films of Michael Moore, for example—recalls the medieval maps that lay out pilgrimages for users to follow, the cartography of conversation suggests what Gilles Deleuze and Félix Guattari call a rhizome. In the introduction to *A Thousand Plateaus: Capitalism and Schizophrenia*, the authors write that "any point of a rhizome can be connected to anything other, and must be" (7). They thus reject the binary logic that governs classical thought, mirrored in the image of the root-tree that serves to organize information in linguistics, for example. In the rhizome, "the laws of combination [. . .] increase in number as the multiplicity grows" (8). Instead of the root-tree—a hierarchizing map with a built-in itinerary—Deleuze and Guattari suggest the "principle of cartography and decalcomania: a rhizome is not amenable to any structural or genetic model. It is a stranger to any idea of genetic axis or deep structure" (12). The rhizome is thus a "map and not a tracing." It is open, not merely a reproduction of "an unconscious closed in upon itself" (12).

The rhizomatic arrangement of the documentaries of Errol Morris and Eduardo Coutinho becomes evident in two projects mapped out without an itinerary: *Vernon, Florida* and *O fim e o princípio*. In the first, the director chooses to film in a quiet town in the southern United States (pop. 500–800), which had become infamous in the 1950s and 1960s as a result of scandals involving potentially deliberate limb amputations for fraudulent insurance payouts. According to Morris, the initial idea had been to focus the conversations on this, which had led Vernon to be dubbed "Nub City." Once he began getting death threats from residents, however, the director transformed the project into a series of conversations with eight peculiar characters, including a police officer, a turkey hunter, and a couple convinced that the sand from a neighboring desert, stored in a jar, was "growing." In *O fim e o princípio*, an even more radical case of a lack of a "genetic axis" or absence of a "structural or genetic model," Coutinho and his team arrive in the backlands of the Brazilian state of Paraíba, as he says at the start of the film, "to *try* to make a film in four weeks without any sort of prior research, on no particular topic, with no particular location."

In both films, "ordinary" conversations with "unknown" people—under exceptional circumstances created by the camera and the arrival of a film crew in a small community—flow into a number of strangely similar veins. From the everyday to the supernatural, personal relationships with religiosity crop up insistently, for example. At the same time, we cannot overlook important stylistic differences that separate the films, starting with the cinematography. In the case of the Brazilian documentary, Jacques Cheuiche's methods seem animated by a rare combination of technique and intuition, with the result being a fluid camera very unlike the rigid framing that marks the US director's earliest work.[9] Moreover, while Coutinho explains the circumstances surrounding the shoot at the start of *O fim e o princípio*, we do not see or hear Morris in either of his first two films. Coutinho tends to lay bare the apparatus of the shoot and include the questions he poses, as well as the answers he gives when asked something by one of his interlocutors. Morris omits what he says, even though the conversational nature of the interactions comes through: in *Gates of Heaven*, one elderly character asks what a place is named; in *Vernon, Florida*, we hear things like "what does a jeweler look for?" or "you ever seen a man's brains?" They are almost always followed by silences that, while disquieting, are not paralyzing, during which we may imagine the director reacting with gestures or facial expressions.

Once again, what brings the two directors together and distances them from the subgenres cited by Bill Nichols is the place of conversation as object *and* organizing narrative principle. The fact that the titles of *Gates of Heaven* and *Peões* come from phrases spoken during the films, for example, attests to how conversations are the axis structuring them. At the same time, as rhizomatic as the conversational process may be, and however manipulated in editing, there is always a linear element to a film: the chronological sequences of pre-production research, encounters, conversations, and shoots. The editing in Coutinho's documentaries did not always follow the order in which events and recordings took place.[10] Even so, unlike the mode of representation that Nichols refers to as observational, neither of the directors shies away from intervening in the relationships with subjects, and thus in the construction of their characters. In the documentary *Capturing Reality: The Art of Documentary* (Pepita Ferrari, 2008), Morris says that a famous scene from *Gates of Heaven*, where we see a character in his office, his desk packed with trophies, had been set up. The director had asked for the trophies to be placed there, since they illustrated the triumphalist discourse of the son of one of the cemetery owners, whose business was enjoying relative success.

On *Edifício Master*, Consuelo Lins, a film scholar and one of Coutinho's collaborators, writes:

> The decision was to follow the order in which the characters were filmed, but in a way that diverged radically from what we'd seen in *Babilônia 2000* [filmed at the turn of the millennium], which respected the chronology of the shoot because the passage of time was crucial. [. . .] In *Edifício Master*, the shooting order was random and in keeping with production logistics, which is exactly why Coutinho found it interesting. But this wasn't a "jail cell" of a rule. The director altered the order when he found it necessary, when it became too connotative: he separated three characters in a row who all sang songs and two older woman who spoke of suicide, and moved the man who sang "My Way" from the end of the film—his had been the penultimate session—to the middle. It would be "emotional extortion" for the viewer, Coutinho says, the quintessential dramatic finale, a true cliché: comforting, gratifying, pacifying, in opposition to the whole of his oeuvre. (156)

In other words, during the editing process, the director chooses to alter the order of the shoots to preserve or connote the "rhizomatic" (dis)order of a conversational mode. The procedure destabilizes the temporal hierarchies that inevitably assert themselves in cinematic narrative: beginning, middle, and end. Even when an *end* crops up by chance, the director decides to avoid it in favor of a more open *ending*, one that is "a map and not a tracing," refusing to reproduce an unconscious that calls for emotional closure, the "quintessential dramatic finale." It is no coincidence that the very title of *O fim e o princípio* operates in a similar fashion—as if to remind us that every end is a beginning, and that every beginning may also be an ending. In *Vernon, Florida*, the title is a place that few would be able to locate with precision, but it stands for a fixed point in a map. *O fim e o princípio* begins with a situated starting point but no known point of arrival, with the title suggesting a return to something that is no longer—as good a metaphor as any for film itself.

V.

In *Cineastas e imagens do povo*, Jean-Claude Bernardet describes a "fetishistic relationship" commonly found in documentary, wherein the character is taken as "the class-based Other." In his words, "whatever the poor person says, goes. Let's not contradict the poor person, because that would imply that we are collaborating with the mechanisms of oppression—poor interviewees tend to be somewhat sacrosanct" (295). In the attempt to invert socioeconomic power dynamics, one asymmetry replaces another. The filmmaker positions himself as inferior to the interviewee, in an ultimately condescending, paternalistic posture. Foucault points to something similar, the idea that different forms of interviews "all involve regulated forms of exchange, with an uneven distribution of power between client and institutional practitioner" (qtd. in Nichols 122).

In much of the recent production of Brazilian documentaries paying tribute to popular music, for example, we find a different sort of asymmetry, against the grain of the "fetishistic relationship" indicated by Bernardet, but with similar consequences. These are films that adopt a reverent tone not only toward the supremely rich realm of Brazilian music, but also to the interviewees chosen to speak about it—in many cases in their condition as participants, witnesses, or creators. While the implicit contract that defines the relationship between viewer and documentary is a central element in reflections on the genre (cf. Salles 58–59), there is little discussion of the implicit contracts between filmmakers and interviewees. To put it plainly: from 2003 to 2010, Caetano Veloso gave interviews for at least twenty different films. With all the potential difficulties and negotiating involved in obtaining a valuable interview with a major figure in Brazilian culture, how could one conceive of leaving them out of the final, edited film? Would any director dare to interview and not include them, or to include scenes that might be unflattering?

Unlike the conversational mode, the logic of the interview thus hierarchizes, predetermining what has value, be it a poor person's opinion or a celebrity's. An interview has a preset point of origin and aims to reach a particular endpoint. Documentaries framed by a "fetishistic relationship," whether sociological or musical in nature, envision a "future" that is, paradoxically, defined a priori: this film will celebrate popular music, or this film will condemn capitalism. This is not to detract from the many moving and important works that fit the description; we must, however, distinguish them from the documentaries that assimilate, recognize, and/or problematize the possibility of an opposition between the metrical and syntactical limits of film.

The documentaries of Errol Morris and Eduardo Coutinho do not limit themselves to being about this or that; they structure themselves around (and through) conversations. Against the grain of journalistic expectations—and, to an extent, those of the film industry—both work toward symmetry in their relationships with the people/characters in their films. Consuelo Lins emphasizes that "what is [. . .] distinctive about the filmmaker's methods is his preference for questions that do not beg for 'opinions'" (148). In an analysis informed by her experience working on *Edifício Master*, she observes how people have an "extraordinary intuition as to what you want": "If the interviewer wants oppositional, 'leftist' answers, he'll get them; if he wants the opposite, he will get that too. That's one of the most important things to break through, not suggesting to the other what it is that you want to hear" (147). Even the gesture of seeking out an opinion presumes a prior judgment—that the interviewee's opinion should illustrate some idea or serve some specific function. In the case of Coutinho's films, it is not hard to imagine the same ambivalent and wide-ranging reactions that Roger Ebert observed among viewers of *Gates of Heaven*.

In this, "not judging the other [and] not objectifying the interviewee" (Lins 157) define the approach for one seeking to establish a minimum of symmetry in encounters between director and characters. This stance, if taken seriously, entails a willingness to be judged as well. In *Edifício Master*, there is a scene in which Roberto, a street vendor who has suffered a stroke, talks about how difficult it is for an "old geezer with all kinds of problems" to find work, and suddenly asks the director: "Want to give me a job?" Caught off guard, Coutinho responds hesitantly: "I don't . . . I don't know what to say." Roberto cuts him off and, looking to the side, as if speaking to another member of the crew, says: "You're very kind and obliging, and I'm very grateful, don't you know." After this ironic aside, he turns back to the director and adds: "but that's it, reality is reality, y'know, man?" The scene reveals the (perhaps inevitable) asymmetry of the encounter, sprung of social or economic differences and shaped by the expectations the conversation gives rise to. At the same time, for a brief moment, there is an inversion of power relations. The person setting the course for the conversation, *directing* the dialogue—at least in this exchange—is no longer Coutinho alone, but Roberto as well.

From a different angle, Salles comes to a similar conclusion:

> [I]n recent years [. . .] documentary cinema has been attempting to discover narrative strategies that reveal right from the beginning the nature of this relationship. They are films about encounters. Not all these films are good, but the best ones attempt to transform the formula "I speak about him/her to us" into "*He/she* and *I* speak about *us* to *you*." Such films do not intend to speak about the other, but about an encounter with the other. They are open films, hesitant in relation to categorical conclusions on the essence of others. They do not abandon the pursuit of knowledge, but merely do not aspire to know everything. (233)

Salles cites the text by Consuelo Lins referenced above, where she writes about a key moment in *Edifício Master*:

> The young student who gives the last interview asks Coutinho "Who are you?" and goes on to say that it is difficult for her to think about what she is going to become in life. She says: "I can't really imagine myself as anything." With this, she produces a final line that fits fully into the trajectory of all of [Coutinho's] films. Hers is an apparently offhand remark, which resonates with the director's conviction that it is impossible to conclude, in the sense of providing a "closing," not only for the document, but also for a character. (233)

There are comparable interpellations in other of Coutinho's films, and these moments place his work closer to the cinema described by Salles than to the documentaries of Errol Morris. In what he leaves as the last exchange in *Peões*, Coutinho is asked if he had ever worked in a factory: "Were you ever a *peão*?"[11] (fig. 10.1). At the end of *O fim e o princípio*, meanwhile, as he says goodbye to one of the locals he had spoken with earlier, Coutinho is praised effusively by the initially withdrawn Chico: "more 'n a detective, announcer, wise man, scientist, you're all that." Chico's insistence seems to embarrass the director, and it becomes clear that he seeks to affirm his own intelligence by identifying in Coutinho the ability to perceive it. Yet it is

Figure 10.1. Geraldo asking Coutinho "Were you ever a *peão*?" in *Peões*. Source: *Peões (Metalworkers)*. Directed by Eduardo Coutinho, Videofilmes, 2004.

precisely these lateral connections where the personal agenda of the other (be it in a spirit of identification or confrontation) usurps the director's cinematographic project, revealing a rhizomatic process. To an extent, the hierarchies, itineraries, and codes of the interview are broken down; for a few moments, the dialogue drifts, unmoored.

Of course, we know that directors' interventions are also made a posteriori. Coutinho decides to keep the aforementioned scenes in the final cut. And yet there is a difference between the editing process in documentaries and in fiction films, which refers back to the potential for enjambment only present in the former, as argued at the start of this chapter. Whatever is left of a fiction film on the cutting-room floor "does not exist." That is to say, the character only "exists" within the metrical limits of the work, which thus coincide with meaning. In documentary, if the director decides to leave out a scene where a person opens up about his or her childhood, it will not cease to exist—neither the childhood nor the exchange.

O fim e o princípio inscribes this opposition—how it becomes impossible for the end of stories or conversations to coincide with the ending of the film—into its encounter-narrative. The documentary ends with the director and his crew promising to go back to show the results of their shoot. There is, in this, a sort of recognition that meaning, "the semantic sphere" or syntactical limits, extends beyond the metrical limits of the film itself. We are left not knowing if the visit will in fact come to pass. Refusing the future, in a sense, keeps the ending (and the film) open. All we can know of the future, after all, is that it never arrives and that it will always remain beyond our grasp. The end may only be possible in fiction and in cinema. Beyond those realms, one might do well to echo Chico's caution when he hears from Coutinho that the crew will be back to show the film: "Can't guarantee I'll be alive."

VI.

Some fourteen months after they finished shooting *O fim e o princípio*, Coutinho and members of his crew returned to the community of Araçás, in São João do Rio do Peixe, for a public screening of the film. A short about it is available as an extra in the DVD. We learn that Chico de Moisés is still alive, but that two others, Leocádio and Zé de Souza, passed away. Documentary subjects, when "anonymous" and unknown, only gain meaning as characters to an audience once they appear on-screen. They at once exceed the boundaries of film and are bounded by it. David MacDougall in *Transcultural Cinema* gets at something related:

> In fiction films, the characters seem to slip away into the past. More disturbingly, the subjects of documentary slip away into the future [. . .]. Films stand still, but their subjects move on. Less than two years after Robert Flaherty filmed Allakariallak (better known as Nanook), he learned he had died of starvation on a hunting trip [. .] Even as a film is being shot, its subjects are in transition, moving toward a future that the film cannot contain. (33)

There are also ways in which films move on, but their subjects stand still. The characters of *O fim e o princípio* return to the unrecorded actions of everyday life, even as the film circulates and gains a life of its own. And of course, to the extent that films stand still—fixated in print or digital media—they have afterlives beyond our own. In one sense, when the cameras are turned off and the film crew leaves, the characters die but the subjects live on. In another, as time goes on and a film outlives those involved in it, the subjects and filmmakers die, but the characters live on.

When Eduardo Coutinho died on February 2, 2014, he left an unfinished documentary, to be titled *Palavras* (*Words*), with young men and women from public schools in Rio de Janeiro. The encounters had been recorded in what looked like a classroom, with only one black chair and a door visible. This spare set confirms the tendency toward austerity of his later films. Two longtime friends and collaborators of the director completed the film: João Moreira Salles, who produced several of his projects, and Jordana Berg, who edited his films beginning with *Santo forte*. Berg wrote a beautiful essay on the process, explaining that the film had been rife with a sense of failure while Coutinho was alive. As she puts it, they ultimately settled on "making our film with his material" (20). It was released in 2015 with a fitting title, *Últimas conversas* (*Last Conversations*). Though Coutinho's passing imbues the title with a sense of finality, in Portuguese it could also have the secondary meaning of Latest Conversations.

In her reflections on watching the footage, Jordana Berg describes the first character, a young woman "with a nervous laugh, as if she were taking an exam that would guarantee her future" (9). Berg identifies in all of the interactions this enduring power of the camera, containing the promise of opportunities for a better life. Most of the public-school students are Black and, we can presume, come from backgrounds with more modest socioeconomic means than most of the crew members. Being in a shoot could mean "a way out," "an escape to the future" (10). Berg's observations recall MacDougall's idea, quoted above, that "even as a film is being shot, its subjects are in transition, moving toward a future that the film cannot contain" (33). In this case, Berg recognizes that it is "a future that might not arrive." Given the often intractable inequities of Brazilian society, the open futures would likely remain latent, a projection of the students onto the encounter with the film crew. The imagined future of opportunities, as Berg notes, "would only reach other young people," those "from private schools" (10). Perhaps Coutinho's sense that the project was failing came from this perceived goal-driven mode of the characters, acting as if they were in an interview, with something to gain, seeking in the film a pathway to success (an itinerary, to return to the cartographic metaphor).

Últimas conversas is credited as a film directed by Coutinho, edited by Berg, and finished by Salles. In it, Coutinho becomes more of a character than he had been in earlier documentaries. The film opens with him, as the first "interviewee," voicing frustration with the shoots up until that point. Throughout the film, we will hear more from him than usual: intervening, opining, quipping, venting. The result, nonetheless, contains some of the characteristic exchanges of his documentaries. Despite Coutinho's misgivings about how "guarded" and "castrated" the teenagers had been, the characters, at least those that made it to the final cut, open themselves up. Though their linguistic repertoire might lack the verve of Chico and his counterparts, they come across, on the whole, as poignant and as captivating as the characters of previous Coutinho documentaries. The notion that these teenagers might be approaching the shoot with an instrumentalizing ethos does not pervade the film. The characters in *Últimas conversas* reveal intimate memories, dreams, aspirations, fears.

The sixth of ten students to appear on the screen, Estephanie, was about to graduate high school—the first in her family. Initially seeming apprehensive, she becomes both warmer and more assertive as the conversation goes on. Estephanie says she was raised by her mother, who had been a prostitute. and her partner—whom she considers to be more of a father figure than her biological father. Coutinho asks, "for the future, what would you most desire in life?" and Estephanie responds: "What do I plan for my future? To be an excellent licensed practical nurse, to be an excellent masseuse, as that's my aesthetic [beauty therapy] course, and to make my mom very happy, which I didn't manage to in the past. To give a good future to my old lady." Her goals are both laudable, and somewhat prosaic. For the very next character, the cut leads into Thiago Theodoro. We see him, but we hear Coutinho: "don't you think that life . . ." Thiago, startled, interrupts: "life?"—as if to confirm that the conversation was about to dive into such a heady, philosophical direction. The juxtaposition with the previous scene jolts us too. Coutinho goes on: "Life, human life [. . .] Isn't it such a strange, such a bizarre thing?"

Here, again, the conversation turns to futures. They discuss the fear of ending up alone. Thiago states that we either have love, or we have death. Coutinho interjects, impatient: "no, you love and die [. . .] life is never love or death—it is love and death." He alternates, throughout the film, between a melancholic and an almost imperious tone. Sometimes sounding vulnerable, here he is certain. Indeed, as far as we know, death in any material sense cannot be preceded by a conjunction that presents alternatives—death is as inescapable as the fact that films need to end somehow. There is no life *or* death, but rather a multiplicity of endings and beginnings. We could think back to Deleuze and Guattari on the rejection of a binary logic and a "genetic axis."

After a lull, during which they both resort to platitudes and seem to have trouble getting through to each other, Thiago unsettles the director again: "Do you know of anybody who came back from the dead?" "No," Coutinho replies, almost sheepish. "So how do you know what death is?" Thiago asks, bringing up the promises of afterlife, and how "it's horrible because we don't know if it's true." A silence of nearly fifteen seconds follows. Thiago breaks it, laughing nervously, "The silence got strange." Coutinho recovers his beat: "Silence has to be strange." Thiago, who had just then been driving the conversation, assuming an air of authority, is now the unsettled one. He asks why, with seemingly genuine curiosity. The reiteration of opinions or set pieces, characteristic of interviews, gives place to the conversational mode: there is movement, openness to difference, and the possibility of shifts in perspective. This converts into a lesson on filmmaking and life, concealed in an apology of silence. "Silence is great," Coutinho says. Perhaps, because it imbues the film with some of life's strangeness.

In some ways, there is little actual communication between Eduardo Coutinho and Thiago Theodoro. It is not clear that they make sense to each other, and the dialogue remains awkward. Differences persist, if anything, heightened. But *something* happens—something other than reproduction and reiteration. We might have, in this conversation, a possibility for transformation—or at least movement—greater than in more fluid exchanges. In conversations, as in life—as in films?—apparent dead ends can sometimes open up futures. The possibility of an opposition between a metrical limit and a syntactical limit in documentaries introduces delicate ethical challenges for filmmakers. How to be truthful to the materials without compromising a subject who will have to live on outside the movie? Coutinho's skepticism toward possibilities of closure and redemption means that his films avoid making promises that cannot be fulfilled. We could say that his conversational documentaries at once intensify the interactions and resolve or reduce what we have deemed as the metrical/syntactical opposition, by lowering the stakes of what the film might mean to the character outside the filmed encounter.

Against logics of productivity and pragmatism, his conversational (poetic?) mode is often marked by detours that lead nowhere, but constitute something. Coutinho's documentaries offer no solutions, but—to paraphrase Donna Haraway—they stay with the trouble. In our contemporary moment, entrenched socioeconomic disparities and ecological doom force us to contend with foreclosed futures and no apparent utopias on the horizon. In Coutinho's conversational mode, we find constant renewal. The last character to appear in *Últimas conversas*, Luiza, a six-year-old from a wealthier background than the others, is probably the youngest in all of Coutinho's documentaries. When he appears in the film as its first interviewee, in a conversation recorded after the fourth day of shooting, Coutinho had expressed regret over not making a film with children. He appears to be fascinated by everything she has to say.

As the conversation with Luiza comes to a close, someone off-screen directs her to "give Coutinho a hug." As she holds his right hand, he gestures with his left hand toward the door—directing her to exit. She unexpectedly high-fives him, to the delight of the director. As she leaves through the door, some in the crew hoot and applaud. But it is not quite over just yet. Luiza returns to take a bow. The room erupts, and as she leaves again, the film ends with the empty room, an open door, and a recording of the last conversations between Coutinho and crew. Among animated back-and-forth comments, he says—"and then that makes me sad, because the film should've been made with children [. . .] children ao léu, ao léu." This is, in many ways, more "the end" than an ending—especially given what we know happened to Coutinho by the time *Últimas conversas* was released. There is a sense of finality here not found in his earlier films. But the director had retained an aversion to any sort of resolution. *Ao léu* is an expression denoting adriftness, wandering without aim.

Notes

1. This chapter adopts the terms cinema, film, and movie interchangeably, avoiding discussions over the implications of digital versus film.

2. We will deliberately sidestep the classic debates and vast bibliography on the topic. See Salles (224–34). After summarizing a number of schools of thought, the documentarian develops the idea that the "true problem of documentary" is an ethical one.

3. We might think of films using nonprofessional actors, for example, or documentaries using professional actors, or cases such as the relationship between Werner Herzog and Klaus Kinski (see Werner Herzog, *Mein liebster Feind—Klaus Kinski*, 1999).

4. The distinction may seem obvious, or merely reiterative, if seen alongside reflections on the ethics of documentary, including issues such as the repercussions of the film to the subject who is exposed, etc. This chapter seeks to reframe the discussion, particularly fertile among ethnographers, by foregrounding formal elements.

5. The chapter appeared in *A indústria radical: leituras de cinema como arte-inquietação*. It was translated into English by Flora Thomson-DeVeaux before going through extensive revision, which included several additions. I would like to thank Flora and João Moreira Salles for their helpful feedback.

6. Though it may be reductive to label them Michael Moore–style documentaries, they generally involve critiques of capitalism and corporations. Just picking from among the Oscar nominees in the category from 2005 to 2009, we can find *Enron: The Smartest Guys in the Room* (Alex Gibney and Jason Kliot), *An*

Inconvenient Truth (Davis Guggenheim), *The Garden* (Scott Hamilton Kennedy), and *Food, Inc.* (Robert Kenner).

    7. Flora Thomson-DeVeaux, while working on English subtitles for *As canções*, recalls how the director lamented the volume of text on the screen.

    8. In an interview published in the winter 2004 edition of *FLM Magazine*, Errol Morris explains that in *Gates of Heaven* he spoke to people with his head leaning up against the camera lens. In later films, with the aim of giving the impression that people are speaking directly to the viewer (in the "first person"), he invented the *interrotron*, where the interviewer talks with the director by way of an image projected in real time onto a teleprompter.

    9. Cinematographer Jacques Cheuiche worked on all of the films by Coutinho referenced here, with the exception of *Santo forte*.

    10. João Moreira Salles relayed this information to me in a series of email exchanges. He worked as a producer on several of Coutinho's films.

    11. *Peão* refers to all sorts of salaried work of low rank, and it initially applied to rural contexts. The word translates literally as "pawn."

Works Cited

Agamben, Giorgio. *The End of the Poem: Studies in Poetics*. Translated by Daniel Heller-Roazen, Stanford UP, 1999.

Berg, Jordana. "Diário de Montagem." *Últimas conversas*, edited by Eliska Altmann and Tatiana Bacal, 7Letras, 2017, pp. 9–22.

Bernardet, Jean-Claude. *Cineastas e imagens do povo*. Companhia das Letras, 2003.

Bloom, Livia, editor. *Errol Morris: Interviews*. UP of Mississippi, 2010.

Bragança, Felipe, editor. *Encontros: Eduardo Coutinho*. Beco do Azougue, 2009.

Deleuze, Gilles, and Félix Guattari. *A Thousand Plateaus: Capitalism and Schizophrenia*. Translated by Brian Massumi, U of Minnesota P, 1987.

Giordano Paz, Ravel, and Fabio Akcelrud Durão, editors. *A indústria radical: leituras de cinema como arte-inquietação*. Nankin, 2012.

Haraway, Donna J. *Staying with the Trouble: Making Kin in the Chthulucene*. Duke UP, 2016.

Lins, Consuelo. *O documentário de Eduardo Coutinho: Televisão, cinema e vídeo*. Jorge Zahar, 2004.

MacDougall, David. *Transcultural Cinema*, edited by Lucien Taylor, Princeton UP, 1998.

Nichols, Bill. *Introduction to Documentary*. Indiana UP, 2001.

Salles, João Moreira. "The Difficulty with Documentary." *Realism and the Audiovisual Media*, edited by Lúcia Nagib and Cecília Mello, Palgrave Macmillan, 2009, 224–34.

Singer, Mark. *Mr. Personality: Profiles and Talk Pieces from The New Yorker*. Mariner Books, 2005.

11

Parting Glances

The Posthumous Coutinho

NILO FERNANDO COURET

In mid-November 2013, Coutinho began production on his final movie, *Últimas conversas* (2015), a series of conversations with graduating high school seniors. Coutinho died during post-production in February 2014, leaving thirty-two hours of unedited footage to be completed under the direction of João Moreira Salles, producer of his previous nine films, and his longtime editor Jordana Berg, a working partner since 1999's *Santo forte*, the start of his so-called "late phase." Its posthumous completion and release have invited much critical debate about the film's authorship. In her mixed review of the film, Consuelo Lins notes that the film "is less *by* Eduardo Coutinho and more *with* and *about* the filmmaker" ("Eduardo Coutinho" 29). Cecilia Sayad recovers the film by including it within a broader career trajectory that always sought to complicate the question of authorship (14). Whether lamenting that this is not *his* film or affirming that *he* is very much in this film, both positions tellingly frame authorship around the question "where does Coutinho end?" In a sense, tracing the authorial signature is always already a thanatological endeavor. In a career that willfully rejected cliché representative categories of identity, Coutinho's death should not simply become a dramatic telos of a search for identity. In this literal death of the author, we cannot use Coutinho as the key to deciphering a hidden meaning.

In lieu of the author, I want to suggest that Coutinho offers the *personagem* (character) as an organizing unity, but one that eludes closure.

Unlike the author, the personagem can never be conceived as preceding the documentary inscription because they are the precipitate of the documentary encounter. If the author is a position (of closure) that grounds meaning, the personagem is more a horizon "which allows beings to *appear* as what they are" (Derrida 144). I emphasize the language of appearance because the politics of the image in documentary studies is usually premised on moving beyond appearance and toward some concealed truth, an epistemology of revelation as exposure. Kaja Silverman reminds us that this repudiation of appearance belongs to the "dream of metaphysics," where truth is achieved by turning away from appearance and to a suprasensual domain (*World* 2). The paradox at the heart of documentary studies lies in its inability to escape the fact of representational mediation. The response to this impasse has been to situate nonfiction practices within institutional and scientistic discourses or to turn to phenomenology and its ostensible return to the world of the senses.

I want to suggest a third response that draws on Heidegger, for whom appearance is not an inaccurate replica of Being but its mode of stepping forth. Thinking documentary studies through Heidegger means lingering in the sensual domain but without the subjectivity of phenomenology; that is, without supposing a subject-object relation grounded on an unmodifiable transcendental present and without appearance figured as mendacious mediation (Derrida 150). When we figure the world as an object with a truth to be exposed, we substantialize the world by giving it semantic latency. Objectification imagines something as temporally and spatially present(-at-hand), something we can possess and/or know. This makes assumptions about the perceiving subject and the perceptual object. It presumes a subject position that could disavow its historicity and partial look, and it presumes a perceptual object that could be available in its totality. To relate to the world in its seeming does not mean to simply accept the image as a copy or metaphoric displacement for something real. I am not arguing for an abandonment of depth in favor of mere surface but rather to allow for the world to be salient. Heidegger compels us to think documentary less as an epistemological tool than an "ontological calling card"; the documentary discloses the world rather than exposes the truth (Silverman, *The Miracle* 11). What would it mean for documentary studies to consider "truth inhering less in the correctness of representation than in the unhiding of the hidden"? (Silverman, *World* 2).

This chapter is loosely structured around a series of questions: (1) How is the Coutinho interview different from a conventional documentary interview? (2) What is a character or personagem? and (3) How are Coutinho's documentaries political? These are questions that have already been answered in the scholarly literature and even by the director himself. Yet my contribution invites us to capitalize on the "failures" of *Últimas conversas* and suggests alternatives inflected by this Heideggerian lens. I develop these questions in conjunction with other films from his late phase as well as a Carlos Nader documentary about the filmmaker produced contemporaneously to *Últimas conversas*. Originally commissioned as a short video piece in conjunction with the anniversary celebration of SESC programming, *Eduardo Coutinho, 7 de outubro* (2013) provides a feature-length glance onto Coutinho as personagem, with Coutinho sitting across from Carlos Nader in the unfamiliar position of interviewee. The death of the documentarian in February 2014 between its festival premiere in late 2013 and its theatrical premiere in March 2015 made this veritable diary entry an unexpected final master class. It is my hope that putting these texts together will yield some new answers to these questions. By encountering *Últimas* posthumously, I argue that Coutinho's late phase is understood not as observational documentaries that unearth what is present in a denunciatory key, but as staging the conditions to make something appear.

The Beginning of the End

Coutinho has been called the master interviewer, and his method has probably been the most remarked aspect of his work. Coutinho attempts to make the documented encounter always his first meeting with the character. After an initial survey by producers and a process of selection in consultation with Coutinho, the filmmaker "empties" himself. Most discussions of this emptying look at this strategy in an anthropological or sociological light, ridding oneself of preconceptions in order to have an open dialogue. Coutinho would call his approach a savage anthropology and this emptiness one that compels his characters to film him (Russo 52). Coutinho long held that filmmakers should avoid giving opinions because it was a sure way to get ready-made answers. *Últimas* marks a departure partly because the frustrated director cannot help but assert his opinions, pass judgment, and explain the interview parameters. Consuelo Lins makes a similar observation about the director's unusual interventions: "A dimensão reflexiva aqui é pequena . . . Não lembro de outras conversas em que Coutinho tenha se colocado de modo tão assertivo e provocado discussões tão abstratas como nesse filme" (Lins, "*Últimas*" 33, 39; The reflexive dimension here is small . . . I cannot recall other conversations where Coutinho inserts himself in such an assertive way and provokes such abstract discussions as he does in this film). For instance, Coutinho begins the film's first interview with Tayna: "We're making a film here that will probably go wrong because lately everything I do goes wrong. We are speaking with high schoolers in Rio. We don't want to make a film about school, but about people. I have some vague information. I'm going to ask you logical questions and some absurd ones, as if I were a five-year-old." What we see in *Últimas conversas* is a Coutinho who breaks his own rules, asking students their opinions rather than asking them to recount experiences, wielding preconceptions as weapons to elicit responses. This is not meant as a criticism of the film; rather, I find that the film compels us to think about emptiness beyond methodology and to tease out the nature of this intersubjective encounter. Here there is a certain inability to empty himself, as though this clearing were a precondition to being connected to the world.

These moments, I contend, are not lapses in Coutinho's method; instead, they are departures from his earlier films because the director uses reported speech in ways that complicate the distinction between the director and his *personagens*. To suppose the director's involvement detracts makes sense given the long-held impression that Coutinho's is a cinema of listening; however, reported speech "crystallizes social relations because [it figures] an active reception of another's speech" (Schwartz 112). During his first interview, Coutinho uses information gleaned from his producers' preliminary interviews: "You write stories and poems," he asks Tayna. When the cynical teenager, who earlier mentioned she was not interested in love, says she writes about love, Coutinho retorts: "Você fala que não sabe sobre [amor] . . . que provoca medo e sofrimento. É isso? . . . Mas a vida provoca medo e sofrimento. Vivir é passar por isso" (You said you didn't know about [love] . . . because it provokes fear and suffering. Is that it? But life provokes fear and suffering. Living is going through that). Coutinho's opinion is couched in indirect speech. Moments later, Tayna shares the journal in which she records the events from her everyday life. Coutinho asks her to find the most interesting story, and she finds a "funny story that is R-rated." Coutinho offers to read it, and the camera cuts to an extreme close-up of the notebook in Coutinho's hands. Coutinho reads the story of two homeless people having public sex and the teenager derisively cheering the couple. This not-quite point of view of the notebook finds the author quoting the teenager's words, underscoring the punctuation—"three exclamation points"—and upper-case writing—"OS

MENDIGOS FUDENDO [sic]" (the homeless people fucking)—both by speaking the graphemes and pointing to the page. From indirect speech to direct speech, the film is unusual because Coutinho is the one speaking another's language. Indirect speech presents the thought of a character in the character's own language without using quotation marks. For Pier Paolo Pasolini (and later Deleuze), the use of reported speech "implies a sociological consciousness . . . in the author" (Pasolini 82). Reported speech can expose socioeconomic differences—"the words of the author and the words of the character are not the same" (87). Indirect speech allows an author to speak in their own voice and another's simultaneously in a mode of appropriation that blurs the distinction between subjective and objective categories.[1] Reported speech is a document of neither the character's subjectivity nor the psychology of the recipient but the social relations between speaker and receiver (Schwartz 113). When the teenaged poet, Breno, explains how poetry is a way to get his feelings on paper, Coutinho again uses reported speech: "Para explicar tua inadequação no mundo" (To explain why you don't fit in the world). This reported speech allows a single linguistic construction within which two differently oriented voices are maintained. The relations between author and character are not so easy to parse. Critics' discomfort with Coutinho's interventions perhaps indicates a certain dissolution of any stable enunciative position. *Últimas*'s uses of reported speech force us to ask whether there might be another way to understand the director's claim that he empties himself ahead of each encounter, one informed by Heidegger, who gives us the tools to think this emptiness as an ontological rather than a methodological or epistemological condition. Through this lens, I want to journey backward to an earlier Coutinho film, *Babilônia 2000* (2000), to argue that Coutinho empties himself not to presume objectivity but to summon relationality.

In *Babilônia 2000*, a well-known personagem from the film, Djanira, is a former housekeeper of a wealthy family that was close friends with former president Juscelino Kubitschek. Although her formal interview was a favorite of Coutinho's, her second appearance proves more insightful. In this unusual return of a personagem, she approaches the crew and thanks them for coming to her home and "levando de mim o que eu tenho e dando de vocês o que vocês têm" (taking from me what I have and giving what you have of yourselves). This later moment to camera is less discussed in the Coutinho literature, yet it characterizes the economy of the encounter between Coutinho and his personagem. Coutinho empties himself not for the sake of objectivity but so that he can take from the personagem what they have; further, this emptying is less a withdrawal or a removal than a giving of himself to the person he encounters.

In a later sequence that departs from the talking heads convention, the film presents a quick succession of scenes where the film crew is greeted as they cross doorways and enter different apartments. Coutinho and his crew are regularly greeted with the idiomatic salutation "*fique à vontade*" (make yourself at home). This Brazilian idiom expresses a summons: *vontade* means will or volition and *ficar* means both to remain or stay *and* to enter and reach a specified state. In coupling temporality and spatiality, this salutation reminds us that our Being cannot exist independently of our relation to the world, we become as we remain (Heidegger, "Building" 154).[2] Coutinho is greeted with a summons to a disposition that complicates his claim that he "empties" himself. Coutinho does not so much empty himself of human agency as he does *ficar à vontade*, dwelling with an intentionality that allows the world to appear. For Heidegger, to empty oneself is a form of caring that is disclosive because it requires allowing the world to come to light but not substantializing it. Care does not make an *object* in implicit opposition to a subject; instead, it allows other beings to be encountered in a way that is constitutive for *appearance*.

Taking Care of Appearance

Appearance in this light is not mendacious because there is no *ultimate* meaning that can be captured. The personagem is less the achievement of subjectivity than a "representational positing" or a projection into the world (Derrida 157). Coutinho traffics in appearances because they shift attention from capturing an essence to disclosing an aspect. Appearance famously comes up in Coutinho's earlier *Babilônia 2000*, where the filmmaker and his crew visit a slum overlooking Copacabana beach on New Year's Eve in 1999. Just before noon, the first personagem is Fátima, a former hippie who used to sell artisanal wares, named her son Siddartha after reading Herman Hesse, and listened to the Beatles and Janis Joplin. The interview ends with a memorable sequence atop a clearing where she sings Janis Joplin's "Me and Bobby McGee." Consuelo Lins has referenced the musical sequence and Fátima's invented English lyrics as exemplar of Coutinho's "savage linguist" interest: "nos deparamos, em muitos momentos, com uma fala vigorosa que inventa sentidos, cria vocábulos, mistura termos de diferentes origens, uma fala que tenta escrever sua própria gramática" ("Eduardo Coutinho, linguista" 51; we come across, in many moments, vigorous speaking that invents feelings, creates words, mixes terms of different origins, a speech that tries to write its own grammar). The fallenness of language provides the ground for a certain kind of naive creativity, what Lins calls the "infancy of language"—i.e., moments of non-meaning where the relation between sounds, words, and things is not defined (42). This infancy, a reference to Giorgio Agamben, refers to a playful openness to signification. Lins, however, does not engage the Heideggerian dimensions of this Agamben idea. For Heidegger and Agamben, metaphysics is not defined by an originary presence but by negativity; that is, presence has always already been removed in order that language can take place. If we agree that Coutinho's work thematically coheres around the "infancy of language," recalling Agamben's debt to Heidegger reminds us that Coutinho's work must have ontological stakes.[3] In other words, Coutinho's films are not simply about finding better ways to signify the real or gesturing toward an ineffable object that exists outside language. In this sense, Fátima's preceding interview proves illuminating. Once Fátima sits opposite Coutinho, the director asks his first question: "What were you doing when we arrived?" Fátima tousles her hair in a medium close-up and explains she was dying her hair: "tem que cuidar da aparência que a aparência é fundamental na vida do ser humano" (you have to take care of appearance because appearance is fundamental in a human being's life). While scholars study the ersatz Joplin performance to argue the performative aspects of Coutinho's oeuvre, the earlier interview reminds us that Coutinho's films explore performance not to belie the truth but to "take care of appearance," to illustrate how Being is not concealed behind appearance but is unconcealment itself.

That Coutinho is less interested in revealing the truth is evident in later interviews in *Edifício Master* (2002), a film that finds the director renting an apartment for one month in a twelve-story building in Copacabana to film everyday life in the building during one week. The first interview is an unusual conversation with Daniela, an English teacher who refuses to *encarar* or face Coutinho. She explains that she has sociophobia and neuroses exacerbated by the bustle of Copacabana and its crowds. Her greatest pleasure is going up or down the elevator alone because she knows she will not have to see or be seen. When Coutinho confronts her about her withheld gaze, Daniela explains, "não porque eu que esteja dizendo não tenha veracidade mas porque eu não sei se tenho a autoconfiança para encará-lo" (not because what I'm saying isn't true but because I don't know if I have the self-confidence to face you). She insists she is not lying and laments that seeing and being seen underwrite truth claims. Must we *encarar* to divine the truth? Daniela recites her poetry and displays her painting. We glimpse Daniela entirely through these mediations as she conceals others facets of herself. These modes of expression are refuges from being "sempre assistida" or always watched. Challenging the documentary injunction that truth is revealed through direct observation, Coutinho's film suggests the need for another way of thinking the true/false distinction, where the truth emerges perhaps in the light of appearance. More famously in *Edifício Master*, Alessandra, a young woman who recounts her teenaged pregnancy and her sex work, ends her interview with an admission: "Eu sou muito mentirosa. Eu conto mentira e eu acho que para a gente mentir tem que acreditar . . . Eu até choro para me acreditar . . . Você sabe que tem mentira que eu acabo acreditando é verdade? . . . Agora não menti nada, não. Ontem menti para eles . . . Sou uma mentirosa verdadeira" (I am such a liar. I tell many lies and I think that for people to lie they have to believe. I even cry so I'll be believed. You know there are lies that I end up believing are true? But I haven't lied this time. Yesterday I lied to them [the producers]. I am a true liar) (fig. 11.1). This liar's paradox speaks to the limits of the interview as a means to arrogate truth value, a limit Coutinho limned in *Últimas conversas*. Alessandra echoes the adolescent Bruna in this final film, who proudly states, "sou loroteira" (I'm a liar!). When Coutinho explains his modus operandi

Figure 11.1. Alessandra, a "true liar," in *Edifício Master*. Source: *Edifício Master* (*Master Building*). Directed by Eduardo Coutinho, Videofilmes, 2002.

to Bruna, he cautions: "I'm going to ask you questions about your life. You can lie or not, it doesn't matter. I don't know if the truth exists." Later, Coutinho even ends his emotional interview with Rafaela, who sheds tears while recalling her domestic abuse, with a final equivocation: "Everything you said is true, isn't it?" I do not take this to mean that Coutinho is a relativist; instead, I want to suggest that Coutinho's encounters are not epistemologically driven but ontologically oriented. Coutinho's *conversas* are less about learning the truth than allowing Bruna or Alessandra to disclose themselves in their seeming.

Últimas unsettles because it encounters a mundane form of adolescent pretension, where pretension refers pejoratively to an inconsistency in appearance. And yet isn't pretension another form of performative language?[4] Coutinho's late phase has long used performance to unsettle the realist documentary project; however, performance is generally taken to be a temporary state, and we otherwise demand consistency between appearance and manner. In this light, *Últimas* is less a departure from Coutinho's method than it finds the director's project at its limits.

The Personagem Appears

Coutinho's interest in performance is less tied to questions of truth or authenticity than to how words are used to describe and define. Coutinho was an avid reader of Walter Benjamin, and Benjamin's reflections on language inform Coutinho's own ruminations on how identities are reinforced and communicated through iteration and how our interpretations of the past assist in the "performance" of the past. In his 2013 interview with Nader, Coutinho explicitly references Benjamin when he recalls his meeting with Leocádio in the interior of the northeastern state of Paraíba during the production of his film *O fim e o princípio* (2005). This scene is the centerpiece of a film that Consuelo Lins argues is Coutinho's most explicitly about language ("Eduardo Coutinho, linguista" 48). Leocádio, one of the few older residents who is literate, engages Coutinho in an esoteric conversation about how "há tanta palavra escrita em vão" (there are so many words written in vain). When Coutinho presses Leocádio to explain himself, Leocádio demonstrates the difference between the common word (a palavra comum) and the true word (a palavra certa). He explains that "in the beginning" there was but one word to designate an object: "por exemplo, uma janela era uma janela" (for example, a window was a window). He raps on the side of his window and continues, "agora janela, meia-porta ou outra coisa" (now it's window, half-door or something else). Leocádio laments the fallenness of language and recounts a peculiar version of the Tower of Babel.

In his later interview with Nader, Coutinho marvels at how Leocádio's explanation evoked Benjamin's essays on Adamic language and the one-to-one correspondence between word and reality. Nader underscores how both Benjamin and Coutinho were interested in what is expressed not *through* language but somehow *in* language: "Ambos partindo da mesma questão fundamental. O que realmente comunica a nossa língua, para além de uma eventual mensagem utilitária?" (62; Both depart from the same fundamental question. What does our language really communicate beyond an eventual utilitarian message?). Nader argues that our essence is communicated in a language that is paradoxically made up of words not belonging to us. To understand this paradox, I want to turn to an earlier moment in the film when Coutinho has yet to settle on his documentary subject. Coutinho explains in this prologue that he and his crew set out for the countryside for four weeks to make a film without having done any preliminary research and without a planned topic or filming location. The filmmaker quickly finds a local, Rosa, who becomes a guide to the region. After a couple of days of using Rosa as an inter-interviewer in neighboring towns, Coutinho resolves to shoot his film in Rosa's hometown because conversations with relative strangers seldom moved beyond questions of daily work and did not create the necessary "intimacy." If we recall Coutinho's interest in surface, intimacy cannot simply be aligned with an insider knowledge that guarantees truth value. As Lauren Berlant explains, intimacy resides between the public-instrumental and private-affective, and this resonates with Nader's earlier discussion of Coutinho on language—"What does our language really communicate beyond an eventually utilitarian message?" ("Intimacy" 283). To answer Nader requires engaging with intimacy and the ways it bears on the categories of experience and subjectivity.

Consuelo Lins and Cláudia Mesquita seem to argue along these lines when they cite the physical proximity of the filmmaker to the town's residents, which "guarantees they do not become mere documentary objects" (54). For Lins and Mesquita, the answer to Nader's query is to argue for a bodily language expressed despite (or because) of the residents' illiteracy. Yet how do we reconcile this embodiment via proximity with the fact that Leocádio, the "messianic Sebastianist," is the least proximate interviewee in the film? Leocádio does not welcome the crew into his home. He does not even come to the door. Rosa moves away from the camera to approach the furtive man at his window. In the next shot, Coutinho and Rosa are at the window on either side, facing Leocádio, who shrinks away from the camera, using his arms, his hands, and even a yellow folder to conceal his face and body. To privilege physical proximity and the embodied language of rural people recalls the more populist strains of subaltern studies that misread Gayatri Spivak's "Can the Subaltern Speak?" As Abraham Acosta argues, Latin American postcolonial thought has responded by saying "yes (the subaltern can speak) *and* no (we just don't listen)" (52). Lins and Mesquita's argument seems to fall into the same trap. Their framework relies on a positive metaphysics; caught up with making the world significant within a conventional linguistic framework, they seek out the real in its semantic latency or valorize each sign as surface for a phenomenological encounter.

"Intimacy" (and not physical proximity) enables us to think Coutinho's project differently. Lauren Berlant continues, "to intimate is to communicate with the sparest of signs and gestures" ("Intimacy" 281). But for Berlant, this is a communication that is less about making meaning—"intimacy only rarely makes sense of things"—than allowing a process of attachment—"a narrative about something shared" (286). This intimacy is a performative language that shapes the relation between private and public because our desire for attachment has a necessarily public dimension—attachment requires a willingness to extend beyond ourselves (281). Coutinho's personagem is a person made public, not to expose some hidden truth or secure some measure of authenticity but to "build worlds [and] create spaces . . . for other kinds of relation" (282). Framed through intimacy, Coutinho's films are less linguistic experiments than ontological solicitations.

In this vein, we can return to Leocádio's telling of the myth of Adamic language following Kaja Silverman. For her, the function of words is not to describe or correspond to the world but to communicate with others how we see that world (Silverman, *World* 21). Through Heidegger, Silverman suggests that "language does not signify, rather it shows" (57). Intimacy avoids thinking language as an obstacle to the recovery of the real or as an entifying representation that yields an object present-at-hand (55). Deploying language in the intimate field means opening ourselves to the world because there can be no precise substitutory transaction in the linguistic exchange, only new possibilities for signifying constellations. Recall that Coutinho characterizes the loss of correspondence between word and object as a "great tragedy" that *also* animates great poetry. When he says "a palavra não é a coisa" (the word is not the thing), we should not presume his intent is to make the word and thing coincide. Perhaps we should delight in their noncoincidence. In this framework, where the function of the word is to communicate how the world is seen, the word is not a mere appearance that denies us the real, but rather a relation between speaker and world that allows the world to appear (55). Coutinho mines language not to find more precise modes of signification but to disclose the world (and the personagem) in its affective relation to himself.

The personagem does not preexist the intimate encounter as identity, subject, or type but emerges through a disclosive relation of care with Coutinho. This is perhaps what Coutinho meant when he claimed that each person was encountered in their singularity: "there is never a generalization or classification [because] the people are not shown as examples of anything else. They are not psycho-social types. The people are not seen as part of a whole" (Lins, "El cine" 45). This suggests a mode of representation that is neither metaphoric nor metonymic. There is no *behind* each figure. To imagine a behind (to appearance, to language) is an effect of a subject before speech and an essence behind appearance. This helps make sense of Coutinho's admonition against depth. He notes: "It's not about depth. I don't like the word deep. I expect it to be very superficial." He derides depth in its German Romantic connotation—that is, an inmost depth as a site of truth—and by extension of the contemplation it would prescribe.

Contemplation and reflexivity entail using things in the world as an opportunity for introspection and removal from the world, instantiating a metaphysics that discovers Truth by concealing the world (Silverman, *World* 17). Instead, Coutinho catches glimpses of the world. I use the term glimpse because every disclosure is a partial concealment; something can *sobressair* only if something else remains concealed, and "nothing ever stands fully exposed before us" (Silverman, *The Miracle* 49). When Coutinho playfully asserts that he is not interested in depth, he encourages us to treat the image for its ontological extrusion rather than its hermeneutic depth.

This means the image signifies neither metaphorically nor metonymically but analogically. Analogy here refers not to sameness or equivalence, where one term functions as a placeholder for another, but as "the authorless and untranscendable similarities [and differences] that structure Being" (11). I derive this understanding of analogy from Kaja Silverman, who thinks the photographic image as an analogy in a network of correspondences (and not a representation or index) to argue that the photograph does not simply refer to an absent real but opens us to receive others in their seeming. In this way, the image is less evidentiary than demonstrative, and the power of the photograph is both ontological and social not because of what or whom is depicted but because of the "ontological thread stitching the seer to what is seen" (88). Coutinho's documentary lights a "pathway [for us] leading back to the world" by using personagens that summon our look (150). Coutinho's emphasis on the singularity of the personagem does not refer to their uniqueness. The character's singularity is less a property of the object than an appearance externalized that summons differential investments of care. The personagem is not simply the substrate or surface of the object—the opposite of depth is not surface but salience—but a presencing. The person becomes personagem in conjunction with our concern (Silverman, *World* 133).

The Transitive Politics of Cine-Catalysis

The Coutinho encounter does not reveal a hidden truth or allow us to get beyond mere appearance because appearance is the locus within which Being unfolds. Drawing on *cinéma vérité*—"Não é a filmagem da verdade é a verdade da filmagem" (What matters is not filming the truth but the truth of filming)—Coutinho stages encounters between the filmmakers and characters, and the camera's presence and his willful participation produce the recorded event. Lins makes this influence explicit, invoking Jean Rouch and his cine-trance to explain Coutinho's approach, one that seeks to produce a filmed event that does not preexist the fact of film and must undergo a transformation (Lins, "El cine" 41). Yet Coutinho rejects the comparison, adding that his films do not seek out (the filmmaker's) transformation. His is less a cine-trance than a cine-catalysis, an intervention that occasions and accelerates a reaction without consuming the filmmaker-catalyst. What we watch is a reaction in transition-state with the personagem as precipitate. The personagem is a visual augmentation, less a misrepresentation than an appearance, "an event which is also initiated from the side of the spectacle rather than from that of the look" (Silverman, *World* 21). Coutinho's process is less about representational content than what it makes room for. Coutinho summons forth each personagem, but not to capture an authoritative portrait. He does not scrutinize in an attempt to arrest the world and make it known.

When Coutinho insists that he remains unchanged in the encounter and the outcome of his interview is not his own transformation, he departs from most considerations of the documentary as heuristic. Can there be a politics that does not seek transformation? To begin to answer this, I return to Coutinho's interview where he remarks, "to know [conhecer] the world is more important than transforming it." I want to note the use of *conhecer* and not *saber*, the former taking a direct object, indicating familiarity with something or someone, and the latter taking a verb, pertaining to knowledge of a some*how*, a mastery. Coutinho advocates becoming familiar with the world. His is a *cinéma vérité* that doesn't imagine the world as deceitful and doesn't imagine appearance as something to shed to arrive at truth (perhaps *cinéma vérité* is a misnomer to begin with). In the Nader interview he notes: "The need to be heard, is one of the strongest human needs. To be heard is to be legitimated . . . But who is worried about legitimating the other? People's concern is to legitimize themselves." In this formulation lies the key to understanding Coutinho's politics, a shift from the reflexive (*se legitimar*) to the transitive (*legitimar*).

Coutinho's films are often celebrated for their self-reflexivity, for foregrounding how his scenarios are staged and how the film crew intervenes in the documentary production. Figured in the conventional language of political modernism, these explanations cast Coutinho's films as steeped in a tradition of critical distantiation that produces an awareness of how meaning is made. Yet this tradition of self-reflexivity is one directed toward and avowing the subject positioned in abstract space. When Coutinho suggests a method that operates transitively and reciprocally, he aspires to militate against a (self-)reflexive disposition. Coutinho does not work in the reflexive (and self-reflexive) mode of an earlier political documentary, which distantiated and evicted the spectator from a narrative space to produce an awareness of how meaning is made. This technique relies on cultivating an ironic disposition that supposes a hidden truth or reality. Instead of the pronominal "se legitimar" and its reflexive pronoun, which avow the subject, Coutinho's method suggests that we legitimate others and, in turn, are legitimated by others. The transitive verb takes a direct object; the sentence is incomplete and has no meaning without its direct object. As we know [*conhecemos*] the world, we invite it into this transitive relation; we legitimate it.

Perhaps we could regard Coutinho in his late phase as turning away from the reflexivity of political modernism in the wake of New Latin American Cinema, emblematized in *Cabra marcado para morrer* (1964–1984). *Cabra* invited us to confront the death of João Pedro Teixiera and arguably the death of a certain political restiveness in the late 1960s. *Últimas* forces us to confront a death of a different sort. Of course, Coutinho's interviews are only "últimas" because of his unexpected death during post-production.

How can this be a film "about death" if death was not thematized during production? Nader observes that in Coutinho's project, "vida e linguagem são sempre indissolúveis" (86; life and language are always inseparable). Yet most critics separate them, spending most of their energies thinking the latter term without considering the former. My turn to Heidegger thinks life (and death) in relation to language in Coutinho's films. *Últimas* showcases these imbricated concerns in Coutinho's interview with Thiago Theodoro. Coutinho asks, "Você não acha que a vida humana é muito estranha?" (Don't you think life is very strange?). Thiago responds with his own example of reported speech: "A friend of mine said to me, 'you think life's just waiting, sleeping and living? No, it's more complex than you can imagine.'" Coutinho eventually thinks aloud: "Viver é sofrer também, não é? Alegria e sofrer são inevitáveis" (To live is also to suffer, isn't it? Joy and suffering are inevitable). A self-professed Romantic, Thiago responds, "É aquela história, ou amor ou morte . . . Ou você ama ou a vida não faz sentido" (It's that [age-old] story, love or death . . . Either you love or life has no meaning). Lins remarks that the director hated the conjunction "or" ("*Últimas*" 39), and Coutinho rebukes Thiago: "Não, você ama e morre, não tem 'ou,' nunca é 'ou,' . . . é vida e morte, e não vida ou morte, não existem duas coisas separadas assim" (No, you love and you die, there is no 'or,' it's never 'or,' . . . It's life and death, not life or death, the two are not separate). Coutinho understands that death is not opposed to life but is "life's 'natural goal'" (Choe 262). In this regard, *Últimas* is a fitting bookend to *Cabra marcado para morrer*, a film whose Portuguese-language title also reminds us that death is immanent to life.

Últimas is an unusual film because death features not in the mortification of the lived body but in the film's posthumous completion (Sobchack 237). *Últimas* is about death not in that it makes death visually present but in that it forces us to confront the impossibility of its presence. Consider Thiago's provocative question to Coutinho: "Alguém voltou da morte?" (Has anyone ever come back from the dead?). Coutinho, now the interviewee, answers monosyllabically, "Não." "Então como você vai saber que é a morte?" (So how will you know what death is?). We cope with this aporia watching *Últimas* (and Coutinho's late phase) when we attempt to locate of the authorial "I" or use semiotic phenomenological approaches that privilege the perceptibility of death. Heidegger teaches us that these mechanisms inscribe both a self-centered relation to the other and time as a present-at-hand phenomenon. For instance, Sarah Wells argues that Coutinho's *Moscou* (2009) is a rumination on the obsolescence of cinema and its related precursors, photography and theater (423). For Wells, Coutinho's late phase is fascinated by ends, almost elegiac in staging the failures of political modernism and the role of cinema as a medium for capturing the present (425). I share with Wells a fascination with these films' concern with untimeliness; however, I want to shift away from obsolescence and toward senescence to avoid thinking time in relation to use-value. Senescence connotes instead maturation and finitude, less a lamentation of "an inevitable loss to come" and more "an affirmative attitude toward death" (Choe 257). I agree that these films reckon with the past, but "this return to the past . . . is grounded in anticipatory resoluteness" (Heidegger, *Being* 352). Unlike Wells, who argues that Coutinho's oeuvre increasingly uses the obsolescence of the film medium to meditate on the past, I want to suggest a posthumous lens that regards Coutinho's late phase as a meditation on the present as the past of the future. To anticipate the end is "to constitute the present not as the origin and absolute form of lived experience but as the product, as what is constituted . . . on the basis of the horizon of the future" (Derrida 188). Thiago's question in *Últimas* stages this existential dilemma and reminds us that there is always something outstanding until the moment of death. For Heidegger, death is not simply "a factual present-at-hand occurrence" (Hammet 168). Heidegger insists we must stop treating death as an object or something alien to the self; however, if death is integral to the self, then there is always something outstanding to the self: "The self as future, as not-yet, is manifested through anticipation" (168). The present is not a self-evident or transcendental present but the past of the future—we are what we will have been. The present is less a "here and now" than a "not-yet."

Instead of attempting to curb this anticipatory comportment, Heidegger proposes we use this anxiety to cultivate a relation to indeterminacy. *Últimas conversas* is effective precisely because this anxiety is at its most salient. Despite Coutinho's reservations, the problem with the teenagers is not that they have no past but rather that they have too much future. So much future is ontologically unsettling, with both personagem and spectator confronting the limits of their sovereignty. The former beckons the future in an apostrophic mode, and the latter confronts a posthumous presence bearing an agency that exceeds intentionality. The interviewee becomes personagem in their seeming, that is, when our beholding renders the personagem posthumously present. In this transitive politics, the film and its viewer are related in a "phenomenologically vitalizing movement of rhetorical animation" (Berlant, *Cruel* 26). The personagem in the Coutinho film is the ontological extrusion of the interviewee prolonged in the spectator. Through this intimate encounter, both interviewee and spectator share a desire for attachment, enacting a form of publicness with a peculiar temporality, where the past is an opening toward the future where it will be made historical past (Derrida 213). By figuring Coutinho's films through the question of ontology and the existential temporality and spatiality of Being, we move away from an epistemology of revelation that presupposes an object we can possess and/or know and is therefore temporally and spatially present(-at-hand). Coutinho's films do not merely yield some ontical knowledge about the world itself [*saber*], they disclose how the world matters to us in one way or another [*conhecer*]. This approach to documentary is less concerned with making its objects known than summoning us into relationality. As we extend beyond ourselves, we are made part of a public that is never *ultimate* because the world steps forth as it solicits and corresponds to our desire so that there is always something outstanding and something that exceeds intentionality. In this way, the *conversas* in Coutinho's final film are not *últimas* because our attachments allow the world to posthumously appear or *sobressair* in an elsewhere and elsewhen.

Notes

1. Francisco Elinaldo Teixeira also recovers Pasolini and Deleuze to rethink the dialogic conventions in Coutinho's oeuvre.
2. The existential spatiality of Being is developed in Heidegger's "Building, Dwelling, Thinking." In this essay, Heidegger uses the concepts of building and dwelling to ruminate on how we exist in the world. Heidegger imagines us not as subjects who master the world by making ourselves its relational center but as dwellers who sustain space by remaining constant with relations to things. This entails thinking space not as an external object or a measurable distance but an intervening space or interval. To dwell remains with the thing itself rather than reducing it to a symbol of its distance from us.
3. Agamben ultimately rejects Heidegger's ontological project because of the correspondence (if not substitution) of Being and language in relation to an ineffable presence outside language. See McLoughlin for more.
4. As Dan Fox argues, pretension is a form of play-acting or pretending (29).

Works Cited

Acosta, Abraham. *Thresholds of Illiteracy: Theory, Latin America, and the Crisis of Resistance*. Fordham UP, 2014.

Berlant, Lauren. *Cruel Optimism.* Duke UP, 2011.

———. "Intimacy: A Special Issue." *Critical Inquiry,* vol. 24, no. 2, 1998, pp. 281–88.

Choe, Steve. "From Death to Life: Wim Wenders, Autobiography, and the Natural History of Cinema." *The Autobiographical Turn in Germanophone Documentary and Experimental Film,* edited by Robin Curtis and Angelica Fenner, Camden House, 2014, pp. 255–76.

Derrida, Jacques. *Heidegger: The Question of Being & History.* Translated by Geoffrey Bennington, U of Chicago P, 2016.

Fox, Dan. *Pretentiousness: Why It Matters.* Coffee House Press, 2016.

Hammett, Jenny Yates. "Thinker and Poet: Heidegger, Rilke, and Death." *Soundings: An Interdisciplinary Journal,* vol. 60, no. 2, 1977, pp. 166–78.

Heidegger, Martin. *Being and Time.* Translated by Joan Stambaugh, State U of New York P, 1996.

———. "Building, Dwelling, Thinking." *Poetry, Language, Thought.* Translated by Albert Hofstadter, Harper and Row, 1971, pp. 141–60.

Lins, Consuelo. "Eduardo Coutinho, Savage Linguist of Brazilian Documentary." Translated by Natalia Brizuela. *Film Quarterly,* vol. 69, no. 3, 2016, pp. 28–34.

———. "Eduardo Coutinho, linguista selvagem do documentário brasileiro." *Galáxia,* vol. 16, no. 31, 2016, pp. 41–53.

———. "El cine de Eduardo Coutinho: un arte del presente." *Eduardo Coutinho: cine de conversación y antropología salvaje,* edited by Grupo Revbelando Imágenes, Nulú Bonsai, 2013, pp. 37–50.

———. "*Últimas conversas*: entre o filme inacabado e o filme possível." *Últimas conversas,* edited by Eliska Altmann and Tatiana Bacal, 7Letras, 2017, pp. 23–48.

Lins, Consuelo, and Cláudia Mesquita. "*O fim e o princípio*: Entre o mundo e a cena." *Novos estudos,* vol. 99, 2014, pp. 49–63.

McLoughlin, Daniel. "From Voice to Infancy: Giorgio Agamben on the Existence of Language." *Angelaki: Journal of the Theoretical Humanities,* vol. 18, no. 4, 2013, pp. 149–64.

Nader, Carlos. "No princípio era o verbo." *Últimas conversas,* edited by Eliska Altmann and Tatiana Bacal, 7Letras, 2017, pp. 49–116.

Pasolini, Pier Paolo. *Heretical Empiricism.* Translated by Ben Lawton and Louise K. Barnett, Indiana UP, 1988.

Russo, Pablo. "Cine de conversación: la restitución de la palabra y el cuerpo del otro en Eduardo Coutinho." *Eduardo Coutinho: cine de conversación y antropología salvaje,* edited by Grupo Revbelando Imágenes, Nulú Bonsai, 2013, pp. 51–58.

Sayad, Cecilia. "Variations on the Author." *Film Quarterly,* vol. 69, no. 3, 2016, pp. 12–18.

Schwartz, Louis-Georges. "Typewriter: Free Indirect Discourse in Deleuze's Cinema." *SubStance,* vol. 34, no. 3, 2005, pp. 107–35.

Silverman, Kaja. *World Spectators.* Stanford UP, 2000.

———. *The Miracle of Analogy: or the History of Photography, Part 1*. Stanford UP, 2015.
Sobchack, Vivian. *Carnal Thoughts: Embodiment and Moving Image Culture*. U of California P, 2004.
Teixeira, Francisco Elinaldo. "Enunciação do documentário: o problema de 'dar a voz ao outro.'" *Estudos Socine de Cinema—Ano III,* edited by Mariarosaria Fabris e João Guilherme Barone Reis e Silva, Sulina, 2003, pp. 164–70.
Wells, Sarah Ann. "Jet Lag: Late Cinema in South America." *Revista de Estudios Hispánicos*, vol. 50, no. 2, 2016, pp. 409–37.

12

The Right Moment

Kairos and the Documentary Cinema of Eduardo Coutinho

Vinicius Navarro

At the time of his death, in 2014, Eduardo Coutinho was the most celebrated documentary filmmaker in Brazil, a towering figure whose influence has yet to be fully accounted for. His seemingly modest cinema, however, could have said otherwise. After the unchallenged critical success of *Cabra marcado para morrer* (1964–1984), it took him several years to define a consistent and coherent documentary practice. When he did so, it was often through films that seemed to lack both rhetorical ambition and narrative complexity.[1] Many of his documentaries were shot on a single location; several consisted mainly of interview shots, lengthy testimonies from ordinary people whose singular identities might have eluded other documentary makers. Interestingly, it was this unadorned and seemingly unpretentious cinema that cemented his status as Brazil's foremost documentary maker. "The widespread critical endorsement of Coutinho's films," writes Cecilia Sayad, "comes largely from the understanding that he could achieve so much with what appeared to be so little" ("Variations" 12). The documentary interview was key to his cinema, but Coutinho managed to reinvent the interview format, turning what could otherwise look like a highly conventionalized procedure into a conversational practice—a method alluded to in the title of his posthumously completed documentary *Últimas conversas* (*Last Conversations*, 2015). Moreover, as Ismail Xavier notes, in Coutinho's films the interview becomes a "dramatic form," combining theatricality and spontaneity, the contrived and the contingent (223).

The pursuit of a conversational cinema was not accidental. In many ways Coutinho's films constitute a timely response to what might be broadly described as a crisis in documentary authority, much of which has involved a need to reevaluate the filmmaker's role as discursive agent in contemporary nonfiction film. As the political culture that inspired documentary makers changed toward the end of the last century, so did their films. Michael Chanan puts it lucidly when he says that "documentary widely abandoned its formerly all-knowing tone of voice, acknowledged the susceptibilities of the camera and its own subjectivity, discarded sobriety and modernised its language to match the loss of the old sociopolitical certainties and the articulation of new preoccupations" (v).[2] In Brazil, these changes presumed a recognition of cinema's limitations as political discourse and a distancing from a "pedagogically" oriented type of cinema associated with the 1960s. They also overlapped with the country's transition from dictatorship to democracy in the 1980s, which in turn allowed for fresh approaches to political filmmaking.

Coutinho responded to these changes not with skepticism but with a renewed interest in the world. Against documentary cinema's penchant for generalization, he created films that affirmed the concreteness of individual lives. To the tired questions of transparency and authenticity in documentary representation, he proposed a cinema that valued artifice, in which the subject documented was directly implicated in the act of filming. And in response to the ethical dilemmas that accompany documentary cinema's approaches to "the other," Coutinho opted for a dialogical cinema that demanded attention to particularity and contingency.

What made all this possible was a consistent interest in the profilmic situation as locus of exchange, an unfaltering attention to cinema's encounter with the world. In Coutinho's films, the profilmic functions not just as source of documentary material but also as creative engine, as site of invention. Despite the films' status as finalized artifacts, it is the process rather than the product that stands out; the moment of creation overlaps with the situation that unfolds in front of the camera. This is a cinema of the present, as Consuelo Lins puts it ("O cinema de Eduardo Coutinho"), where the relative unpredictability of the profilmic event often receives more attention than the alleged certainty of the documentary record. Coutinho's cinema, in this sense, goes against documentary orthodoxy, which privileges the pastness of the record, the *elsewhere* and *else-when* of the world documented.[3] Documentaries are expected to "[carry] fragments of social reality from one place or one group or one time to another," as Jonathan

Kahana writes (2). Yet Coutinho's cinema of the present is not a cinema unconcerned with the past or oblivious to the affinity between documentary films and historical narratives. One need only look at *Cabra marcado para morrer* (*Twenty Years Later*, 1984), which explores different layers of collective and personal histories, to appreciate the mutual implications between present and past in Coutinho's work. Similarly, his films show no pretension of treating the present as if it existed independently of the mediating process. The opposite is true, in fact: the present is clearly entangled in the process of mediation. Ismail Xavier's often quoted term, "the camera effect," suggestively evokes the mutual dependence between the act of filming and that which is filmed (223).

My interest here is in looking at how Coutinho's cinema of the present restores the authority of documentary discourse even when—or precisely because—it challenges documentary orthodoxy. More specifically, I am interested in discussing the significance of *the occasion* in his cinema, the propitiousness of the moment that connects the documentary process and the subject documented. Indeed, if it is possible to talk about a cinema of the present, it is because Coutinho values the inconclusiveness—and the fecundity—of a moment still in the process of becoming. Instead of continuity and finality, what stands out is the specificity of that moment, the occasion that mobilizes the filmmaker's attention: *kairos* rather than *chronos*, to evoke two distinct notions of time, one associated with the particularity of the occasion, the other with duration and progress. This chapter turns to the former as it explores Coutinho's cinema of the present, his seemingly modest yet decisive contribution to the history of contemporary documentary. I look at seven of his films, most of them made in the last fifteen years of his career.[4]

Kairos is one of the ancient Greek words for time. While *chronos* refers to linear time—the continuous temporality of the story events in a narrative, for instance—*kairos* designates the unique and provisional time of a particular occasion—the *here and now* of the profilmic situation, to use a familiar example. *Kairos* is commonly understood as the right time or the opportune moment. In rhetorical theory, it usually refers to the critical moment when the rhetor must act (White 13–14, Rickert 74). Other meanings attributed to *kairos* in classical rhetorical thinking include "symmetry, propriety, occasion, due measure, fitness, tact, decorum, convenience, proportion, fruit, profit, and wise moderation" (Sipiora 1). The importance of *kairos* in classical rhetoric contrasts with its apparent neglect in post-Enlightenment thinking, whose emphasis on rationality was at odds with *kairos*' affinity with improvisation. By contrast, *kairos*' resurgence as a major concept in rhetorical theory during the last quarter of the twentieth century overlapped with a newly found interest in knowledge that is contextual, situated, and provisional—an interest shared by a variety of disciplines, including documentary studies.[5]

My use of the term *kairos* derives from an interest in qualifying the present in Coutinho's cinema. *Kairos* resonates with experiences that cannot be reduced to the imperatives of narrative development and argumentation, neither of which finds strong expression in Coutinho's films. In its affinity with the *here and now*, it also sheds light on Coutinho's interactions with the subjects in his films, the propitious encounter that serves as the basis for his documentaries' claim to the real. And insofar as it prescribes a specific attitude or disposition toward the present—"a way of being in the world" (White 151)—*kairos* can offer insight into the ethics of Coutinho's cinema as well, a cinema attentive to *the moment*, whose attunement to the present cannot be reduced to a methodological choice. More broadly, attention to *kairos* can provide an alternative to—or an expansion of—the interest in duration that characterizes many aspects of Coutinho's cinema (Brizuela). In this case, *kairos* presupposes *chronos*, as the opportune moment arises from within the prolonged exchanges between the documentary maker and the documentary subject. The focus, however, shifts from the sustained presence of the world to the particular nature of the occasion, as Coutinho himself suggests in a memorable testimony captured during the making of his last film.

The Right Moment

It is ironic that the scene we are likely to remember most vividly from *Last Conversations* is one that might not have been included in the film had Coutinho lived to finish it, his brief appearance at the very beginning of the documentary. *Last Conversations* consists mainly of interviews with adolescents from the public school system in Rio de Janeiro. It was completed after his death by longtime collaborators João Moreira Salles, the film's producer, and Jordana Berg, Coutinho's editor since *Santo forte*. The scene mentioned here, recorded at the end of the fourth day of shooting, serves as a prologue to the documentary we are about to watch. In it Coutinho comments on how difficult it is to engage with the teenage subjects in the film and laments the fate of what strikes him as a failed project: "It's really better not to do it than to make a seventy-minute film you don't believe in. . . . I've lost my connection with the world I had, or could have had. . . . Having faith is hard. Regaining faith is very hard." Coutinho is alone in the frame, sitting in a chair, the only piece of furniture in a large room, the same room in which he recorded the interviews we watch subsequently. Although he speaks as the film's director, the speech momentarily puts him in a different place: Coutinho takes the seat of the interviewee. In addition to ruminating about the shooting of the film, he answers off-screen questions from Jordana Berg, who now tries to reassure him of the worthiness of his project.[6] The edited conversation lasts about six minutes, at the end of which Coutinho orders the crew to cut. It is then that the interviews with the adolescents begin (fig. 12.1).

There are different reasons why the scene stands out. The man on the screen never got to see the film we are now watching, the project that so troubled him during the shooting process. Placed at the very beginning of the documentary, this brief sequence becomes a small tribute to a filmmaker who is now gone. There is also the distressed, annoyed tone of his speech, which contrasts with the image of the poised filmmaker we see in his other films, just as the punishing moment of self-doubt disagrees with Coutinho's status as Brazil's most celebrated documentarian (Sayad, "Variations" 14–15). The most revealing aspect in this sequence, however, may have less to do

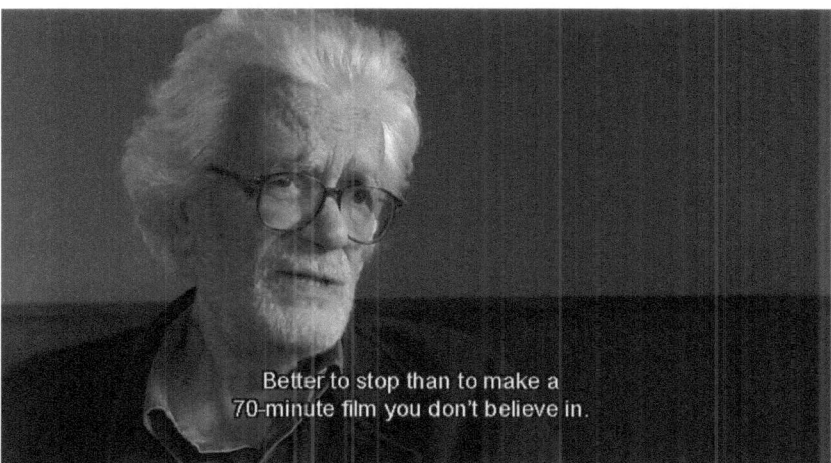

Figure 12.1. Eduardo Coutinho in the opening sequence of *Last Conversations*. Source: *Últimas conversas* (*Last Conversations*). Directed by Eduardo Coutinho, completed posthumously by Jordana Berg and João Moreira Salles, Videofilmes, 2015.

with this unusual screen appearance than with what Coutinho's speech tells us about his cinema in general. What Coutinho misses—the apparent loss that becomes the source of his frustration—is that special connection with the documentary subject he was well known for, the famed encounter with the world that has so often been described as a defining feature in his cinema.[7] That encounter was not meant to scrutinize or decipher the world in front of the camera. The purpose, rather, was to attend to a particular moment, just as that moment itself was coming into being. Missing that moment entails missing what is particular to the occasion—the *kairos* of the profilmic situation.

Philosopher John E. Smith refers to *kairos* as qualitative time, in contrast with time that can be quantified, measured in its duration—chronological time. *Kairos* "points to . . . a season when something appropriately happens that cannot happen just at 'any time,' but only at *that* time, to a time that marks an opportunity which may not recur" (Smith 47, emphasis in the original). *Kairos* assumes, then, a situation that is distinct from a random occurrence but also less predictable than a ritual. It commands attention and, perhaps more important, calls for action. Because it privileges the uniqueness of the occasion over the steadiness of chronological development, *kairos* is sometimes associated with chance. Smith refutes this analogy, though, arguing that chance may happen at any moment—not just at the right moment (54).

Kairos was a major concept in ancient Greek culture, spanning different areas and spheres of activity, including ethics and aesthetics, theater and poetry. It played an important role in Greek philosophy, from pre-Socratic to Aristotelian thinking. But it was in classical Greek rhetoric that it gained the greatest significance (Sipiora 3). *Kairos* was a key concept for the Greek Sophists, who believed in the "necessity of adapting [speech] to rhetorical circumstances" (Sipiora 4). Meaning was not to be dissociated from context, the persuasive force of speech being directly dependent on the situation of which it was part. Eric Charles White, in his influential study of *kairos* (suggestively titled *Kaironomia*), recalls the rhetorical thinking of Gorgias of Leontini, a sort of father figure among the Greek Sophists, for whom "*kairos* stands for a radical principle of occasionality" and the production of meaning appears as "a process of continuous adjustment to and creation of the present occasion" (14). The key words here are "adjustment" and "creation." The first suggests that a certain situation exists in the world and commands our attention; the second speaks of our capacity to produce that occasion. The distinction is not always clear, though, as occasions both shape and are shaped by the parties involved. In fact, contemporary approaches to *kairos* tend to wrestle with this distinction: where do we draw the line between opportunity "as discerned" and opportunity "as defined" (Miller 312), between discovery and creation? Are the rhetor and the environment not mutually implicated? (Rickert 75–77). For documentary filmmakers, the overlapping terms might be contingency and contrivance. We can think, for example, of the tenuous distinction between responding to a particular moment and creating that moment through the act of filming.

This interplay between contingency and contrivance helps us understand the emergence of the opportune moment in Coutinho's cinema. There, too, the line between discovery and creation is often unclear. Or, rather, the dichotomy itself loses its grip over the kairotic situation, as the act of invention and the world that surrounds it become mutually implicated. The interview setup in Coutinho's films, to use an obvious example, does not so much define the opportune moment as create the conditions of possibility for that moment to arise (an uncertain prospect, to be sure, as he contends in the aforementioned scene from *Last Conversations*). The same could be said about the specific locations he chooses for some of his films (a garbage dump, a building in Copacabana). Coutinho himself does not determine what happens in front of the camera. Rather, the profilmic situation invites the world "[to react] to the director's presence" (Sayad, "Variations" 14). Because the kairotic moment can be uncertain, we may end up grappling with the elusiveness of its form. Or we may argue, more generally, that *kairos* resists formalization (White [20] says precisely that). This argument is not without reason, but it risks overlooking the emergent particularities of the kairotic situation, the coming together of the various participants involved in it, the interactions between filmmaker and documentary subject—all of which suggests some level of formalization, however provisional that might be. What we have, then, is a situation in which a moment that might otherwise seem unremarkable is given salience, in which it becomes recognizable as such.

Think about *O fim e o princípio* (*The End and the Beginning*, 2005), a project that took Coutinho back to the Northeast of Brazil, where he shot the original *Cabra marcado para morrer* in the 1960s.[8] When the 2005 film starts, Coutinho is on the road with his crew, traveling in the sertão, Brazil's arid hinterlands, trying to find material for his documentary. We see a shot of a roadside taken from a moving vehicle and listen to the filmmaker's voice-over narration as he explains the project: "We came here to make a film in four weeks, with no previous research, no particular topic, and no particular location. We want to find a rural community we may like, and which may also welcome us. . . . Maybe we won't find any. Then the film will become a search for a location, a topic, and, above all, characters." The voice-over narration comments on the tentativeness of the project, implying that the opportunity Coutinho is seeking may not arise. Although the tone here is casual, even hopeful, this sequence now appears as a curious companion to the one at the beginning of *Last Conversations*. (There, too, it was the elusiveness of the occasion that concerned Coutinho, despite the fact that there was no search involved.) As we soon find out, however, in *The End and the Beginning* the right moment does come about; Coutinho ends up finding the community he is looking for. We watch a series of lengthy conversations with the (mostly) elderly citizens of that small rural community. And what once seemed formless and vague—a film that might not happen—now takes the form of a series of occasions involving the filmmaker's interactions with local people. The irony, for those who have watched *Last Conversations*, is that there too the promise of the occasion does not go unfulfilled. Despite the generational gap that separates Coutinho from the adolescents in the film, and a momentary awkwardness in their interactions, the conversations produce moments that are typical of his cinema, the "qualitative time" that characterizes the encounter between the camera and the documentary subject, the interplay between creativity and contingency, provocation and surprise.

The Occasion and the Archive

In some respects, *The End and the Beginning* distills qualities commonly attributed to Coutinho's films. The project begins to take shape when he meets Rosa, a young woman who serves as liaison between him and the local community. Coutinho is interested in hearing about their lives, in listening to them. And they willingly, if also reluctantly at first, comply. What started out as a film without a topic turns out to be precisely what we have come to expect from a Coutinho documentary: a film whose "design" depends largely on the here and now of the filming process. Accordingly, knowledge produced from these exchanges is contextual and inconclusive, but it is no less legitimate for that matter. More than gather information, the conversations submit the production of knowledge to the occasion that arises together with the filming process.

Two of Coutinho's most memorable documentaries, however, complicate this argument by including prerecorded material and directing our attention to historical events: the groundbreaking *Cabra marcado para morrer* (*Twenty Years Later*, 1984) and *Peões* (*Metalworkers*, 2004; shot in 2002), both of which rely on preexisting documentation, as archival documentaries are supposed to do. The former revisits the making of Coutinho's 1964 unfinished film—also called *Cabra marcado para morrer*—as well as the history of Brazil's military dictatorship (1964–1985). The latter looks at Brazil's labor movement of the late 1970s and early 1980s. In *Twenty Years Later*, Coutinho reconnects with the nonprofessional actors who participated in the making of the first *Cabra marcado*; in *Metalworkers* he goes looking for the worker-activists who anonymously contributed to the history of Brazil's labor movement more than two decades before the making of the film. As incursions into the country's recent past, both documentaries attempt to reclaim a piece of history that might have been silenced by the dictatorship, omitted from official narratives, or simply overlooked.

Twenty Years Later includes several images from the unfinished fictional film shot in 1964. Coutinho also uses still photographs, newspaper clippings, and footage of political demonstrations involving rural workers in the early 1960s. Similarly, in *Metalworkers* he turns to photos and press material, as well as existing documentaries about the Brazilian auto industry worker strikes. In some ways, the films do work like archival documentaries; they recontextualize and repurpose existing material. Yet the analogy with the archival film goes only so far. For whereas compilation documentaries are likely to place archival material within relatively linear narratives, Coutinho's films open the archive to the loosely structured events of the profilmic situation. Moreover, if traditional archival documentaries are expected to assign a specific meaning to the historical document, Coutinho's films refuse to constrain the life of the record. And while elsewhere archival footage may be prized for its value as photographic evidence, here the archive becomes part of the "mise-en-scène" (Furtado 17). The archive, in other words, helps create the occasions that breathe life into the films. Both *Twenty Years Later* and *Metalworkers* turn the alleged semantic insufficiency of archival material into an opportunity to connect present and past, to revisit history in the here and now that constitute the province of kairotic time.[9]

The famous opening shots in *Twenty Years Later* foreshadow what we later recognize as one of the film's most salient features: the use of preexisting documentation to facilitate Coutinho's interactions with the documentary subjects. Running for just over twenty seconds, these initial shots show a projectionist setting up an outdoor screening of footage from the unfinished *Cabra marcado*. Nearly two decades after the shooting of the original film, Coutinho located the nonprofessional actors who had worked in it—peasants from northeastern Brazil—and invited them to an improvised screening of the footage shot in 1964. The filmmaker then used the screening as a catalyst for his conversations with the "actors." In a sort of amplification of what would later be recognized as a defining characteristic in Coutinho's work, the dialogue between the filmmaker and the documentary subjects becomes also a dialogue "between the recorded images of the past and a present time of filmmaking," as Gustavo Furtado writes (11). Coutinho used similar methods in *Metalworkers*, although in this case he had no previous contact with the subjects he tried to locate. First, he met with a group of former worker-activists in a small room where he screened video footage of assemblies and demonstrations that had taken place more than two decades earlier. The workers in the room soon started naming the anonymous subjects in the videos, all potential participants in the film that would become *Metalworkers*. Later, Coutinho met with workers in their homes and shared photos and moving-image footage shot in the late 1970s. In these later interactions, reflections on personal experiences commingle with memories of collective struggles, and individual stories overlap with the country's political history. As with *Twenty Years Later*, the archival material does not simply provide a record of the past; it allows history to resurface in the moment of shooting (figs. 12.2 and 12.3).

Each film submits history to the power of the occasion; each one functions as a node in which the present converses with the past. *Twenty Years Later* was shot in 1981–82, a time when Brazil was transitioning from military dictatorship to democracy. Its impact and relevance are inseparable from that particular context. (Remember that the making of the first *Cabra marcado* was interrupted by the 1964 military coup.) More than recovering a history silenced by the dictatorship, the new film connects two historical moments: the onset and waning of military rule in Brazil. *Metalworkers* reveals a comparable scenario. The search for the anonymous worker-activists was also "framed" by an event contemporaneous with the shooting of the film. What instigated the making of the documentary was the imminence of the 2002 Brazilian presidential election, from which Luiz Inácio Lula da Silva, who had entered the country's political scene as a labor leader in the late 1970s, emerged victorious. The presidential campaign functioned as a catalyst for Coutinho's film, his search for Lula's former "comrades"

Figure 12.2. Archival material included in a scene from *Twenty Years Later*. Source: *Cabra marcado para morrer* (*Twenty Years Later*). Directed by Eduardo Coutinho, 1964–1984. Instituto Moreira Salles, 2014. DVD.

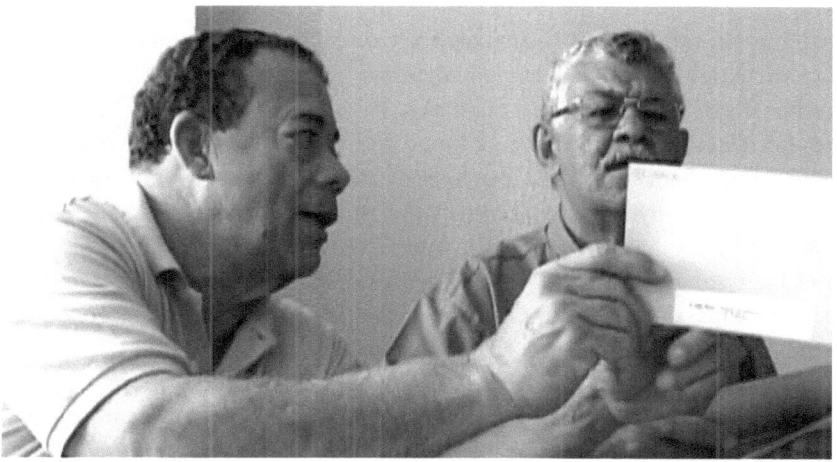

Figure 12.3. Archival material included in a scene from *Metalworkers*. Source: *Peões* (*Metalworkers*). Directed by Eduardo Coutinho, Videofilmes, 2004.

and the conversations that followed it. With each film, then, there are at least two opportune moments to consider: the historical circumstances that prompted the development of the projects (the transition to democracy in one case, the 2002 presidential campaign in the other) and the profilmic exchanges with the documentary subjects. In practice, the two occasions tend to overlap during the making of the films.

What emerge from these experiences are not conclusive narratives but histories made up of fragments held together by the opportune moment. Echoing a theme recognizable in several of Coutinho's films, the emphasis falls on the fragment, and it is the fragment itself that connects present and past. Coutinho's films crack open the archive not to dismiss its significance but to find new uses for it. The result is less a revisionist narrative, an effort to correct the past and rid history of its omissions, than a recognition of those critical moments when the past can resurge and be seen anew.

Performance and Artifice

Toward the end of his career, Coutinho made three documentaries in which the use of preexisting textual material helped shape the profilmic situation: *Jogo de cena* (*Playing*, 2007), *Moscou* (*Moscow*, 2009), and *As canções* (*The Songs*, 2011). In some ways, all three recall Coutinho's use of archival images in the films discussed above, although what counts as archival material here—a song, for example—might seem unusual in the context of documentary filmmaking. The three films also include a strong theatrical component, a more explicit emphasis on performance than was apparent in any of Coutinho's earlier films. In *Playing*, the filmmaker has six actresses reenact previously recorded testimonies from women who had agreed to share their life stories with him; *Moscow* entwines the lives of the characters in Chekhov's *Three Sisters* and the lives of the actors in the Brazilian theater company Grupo Galpão; in *The Songs*, the subjects interviewed by Coutinho choose to sing Brazilian songs that evoke personal memories (often involving romantic relationships). Much like what happens in the earlier films, the occasion we attend to arises through these encounters with "the archive."

Playing, the first film in the trilogy, explores intersections between acting and lived experience by bringing together testimonies from ordinary women and performances by professional actresses. At first, we assume Coutinho is simply interviewing women recruited through an ad posted in a local newspaper: "If you are a woman, eighteen or older, live in Rio de Janeiro, have stories to tell, and would like to audition for a documentary film, please contact us." The ad appears at the very beginning of the film, preceding a series of interviews recorded inside a theater in Rio, the Teatro Glauce Rocha. We hear from thirteen women who share stories of suffering and resilience, of bereavement and hope, not unlike those we may have heard in other films by Coutinho. That we may be looking at a more complicated scenario becomes clear approximately seven minutes into the film, when we first see the well-known Brazilian actress Andréa Beltrão and realize she is reenacting a testimony from the woman in the previous scene. Like Beltrão, five other actresses—not all as famous or easily recognizable—reenact testimonies recorded three months earlier. Sometimes the reenactment is intercut with the original interview, but sometimes we cannot tell one from the other. The distinction between what is reenacted and what is not becomes blurry. What prevails is the reality of staging itself (Sayad, *Performing Authorship* 98).

The reenacted scenes do more than highlight the film's emphasis on performance. They produce new material for the documentary. The reenactments create a new experience (Page 74). Take the scene with Andréa Beltrão, for instance. Toward the end of her "testimony," the actress breaks into tears, unable to control her emotions. The crying scene, however, was not in the script. The woman whose testimony is being reenacted did not cry. The tears Beltrão could not hold back are in fact her own. (She later comments on how the other woman's experience affected her emotionally.) The episode challenges the conventions that have typically defined authenticity in documentary: the distinction between premediated and uncontrolled behavior, for example, or between artifice and lived reality. Yet the scene does not undermine the credibility of the film. Beltrão's act does not so much depart from the script as it expands the realm of the real. The actress becomes a new documentary subject, a character—to use the term Coutinho favored for his documentary subjects—whose status is defined relationally, that is, in "conversation" with a woman Beltrão never really met.

This is where *Playing* resembles the archival documentaries discussed earlier. Prerecorded material helps bring about a situation that might not have existed otherwise, the basis of which is the "encounter" between two women. Rather than mimic a prerecorded testimony, the reenactments produce reverberations that carry over from one life experience to another. This encounter shifts attention from the individual testimonies to the relations that form between them, from the events narrated to those prompted by the reenactments, and from the alleged certainty of the past to the promise of the occasion that emerges with the filming process.

Playing is sometimes described as a companion piece, or a predecessor, to *The Songs*, the last film in the trilogy, which uses a similar setting—a stage—and follows a comparable format—a series of interviews that combine theatricality and ordinary life. Besides the usual interactions between the filmmaker and the documentary subjects, the interviewees sing a song of their choice, a gesture we may recognize from other films by Coutinho but which becomes a central component in *The Songs*. Seventeen people sing in front of Coutinho's camera. Thirteen of those also tell personal stories, the songs serving as opportunities to revisit a particular life experience. This resonance between the songs—a sort of popular cultural archive—and the characters' life experiences offers yet another variation on the use of archival material in Coutinho's cinema. But the songs play a more decisive role in the structure of the film. The singing performances interrupt the flow of information, emphasizing dramatic intensity over causality. As a structuring device in the film, the performances thus help define a particular temporal logic for the documentary, one that privileges the discontinuous, fragmented nature of kairotic time over the relative predictability of chronological progress and narrative development. For Coutinho, this logic helps produce a melodramatic quality that the testimonies may not deliver by themselves. In fact, in the Brazilian DVD audio commentaries, he repeatedly refers to his interest in the melodramatic character of the songs: "What interests me is the world of passion," he says in response to a question from filmmaker João Moreira Salles, the producer of *The Songs*. Punctuating the entire film, the songs—more specifically, the singing performances—reveal the extraordinary in the mundane and, in this sense, reiterate the qualitative difference that distinguishes the kairotic moment from the ordinary flow time (fig. 12.4).

The theatrical and the fragmented are at the center of *Moscow* as well, the most unusual of the documentaries in the trilogy, perhaps the most atypical of all of Coutinho's films, a documentary that has been described as a failed experiment and, for this very reason, an opportunity to reexamine the concept of *kairos* in Coutinho's cinema. In February and March 2008, Coutinho spent three weeks with the Brazilian theater company Grupo Galpão as they worked on Chekhov's *Three Sisters*. The group convened specifically for the making of the film; the play was not staged for a theater audience. What we watch are rehearsals and, occasionally, interactions among the actors. Coutinho himself hardly engages with the subjects in the documentary. Apart from a brief appearance at the beginning of the film,

Figure 12.4. Singing performance in *The Songs*. Source: *As canções* (*The Songs*). Directed by Eduardo Coutinho, Videofilmes, 2011.

he seems to abandon the role of filmmaker-interlocutor, the same role he had been refining throughout his career as a documentarian. This deliberate departure from what had until then been a recognizable feature in his cinema largely accounts for the documentary's atypical character and partly explains the disappointment felt by some of the film's critics. Longtime collaborator Eduardo Escorel lamented Coutinho's "absence" from the scene, noting that "he has taken the place of a privileged spectator of the drama and incorporated the conformism of Chekhov's characters."[10] The film, according to Escorel, fails to produce the connection with the documentary subjects we have come to expect from Coutinho's films. "During the shooting of *Moscow*, nothing happened," he writes.[11] Of course, that's not true. There was much going on in front of the camera: rehearsals, informal conversations, brief autobiographical monologues. Yet Escorel's critique is not without reason. What it reveals, to return to a familiar topic, is a concern with what looks like a missed opportunity, a concern not unlike the one Coutinho expresses in the opening scene of *Last Conversations*. What fails to materialize, if we take Escorel's perspective, is the opportune moment when something that might not have happened does come about.[12]

There are other ways to look at the film, though. Even if it departs from some of the most recognizable procedures in Coutinho's cinema, *Moscow* shares a number of features with the other two films in the trilogy. In his early and only appearance in *Moscow*, Coutinho explains the project this way: "We are going to try to put together at least parts of this play . . . The unfinished, the fragment—which is Chekhov himself—is fantastic. We don't want a finished play." As happens in the other two films, what is privileged here is the particularity of moment, the promise held by the inconclusiveness of the fragment. The actors' performances create oblique means to engage with lived reality, as was the case with the singing numbers in *The Songs*. There are also moments in *Moscow* when the separation between the characters in Chekhov's play and the actors playing fictional roles becomes muddled, a feature reminiscent of the reenactments in *Playing*. As Joanna Page puts it, "There is no clear distinction between rehearsal, performance, and real life. . . . Acting becomes a means of sharing experience" (81). What is more, the point of contact between acting and lived reality is not given beforehand but emerges through the actors' performances, the occasions brought about during the filming process. All this recalls the exploratory character of Coutinho's cinema and his unorthodox approaches to lived reality in the films that form this trilogy.

Whether or not *Moscow* was a failed experiment remains open to debate. What is certain is the opportunity to examine issues that became especially prominent in the last years of Coutinho's career: the use of artifice as a catalyst for the encounter with the world, the slippery nature of lived reality, the elusiveness of the propitious moment. *Moscow* may be more than just a reflexive documentary, as Joanna Page argues. But it is a reflexive film nonetheless, exuberantly so as a matter of fact.[13] As such, it invites consideration not just of the filming process but also of the nature and limits of documentary filmmaking. *Moscow* remains an intellectually engaging documentary even if we accept Escorel's claim that nothing happens in it, for when we do so we also start speculating about what might or should have happened. We invoke the promise of the kairotic moment and its place in documentary cinema.

Kairos and Ethics in Coutinho's Cinema

Moscow's departure from Coutinho's other films, wherever it exists, draws attention to yet another important aspect in his cinema. What remains consistent in most of his films is a particular attitude toward the world, an ethos that exceeds considerations of methodology and style. This attitude can be described as attentiveness to the moment, as attunement to the situation that emerges along with the filming process. Put differently, in Coutinho's cinema, *kairos* is elevated to an ethical dimension, not as the pursuit of an opportunity to be taken advantage of (the word opportunistic carries negative connotations for good reason) but as a way of embracing what the moment has to offer—and becoming part of it.

Ethics is central to Coutinho's cinema, and his films have contributed to the debate on documentary ethics in various ways, starting with the demystification of the film production process. More significant perhaps was his determination to withdraw judgment on his subjects, which made it possible for him to converse with a wide range of characters—and earned him their trust. Yet Coutinho's cinema ultimately exceeds these familiar concerns and offers yet another perspective on the ethics of documentary filmmaking. *Kairos* demands that we revise the terms that have traditionally defined ethics in documentary cinema, shifting the focus from the filmmaker's relationship with the filmed subject to the situation in which they are both involved. This is not to relieve the filmmaker of responsibility. But it is to think of responsibility as emergent and distributed, to think of it in relation to the situation that arises along with the act of filming.

Consider this often-remembered scene from *Twenty Years Later*, Coutinho's first conversation with Elizabeth Teixeira, the widow of the labor activist João Pedro Teixeira assassinated nearly two decades earlier, whose story was the subject of the first *Cabra marcado*. Fearing persecution from the military regime, Elizabeth Teixeira had been living clandestinely under a fictitious name for more than a decade, separated from most of her family. The meeting with Coutinho takes place at her home, where she is surrounded by her neighbors and two of her sons. She looks at stills from the shooting of the earlier *Cabra marcado*, in which she played herself in the reenactment of the events that led to the assassination of her husband. She then speaks somewhat reluctantly about living clandestinely and escaping political persecution. At one point her eldest son, who is sitting beside her, interrupts and gives a speech that is supposed to deflect attention from the history of political resistance the meeting inevitably evokes: "All [political] regimes are the same if you don't have political protection. . . . All political parties forgot Elizabeth Teixeira simply because she had no power." The son then challenges Coutinho to keep his disgruntled speech in the finalized film, fearing he could edit it out. Coutinho assures him that his voice will be heard. And the edited film confirms the filmmaker's deference to his request.[14]

Besides showing respect for the documentary subject, what the sequence reveals is a disposition to welcome the situation as it unfolds. Respect for the "other" is subsumed under responsiveness to the moment. Moreover, what might have seemed like a reluctance to intervene on the part of the filmmaker shows in fact a disposition to adjust, to be in the moment. As Thomas Rickert puts it in his study of ambient rhetoric, the "situation *gives back*" (87, emphasis in the original). That situation is shaped not by one person or another but by an ensemble, even if each participant plays a different role—and enjoys a different level of authority. In addition to the individual participants, the situation in Elizabeth Teixeira's house involves the act of filming, the unexpected arrival of Coutinho and his crew, and the memories triggered by their conversation. "Kairos is not about mastery but instead concerns attunement to a situation, with attunement understood . . . as an ambient catalysis . . . a gathering that springs forward" (Rickert 98).[15] Attunement evokes the emphasis on listening often associated with Coutinho's cinema. More generally, it also calls for a different way to approach documentary authority. As an ethical principle, *kairos* locates the source of authority neither in the voice of the filmmaker nor in the reality documented but in the situation that joins one to the other.

It seems fitting to conclude a discussion of Coutinho's films by turning to the ethics of his cinema. For it is through the lens of ethics that his general attitude toward documentary film seems most coherent. An ethical approach to documentary cinema usually presumes an ethical approach to the world documented as well. In Coutinho's cinema, this ethos crystallizes in his openness to the situation that unfolds in front of the camera. Or, as he himself might have put it, in his desire to remain curious. (In that famous opening scene from *Last Conversations*, he worries: "Other people felt I was curious. Do you think [these kids] feel I am not?" . . . If I'm not curious, then why talk?") This looks like a modest way to characterize a cinema that has elicited so much critical attention, or too simple a term to describe films that often function as critical texts in their own right. But curiosity does say a lot about Coutinho's cinema. It honors the promise of the occasion, welcomes both uncertainty and opportunity, and in the end affirms the importance of *kairos* in documentary cinema.

Notes

1. *Santo forte* (*The Mighty Spirit*, 1999) stands out as a significant moment in this trajectory, both in terms of style and methodology. Although many of the traits we recognize in Coutinho's oeuvre were already noticeable in *Cabra marcado para morrer*, starting with *The Mighty Spirit*, as Cecilia Sayad explains, he "steadily solidified his carefully conceived approach to nonfictional filmmaking" ("Variations" 12). With the exception of *Cabra marcado para morrer*, all the films discussed in this chapter are also from the period that follows the making of *The Mighty Spirit*.

2. Chanan lists a number of political developments that help contextualize this crisis in authority: "On the one hand, the heartlands of capitalism saw the demise of traditional class politics and the gradual demoralisation of the organised left in the face of neoliberalism; on the other, came the rise of second-wave feminism, identity politics and the new social movements, all of which have global resonance" (v).

3. Coutinho's cinema of the present recalls in some ways Bill Nichols's definition of the performative documentary, a cinema in which the "world is itself brought into being through the very act of comprehension" (*Blurred Boundaries* 102). There, too, the present "intrudes" into documentary discourse.

4. In his discussion of Coutinho's work and its dialogue with modern cinema, Ismail Xavier refers to the importance of the fragment and the potency of the instant in Coutinho's films (226–27).

5. For a discussion of scholarship on *kairos* that precedes this English-language resurgence of the concept, see Rickert (83–90).

6. Jordana Berg would go on to edit *Last Conversations* as well after Coutinho's death.

7. On Coutinho's dialogical cinema, see Lins (*O documentário*); Sayad (*Performing Authorship*, "Variations on the Author"); and Xavier, among others.

8. Coutinho also shot the initial sequence of *Peões* (*Metalworkers*, 2004) in the Northeast of Brazil.

9. Archival footage is also used in more conventional ways both in *Twenty Years Later* and in *Metalworkers*. When it is edited into the films, however, the archival material tends to serve mainly as illustration. The most ambitious uses of existing documentation take place within the profilmic situation.

10. "Coutinho se acomodou no lugar de espectador privilegiado da ação e incorporou o conformismo das personagens de Tchekhov."

11. "E na gravação de *Moscou*, nada aconteceu."

12. For a different perspective on the film's alleged failure, see Feldman.

13. Bill Nichols defines reflexive documentaries as texts that are "self-conscious not only about form and style . . . but also about strategy, structure, conventions, expectations, and effects" (*Representing Reality* 57).

14. Consuelo Lins offers a detailed analysis of this sequence, focusing specifically on the exchanges between Coutinho, Elizabeth Teixeira, and her son (*O documentário de Eduardo Coutinho* 45–47).

15. On *kairos* and attunement, see also Lipari.

Works Cited

Brizuela, Natalia. "Conversation and Duration in Eduardo Coutinho's Films." *Film Quarterly*, vol. 69, no. 3, 2016, pp. 19–27.

Chanan, Michael. *The Politics of Documentary*. BFI, 2007.
Escorel, Eduardo. "Coutinho não sabe o que fazer." *piauí*, no. 35, 2009, https://piaui.folha.uol.com.br/materia/coutinho-nao-sabe-o-que-fazer/. Accessed 4 June 2022.
Feldman, Ilana. "O filme que não acabou." *Eduardo Coutinho*, edited by Milton Ohata, Cosac Naify, 2013, pp. 638–49.
Furtado, Gustavo P. *Documentary Filmmaking in Contemporary Brazil: Cinematic Archives of the Present*. Oxford UP, 2019.
Kahana, Jonathan. *Intelligence Work: The Politics of American Documentary*. Columbia UP, 2008.
Lins, Consuelo. "O cinema de Eduardo Coutinho: Uma arte do presente." *Documentário no Brasil: Tradição e transformação*, edited by Francisco Elinaldo Teixeira, Summus, 2004, pp. 179–98.
———. *O documentário de Eduardo Coutinho: Televisão, cinema e vídeo*. Jorge Zahar, 2004.
Lipari, Lisbeth. *Listening, Thinking, Being: Toward an Ethics of Attunement*. Pennsylvania State UP, 2014.
Miller, Carolyn R. "*Kairos* in the Rhetoric of Science." *A Rhetoric of Doing: Essays on Written Discourse in Honor of James L. Kinneavy*, edited by Roger D. Cherry et al., Southern Illinois UP, 1992, pp. 310–27.
Nichols, Bill. *Blurred Boundaries: Questions of Meaning in Contemporary Culture*. Indiana UP, 1994.
———. *Representing Reality: Issues and Concepts in Documentary*. Indiana UP, 1991.
Page, Joanna. "Beyond Reflexivity: Acting and Experience in Contemporary Argentine and Brazilian Cinema." *New Argentine and Brazilian Cinema: Reality Effects*, edited by Jens Andermann and Álvaro Fernández Bravo, Palgrave Macmillan, 2013, pp. 73–85.
Rickert, Thomas. *Ambient Rhetoric: The Attunements of Rhetorical Being*. U of Pittsburgh P, 2013.
Sayad, Cecilia. "Variations on the Author." *Film Quarterly*, vol. 69, no. 3, 2016, pp. 12–18.
———. *Performing Authorship: Self-inscription and Corporeality in the Cinema*. I.B. Tauris, 2013.
Sipiora, Phillip. "Introduction: The Ancient Concept of *Kairos*." *Rhetoric and Kairos: Essays in History, Theory, and Praxis*, edited by Phillip Sipiora and James S. Baumlin, State U of New York P, 2002, pp. 1–22.
Smith, John E. "Time and Qualitative Time." *Rhetoric and Kairos: Essays in History, Theory, and Praxis*, edited by Phillip Sipiora and James S. Baumlin, State U of New York P, 2002, pp. 46–57.
Xavier, Ismail. "Indagações em torno de Eduardo Coutinho e seu diálogo com a tradição moderna." *Cinemais*, vol. 36, 2003, pp. 221–35.
White, Eric Charles. *Kaironomia: On the Will-to-Invent*. Cornell UP, 1987.

Part V

Coutinho in His Own Words

Introduction

Krista Brune and Natalia Brizuela

During his filmmaking career from the late 1950s until his death in 2014, Eduardo Coutinho rarely wrote about his thoughts on cinema. Unlike renowned Cinema Novo director Glauber Rocha, Coutinho did not publish extensively as a film critic prior to becoming a director, nor did he articulate his theories and methods of filmmaking in manifestos and treatises. The documentarian's comparative disdain for writing about how he saw film, whether the work of other directors or his own practice, makes the few texts that he did publish more significant. This section consists of four pieces that Coutinho wrote and published on film, which were previously included in Milton Ohata's 2013 edited volume *Eduardo Coutinho*. Written at different moments of Coutinho's career, these texts offer insight into his relationship with cinema as a viewer and a director. They reveal interests and concerns that recur in his documentaries as he refined his distinctive style of a cinema of conversation.

Fascinated by spoken words and oral expression, Coutinho distanced himself from writing as his career progressed. In fact, Coutinho's 1992 "O olhar no documentário. Carta-depoimento para Paulo Paranguá,' translated here as "Gaze in Documentary. Statement/Letter to Paulo Paranguá," begins with the director's distress at having to write four to five pages about the topic of the documentary gaze. Part of this lament has to do with his view that defining documentary was too general and that it was more appropriate to think about the specific people and places in his films. It also betrays his frustration with and eventual rejection of the written text. We open the section with this "statement/letter," which is one of Coutinho's only written reflections on his filmmaking practice and on the relationship of documentary cinema to the real and to fiction. He continued to comment on his approach to filmmaking in interviews until the end of his career, but he did not formulate these views in written texts.

The director did not always eschew the written word, however. After initial experiences with filmmaking as a student in Paris in the late 1950s and with the CPC in the early 1960s, Coutinho worked as a screenwriter. His writing process was often connected to forms of dialogue. For instance, he based the script for the original 1964 version of *Cabra marcado para morrer* on conversations with Elizabeth Teixeira during his three months in Paraíba in 1963. As he listened to her talk about the life of her husband, João Pedro, and their participation in the Ligas Camponesas (Peasants' Leagues), Coutinho took notes that served as source materials for the subsequent screenplay (Mattos 51–54). Even in his work as a writer, Coutinho occupied the role of a listener, whether he was in conversation with Elizabeth or in dialogue with the written words of playwrights and novelists. He cowrote the screenplay for *A falecida*, a 1965 film adaptation of Nelson Rodrigues's play. In 1967, he contributed to the screenplay of *Garota de Ipanema*, which was inspired by the eponymous song by Vinícius de Moraes and Tom Jobim. He drafted a rejected screenplay for *Engraçadinha depois dos trinta* as a film adaptation of Rodrigues's novel *Asfalto selvagem*. He collaborated with Armando Costa to write the script for *A vingança dos doze* in 1969. The following year, he wrote and directed *Faustão*.

Coutinho entered his most intense period of writing in the early 1970s. From 1972 to 1976, he cowrote screenplays for three fictional feature films: *Os condenados*, an adaptation of the novel by Oswald de Andrade directed by Zelito Viana; *Lição de amor*, directed by Eduardo Escorel and adapted from Mário de Andrade's novel *Amar, verbo intransitivo*; and *Dona Flor e seus dois maridos*, an adaptation of Jorge Amado's novel directed by Bruno Barreto. As a cowriter of these filmic adaptations, Coutinho was in conversation with his fellow screenwriters and with the esteemed authors who penned the source materials. At the same time, from 1971 to 1974, he worked for the *Jornal do Brasil*. After two years at the copydesk, Coutinho joined the team of film reviewers alongside Ely Azeredo, José Carlos Avellar, Alberto Shatovsky, and Alex Viany. Between August 1973 and December 1974, Coutinho wrote forty articles, ranging from film reviews and commentaries to profiles of Hollywood stars. Ohata compiled these pieces and reprinted them in their entirety in chronological order in his edited volume. Within this corpus, only one article, "As riquezas do subdesenvolvimento" (The Riches of Underdevelopment), directly addressed Brazilian film. Coutinho's journalistic production instead focused on mainstream Hollywood films, westerns, and literary adaptations. Because of his contemporaneous work as a screenwriter, he brought unique insight to the challenges of adapting literary works to screen in, for instance, his pieces on Ingmar Bergman's *The Seventh Seal*, Luis Buñuel's cinematic use of surrealism, and screen versions of Henry James's comedies. Above all, his writing explored the highs and lows of the film viewing experience (Ohata 49–50).

From this interest in the spectator's response, Coutinho expanded to think about the geopolitical inequalities in the world cinema system. He commented on the values and aesthetics that were either imposed on or desired by directors and traditions outside the Hollywood machine His writings revealed a fascination with and a deep love of classic films, even as he criticized the industry that produced them. To give a sense of Coutinho's distinctive approach to film criticism, this section features three pieces originally published in the *Jornal do Brasil* and now translated for the first time into English. "A melancolia do crepúsculo" ("The Melancholy of Twilight") demonstrates his ability to explore broader themes, such as aging and fame, via the study of a specific place or person, in this case, Charlie Chaplin. This technique defines his filmmaking, most notably as he examined the idea of Brazil, its democracy, and its people through his conversations with Elizabeth Teixeira and her children in *Cabra marcado para morrer*. The spatial and temporal confines to which he subjected himself when making *Seis dias de Ouricuri, Santa Marta—duas semanas no morro, Babilônia 2000*, or *Edifício Master* offered a similar template where the filmmaker moved beyond these limitations to consider more general topics and questions.

Although Coutinho is best known for his independent and nonprofit documentaries, he approached cinema as a global industry with commercial pressures and financial strains in his roles as a viewer and a critic. Attempting to write and direct fictional feature films during the 1970s exposed him more directly to the processes of financing, producing, and distributing films. He also examined these questions in his essay "Uma Hollywood Latina em busca de mercados," translated here as "A Latin Hollywood in Search of Markets." News of a recently signed economic and cultural agreement between Mexico and Brazil led Coutinho to reflect on the unique status of Mexican cinema as a state-sponsored industry positioned between Hollywood, Latin America, and the global market. Coutinho also considered how the fame and prestige of a director influenced the circulation and reception of their films, as the opening paragraphs of his essay "Uma partida de xadrez entre a morte e o cavaleiro," which is translated here as "A Chess Match between Death and the Knight," indicate. After noting that nearly two decades passed between the 1956 production of *The Seventh Seal* and its Brazilian release in 1974, the essay contextualizes the film in Bergman's career and delves into an astute analysis of the film as a work of adaptation. Coutinho's attentive reading of the theater piece in relationship to the screenplay and the final film showcases his multiple perspectives as a spectator, a writer, and a filmmaker fascinated by performance. Decades later in *Jogo de cena*, he further explored the porous lines between the person and the character and between a real setting and the fictional mise-en-scène as one performs versions of themselves, or others, on stage and on-screen. Coutinho's writings on film provide insight into the cinephile that he had been since childhood and the documentarian that he would become.

Works Cited

Mattos, Carlos Alberto. *Sete faces de Eduardo Coutinho*. Boitempo, 2019.
Ohata, Milton. "Era uma vez um crítico." *Eduardo Coutinho*, edited by Milton Ohata, Cosac Naify, 2013, pp. 49–54.

13

Gaze in Documentary
Statement/Letter to Paulo Paranaguá

EDUARDO COUTINHO,
TRANSLATED BY FLORA THOMSON-DEVEAUX

Editors' note: This statement/letter to Brazilian film historian and journalist Paulo Paranaguá first appeared in the catalogue of the 1992 Cinema du Réel, a documentary film festival held annually in Paris. By defining his idea of a "cinema of conversation," Coutinho unpacked a concept central to his trajectory as a documentary filmmaker. This brief text introduces key themes, including the gaze, the conversation, and the encounter, that reappear throughout Coutinho's work.

Faced with the responsibility of writing four or five pages about gaze in film and television documentaries, I feel inordinately anguished. Before the blank page, which is demanding to be filled up with ideas and words, I'm unable to repeat the broad definitions of television as the site of the simulacrum, of non-gaze and non-contemplation, the destruction of memory, of the imaginary, of any experience of the real. Even if I decide to write from a purely personal perspective, there's still the difficulty of choosing words and ideas in the abstract, since I have no idea who it is that may be reading me. I usually wind up giving in to these sorts of commitments and producing, however laboriously, something that is an "average" of my opinion, directed to an "average" foreseeable reader. When it's done I feel cowardly, remiss, and superficial, and I pray to the gods that I won't be interpreted or understood by way of these pieces written on demand, these bloodless, passionless, "average" essays.

In my case, apart from any passing or permanent neuroses, my struggles have to do with the fact that I chose documentaries—and one particular kind of documentary—some fifteen years ago. Through the structure of a "cinema of conversation," I chose to be nourished by the speech-gaze of singular events and people, immersed in the contingencies of life. Inasmuch as possible, this had the effect of doing away with broad ideas—which rarely inspire good cinema, documentary or otherwise—as well as the immediately, intelligibly symbolic "types" that are made to stand in for a social class, a group, a nation, or a culture. Improvisation, chance, and the friendly, at times tense relationship between the people in conversation, who are, at least in theory, placed on either side of the camera—this is the essential stuff of the documentaries I seek to make. That doesn't mean that there can't be a central idea preceding the shoot, of course. It can structure the film, but it's ultimately just a working hypothesis, one that is tested out in practice through successive encounters with flesh-and-blood characters.

In this sense, I never wrote scripts for my documentaries. I researched, read, and gathered information. From all that, I drew up "itineraries" for journeys, encounters, and, above all, questions.

Working notes, in other words, private annotations for my own use. But this, right here, is about writing thought-out thoughts, with no improvisation—definitive words, to be printed, made available for public use. There's nothing to nourish me but an abstract relationship with unknown readers who may or may not be interested in what I have to say. It's very little, it's vague; it means that what I have to say will be normalized in one way or another.

Ah, word choice, a metaphysical problem. Words are nearly infinite—just as the number of camera positions in a given environment, you might say. At least in the sort of films called fiction. In the sort of documentaries that I chose to make, I cut this dilemma down to the bare minimum. The limitations imposed by improvisation, by the need to capture events in the moment, by the essential eye contact between the people in conversation that so often requires the director's utmost attention—all these contingencies make the position of the camera so utterly dependent on the real that it is no longer an open-ended choice, as might be the case in fiction. In short, let me make this painful confession: I chose documentary so as not to be forced to choose where to place the camera. That's why the hardest part of cinema for me is coming up with the narration—when it can't be eliminated altogether, that is. And that's why, if it weren't for the unavoidable commitments that crop up here and there, I would now choose silence. Or, at most, oral expression, which is improvised and precarious by definition.

That said—or, rather, that written—I'm almost regretting this. But I believe that, however the previous paragraph may seem reductive or extremist, it stands as both a provocation and something I wanted to get off my chest, an outburst that is sincere, personal, and non-transferrable. I believe that this is a way, however roundabout, of fulfilling the commitment I mentioned at the start. I'm talking about my "real," and how I need the "real" of others to inspire associations and structures. I'm talking about the real, the gaze, documentary.

I could finish up here, and I'd suffer less, and it would be more honest. But since I must, I'll put down a few notes, plucked by chance out of the chaos of personal experience, without knowing beforehand if they'll make sense—because I can't plan what I should select, underline, or structure. I'll improvise, in a way, if that's possible. And let them be independent blocks, not necessarily connected in one overarching, neatly rounded off argument.

In August 1975, I joined TV Globo in Rio to work on *Globo Repórter*, a weekly documentary and news show, the only one of its kind on Brazilian television. This was in the thick of the military dictatorship, for all the talk of a "safe and gradual" political opening—a process that would take ten years before it was done. I was coming off a series of frustrations in fiction films (three features and a few scripts), first as an activist for the Centro Popular de Cultura (People's Cultural Center) of the National Students' Union, and then in the so-called film industry. I'd never done documentaries. Political and personal disillusionment, among other things, helped spark an immediate passion for one simple thing—looking at and listening to people, generally poor people, whether in the country or the city—the social and cultural Other. Trying to understand the country, the people, history, life, and myself, but always focused on the concrete, the microcosm.

It's become a truism in Brazil to say that cinema is an archaic form and that video, electronic equipment, stands for progress and modernity. What I saw at *Globo Repórter* was a testament to the danger of purely technological analyses that are blind to social and political conditioning. In the late 1970s, all of Globo's production, including journalism, was done on videotape; *Globo Repórter* was the lone exception. We worked with reversible film, with no rushes, using material that was prone to getting dirty and scratched in the Moviola. That widened the gap between the technically "clean" products that represented the "Globo standard of quality" and *Globo*

Repórter. In short: back then, in spite of the dictatorship, we had a niche inside the station where more autonomous, slower-paced work was possible, with greater room for controversy and a degree of experimentation.

In 1982, the show entered the electronic age. Suddenly, control was easier and tighter—all someone had to do was go into the editing room, grab a tape with the latest version of the product, and take it to be judged by the higher-ups. The documentaries soon became news pieces, just like the content coming out of the station's other journalism departments. Now they were antiseptic, integrated, neutralized. The logic of the industrial process in the form that it takes at Globo and on television in general, the logic of homogenization and profitability at any price.

In the 1970s, in the thick of the dictatorship, it was more interesting to do journalism at Globo than it is today. Back then, the censorship was external; now it's internal, and it doesn't just affect content, but language as well. One experience of mine is a prime example. For a show on the endless droughts in the Northeast in 1976, I shot a three-minute, ten-second scene in which a drought-stricken resident talked about the many sorts of roots he'd been forced to eat during the dry spells he'd lived through. He spoke and showed us the roots. The show, as well as the scene, aired intact and duly approved, having gone through the external censorship. That would be impossible today, but more for reasons of form than of content. A three-minute shot—what does that mean? The Globo Manual says: "When someone talks for more than thirty seconds, think twice." In journalistic pieces, the average shot is three to four seconds long; when the camera is moving, that can go up to seven or eight seconds; and people don't talk for more than thirty seconds in newscasts or for more than a minute in in-depth pieces. These are unwritten rules, of course. It's simply become a consensus among professionals in the field.

Silence is forbidden on Brazilian television because it's dead time, it may lead audiences to think there's been a technical problem, and it makes viewers change the channel. The only thing worse than breaking that taboo is to reveal that the film is a film, and not reality. In all its virulent naturalism, saying "this is real, we were here, this really happened," what our television abhors most of all is to show the negotiations that guide a shoot, the confrontation between the two entities placed on opposite sides of the camera. As more learned men might put it, to reveal the work of enunciation is a crime against credibility.

The broadcast licensing system and the way television works in Brazil is the product of collusion between the State and the private sector, riddled with secret rules, backroom dealmaking, and political pressures on top of the pressures of the market, where audience ratings are the be-all, end-all, a perverse system of controlling information and advertising funds, in which the government plays a major role. In the states, local oligarchies buy licenses for stations that become synonymous with political and economic power. How to make all this intelligible for a European? How to go about discussing gaze, the alleged topic here, when the common people are shown on TV either like some rare variety of orchid, to be admired at a distance, or scrutinized up close as the naive repositories of folklore and "wisdom"?

The myth of balanced, impartial information. Objective information. In its name—although no attempt is made to honor that name—any product with a patient, respectful gaze is automatically tossed out. If it isn't "information," it's useless poetry, pretentious anthropology, elitist navel-gazing.

Sometimes, documentaries are shown on television. They're generally produced by major government agencies or private companies, made for prestige or for institutional motives. They buy the time, and the station gets the money for practically no work. You might say that companies and stations buy "protection," like the mafia in the old days—and in the new days, too. Alibis.

People speak of gaze, which presumes listening. All foreign documentaries made in Brazil, even when they have the best of intentions, wind up reproducing ethnocentric stereotypes or giving reality a wide berth in one way or another. How can you dialogue with an interlocutor if you haven't mastered their language? Words conceal secrets and traps that lead to hesitations, silences, missteps, rhythms, inflections, different restatings of the same idea. And then there are the gestures, the pursed lips, furrowed brows, looks, breaths, shrugs, etc. Faced with all this, someone who doesn't know the language can only survive if, instead of trying to get around these issues, they turn their full attention to them and make that difference a source of power, make that strangeness a path to learning. The rest is folklore.

In my experience, I saw the extraordinary richness of the way that illiterate people expressed themselves, especially in less industrialized regions. This makes it more tempting to investigate an unassuming part of everyday life in the Brazilian Northeast, say, than a major topic in São Paulo. In regions where an oral, popular culture is still alive, enriched with all its impurities, even literate people will put all of their resources of expression into their speech. This is not a defense of the hateful culture of poverty and illiteracy. It merely exposes a contradiction: what took place when the model of Brazilian industrialization rapidly moved individuals from oral culture into mass culture, such as it is here, without going through any sort of school worthy to be called one. The name of that is catastrophe.

Many so-called progressive documentaries, whether leftist or at least remotely interested in social issues, tend to film only the events or listen only to the people who confirm their own previously held ideas about the topic in question. The result is a film that accrues data and information without producing surprises, anything new or unpredictable. Chance, the flower of reality, is shut out. I believe that a documentary's greatest virtue is its ability to be open to the other, such that it may ultimately give the (accurate) impression that the interlocutor is always right. Or that they have their reasons. This is a rule of supreme humility that must be rigorously observed, and in which one can take tremendous pride.

Always film irreplaceable events, the kind that have never happened before and will never happen again. Even if they're brought about by the camera. Even if they're not true. Without the feeling of urgency as to that which will certainly be lost if it's not filmed in real time, why bother to make cinema—an activity that is, after all, slow, tiring, and far from profitable?

Reality can only be subverted, in cinema or anywhere else, if one first accepts everything that exists, by virtue of the simple fact that it does exist.

Yours, Eduardo Coutinho.

P.S.: This is probably bad, and too long to boot. Cut whatever you think should be cut, you'll do a better job. I'll wait for you to let me know if it's all right.

14

The Melancholy of Twilight

EDUARDO COUTINHO,
TRANSLATED BY FLORA THOMSON-DEVEAUX

Editors' note: Published in the Jornal do Brasil *on August 29, 1973, this article responds to news of Charlie Chaplin's announced return to filmmaking at the age of eighty-four by commenting on Chaplin's career and, more generally, the place of an aging director in cinema. Coutinho expresses compassion here for veteran directors as they attempt to remain relevant. In doing so, the documentarian reveals a concern with aging and mortality that would continue to vex him until his untimely death. Two films made during his final decade,* O fim e o princípio *and* Últimas conversas, *offer meditations on coming to the end of one's life and career. The empathy evident in those films also marked Coutinho's reflections as a younger man writing this piece.*

The news that Charles Spencer Chaplin (84) is preparing his return to cinema indicates that the legendary comedian is up against the greatest challenge of his life. Thirty-two years after setting aside the Little Tramp's cane, seven years after his last film—the disappointing *A Countess from Hong Kong*—he is tired, secluded from the world in his Swiss villa. In the film world, directors have a relatively short life span and need to have iron constitutions, if Vittorio de Sica's recent operation, the gastric ailments of Luís Buñuel—the most brilliant of the septuagenarians—and the semiretirement of all of the great masters of American cinema are any indication.

> All I can do is bear up the best I can under my own old age and thank God. I can't do much anymore. And the days are long. I often drift off while I'm sitting. Sometimes I'll admire the landscape, the mountains, through the window. It's lovely, restful. And that's just what I need right now.[1]

These words of Chaplin's in an interview from December 1972—the words spoken quite slowly, after long moments of reflection—indicate just how difficult it will be for him to resume his place behind the camera, seven years after the failure of *A Countess from Hong Kong*. In his mansion in Vevey, Switzerland, he has apparently devoted the past few months to a single activity: composing music for his silent classics, which, as they're gradually shown across the world, have begun winning over a generation that only knew them from the mutilated shorts shown on TV.

The still-living myth of Chaplin the Tramp, as well as his millions, may ease his return to the hustle and bustle of the studios. It might well be an unprecedented event in the history of cinema, which has seen the retirement of its octogenarians and most of its septuagenarians, and the creative—or commercial—decline of illustrious sexagenarians. Indeed, the machinery of cinema, with all of its financial and bureaucratic trappings on top of the life-draining mission of directing a team of technicians and artists in the exhausting work of filming, is merciless on the aging. And producers are wary of putting their capital toward a film that may be interrupted by a heart attack from the boss (the situation that De Sica and his producer Carla Ponti now find themselves in).

Since his cinematic last will and testament—*Limelight* (1952), in which Calvero-the-Tramp remarks with dignified resignation on the "melancholy of twilight"—Chaplin has only made *A King in New York* (1957) and *A Countess from Hong Kong* (1966). Both show the artist striving to keep up his connection with audiences, but only managing to do so when autobiographical elements bleed into fiction and lend it another sort of truth.

The announcement of Chaplin's return may thus be considered, if not a false alarm, then at least an attempt unlikely to come to fruition. If that's the case, he'll continue to express his creativity in music—which is, like painting, an art that goes much easier on its practitioners. It frequently grants them a second youth denied to filmmakers, a common phenomenon that may be summed up in the final works of the late Stravinsky and the tireless, record-breaking production of Pablo Casals at age 92.

Almost none of the great directors in decline will have the consolation of music or the pleasures of a refined lifestyle. At most, they can turn to the hobbies that set the pace of life for so many retirees, as have William Wyler (70) and George Stevens (69), who seem tired and relatively uninterested in new projects. With *Frenzy*, his latest film, which recently premiered in Rio, Alfred Hitchcock (74) proved that the commercial and artistic appeal of his fascinating forms has stood firm against the passage of the years; even so, it seems likely that he will only direct intermittently, carefully picking his plots.

George Cukor (74), famous for the sophistication of his mise-en-scène and for his work directing actresses (*Gaslight, Adam's Rib, A Star is Born, My Fair Lady*) is one who hasn't resigned himself to dormancy. Despite having been off the sets for a few years, he's still making the rounds at studios and producers' offices in search of a chance, like an ambitious greenhorn drawn in by the lights of Broadway. In the throes of unemployment, he stands as the pathetic symbol of a tired old man who still wants to—and may even know how to—create.

Of all the great Hollywood directors who started out in the silent era, Howard Hawks may have held up the best. At age 77—he debuted in 1926, with *The Road to Glory*—he's kept busy, albeit somewhat sporadically, with *Eldorado* in 1966 and *Rio Lobo* in 1971, two Westerns that, while they may not add much to his glory, are a credit to his virtues. Genre may have played a part in his longevity: the Western has survived all fads, reaffirming its near-immutable simplicity since the dawn of American moviemaking. In a 1971 interview, Hawks said:

> The action should be surprising and logical. There are no new Westerns because there are no new plots. [. . .] A filmmaker should tell simple, true stories. Life, love, death. The Western seems particularly well suited to those requirements. [. . .] Audiences' ability to absorb that sort of thing seems nearly inexhaustible.[2]

It was also cut on the plains of the American West, crisscrossed by pioneers, Indians, soldiers, and buffalo hunters, that John Ford forged a style and created a world that are both recognizable at a glance—hence the introduction of the adjective "Fordian" into critics' and cinephiles' vocabularies, setting trends and sparking controversy as it came. At age 78, deaf (like Buñuel), blind in one eye, and wearing an eye patch à la Moshe Dayan (and like Raoul Walsh and Fritz Lang, both octogenarians), he was awarded the highest honor that the government of the United States can bestow on a civilian. During the ceremony, at the Beverly Hilton, a wheelchair-bound Ford exchanged pleasantries with Nixon while Jane Fonda, outside on the sidewalk, led protests against the president. Nixon called Ford one of the "geniuses of his profession," while Ford recalled that, when he saw American POWs coming back from Vietnam, he cried out: "God bless Nixon."

He may be the most famous American director alive, but Ford has been dormant since 1966, when he brought out the mediocre *7 Women*. In 1964 he had directed a project in his native Ireland (*Young Cassidy*), but had to leave the set early for an operation, and the movie was finished by Jack Cardiff. Though he may film again—there's no shortage of projects—all signs seem to indicate that his swan song was *Cheyenne Autumn*, which debuted in 1964 and was screened at the Rio de Janeiro International Film Festival the following year.

But it seems clear that the only filmmaker who has been able to keep up the quality and vigor of his work, fully retaining its contemporary edge, is Luis Buñuel. Almost as hale as his fellow Spaniards Picasso, Miró, and Casals, he has turned 73 in rare form. His last movie, *The Discreet Charm of the Bourgeoisie*, not only brought him the Oscar for Best Foreign Language Film—which he declined to accept in person—and the distinction of Film of the Year from the National Society of Film Critics, but it was a box-office success as well as a critical one.

Buñuel, having gone almost completely deaf years ago—which hasn't left a dent in his good spirits, and which allows him to become even deafer when he's in uninteresting company—has maintained an exemplary level of aesthetic and thematic coherence ever since his explosive debuts, *Un Chien Andalou* (1929) and *L'Âge d'or* (1930), even as his initial iconoclasm has given way to a subtler sort of cruelty. But not even he is impervious to the maladies of old age. This month, according to news from Mexico, Buñuel gave up on directing *The Phantom of Liberty*, a project for the same producer as *The Discreet Charm*. The reason: a gastric complaint, nothing more serious. The same report had the director saying that he wouldn't do any more adaptations and would only film his own ideas in the future.

Hospitalized for the extraction of a pulmonary cyst, according to some, or a benign tumor, according to his wife, Vittorio de Sica (72) harbors hopes from his sickbed that producer Carla Ponti will wait for him to recover to start shooting on *Il Viaggio*, with Sophia Loren and Richard Burton. De Sica, who made a name for himself as a director of neorealist cinema with *Shoeshine* (1946) and has 150 films to his credit as an actor, has gone downhill over the past twenty years and only recently garnered critical interest with *The Garden of the Finzi-Continis* (1971), which earned him yet another Oscar.

Among the filmmakers approaching the dangerous 70-year mark are John Huston, Billy Wilder, and Luchino Visconti, all age 66. While they're still active, it's undeniable that their latest films lack the vigor of mature work like *The Treasure of the Sierra Madre*, *Sunset Boulevard*, or *La Terra Trema*.

And if cinema is unforgiving in general, it only follows that things are even harder in Brazil. Out of all our directors who have passed that crucial benchmark, Cavalcanti (76) is living in Europe and writing his memoirs, having directed his last feature in 1958; Humberto Mauro (76) is retired and back in his native Volta Grande, planning to make *A noiva da cidade*, an old project of his; and Luís de Barros, who'll turn 80 this year, also has plans for a return, but in the meantime he's also delving into the past to finish his memoirs. The last of the pioneers to direct a feature film was Ademar Gonzaga (73), with *Salário mínimo*, in 1970. Given its paltry infrastructure—there are hardly any studios, which forces directors to do grueling on-location shoots—Brazilian cinema would certainly finish off many of the septuagenarians who are still working away in the studios of Hollywood or Cinecittà.

Notes

1. Translator's and editors' note: this quote is translated from Coutinho's Portuguese version of Chaplin's quote, as we were unable to locate the original English-language source.

2. Translator's and editors' note: this quote is translated from Coutinho's Portuguese version of Hawks's quote, as we were unable to locate the original English-language source. It is worth noting that the quote in Portuguese is quite formal compared to Hawks's tone in other interviews, such as the one with Joseph McBride and Michael Wilmington published in the spring 1971 issue of *Sight and Sound* and reprinted on the British Film Institute website in 2021. See https://www.bfi.org.uk/sight-and-sound/interviews/audience-howard-hawks-1971.

15

A Latin Hollywood in Search of Markets

EDUARDO COUTINHO,
TRANSLATED BY FLORA THOMSON-DEVEAUX

Editors' note: This undated commentary from the Jornal do Brasil *differs from Coutinho's other criticism, which focused on directors or films from Hollywood or Europe. This piece surveyed Mexican cinema from its Golden Age of the 1940s and the 1950s to its current state as an industry in search of markets, per Coutinho's assessment. State control of Mexico's film industry posed a challenge for experimentation, thus putting it at odds with viewers' preferences during the 1960s and 1970s as trends like New Latin American Cinema emerged. Coutinho contemplated how films could survive outside Hollywood, despite uneven dynamics of production and reception. His own documentary practice similarly navigated how to create films within and outside established systems.*

Among the economic and cultural accords signed yesterday between Mexico and Brazil, marking the high point of the Mexican president's visit here, one was an agreement on cinematographic co-production, to be implemented by the Instituto Nacional do Cinema. Meanwhile, a selection of the best in the latest crop of Mexican films was screened in a number of state capitals across Brazil, a sign of attempts to overhaul a film tradition both privileged by the protection of its government (which manages internal and external distribution as well as exhibitions) and hampered by official and union bureaucracies that are less than fully receptive to innovation.

"This film was created by members of the Mexican Republic's Union of Film Production Workers." These words, which appear at the end of the three Pelmex films currently showing in Rio, may have gone entirely unnoticed by Brazilian viewers. They must be included in nearly every domestic production distributed commercially in Mexico, however, and are a sign of the unique nature of that country's industry: a sort of Latin American state-run Hollywood whose ponderous gears have been modernized over the past four years to meet the new demands of the market.

In Mexico, the government controls all the elements of what could potentially be a genuine film-production policy geared exclusively toward the national interest. For years, this compact structure bolstered a continuous line of production that guarded against the advance of foreign films and won over audiences—in 1972, as had already happened at the Mexican industry's peak, box office revenues there surpassed figures for the United States. At the same time, however, this system has worked to stamp out nearly every spark of original work or nonconformity. This is made possible by the collusion (despite a lack of explicit coordination) of two sources of inertia: the intractable bureaucracy of government on one hand and the staunchly monolithic nature of unions on the other. As French critic Louis Marcorelles wrote in *Le Monde*, commenting on a ceremony presided over by the current head of the industry, Rodolfo Echeverría, Mexican cinema is both "state business and a family affair."

The Mechanisms

Around thirty years ago, the two fundamental mechanisms that control the industry were founded: the National Film Bank and the Union of Film Production Workers. Both entities were born with the best of intentions: to encourage the expansion of the industry and build an audience (in 1938 alone, Mexico produced a respectable 57 films), and to protect the rights of workers and technicians in a field naturally prone to cyclical crises. The short-term results of the policy were extremely rewarding: production for 1950 set a record, 122 films, making Mexico one of the five largest producers in the world. Laboratories and studios, all government-owned, were built and improved, and are now the best in Latin America. The government also saw about setting up an official network of distribution and exhibition, which tends to be the Achilles heel of the film industry in developing countries. They took advantage of the existing linguistic and cultural community—a state-run company, Pelmex, moved to occupy privileged spaces in the market abroad, across the countries of Spanish-speaking Latin America (Brazil was also an avid consumer from 1945–55), and the United States, with its Chicanos and Puerto Ricans. During the 1950s, Mexican productions beat out France and Italy on multiple occasions at the US box office.

Financing for production was the last link in the chain of this "infallible little machine," to borrow the words of Mexican critic Tomás Perez Turrent. He described the system as follows in a clear-eyed, implacable article published in *Mundo Nuevo* in December 1970: "The National Film Bank financed films that promised immediate, safe returns, based on a calculation of 'commercial values' (the popularity of the actors, genres, and reliably popular topics, songs, etc.) The loans were covered by the advances on distribution in major markets, based on the same calculations. The films were made quickly, with no effort to ensure even minimal artisanal quality. By the time the product was ready, it had already been paid for; the producer would invest the profits in real estate or other businesses and would start all over again."

Rumbas and Villains

This was the age when Brazilian audiences drank in the comedies of Mario Moreno, better known as Cantinflas, that extraordinary phenomenon of popular communication, and explosive melodramas dotted with musical numbers featuring *rumberas* like Niñón Sevilla and María Antonieta Pons, or crooners like Pedro Vargas. At a time when bolero rivaled the popularity of samba in Brazil, *Pecadora*—a feature buoyed by its titular song—could be seen steamrolling its American competitors in movie theaters across São Paulo. Enchanted by the songs, moved by the tearstained tales of sordid villains from the city's underbelly and prostitutes with hearts of gold—who, alongside long-suffering mothers, were inevitably the movies' great heroes—or won over by Cantinflas's mangled diction, the Latin American masses saw themselves in this world, which was, one way or another, connected to their roots.

Within the unions, all this was cause for righteous euphoria. Work proceeded at full bore, with project after project being filmed on studio lots. Even so, the Union would become a sort of fiefdom from the start, set aside for an elite that fought to defend its privileges and reject any new element. The creative stagnation brought on by this structure (the lone escapee from it being Buñuel) may be attested by a single metric. From 1938 to 1944 (one year before the foundation of the Union), 69 filmmakers put out their first films. From 1945 to 1958, that number was just 14, most either from within the organization itself—former editors, ex-directors of photography, etc., or relatives of industry higher-ups.

While Hollywood braved the industry crisis—the growing threat of TV and the rebirth of European cinema, with neorealism, Mexican cinema remained unchanging, even as its profitability plunged (by 1960, production had shrunk to fewer than 60 films). As in South America, economic growth had created a broader, increasingly sophisticated urban middle class, whose children were entering universities in larger numbers. Two consequences of these social transformations left a mark on film: large portions of the public began demanding films where they could see themselves represented, and started looking critically at *chanchadas*;[1] and young people with college degrees—architects, writers, and journalists—were drawn to the overarching term *nuevo cine*, determined to fight for a cinema that would be more open to formal invention and meaningful subjects.

The First Crack

Even as they bled money and prestige, the state and union bureaucracies resisted any change until, impelled by the biological imperative of survival—as Turrent puts it—they were forced to open up the system just a crack. In 1965, the STPC introduced its First Experimental Feature Film Competition; forty films were presented but, given the difficulties in obtaining financing, only twelve were produced. In any case, seventeen filmmakers were able to make their first films. Two years later came the second edition, with slightly less robust results: seven films, five new directors. The grand hopes inspired by the first competition faded away, bit by bit: new arrivals either adjusted to a flawed system or confined themselves to rare incursions with marginal producers and struggled to find a foothold in the market.

Nor was the economic crisis facing Mexican film placated by these timid measures. It was then that, in late 1970, Rodolfo Echeverría, the Mexican president's brother, became the head of the industry. Dynamic and well-intentioned, a highly popular former actor, he introduced sweeping structural reforms, including the creation of distribution offices in Paris (Cimex-France) and the Middle East, making the recruitment process more flexible and facilitating coproduction with technicians and workers. This led to a renaissance in Mexican cinema, as seen at the weeks of screenings put on in Europe. The Paris selection, for example, presented eight films chosen without any official interference—something nearly unprecedented in an arena in which more independent-minded directors limit themselves to drawing up screenplays, which are immediately rejected by the higher echelons in the union or the industry.

But from what arrived in Rio as a sample of this new crop, and from the observations of critics like Marcorelles and Turrent, it seems evident that the persistent rigidity of the system has erected very strict bounds around a renewal that must be both broad and ongoing. Turrent goes so far as to deny the emergence of a *nuevo cine*, while his French colleague, investigating in loco, has concluded that impasses persist, forcing more creative, aggressive auteurs to take refuge in the Universidad Autónoma de México's Centro Universitario de Estudios Cinematográficos. The films produced there, which generally make direct reference to the state of the country, its crises and its challenges, are accessible to college students but have failed to penetrate the blockade around commercial exhibition.

Even if Echeverría is able to finally conciliate entrenched interests with the need for a radical change, Mexico seems to offer an essential lesson, one that may prove quite useful now that our official film agencies are taking stronger stances in a market dominated by foreign distributors and the theater owners they work with. The challenge will be to absorb the notion that intervening in defense of our interests—in accordance with producers' justified demands—cannot imply control over or further limitations on the creativity of films or filmmakers' freedom of choice. After all, these are the factors underpinning the cultural health, and ultimately the economic health, of any film industry in search of national affirmation as the vehicle for the desires of the population in all its diversity.

Note

1. Editors' note: the *chanchada*, a genre of popular dramas, risqué comedies, and musicals that were modeled on and often parodied Hollywood films, dominated Brazilian cinema from the 1930s to 1950s.

16

A Chess Match Between Death and the Knight

EDUARDO COUTINHO,
TRANSLATED BY FLORA THOMSON-DEVEAUX

Editors' note: Published on October 19, 1974, this review of The Seventh Seal *was one of Coutinho's final pieces for the* Jornal do Brasil. *By situating the film within Bergman's career and, more broadly, Swedish national culture, the article highlights how creative and cultural influences, from Protestant puritanism to August Strindberg's writings and Victor Sjöström's films, shape this cinematic adaptation of a play written two years before the film. For Coutinho, analyzing the play, screenplay, and movie together underscores how the written text gains meaning via its staging. This recognition of the role of the mise-en-scène in theater and cinema anticipated the experimentations with performance and playing at the end of Coutinho's career. The piece also reveals the documentarian's long-standing fascination with language and mortality.*

The 1956 film *The Seventh Seal*, by Ingmar Bergman, will have its Brazilian premiere tonight, at midnight, at Cinema-1—as part of a retrospective of the director's work—and will begin screening commercially on Friday. At a time when *Cries and Whispers* is winning over audiences, the vision presented in *The Seventh Seal*—an adaptation of a one-act play by Bergman himself—may help shed some light on the evolution of a filmmaker whose thirty-year career has seen 45 productions (feature films, shorts, screenplays, and films for TV) marked by remarkable stylistic and thematic coherence.

Shot between *Smiles of a Summer Night* (1955), which garnered him a belated special award at Cannes by way of definitive international recognition, and *Wild Strawberries* (1957), *The Seventh Seal* can be seen, in the arc of Bergman's filmography, as the beginning of his metaphysical period. In this phase, setting aside a few minor works such as *Brink of Life* and *The Virgin Spring*, the anguished interrogation of a sky that remains empty and silent will give rise to the trilogy of *Through a Glass Darkly*, *Winter Light*, and *The Silence* (1963), where the impossibility of transcendence leads the director's characters to accept their inevitable solitude.

Choosing the Middle Ages as his time frame—the plague-wracked thirteenth century, to be specific—Bergman shuns decorative period reconstructions and frames the film as an allegory of the modern world. The plague, like the threat of the atomic bomb in the 1950s, was the mass destruction that reduced men to moral nakedness and to the sinister masks of superstition and official religions, which were left powerless to restore any connection to the divine. Bergman—the son of a Protestant pastor, who got "an early picture of behind the scenes of life and death"—is an intrigued observer of the rituals that punctuate human existence from birth to passing. From the title of the film onward, he underscores the sameness between the Middle Ages, with its mystical half-light, and the perplexity of the modern intellectual, who has lost faith in progress and reason but remains chained to the religious forces of the past.

"And when the Lamb broke the seventh seal, there was silence in heaven for about the space of half an hour," recounts John of Patmos in what is both the last book in the New Testament and the only prophetic one, containing the symbolic revelations of things past, present, and future. At the end of the film, Karin, the Knight's wife, recounts the list of disasters that befall the world as the angels blow their trumpets in the preamble to Judgment Day: rains of hail and fire, and the fall of the star Wormwood (symbolizing the liberation of Satan and the beginning of the end). Karin's narration concludes after the third angel, sparing us the horrors of the beast with seven heads, but also depriving us of the redemption of the New Jerusalem, with the triumph of the Church and the innocents: "And they shall see his face; and his name shall be in their foreheads." For Bergman, in the original play, the cataclysm leaves no survivors. But in the film, the ingenuity of the questioning man (the Knight) allows him to trick Death and steal away three of the simple in spirit, who will find, if not heaven, then life in all its precariousness: the juggler Jof, his wife, Mia, and their son, Mikael.

As with Bergman's best films, the project for *The Seventh Seal* was apparently born from an image, or a number of them—the traditional iconography of the Middle Ages, with its acrobats, plague, processions of flagellants, Death personified, witches burned in exorcisms, the end of the world as a real inevitability, sex as the creation of the devil, and the end of the age of the Crusades, when knights returned from the East just as shaken in their faith as soldiers returning from wars today are doubtful of the meaning of their participation. And so the Knight proclaims: "I want knowledge, not faith, not suppositions, but knowledge."

Perhaps more than any of Bergman's other films, *The Seventh Seal* reveals its roots in Swedish culture: in addition to the general aura of Protestantism and Puritanism that marked his childhood in Uppsala, we find the looming shadow of Strindberg, and above all of Victor Sjöström, the master of Swedish silent film. The specific inspiration here is *The Phantom Carriage* (1921), which Sjöström adapted from a book by Selma Lagerlöff. The difference being that Bergman is consoled neither by faith nor by their pantheism.

The matter of faith, however, is hardly uncomplicated for him. In 1958, before beginning filming on *The Magician,* he told Jean Béranger: ". . . [my father] liked *The Seventh Seal* a great deal. He knows that I only ever say what I think sincerely. It should be clear that I believe in God, not in the Church, Protestant or otherwise. I believe in a superior idea that we call God. I want to and I have to. I believe it is absolutely necessary. Integral materialism could only lead humanity to an impasse without warmth."

Darkness and Blood

In the play, written two years before the film, the knight, Antonius Block, remains silent throughout, only exploding at the last second as he cries out to the "Stern Master": "Every morning and evening I reach out toward heaven, toward God. I call on the Saints, I fill their ears with my cries, and again and again my heart overflows with faith. Across a spiritual desert, I feel God's nearness like the vibrations of a mighty bell. Suddenly my emptiness is filled with music of no tone, as if in waves of innumerable voices. In the great darkness I cry out, and my cry is like a whimper. For your glory, oh God! I live for your glory! So I call out in the dark. Then a terrible thing happens in every fiber of my body . . . the flame of my faith dies suddenly as if someone had blown it out. The great bell falls silent, the darkness throbs and thickens, it presses against my mouth and forces itself down my throat." Further along, he concludes: "And the darkness is splattered with blood . . . and my old wounds run with gore."

The silence that follows is broken by the lighthearted intervention of his squire Jons: "Wash away your tears and let your face reflect your indifference. I could have given you some herbs to clean out your troubles with eternity, but I suppose it's too late now. Anyway, in your very last minutes, you will feel a terrific triumph at being able to roll your eyes and wiggle your toes"—movements that he executes with evident glee at the end of his speech.

In the film, the Knight, who becomes the center of the action and the conflict, hashes out his doubts in much more explicit fashion, and is likewise met with impenetrable silence. Contradictorily, however, he does manage to save his three protégées from Death, opening a door of hope that may be read from a religious perspective, or from another angle—as the only humanism available to a filmmaker racked with doubt.

Play and Screenplay

An examination of the play and the screenplay, written a few years apart, gives us a rare opportunity to see how the filmmaker worked to move from a theatrical staging to a pre-cinematographic version, which is ultimately what a screenplay is: a skeleton that will only take on life through the mise-en-scène, a pre-text that has ceased to be literature but is not yet anything in its own right. In this limbo prior to the establishment of a literary genre, the screenplay, thanks to its relation to the original play, can provide observations as to the author's evolution, his vision, whether recurring themes and concepts are preserved or not, and even his relationship to cinema as a language that is only expressed definitively through shooting and editing.

By the mid-1950s, Bergman was already a consummate theater director, and a filmmaker only unrecognized by the blindness of the festival circuit. In the former role, he didn't stick to putting on both classic and modern works—from *Macbeth*, his great passion, which he staged three times, to Strindberg. He also wrote plays, "twenty-three to twenty-four, the first when I was seventeen." Six of them were published or put on. *Tramaning* (*Wood Painting,* or *Peinture sur bois* in the French adaptation), written in 1954 for his students at the Malmö Municipal Theater, is a one-act play in the form of a medieval mystery, a modernized morality play. At the start of the play, the narrator justifies the title: the story is nothing but the dramatic representation of a mural on the wall of a Swedish church, inspired by the plague and painted by an unknown artist.

The narrator concludes his introduction as follows, by saying that the story "begins at the small windows of the entryway, where the sun is playing over the quiet green landscape, and ends twelve feet away in a dark corner where the final incidents occur in the grayish, rain-laden dawn . . ." The twelve feet of the mural indicate the bounds of the mystical, spatial, and temporal journey that the characters will undertake with the help of the narrator, who is called upon to alert the audience as the landscape changes—here a village, there a forest, now a clearing.

It is a "short, quite concentrated" play. A wood painting can do without a realistic depiction. This world must operate in a limbo between life and death, as is the case, to a degree, in *Wild Strawberries* and *Cries and Whispers,* driven forward by archetypal characters whose names, identifying as they are, might only exist in the stage directions: the Knight; Jons the Squire, with all the common sense of Sancho and the sensitivity of Falstaff; the Witch; the Smith; the Actor. There are ten in all, more concepts than living, breathing, psychologically differentiated people.

The Angel and the Knight

The screenplay adds more characters, changes a few of them, and some actions only described in the play are depicted—the procession, the burning of the Witch, the scene of the Actor being attacked. Above all, it changes the narrative focus. In the play, Death is an invisible presence whose domain expands bit by bit, eventually sweeping all of the characters into its macabre dance. Its servant is the Girl, who meets the Knight as he arrives in the land of the plague and invites the Actor to play his lyre at the final ballet; in the film, the initial encounter between the Knight and the Angel of Death on a deserted beach—the angel dressed in black, face painted white—sets the rules of the game from the outset: this will be a chess match. The Knight says: "The condition is that I may live as long as I hold out against you. If I win, you will release me. Is it agreed?" Death draws the black pawn ("very appropriate"), the Knight makes his first move, and the film begins there.

The abstract, conceptual nature of theatrical morality gives way to the clear-cut struggle playing out on the board. The game of chess lends dramatic flair to something that, were it on stage, might tend toward the philosophical, a mere discussion of ideas. The effect is to make the debate visible and tangible. The Knight (Max von Sidow) begins interfering in the action; he joins the couple of jugglers and takes an interest in their son, tells them of his past and his wife, who awaits him at the end of his journey, and relieves the suffering of the Witch, but never ceases to interrogate the mystery: "No, I'll never stop [asking questions]." In between these episodes, his game with Death continues.

The other characters also take on greater weight, especially Jons (Gunnar Björnstrand), who comes into focus as the agnostic, commonsense antithesis of his master. In a world of misery, desolation, barbaric superstition, oppression, and torture, the only light that the Knight finds comes from Jof (Nils Poppe) and Mia (Bibi Andersson), the juggler with his uncontrollable visions of God and the Devil and his wife rooted in a purely earthly simplicity, bolstered by the love of her husband and their small son.

And the Knight finds meaning in his journey, which comes forth in the scene of the meal on the grass: "I shall remember this moment. The silence, the twilight, the bowls of strawberries and milk, your faces in the evening light. Mikael sleeping, Jof with his lyre. I'll try to remember what we have talked about. I'll carry this memory between my hands as carefully as if it were a bowl filled to the brim with fresh milk. And it will be an adequate sign—it will be enough for me." This confession will later echo in the resigned reflections of Agnes at the end of *Cries and Whispers*, as well as in the denouements of films as different as *Smiles of a Summer Night* and *Wild Strawberries*.

Visions and Dreams

Jof and Mia don't exist in the play, and this is the most significant difference between it and the screenplay. Their introduction tracks with a more optimistic perspective from Bergman, who is now eager to save something from the all-encompassing destruction. They are saved not only by the Knight's intervention, but also by Jof's visionary powers and by the elemental connection between himself, Mia, Mikael, and nature. The juggler describes the Dance of Death as Mia smiles in disbelief: "You with your visions and dreams . . ."

The Seventh Seal is one of the rare Bergman films where the protagonists are men. They don't tend to occupy the foreground unless they're half of a couple in crisis. To recall Pierre Marcabru on *Cries and Whispers*: "Indifferent and weak, men appear as objects from which the women extract a handful of complaints and few shouts, but from whom they can expect no help. Just as useless and distant as a drone in a hive."

From a reading of the play and the screenplay, it seems to me that *The Seventh Seal* has been weakened by a structure that is more conceptual than intuitive, exacerbated by the absence of the woman as the metaphysical or sensuous "revealer" of knowledge. The screenplay is still a philosophical essay, and as such it can't go far. It remains to be seen whether the magic of the director's mise-en-scène has been able to overcome these obstacles.

Part VI

Critical Insights from Coutinho's Contemporaries

Introduction

Krista Brune and Natalia Brizuela

Until recently, criticism and scholarship of Eduardo Coutinho in English has been relatively scant. However, in Brazil, the director's films have received critical praise and attention since the watershed moment of *Cabra marcado para morrer*'s 1984 release. Reading examples of how Coutinho's contemporaries responded to his documentaries at the time of their release or remembered their production allows us to better understand the director's contributions to documentary film and Brazilian cinema. This section opens with a remembrance by Brazilian poet Ferreira Gullar, who participated in the CPC and who provided voice-over narration for *Cabra marcado* and *O fio da memória* (1991). Gullar portrays the CPC as a collective effort where participants exchanged ideas on art and politics. At the request of playwright Oduvaldo Vianna Filho, Gullar wrote a *cordel* poem titled "Cabra marcado para morrer," which Coutinho subsequently used, with Gullar's permission, as the title for his film. The poet's memories of this formative period remind us of Coutinho's collaborative work throughout his career. Even though the CPC was a short-lived experience for Coutinho and his fellow artists, it would prove to be foundational for his ongoing interest in making films with, rather than simply about, people.

This section also features chapters by Brazilian film critics José Carlos Avellar and Jean-Claude Bernardet. Avellar's relationship with Coutinho dated to the early 1970s when both worked for the *Jornal do Brasil* as film reviewers. Their professional paths crossed again in the late 1990s when Avellar was the director of RioFilme, the municipal agency that supports the production and distribution of films made in the city. Coutinho received funding from RioFilme to make *Santo forte*, which examined the religious attitudes of residents of Vila Parque da Cidade. The film marked a transition in Coutinho's career as he refined his approach to a cinema of conversation grounded in attentive listening. Moreover, the director's collaboration with

Videofilmes as his production company began with *Santo forte* and lasted for the rest of his career. Though this 1999 film represents an important moment in Avellar's connection to Coutinho, his essays translated here focus on earlier works, namely *O fio da memória* and *Boca de lixo*. Other pieces by Avellar have previously appeared in English, including "Seeing, Hearing, Filming: Notes on the Brazilian Documentary" in *Brazilian Cinema*, edited by Randal Johnson and Robert Stam; and "The Emptiness of the Backyard: An Interview with Eduardo Coutinho," in the 2016 dossier in *Film Quarterly*. The essays in this section, "Brazil by Our Own Selves" and "Mouth Full of Trash," have not been previously published in English. Together, they offer readings of Coutinho's documentary method and its investment in conversation that anticipate the work of subsequent critics. Avellar identifies an element of refined listening in the director's encounters with his subjects beginning with *Cabra marcado para morrer*. Coutinho's role as a listener is central to his filmmaking and to critical interpretations of his work, as Natalia Brizuela highlights in her introductory chapter to this volume. With his commitment to listening, the director developed skills analogous to those of an untrained anthropologist, in his own estimation, or a savage linguist, in Consuelo Lin's assessment.

Beyond this framing of Coutinho as a listener, Avellar recognizes the documentarian's interest in Brazilians whose memories and lived experiences differ from his own. Although the filmmaker selected the people and places to film, asked the questions, and made the final edit, the voices and images of his diverse subjects governed the shape of his documentaries. By analyzing the subject and narrative structure of *O fio da memória*, Avellar observes this dynamic at play. The words of a Black man, Gabriel Joaquim dos Santos, as narrated by actor Milton Gonçalves, determine the structure and the emotional weight of the documentary, even though Coutinho wrote a more didactic narration read by Ferreria Gullar of the history of slavery and the Black movement in Brazil. These two narrators, with their contrasting views and experiences of Brazil, exemplify the encounters that unfold in Coutinho's documentaries between the director and the people whom he films. The dynamics of the encounter are also evident in *Boca de lixo*, as Avellar assesses in "Mouth Full of Trash." By recording the scavengers' responses to why they are at the dump, Coutinho captures their voices and varied ways of speaking Portuguese. Avellar's analysis of these scenes stresses how the director renders their humanity and creativity on-screen. The chapters by Luz Horne and Fernando Pérez Villalón in this volume expand on this reading of *Boca de lixo* as a key work in Coutinho's oeuvre. As Avellar rightly surmises, the often-marginalized subjects of Coutinho's films whose lives differ from his own reveal a portrait of, in the words of Gabriel, "o Brasil por conta de nós próprio" (Brazil by our own selves).

The remaining chapters in this section by eminent Brazilian film critic Jean-Claude Bernardet contribute to a deeper understanding of Coutinho's importance as a filmmaker in Brazil. Bernardet's criticism has appeared in English translation with "A New Actor: The State" in *Framework*, "Trajectory of an Oscillation" in Johnson and Stam's *Brazilian Cinema*, and "The Voice of the Other: Brazilian Documentary in the 1970s" and "The Sociological Model or His Master's Voice: Ideological Form in *Viramundo*" in Julianne Burton's edited volume *The Social Documentary in Latin America*. While these pieces offer an introduction to Bernardet's unique voice, his book-length essays, such as *Cinema brasileiro: Propostas para uma história* (1979), which studies relationships between the production, distribution, and reception of Brazilian film; and *Cineastas e imagens do povo* (1985), which examines how Brazilian documentaries of the 1960s and 1970s represented the popular, have not been translated into English. The translated essays exemplify Bernardet's skill as a critic to contextualize Coutinho's documentaries within Brazilian film history. His review of *Cabra marcado para morrer*, translated here as "Victory Over the Ash Heap of History," highlights the historical significance of the project and, more importantly, considers the theory of history that the film proposes. In Bernardet's reading, the film's distinct chronology, grounded in the recovery of and reflection on archival materials from 1964 in the contemporary moment of the 1980s, prevents an overly romanticized view of Brazil's history. The resulting documentary recognizes both ruptures and continuities within the main subject of Elizabeth Teixeira and her family, and the broader theme of Brazilian society. Bernardet astutely conceives of the fragmented and displaced family within *Cabra marcado* as symbols of the fractured Brazilian nation. This mode of analyzing the film serves as an antecedent to the readings that Krista Brune and Gustavo Furtado offer in their contributions to this volume.

Even as Bernardet's vision has deteriorated with age, he has remained a lucid critic of Brazilian cinema with an interest in film as a spectacle of performance and as a venue for examining social differences and lived experiences. During the early 2000s, he maintained a blog where he reflected on the films that he was viewing. Writing a personal blog suggests an effort to adapt to a shifting critical landscape and, in doing so, reach a different readership. The format invites Bernardet to capture his affective experiences as a spectator, to rehearse ideas, and to refine his critical lens, as his entries about *Jogo de cena* and *Moscou* illustrate. Through these blog posts, which are included in this section in English translation, Bernardet processes his responses to Coutinho's experimental films and reflects more broadly on performance, play, documentary, and fiction. These vignettes exemplify how the critic thinks through writing. As readers of the blog, even in its edited and reproduced form, we accompany Bernardet as he fleshes out his critical interpretation. This playful and essayistic form, with its digressions and repetitions, is especially appropriate for analyzing films that interrogate the line between "real" life and fictional performances. The chapters in this volume by Luz Horne and Brenno Kenji Kaneyasu dialogue with Bernardet's writings on *Jogo de cena*. Although translated into English infrequently, the voices of Gullar, Avellar, and Bernardet as Coutinho's contemporaries in Brazil cast a long shadow over the current scholarship about the director. Reading these translated pieces alongside the other chapters in this volume will establish a rich and lively conversation about Coutinho's documentary cinema.

Works Cited

Avellar, José Carlos. "Seeing, Hearing, Filming: Notes on the Brazilian Documentary." *Brazilian Cinema*, edited by Randal Johnson and Robert Stam, Columbia UP, 1995, pp. 328–39.

———. "The Emptiness of the Backyard: An Interview with Eduardo Coutinho." Translated by Krista Brune. *Film Quarterly*, vol. 69, no. 3, 2016, pp. 44–55.

Bernardet, Jean-Claude. "A New Actor: The State." *Framework*, no. 28, 1985, pp. 4–19.

———. "The Voice of the Other: Brazilian Documentary in the 1970s." *The Social Documentary in Latin America*, edited by Julianne Burton, U of Pittsburgh P, 1990, pp. 87–108.

———. "The Sociological Model or His Master's Voice: Ideological Form in *Viramundo*." *The Social Documentary in Latin America*, edited by Julianne Burton, U of Pittsburgh P, 1990, pp. 217–38.

———. "Trajectory of an Oscillation." *Brazilian Cinema*, edited by Randal Johnson and Robert Stam, Columbia UP, 1995, pp. 281–89.

17

On the Film that Never Was

Ferreira Gullar,
translated by Flora Thomson-DeVeaux

Editors' note: This essay appears in Ohata's edited collection in the "Memories and Portraits" section, which features reflections from Coutinho's friends and creative collaborators such as Rolf Orthel, Zelito Viana, Vladimir Carvalho, and Jordana Berg. These contributors met Coutinho at distinct moments of his career and often continued to accompany his trajectory. Gullar shared with Coutinho the formative experience of the CPC in the early 1960s as a venue for politically and socially committed art. His brief piece situates the initial vision for Cabra marcado *within the project of the CPC and praises Coutinho for creating a classic of Brazilian cinema by repurposing the footage of the unfinished film.*

At every turn, I see the extent to which random factors—the sum of which is also called chance—influence or help to shape that which we do, and even our own lives. In art, these factors play a decisive role, precisely because artistic creation does not obey the same logic as any old daily chore.

I'm moved to this reflection by remembering the film *Cabra marcado para morrer*. In this case, in addition to the random factors that normally play a part in artistic creation, others interfered as well, determined by the moment in history when the film was begun: the year 1964, when a military-led coup toppled the government of President João Goulart.

To give the reader a better sense of the situation in which the film was born, it may help to recall that Eduardo Coutinho was then a young filmmaker, a member of the group behind the Centro Popular de Cultura (CPC, People's Cultural Center) and the National Students' Union (UNE).

The CPC, in a variety of artistic fields, sought to help make a change in Brazilian society. Land reform, a key issue at that point in time, was a constant theme in the group's activities, whether in plays, poetry, folk art, or in cinema. On the urban front, it had recently produced the film *Five Times Favela*, a sequence of shorts by several young directors. Coutinho's film, *Cabra marcado para morrer*, was the CPC's second film; but unlike the first, it depicted the peasants' struggle for land reform—specifically, the story of peasant leader João Pedro Teixeira, who had been assassinated in 1962 at the orders of local landowners.

I was active in the CPC, and, at Oduvaldo Vianna Filho's request, I had written a *cordel* poem on the struggle for land reform. The title I gave that poem, which was published back then, was *Cabra marcado para morrer*—which, with my consent, Coutinho took for his film.

Circling back to the start: I see the film as an example of how chance works on our lives and what we make of them. It so happened that Coutinho's shoot for *Cabra marcado para morrer* was interrupted by the military coup, which meant that the film that bears that name today is not the film that was being shot at Galiléia Farm in Pernambuco, in 1964. Back then, a few of the crew members were arrested, others escaped, and Eduardo Coutinho was able to save the material he had already filmed; he had sent the negatives to a laboratory in Rio de Janeiro a few days earlier. The footage would only be recovered some time later, but the story in the film's original screenplay could no longer be told. The situation in the countryside had changed under the military regime, and the fight for land reform was stamped out. In any case, given the repression that had fallen over the country, a film like that would have been impossible.

The truth is that the film could only be made seventeen years later, but the screenplay could not be the same as the one back then. Random factors—which, of course, weren't foreseen in the original script—now shaped a new story: the story of the film that could not be made, and of the characters who changed the courses of their lives to escape repression, such as Elizabeth Teixeira, João Pedro's widow, who went underground, living in another state, under another name.

This film, about the film that could never be made, became a classic of Brazilian cinema.

On the Film That Never Was | 323

Figure 17.1. Participants watching footage of the aborted 1964 film in *Cabra marcado para morrer*. Source: *Cabra marcado para morrer* (*Twenty Years Later*). Directed by Eduardo Coutinho, 1964–1984. Instituto Moreira Salles, 2014. DVD.

18

Brazil by Our Own Selves

José Carlos Avellar,
translated by Flora Thomson-DeVeaux

Editors' note: This text was first published in Comunicação e Política, *edited by the Centro Brasileiro de Estudos Latino-americanos, volume 2, number 4, August to November 1995. The essay was reprinted in Ohata's edited volume in the section "Routes and Detours of a Filmmaker," which contains essays and reviews by Brazilian critics and filmmakers. Through a close reading of* O fio da memória *and its use of two narrators, Avellar examines how Coutinho approaches the interview in his documentaries. This movement between analyzing a specific film and discussing broader trends offers a model for criticism that scholars continue to employ when analyzing Coutinho's work, as the chapters in this volume indicate.*

Everything ready for the interview to begin, camera and recorder rolling, and the interviewee remains silent. Head down, eyes on the ground, not a word. No sign of movement. The director prods quietly: he can talk now. Silence. Again: they can keep on talking, just like before the camera was turned on. But whatever has muzzled the interviewee is still there, hanging heavily. The camera and recorder await, silently but lightly, at their stations. The final edit included this empty space prior to the outburst, almost an emotional explosion, that finally unleashes the interviewee's words. *Cabra marcado para morrer* (1964–1984) preserves the wait, a pause that apparently says nothing of what the film seeks to convey. In this space devoid of words, only the image can speak. It says that this essential emptiness serves to understand what the interviewee in this scene in particular and the film as a whole are telling us. The interviewee is not reduced to a person telling us about a given event that happened in another time or another place. He is a living person, heart and mind there, in the present, and the film, just then, is about him. About his presence there, about the encounter with him, about the present overshadowed by the past, by the past now, not what happened then. We might say that something new in Eduardo Coutinho's films begins here. A keen ear, cinema being winnowed down to a few expressive figures, making way for an equally radical expansion of what documentary has to offer in terms of turning oneself over to the other. The cinematographic gesture that underpins the films beginning with *Santo forte* (1999)—for example, the image of the empty backyard after Thereza says that the spirits are everywhere—may have begun to coalesce here. And in *Cabra marcado para morrer*—the film interrupted in 1964, with real participants, not actors, performing the story of João Pedro Teixeira, and the 1984 film, with interviews of dramatic intensity to rival João Mariano's silence—here may be the root of the structure of *Jogo de cena* (2007).

O fio da memória (1991), a reflection on the fragmentation that Brazilian society has imposed on blacks and on itself, may be seen as a key element in this process, which ran from just before *Cabra marcado para morrer* to just after *Jogo de cena*.

Rio de Janeiro, May 13th, 1988, one o'clock in the afternoon, Avenida Treze de Maio [May Thirteenth Avenue]: "the thirteen members of the Confraria do Garoto [Garoto Brotherhood] celebrate, in their own fashion, the hundredth anniversary of the abolition of slavery"—says the narrator, over footage of an animated group dancing to the sound of "Cidade Maravilhosa." The festivities will include—the narrator goes on—the coronation of the Queen of the Centenary of Abolition in front of the Church of Our Lady of the Rosary and Saint Benedict. What comes next is an image moving in all directions at once, each sliver of it bearing countless pieces of information. It takes viewers by storm, giving them no chance to organize what they are seeing.

In the foreground, the coronation: Fátima Ju—who, some years before, had been crowned the most beautiful *mulata* in Brazil on Chacrinha's variety TV show—is bedecked with the sash and crown of the Queen of the Centenary of Abolition. Going on behind the coronation is another celebration, this one in honor of the slave Anastácia, at Our Lady of the Rosary. People are gathering at the church in the name of the miracle-working slave, the woman whom many, like the student interviewed in a classroom, believed to be the real force behind the end of slavery. In their eyes, she was the one who truly fought for freedom. She, Anastácia the slave, on a May 13th—her day—not Princess Isabel, who only signed the law that put an end to the regime.

At the raucous celebration in the foreground, someone puts a toddler in Fátima Ju's arms and tries to put the crown of the Queen of the Centenary of Abolition on the child's head. The little boy wriggles and cries. Behind them, in the background, is the less boisterous celebration in the church. Between the two, many people wander by and are drawn to the music and the knot of people with TV cameras and recorders around Fátima Ju. The three layers run together in the shot, and from time to time something that the framing seems to want to push into a corner, or into the background, seems to assert itself with even more life, leaping out and seizing viewers' attention, although not for too long. Suddenly we lose Fátima Ju from sight and find ourselves before a group gathered round a black woman who cries out in protest: "The evidence is there, slavery never ended!" Her voice is strong and she moves as she speaks, seeming to guide the camera. The cameraman is carried along on her words and follows her. The shot, which has seemed disorientingly open, now seems to concentrate on one thing—but things aren't so simple. The chaotic blend, Fátima Ju's laughter, the wails of the baby boy with the crown on his head, the cheery music, the black woman's irritated, clarion voice, the ironic glances that passersby cast on the half-naked queen, the serious look of those going to the church in the name of the slave Anastácia, the smiles of those stopping in front of the camera and sticking out their necks in hopes of getting into the shot—disorder, in other words, continues to reign.

Disgusted at the celebrations, the black woman says, and says again: "Prejudice won't go away." She says that the queen is so skinny, she looks more like a man than a woman. She says that she can "prove and prove again, from the bottom of my soul, that whites just don't like blacks." And she keeps on protesting, even as her sentences are cut off midway through. She is unable to complete her train of thought because a white man breaks into the conversation, determined to show that racial prejudice actually doesn't exist in Brazil. He interrupts the black woman but can't make himself heard because she doesn't stop speaking. He tries once—"fifty-one percent of the Brazilian population . . ." but she ignores him. In a brief pause between one thought and the next, he tries again. He starts talking over her again, and, once again, nobody listens to him. He can barely get out the first few words: "Fifty-one percent . . ."

The black woman couldn't care less about him. She says she's not talking to him; she's talking to the reporter. People standing around get into the discussion, talking over one another. Nobody can hear anything, and nobody finishes saying anything. The microphone picks up this confused mass of voices, everyone talking at the same time and nobody listening to anybody until, during a slightly larger break in the yelling, the white man takes a breath and bellows, almost managing to get the whole sentence out: "Fifty-one percent of the Brazilian population is black. In any company, whoever has fifty-one percent of the shares controls the company. If blacks can't manage to control the country, it's . . ." Then he seems to say something like, "because they can't manage it" or "because they can't organize," or some other "because . . ." But he can't get it out; at this, everyone around him starts clamoring again. They've guessed where he's going and . . . (precisely there, when the action starts heating up), a cut interrupts the scene and the film changes topics.

A fragment. More precisely, a scene that frames itself as a fragment: it begins just after it has begun, and it ends right before it actually ends. Not enough to give us a precise sense of this documentary, begun on the eve of May 13th, 1988, and finished three years later—ironically, in a distortion of the market, at a time when Brazilian cinema was being cut off much like the indignant woman on Avenida Treze de Maio. After citizens' savings accounts were confiscated and the mechanisms for the production and distribution of culture were dismantled under the Collor administration, the film—like the vanishingly few features completed in the early 1990s—barely circulated. And so this scene, cut off midway through, may also be seen (after we understand what it truly is, a debate about racism fueled by the presence of the camera on the hundredth anniversary of abolition) as a portrait of the relationship between Brazilian cinema and viewers in the Collor era. Maybe. It can certainly be read as a representation of the compositional structure behind *O fio da memória*, a structure that is open to all sides and intentionally fragmented. What we see here seeks to exist as a part, not as a whole. Parts and pieces, implying the existence of something outside the frame, incompleteness; this compositional method, this form represents the condition imposed on blacks. It is as if the camera, which tends to be all ears, were also testifying in its own way: in the shape and texture of the image.

The first sign of this fragmentation: the presence of two narrators. One narration, two narrators. The first springs from the desire to reflect on blacks in Brazil; the second, from the desire to let the topic determine the way one thinks.

The first narrator—the words are Coutinho's, the voice is Ferreira Gullar's—gives us immediate information, briefly guiding us into a variety of situations, such as the festivities put on by the Confraria do Garoto. He says at the very start of the film that after abolition, black Brazilians, left illiterate and uprooted from their cultures, deprived of citizenship and of their families, had to fight to stay together and sweep up the fragments of their identity. This first narrator returns later on, introducing a march of members of the black movement in Rio de Janeiro to mark November 20th, the anniversary of the death of Zumbi dos Palmares, as the Day of Black Consciousness. He also pops up here and there to introduce interviewees in a few words. The first narrator says very little, but lets the interviewees speak at length. Like Manuel Deodoro Maciel, a former slave, at age 120; like the family that created the now-venerable Carnival street party Cacique de Ramos; and like the juveniles in the triage center for abandoned girls in Niterói, across the bay from Rio. And finally, the first narrator introduces the second, Gabriel Joaquim dos Santos, who lived in the district of Vinhadeiro in the municipality of São Pedro d'Aldeia, close to Cabo Frio, less than 200 kilometers from Rio de Janeiro. He was born on May 13th in 1892 and died in early 1985, at age 92. The first narrator introduces the second narrator and practically bows out in favor of him.

The second narrator is voiced by Milton Gonçalves. His words come from a conversation recorded in the late 1970s, and from the notebooks in which Gabriel jotted down events from his everyday life, the history of the region and the history of Brazil, ever since, around 1926, having joined the Baptist Church, he met "a real smart young man" who taught him "something about reading" using a "schoolbook." The words of this second narrator are neither precise nor objective. He talks about everything, and everything blends together. The information he provides doesn't come so much from what he tells us but from how he tells it. He jumps from one sentence to another, one topic to another, weaving together a discontinuous narrative. One annotation is freely tacked on to another, much like an edited film places one image beside another (a montage of attractions and conflicts, as Eisenstein once suggested while trying to explain how a silent film speaks to viewers). In fact, Gabriel's writings help shape O fio da memória, or at least point to the model for structuring the film. At some point in the process, the man with the camera saw Gabriel's life, his way of speaking and doing things, as a sort of cinema in the rough, and as an image of the situation of blacks in Brazil, and of all the Brazilians who, like he, exist on the margin of their nation, all those who build their lives just like Gabriel built his "Casa da Flor" (Flower House), with pieces of all sorts of things fished out of the trash:

> When I finished work on the house, then I got the idea to decorate it. Decorate it how? We didn't have money to buy certain things, so I thought up the idea to pick broken dishes out of the trash. Pieces of glass to make glass flowers and nail them up on the wall. That's what came into my mind. Just pick up the pieces, what's left over from the building of the city.

When talking about how people from the city visit him, Gabriel says that "folks from Rio come here and I tell them, there's so many beautiful things in Rio. And they say, no, that all's not beautiful, we just accept Rio de Janeiro because it has the power of wealth, the power of engineering—there's houses there, mansions, all that organized stuff that wealth makes. They come here to see the power of poverty. I want them to admire the power of poverty."

He writes down in one notebook that he started at the saltworks in 1912 and that he "left there in the year 1960, tired out and thrown over by the institute." He recalls what the workers earned per day, back then: "in the year 1912, two cruzeiros; in 1920, three cruzeiros; in 1930, six cruzeiros; in 1940, seven cruzeiros; in 1950, it got up to sixty cruzeiros." Then he writes: "the laws of slavery in Brazil begun back in colonial times, in the year 1532." And he goes on, putting together images, gathering up fragments: "Guilherme gave me a vintém coin from 1869. He gave it to me on April 30th, 1955. The price of goods in 1963: one kilo of meat, 700 cruzeiros; one kilo of beans, 180 cruzeiros; one kilo of sugar, 140 cruzeiros; one kilo of rice, 200 cruzeiros; one kilo of flour, 70 cruzeiros; a loaf of bread, 15 cruzeiros. On April 17th, 1963, the strike started at the saltworks. The pope of Rome died on July 3rd, 1963."

And on it goes, with the editing of the notebook potentially taken as a script and a jumping-off point for the editing of the film:

> José de França took up with Almerinda on February 12th, 1964. Santos Dumont took the first airplane flight in 1906. Land reform was signed on March 13th, 1964, by the President of the Republic. João Goulart signed it at four o'clock in the afternoon in Rio de Janeiro. The order is, whoever doesn't obey goes to the Ilha das Flores. Marshal Castelo Branco took office as President of the Republic at the start of April 1964. Getúlio

Vargas sent the Brazilian army to war in Europe on the 13th of November 1943.

The narrative above, we might say, follows a structure just as unruly as the scene of the coronation of the Queen of the Centenary of Abolition on Avenida Treze de Maio. The footage around the festivities—the film as a whole, one might say—is like the paragraph above. And because of that, it leads viewers to feel (without directly stating, demonstrating, or explaining; it suggests, and, perhaps unconsciously, it leads us to feel) that he has transformed the disaggregation imposed on blacks into a different form of aggregation, a new process of editing, one that makes it possible to express oneself and live creatively. By selecting a passage in which Gabriel says that he is guided by his dreams, *O fio da memória* opens up a space for him to explain himself. It is, as always, interested in merely hearing him out. But then, at the same time, the film explains—consciously or not, it hardly matters—the principles behind its dramatic structure:

> I lie down real early. Not to sleep: to think. My thoughts are alive. My thoughts are alive, and when midnight comes, I fall asleep. I dream every night, I'm made to do these things in my thoughts or in my dreams. Here, I made everything with my own hands. Nobody taught me, it's spiritual. Did you ever think I'd be intelligent enough to do that, ma'am? I'm the one doing it, it's a wonder to me, too.

Imagining a documentary (a form of making cinema that is, at least in principle, as objective, direct, and governed by reason as possible) as a form governed by dreams brings the main matter at hand closer to us. The driving force behind this film, which develops as a dialogue between its two narrators, is the desire to speak with people in front of the camera at the moment of filming, and with viewers in the projection room once the film is ready. Speaking without knowing what will be said. Listening more than talking. During the filming, a brief intervention to encourage the people before the camera to speak. During the projection, editing fragments together to encourage the viewer to speak (internally, but speak nonetheless—this is a conversation without which the film is not fully realized). What is uncovered here is the process, the living moment of this quest. The filmmaker might echo Gabriel's words: "I'm the one doing it, it's a wonder to me, too."

There is one thing that can be known—a work method—but this method and this knowledge are on another order, more of a hypothesis to be investigated than a conclusion to be demonstrated. The cinematic image, here, is engaging with what is in the frame and what falls outside it. It is, essentially, a composition designed as a fragment—a fleeting vision of something in movement, not an attempt to truly frame the people and action it films. Indeed, the film doesn't seek to frame, but rather to free its subjects from frames, leaving them at ease, both in the shot and half out of it. We see a piece of them, not exactly what they are, but quite precisely what they are at that moment. The image is all openness and ambiguity, which allows us to glean a second sort of information from the interviewees' words—a quasi-representation of the dialogue between the two narrators in the film.

Now and then there comes a long shot, seeking to let the interviewees reveal themselves in the conversation: not only do they tell us something, but they also tell what they are, reveal themselves through their gestures, their expressions, the way they speak, the way they tell us of their dreams. Now and then the conversation is brief, because one or two sentences are enough to leave us with a lump in our throat: we are looking at people who have been stripped of even the ability to dream, as is the case with the abandoned children in social triage centers.

When she is asked how she came downtown, the girl answers, head hung low, that she didn't come here: she's been here forever.

With his face hidden in shadow, the boy says he's "done a lot of things in this life," he's stolen, killed, sold drugs.

Whether long or short, the conversations are free-flowing, as open as first encounters. The interviewee doesn't repeat a previously rehearsed spiel before the camera. He's never met the director before (Coutinho sends an assistant to schedule the conversation but only meets the person he's going to film just as they begin shooting, and he starts rolling as soon as he arrives, without rehearsing any part of the conversation). Interviewer and interviewee are surprised at the same time, surprised by one another. Something new, unique, unforeseen unfurls then, as untethered as the free-for-all outside the Church of Our Lady of the Rosary just after one o'clock in the afternoon on May 13th, 1988.

It's altogether likely that the viewer may not notice this architecture, this deconstructed structure, right away. It's also quite likely that viewers won't realize that they're seeing things in this fragmented way. Whether because the fragmentation is inspired by what they are seeing and hearing on-screen, the Casa da Flor, Gabriel Joaquim dos Santos' writings, or because fragmentation is an image of the topic that inspired the film; or because, if the viewer is a Brazilian confined to the time and space of the film, he or she may see something on the screen that is both natural and familiar to him or her. Another possibility: they may not see it because the film flows freely, like a rambling conversation with no specific aim—the aim being, or so it would seem, to shoot the breeze.

It's quite certain that while the film is on-screen, our attention isn't held by the camera, but by the people before it. The interviewees are at ease, holding sway over the image. The placement of the frame, the way the film is organized as a whole, only becomes clear after the screening is over, when we recall Gabriel's words, the first and last in the narration:

> Brazil used to be bossed around by Portugal. Brazil used to be a Portuguese farm. This place here has been everything. People were captive here, it was real dangerous, the Portuguese bringing blacks from the African coast to hoe the land here. All those things passed. Then the Portuguese gave it over. Pedro I made us independent. He put Brazil over here and Portugal over there. And what was left was Brazil by our own selves.

This way of putting it (incorrect grammar? correct meaning?) may be the best formulation of the invitation to participate in the creative process of cinema: to not only witness the images registered in the film during the screening, but also to dialogue with the structure that organizes and lends meaning to those images. A keen ear, the decision to cast oneself as a person who doesn't know things beforehand and is open to learn. *O fio da memória* reveals how a sensibility on the margin of material well-being, cast aside on the margin of history, invented a new world on its own, even as it invites viewers to do the same, let themselves be guided by their dreams and make the world (or at least the world of cinema) on their own.

The keen ear that began in *Cabra marcado para morrer*, en route to the later leap in *Santo forte*, moves through the house and the diaries of Gabriel Joaquim, with their modest lesson about things behind the apparent chaos of an entry (for example) about Santos Dumont's first flight next to the entry about when José de França (on his first flight?) took up with Almerinda.

As the beginnings of an idea, as the ground from which to set flight for the first time, we may bring Gabriel's words—Brazil by our own selves—and Coutinho's film to bear on Brazilian cinema as a whole, just as we took a single scene to conceive of the film as a whole: we may be able to conclude (with a dose of exaggeration) that cinema devoted to the poor and working classes was put under a pressure not unlike the pressure to which blacks in Brazil themselves have been subjected. The fragmented style, here, may arise from a desire to snatch up the lost thread of the memory of a strategy for the survival and affirmation of Brazilian blacks, and, to an extent, a strategy for the affirmation of Brazilian cinema as cultural expression. No matter which thread you pick up, you'll see that it's cut off soon thereafter. It's worth repeating: not so long ago, in the early 1990s, Coutinho was finishing up this documentary on the centenary of the abolition of slavery even as Brazilian cinema was being cut to the bone. We might say (allowing for a dose of hyperbole here and there) that Eduardo Coutinho set about assembling *O fio da memória* like Gabriel Joaquim dos Santos built his Casa da Flor: working with broken dishes picked out of the trash. Gabriel didn't have the money to buy certain things, and he wanted to follow through on the idea of decorating his house. Coutinho, to produce this film and compose its narration, made use of shards picked up here and there out of what the system tends to leave on the margins. You might say that the character and the film in which he appears are typical examples of the power of culture on the margins of the power of wealth—operating outside the grammatical order because, in light of the nonexistent, discontinuous space that it is accorded, if it is to say what it needs to say, it must defy the seemingly good order of the status quo.

19

Mouth Full of Trash

José Carlos Avellar,
translated by Flora Thomson-DeVeaux

Editors' note: This essay was initially published in Rio Artes, number 12, in 1994. It was also included in Ohata's edited volume, immediately after Avellar's essay "Brazil by Our Own Selves." This order follows the release dates of the main film analyzed in each piece, rather than the chronology of publication. Avellar's reading foregrounds Coutinho's relationship to the people and the places that he films in Boca de lixo *and, secondarily,* Cabra marcado para morrer. *By examining how these power dynamics unfold on film, Avellar interrogates the function of conversation in Coutinho's documentaries, establishing fertile grounds for subsequent criticism.*

The first thing that appears is the nigh-impossible relationship between the camera (to be more precise: the man with the camera) and what it sees: trash (to be more precise: the people who live in the trash). How to film those who don't want to be filmed as they pick up cans, paper, fabric, plastic, shards of glass, wood, shoes, scraps of food? The question contains a mode of representation that drives and structures *Boca de lixo*, by Eduardo Coutinho: how to film the unfilmable? How to go beyond what is immediately visible in these images, when the images simply aren't enough to document the everyday life of trash-pickers? We might say that in *Boca de lixo* (1992), Eduardo Coutinho follows through on and takes to new and radical heights the lesson learned with Gabriel Joaquim dos Santos in

O fio da memória (1991): he has imagined a cinema built with shards, like the Casa da Flor built by Joaquim.

From the very start, almost serving as an introduction, we find something that is present in the experience of documentary cinema but rarely presented to the viewer: the negotiation between those who want to film and those who do not necessarily want to be filmed, the prior consent, immediate at times, halting at others, which precedes the filming and makes it possible. We might say that Eduardo Coutinho's documentaries begin just before they begin and incorporate what other documentaries tend to toss out in the editing process: the eye-to-eye contact, the words exchanged before the shoot. And we might also say that *Boca de lixo* adds another question onto the question of documenting (this second question being essential in order for us to perceive the first): it asks what it is that a documentary ultimately documents.

In the film, there is nothing of the somewhat naive curiosity that leads people on camera to do whatever they can to get their faces into the shot, to show up on television (because the people being filmed know, in one way or another, that television signifies true power and they want to be important, subvert the order even if for just a little while, a second, less than a second). What's more: there is no certainty on the part of the person filming, no confident reporter guiding the interviews. Here, the filmmaker is aware of the power dynamic that the camera creates between people, aware that relationships founded on the certainty of knowing ahead of time just how to film will distort the image. Here, the filmmaker is aware that the only chance of filming correctly is, shall we say, to film without knowing how. Behind the camera, a person who doesn't know (because he or she refuses to know ahead of time) how to film; in front of the camera, people who don't want to be filmed: they flee from the camera, they turn their backs, cover their faces, protect their bodies, and, with a gesture in the air, push the filmmaker away.

How to speak with those who don't want to say anything? Who cover their faces so as not to be seen? Does reality always hide from the camera like this, even at the moments when it seems to move contentedly into frame?

At the start of *Boca de lixo*, the camera walks, head cast down, across the shapeless mound covering the ground. An emaciated, tossed-out horse; vultures circle low in the sky. When the camera raises its head, all it sees are the inquisitive eyes of people covering their faces with whatever rags they can find. The first attempts at conversation are faltering, with an awkward question—"What's it like, working here? Good?"—and a half-mumbled answer—"Good it ain't. But this is where we get our money. There's no other way. Gotta get it here." Conversations in which the interlocutors want to change subjects, or in which the interviewee interviews the interviewer. "What are you getting out of this?"—asks one boy in the landfill, his face bare, staring down the camera—"Why are you putting that thing in our faces?" The answer, which is both true and sincere—"To show your lives," sounds just as mumbled as the words of the trash-picker just a few scenes earlier: sticking the camera into the trash, working there, "good, it ain't."

In *Cabra marcado para morrer* (1964–84), conversations began with the screening of images filmed twenty years earlier. Here they begin with photographic records, photograms transcribed from images shot in video: "not a very good photo, a kind of photocopy," the director explains to the subjects of the photographs. At any rate: the conversation begins without words. It begins with images (fig. 19.1). Because the first thing that the people filmed here want to know is this: what will be done with their images, and how and to what end those images will be spread across the world.

Figure 19.1. The conversation begins with images in *Boca de lixo*. Source: *Boca de lixo* (*Scavengers*). Directed by Eduardo Coutinho, CECIP, 1992.

Boca de lixo is about the people who survive off trash in the Itaoca landfill in São Gonçalo, in the Rio de Janeiro metropolitan region. Since the refuse that came there had already been picked through and everything usable had been carried off, all that is left for them is the trash of the trash. Having overcome the difficulties on both sides and gotten past the initial awkwardness, there come long, free-flowing conversations with five pickers: Nirinha, Lúcia, Cícera, Enock, and Jurema. They start out in the trash and continue in each interviewee's home. Long segments, separated by intermissions that are often posed in the form of a question—"What are you doing here in the trash?"—and answer—"Earning my daily bread." Others look almost like music video montages—the image, a bashed-in, upside-down globe fallen among other pieces of things in the trash, accompanied by a percussion that sounds as if it were being played on old cans with pieces of wood and shards of glass. And the others: a fragment of conversation, a glancing record of weighty things: a woman hurt her foot on a syringe from the hospital trash, "but she's all right"; the unemployed man waiting for the trash from the supermarket, a bag of rice or pasta, a potato, a chayote or a carrot, "that'll be a help."

What really matters are the conversations. Conversations, not interviews; an open exchange, rambling, unruly, apparently aimless; what is registered is the moment of knowledge, the encounter between two people; one of the people bears a camera and looks at the other one, eye to eye, but through a camera lens.

Nirinha says how many kilos of paper, cans, and plastic she hauls every day.

Lúcia says she thinks working in the trash is good because everyone there is friends and she feels at ease, she can talk, yell, mess with everybody, and she gets sad when she's not there.

Cícera says that she worked in plenty of rich ladies' houses, but she prefers the trash because she doesn't like being bossed around.

Enock says that he's worked on farms, construction, in the city, in the country, all sorts of jobs, and that trash, the end of everything's working life, is also where everything begins again.

Jurema says that trash is what gets her through, it's her backbone. She's lived there for thirty years, was born there, and educated all seven of her children thanks to her work in the trash.

The conversations without words are equally important—the things the camera says by lingering on especially meaningful details. Sometimes they border on the ironic: the woman excavating the trash heap is wearing a T-shirt with the logo of an institute of archaeology. Others are almost impossible to translate into words. Leisure during a work break: a group plays cards. Farther along, someone is listening to music on an old radio. The younger ones are playing a pickup soccer game. The tired ones slump down onto what's left of an armchair and read a page of a magazine or a piece of an old newspaper. On a bench, the pickers have something to drink or a bite to eat; next to them, children are playing marbles. There, where nothing seems possible, social life has come into form. These people are thrust outside of the world by unemployment, like useless scraps, and mountains of trash are dumped on them several times a day, and they throw themselves on those scraps to find whatever can still be used, whatever can still make life livable. As Enock says, while it's the end of the road, trash is also where everything begins again.

We might say that, just like Nirinha, Lúcia, Cícera, Enock, and Jurema, the camera is also one of the protagonists in *Boca de lixo*. Not only is it a witness and a tool, it is a living presence (in the shoot as an extension of the filmmaker, during the screening as an extension of the viewer) that interferes, tips the scales, provokes, calls for a reaction—either acceptance or rejection—from the person being filmed. The camera provokes behavior that would not exist in its absence. Eduardo Coutinho's films are forged from the conflict, harmony, understanding, and misunderstanding that arise in the moment when the eye of the camera meets the eyes of the person before it. The camera gets as close as possible, trying to see and hear the trash trucks drawing up to the Itaoca dump. It can't see clearly, in part because so many people are throwing themselves onto the trash, and in part because what it sees is blotted out, not only by the people leaping onto the stuff falling from the trucks, but also by the exhaust, the dust, the water, the greasy mud oozing from the trash. It can't see clearly because it is seeing with a knot in its stomach, feeling a twinge of shame. It still sees, but it seems as though it would like to turn its eyes away from the pickers in the middle of the trash, just as they would like to not be filmed. It speaks with a lump in its throat. As it speaks, it swallows hard—or, we might say: as it speaks, it swallows the trash. This is how it sees, and the viewer feels that this is the only way it is possible to see people who have been thrown in the trash, who throw themselves on it. The viewer feels this because he or she has already seen the images that discuss the relationship between the camera's gaze and the thing it sees. "People are ashamed to be on TV. I'm ashamed," says Jurema, and she explains: plenty of what they take from the trash is used at home, "fruit, vegetables, pasta, a good piece of meat, a good chicken," food for the pig in the yard or for the folks in the house, "but the TV doesn't need to go blabbing about it like it does."

Not talk about it like television does: the people for whom trash is a means to get by, a backbone, a living, feel that television is somehow a part of the status quo that, in seeking to preserve its own comfort, has pushed them all to this place. They cover their faces, move away, don't want to talk, grit their teeth, and mumble the justification that is repeated multiple times in the first part of the documentary: they say that they're working, that nobody's stealing anything, that they're not ashamed to be there because they're at work, after all, not stealing or begging. This is the root of it—they're all workers, each of them a common worker, as uncommon as work in a dump may be—and that's why, when he reappears at the end of the film, picking through trash with the others a few days after losing his job, Lúcia's husband (who had spoken frankly in the first interview, his gaze satisfied and confident) practically shrinks, a hat jammed onto his head as he speaks, seemingly dejected.

The issue at the heart of it all is how to translate all this life in the middle of the trash into images. Here, Coutinho is forced to tackle a challenge that, to an extent, he invented himself, or had at least posed since *Cabra marcado para morrer* (1964–84)—the first step toward a way of filming that casts aside almost all contextualizing information, a way of filming that privileges the moment at which the man with the camera encounters a fragment of reality. Cinema, here, does not cast itself as the account of an investigation concluded before the shoot begins, but as the very moment of that investigation, not so much a discovery as the search itself, not so much an answer as a new question: is the experience of the worker in the trash an image of the common worker, caught between the end of usefulness and the moment when everything can begin again?

20

Victory Over the Ash Heap of History

JEAN-CLAUDE BERNARDET,
TRANSLATED BY FLORA THOMSON-DEVEAUX

Editors' note: The first part of this essay was initially published in the Folhetim *of the* Folha de S. Paulo *on March 24, 1985. The "2003 Note" was added when the text was included in the 2003 edition of Bernardet's monograph* Cineastas e imagens do povo, *published by Companhia das Letras. Ohata's volume includes this essay near the beginning of "Routes and Detours of a Filmmaker." This analysis of Coutinho's masterpiece* Cabra marcado para morrer *centers on questions of history. Bernardet comments on the chronology of the film's production and reception at two moments: after its initial release and nearly twenty years later. This retrospective view allows Bernardet to further interrogate the relationship between fiction and documentary in Brazilian cinema, and between the historical and the conditional in the trajectories of Coutinho and Brazil.*

Thank God, here I am today, telling the story.

—Elizabeth Teixeira

Nothing further from Eduardo Coutinho's mind than to tell the story of the last twenty years in *Cabra marcado para morrer*. No thought of lining up facts on the skewer of chronology and tying them together with the twine of cause and effect. Which historical films in Brazil have escaped the illusions of historicism? Very few, if that many. But among them, certainly, is *Cabra marcado para morrer*.

What history does this film propose to us? Perhaps in light of my age—about the same as Coutinho's—I see a historical project concerned with constructing a bridge between the "now" and the "before," so that the before isn't left without a future and the now isn't left without a past. Between before and now, a rupture: 1964. After that rupture, the ideological and cultural project that existed before 1964 ran the risk of being left hanging, meaningless, tossed on the ash heap of history. Just as the present runs the risk of losing its meaning if it fails to root itself in a meaningful past, *Cabra* rescues the detritus of a broken, defeated history. More than that: *Cabra* is the twofold redemption of a twofold defeat. The first *Cabra*, the 1964 film of which only a few vestiges remain, was itself redeeming a defeat: the assassination of João Pedro, the leader of the Peasants' Leagues. Not even a photo was left of him in life; that film, in staging his story, brought him back to life and placed him in history. Today's *Cabra* redeems the interrupted film—and João Pedro, too—along with his wife and family.

The idea of a rupture and the historical work that follows as redemption are quite strong in the film—hence, as I see it, the insistent presence of the "last." A shot is shown (twice, actually), and the commentary tells us that this was the last shot filmed in 1964. At another point, we see footage that is presented as Elizabeth's last appearance at a rally. It's the notion of the "last" that has to be overcome, destroyed: the need to create something after the last. The thing setting off these mechanisms of recovery and the notion of the "last" is 1964, but they aren't tied to it; they frame a conception of history. Along with contemporary shots of an emptied-out São Rafael, the city where Elizabeth took refuge, the narration informs us that the town will soon be flooded by the construction of a dam and that the residents are fighting for compensation, which they have been denied. Everything is always the last, and history, once defeated, must be constantly redeemed: it seems to me that there is no other way to understand the end of the film. Some time after having seen it, viewers are often left with the impression that the film ends with Elizabeth and Coutinho saying goodbye to one another. It would be a perfect ending. The camera is inside the car and the two protagonists are on-screen: the director in the car and Elizabeth, who speaks like she's never spoken before. "The fight goes on," she says. Those words create a link between before-the-coup and now, and they project the film forward into the future. It would be perfect; but the film doesn't end there. After the goodbyes, there comes a short sequence—which is, indeed,

Victory Over the Ash Heap of History | 343

the final one—of scenes showing José Virgínio and his son. The commentary informs us that Virgínio died a month later. This image is much less powerful and conclusive than the final images of the goodbyes. It gives us information that is undeniably important for Virgínio himself, of course, and for the film, which has set out to track down the peasants from 1964. But to my eye, the information is not so decisive that it couldn't have been placed after the conversations with Virgínio and his children, not so decisive as to justify its position at the very end of the film. Except for one thing: this is the last recording of Virgínio. By finishing that way, the film reaffirms its concept of the work of history.

This process of redeeming history leads to a mise-en-abyme in which the work is framed within the work, the film within the film. It is, in fact, the existence of the vestiges of *Cabra '64* that sets off *Cabra '84*; the search for the non-actors who took part in the first shoot, as well as Elizabeth and her children, drives the second film. This drive is made something of a whirlpool by the rereading of the preface of *Kaputt*, a book found by chance among the crew's belongings. Within *Cabra* is an echo of Malaparte's novel; it, too, was hidden in pieces to escape repression, left with a number of the author's friends, including a Polish peasant, and it is peasants who hide the camera used to shoot *Cabra '64*, and a peasant who once again hides *Kaputt*, now in its Brazilian version. The film highlights this episode by returning to the scene in which José Virgínio's son takes the book out of the suitcase where it was stowed away, and this connection is reinforced by Coutinho's question after the reading of part of the preface: "Did you connect it to the film?"

The whirlwind of redemption: what can redeem history? Spectacle. Artifice is present at every step, with the dates of the multiple shoots, documentation of the crew's trips, the presence of the director, etc., confirming the statement made by the masterful opening shot. A landscape at dusk, hills in the background, the dark lower part of the shot set off by the natural light above the hills; then lights—artificial lights—snap on and the landscape is unexpectedly transformed into a vast movie theater the size of nature itself. The show can begin, and the show is what will ultimately guide the work of the redemption of history. History is revived, becomes coherent and meaningful, thanks to the spectacle. Beyond the opening shot, the spectacle as the redemption of history produces other brilliant, moving moments. For example: Coutinho interviews one of the people who took part in *Cabra '64*, who has since settled in Limeira, São Paulo. The director asks the man if he remembers his lines from the film. The man does. We hear the response: "Jerky's awful expensive . . ." The line will appear once again, not over the later interview with the peasant, but over mute footage of his younger self, uttering the same words in 1964. The words of 1984 are dubbed over an image seventeen years younger. Dubbing, which is still frequent in fiction films, would have been the only way to add sound to *Cabra '64*, since at that time standard equipment in Brazil was not capable of capturing direct sound.

The work of redemption may find obstacles, and it may be halted. This is what happens to the peasants who refuse to overcome that rupture, who don't want to talk about the past (like the one who's moved up in life and wants to sell his farm). How castrating it feels! This internal block produces a moment of great dramatic beauty in the interview with Mariano. He dismisses the idea of "joining the revolution again." This is so violent, and goes so frontally against the film's process, that the spectacle itself seems to stutter: the interviewer cuts off the interviewee momentarily because of a technical problem that may be happening with the sound. Once the soundman has been consulted, the interview goes on, but Mariano finds it difficult to pick up where he left off.

In light of this difficulty, Mariano appeals to the visual element of the spectacle as proof of his sincerity: he says that people can see in his expression that his dedication to the movement is not the same. All this—in a single shot—becomes even more dramatic when one recalls that Mariano was the actor who played the part of João Pedro himself in *Cabra '64*. The irony: all that is left of João Pedro (not even a photograph in life) is one living image, portrayed by Mariano in the spectacle.

How does the spectacle function? It connects the author of the film and his project, on the one hand, and Elizabeth Teixeira and her family on the other. It would probably be incorrect to say that Elizabeth is the main character in *Cabra*. The main characters are divided along two axes: one led by Elizabeth, with the peasants who took part in *Cabra '64* and the Teixeira family, and the other led by Coutinho, made up of the newly emerging film. Both axes are oppressed, be it as peasants or as intellectuals: the redemption of oppressed history. The dominant classes, their presence constantly felt in the film in terms of the structure of the countryside, terrorist attacks on the peasants, or the military's part in the coup, are only seen in the bare minimum of images needed to narrate the relevant events. And that is a clear decision: to not show political figures from the dominant classes. Not for lack of opportunity: on more than one occasion, it would have been possible to introduce documents relating to political actors during the dictatorship, or even prior to 1964—when, for example, Elizabeth says that she went to Rio de Janeiro and Brasília to speak before a congressional committee. This decision clearly sets a project like *Cabra marcado para morrer* apart from the structure behind *Os anos JK* or *Jango* (Sílvio Tendler), or, to a lesser extent, *Jânio a 24 Quadros* (Luís Alberto Pereira). Even so, the choice is neither automatic nor dogmatic: the film does include Elizabeth praising General Figueiredo's amnesty law.

A structure of this sort—author/character, both oppressed and both mediated by the work—had already been seen in *O homem que virou suco*, directed by João Batista de Andrade, and *Memórias do cárcere*, by Nelson Pereira dos Santos. The latter film, based on the book by Graciliano Ramos, addresses the relationship between the writer and his fellow prisoners/the people; in the former, the poet/worker Deraldo is able to relate to the murderer/worker through his poetry. In both cases, the film bears the same title as the work written by the main character. *Cabra* takes this to new heights: the work that structures the narrative is not a fictional element, but the film itself. In this process, the intellectual engages with the people through his artistic production, which is explicitly examined in the films. Hence the epitomic power of the final sequence of the goodbyes, as already mentioned here: the camera inside the car, showing the director of the film (who is already inside the car himself) and Elizabeth—a frame within a frame—through the window. The two axes are here in this clearly structured image, implying that this could easily have been the ending to the film, which only underscores the strangeness of the fact that the editors chose a different conclusion.

Of what matter is this spectacle made? In the history that is defeated, reality shatters into a thousand fragments. These are pieces of reality, vestiges, the all-but-buried ruins of history. *Cabra '84* unearths *Cabra '64*, it reveals Elizabeth underneath Marta (the pseudonym she adopted while living underground). The spectacle's task will be to work with these vestiges, bring them to light and organize them into some sort of coherence—a bridge—without abandoning their fragmentality. Fragments are not an arbitrary function of style; they are the very form of defeated history, which is why, even in the search for coherence and meaning, the fragmentary form can never be abandoned. *Cabra* does this admirably. Its fragmentary editing stems naturally from the diversity of material that makes up the film, but goes beyond it. Certain scenes that might have been placed together were instead distributed throughout the narrative, including the peasants watching the leftovers from 1964 and the interviews with Elizabeth in her home or in her backyard.

Nor does the edited material provide any stylistic homogeneity. *Cabra '64* has a touch of neorealism tempered with didacticism: its hieratic spirit recalls the "Pedreira de São Diogo" segment directed by Leon Hirszman in *Cinco vezes favela*, coproduced by the National Students' Union in the early 1960s. The interviews with Elizabeth do not stray far from the style of filming we see in documentaries from the mid-'60s like *Opinião pública* (Arnaldo Jabor). The interviews shot on the outskirts of Rio with Elizabeth's sons and daughters, meanwhile, betray a certain emotional sensationalism that allies them with the sensibilities of modern-day TV reporting. With this variety of styles, the passage of time itself is revealed. Not least among these differences is the deliberate presence of the director: for the author to place himself in the foreground, with the same weight as his character, would have been unthinkable at the time of *Cabra '64*. The author existed then but remained hidden, a transparent vehicle of reality and the message he bore. The author becoming the explicit mediation between the real and the viewer, the author exposing himself within his work as a maker of cinema, all this signals a personalization of the spectacle and its relationship to the audience that contradict the ideological and aesthetic stances taken by *Cabra '64*. Another attitude that stands as a bright line between the proceedings in 1964 and 1984: *Cabra '64* had a written screenplay—and how!—of which we see a page on-screen. Meanwhile, the commentary informs us that *Cabra '84* had no screenplay. For that matter, it should be said that the editor of *Cabra '84*, Eduardo Escorel, must have had as much of an auteurial hand as the director himself, given the complexity and sophistication of this edit.

Cabra '64 is fragmented; it is neither a film nor a part of a film, but an array of pieces; the commentary lets us know early on that it was never edited together. Elizabeth's family was left similarly fragmented after 1964, scattered across Brazil. As were the peasants who acted in the 1964 film. In the face of this shattering, the task is to gather the pieces and bring them together without stripping them of their fragmentary nature. Bring together the peasants in Galiléia before the scenes they shot. Bring the family back together. Here, it seems that within the structure of the film, these efforts are almost competing: Elizabeth wants to find her children (she expresses this desire, having sent a letter to one of her daughters), and the film also wants to find Elizabeth's children. Close to the end, we are informed that as the narration was being recorded, some time after the shoot, Elizabeth had only reunited with two of her children, while the film crew had already recorded all of her surviving children. The spectacle has outrun Elizabeth. At the same time, it helps open the way for her to follow behind it, in a sense, since the film is what prods her into leaving her assumed identity. They are in competition, unless . . . Unless this reunion only ever happens in the film, and the fragments scattered throughout reality are only gathered together in the realm of the spectacle, this being the imaginary consummation of potential scenarios that never materialized. Only the spectacle can allow Elizabeth to reencounter herself, in the shot in *Cabra '84* in which we see her from behind, looking at her own frontal image in *Cabra '64*. Here, all of Elizabeth's facets come together: Elizabeth as a person, having shed her false name, Marta, and as a character in *Cabra '64*, standing before Elizabeth the actress playing Elizabeth Teixeira. It was the spectacle that brought the peasants to gather again at Galiléia. Only in that 1984 spectacle, and in no other situation, can the character from 1964 say: "Jerky's awful expensive . . ." These things are only possible in the spectacle, which is thus lent its true power.

I've alluded multiple times here to repeated shots or scenes in *Cabra marcado para morrer*. There are many more. Just to list a few borderline obsessive cases: three shots presented consecutively of a scene in *Cabra '64* showing a hired gun leaving a house on horseback and breaking a vase at the feet of a peasant; or the words from the last scene shot in 1964, the sound for which wasn't recorded in 1964—"there's someone outside"—which is repeated four or five times by the peasants in 1984. Just as it is marked by the move toward redemption or the notion of the "last," *Cabra* is marked by repetition. This repetition mainly comes forth in the material or situations relating to 1964, but appears elsewhere as well: the scene in which José Virgínio's son looks for the books in the suitcase twice is contemporary. Each of these repetitions is driven by a different motive: the first time we see Elizabeth at the rally is inserted into the scene where she refers to her life after João Pedro's assassination, while the second reinforces the idea of the "last"; and the repetition of the scene with *Kaputt* underscores the relationship between the film and the novel—the idea of the work that is hidden to escape repression, and the work of history as redemption; and three shots of photographs of João Pedro's body ensure that the man of whom no images were taken in life may be present here. The procedure is so relentless that in addition to case-by-case explanations, there must be a stronger motivation. The repetition reaffirms the fragments, to the detriment of continuity. But I have the impression that its overarching function is to proclaim victory over the ash-heap of history. This was rescued, this was saved, and so the film says again and again that this fragment was unearthed, won back, drawn back into the fold of history, let there be no doubt; and it is repeated again and again in order to cling to it, so that it cannot disappear again, staving off any fresh losses.

The project behind *Cabra marcado para morrer*—to build a bridge over the rupture in history, to lend meaning to the past and life to the present—didn't spring full-fledged from Coutinho's head. Quite the contrary; here, I see a collective project that had first manifested itself clearly around ten years earlier in Ruy Guerra and Nelson Xavier's *A queda*. In it, the characters are workers building the subway in Rio de Janeiro. The authors, asking themselves what sort of past these men might have, imagined that a decade before the events in *A queda*, they had served in the military in the Northeast and subjected starving peasants. Or, in wondering about the future of those young soldiers back in 1964, they found subway construction workers. To create that past, *A queda* includes fragments of the film that Ruy Guerra had finished in early 1964: *Os fuzis*. The excerpts from *Os fuzis* give a past to the characters in *A queda* and a future to the young soldiers, but they also give a past to *A queda* as a film and a future to *Os fuzis* as a film, as well as to the phase of Cinema Novo that was broken off in 1964. *A queda* clearly expressed the desire to find—or, rather, to construct—some sort of coherence between the world before and after the rupture, to make a trajectory out of that which ran the risk of becoming the shrapnel of history.

But *A queda* was not alone in this. The same drive is undeniably present in *Eles não usam black-tie*, by Leon Hirszman, an adaptation of Gianfrancesco Guarnieri's 1955 play, which affirms that the project behind the play and the playwriting seminar put on by the Teatro de Arena remains, both in its original identity and in its changes (for example, the change in the focus on the strike, and the fact that Guarnieri goes from playing the son in the play to playing the father in the film). And *Memórias do cárcere* seems to be linked to the same project: the metaphor of the intellectual in contact with the people, the figure who speaks on behalf of the voiceless, they who appear in the intellectual's work. This is the reaffirmation of an ideal nurtured by much of the intellectual left in the 1950s and 1960s, and by Cinema Novo.

But unlike *Cabra*—and, to an extent, unlike *A queda*—neither *Black-tie* nor *Memórias* is fragmentary; they offer continuous narratives. This itself is neither an advantage nor a disadvantage, but it does reveal another approach: rather than clinging to the redemption of history and working with defeat and rupture, these two films are concerned with their messages. What underpins their homogeneity, their unity, their continuity is the ideological project that defines them. Their fragmentary nature does not come forward because in them, history is shaped by the message to be delivered in a didactic, dogmatic vessel. These works seek to illustrate a concept that precedes them. I may explain myself better by using a comparison. There's a moment in *Cabra* that makes me think of a sequence in *Memórias*, during the first interview with Elizabeth, in her living room. Eight photos of *Cabra* '64 are left, eight fragments; they are seen by Elizabeth and her son Carlos; and then they are passed from hand to hand, with a few young people pointing out things that draw their attention. Though the situations are incomparable, I see a relationship between these scenes in *Cabra* and the sequence near the end of *Memórias* in which the prison guards threaten to confiscate Graciliano Ramos's manuscript: the sheets of paper are handed out among the prisoners, who hide them in their clothes. This scene epitomizes the ideal put forth in the film: the people—symbolized by the community of prisoners—takes up the work of the intellectual, just as the writer hands over his work to the people; in the face of repression, the work spreads out and is atomized into a thousand pieces, even as it finds a sort of unity in becoming fused with the people. Just as the eight photos are taken up by those present. The great difference, as I see it, is that in *Memórias* the meaning of the scene exists before the scene, the scene is born freighted with meaning, serves to express the metaphor, and is dominated by that metaphorical meaning; in *Cabra*, meanwhile, first the scene is described and then the metaphor blossoms from it; rather than imposing itself, it arises, fragile, unimposing, not taking on the mantle of a set message.

> A chronicler who recites events without distinguishing between major and minor ones acts in accordance with the following truth: nothing that has ever happened should be regarded as lost for history. To be sure, only a redeemed mankind receives the fullness of its past—which is to say, only for a redeemed mankind has its past become citable in all its moments. Each moment it has lived becomes a *citation a l'ordre du jour*—and that day is Judgment Day.
>
> —Walter Benjamin

Note [2003]

If . . .

The "bridge"—a metaphor that I still feel is applicable to *A queda* and *Cabra marcado para morrer*—does not eliminate the rupture. The work of redemption does not restore what has been lost.

Let us wonder, passing through the magical portal of "if": would we who, thank God, are here to tell the story, tell it the same way if Eduardo Coutinho had finished *Cabra marcado para morrer* before the military coup of 1964?

The scenes from *Cabra '64* shown in *Cabra '84* indicate a stylistic language far removed from that which shapes the major works of the Cinema Novo in 1963–64. *Deus e o diabo na terra do sol*, *Vidas secas*, and *Os fuzis* have long shots, a persistent spatial continuity, a camera that follows the actors, whether they're walking (as in famous shots in *Vidas secas*) or standing still (Corisco in *Deus e o diabo*). The style of *Cabra '64*, which is closer to the camera work and editing of Leon Hirszman's *Pedreira de São Diogo*, might not have had much of an effect on the ongoing transformation of the language of Brazilian cinema at that time.

Then again, the dramatic structure of *Cabra '64* was innovative for the period. Not only did it use non-actors, but, above all, those actors were directly implicated in the real events that the film was translating into fiction. Never before in Brazil had a person played themselves in a fictional role, as was the case with Elizabeth Teixeira (Jean Rouch had done it in the late 1950s). *Cabra '64*'s work on the complex borders between documentary and fiction opened doors for both fiction and documentary film that might have been followed up on and transformed by Brazilian directors in the mid-1960s. Or maybe not. I believe that the interruption of the shoot led to a loss, a loss that can be worked through (this is exactly the function of the above-mentioned scene in which Elizabeth/Marta looks at the photo of Elizabeth/actress playing Elizabeth Teixeira), but which cannot be restored.

I also believe that the ideological history of Cinema Novo circa 1963–64 would have been told differently if *Cabra marcado para morrer* had been finished.

As it was, the stylistic and ideological hegemony of the period remained with the three films by Glauber Rocha, Nelson Pereira dos Santos, and Ruy Guerra, as mentioned here. They took a humanistic approach that had an international impact. It underscored the poverty of a suffering, apathetic peasantry, not only in the Brazilian Northeast but in the Latin American countryside and the Third World in general—the oppressive permanence of a latifundiary agricultural structure—and gestured toward a vague utopic hope, especially Glauber and Nelson's work. But these films ignored the situations that were developing in the Northeast at the very time that they were being shot. *Deus e o diabo* and *Vidas secas* were prudently set in the 1930s. This lent them an abstract air, which contributed to their impact and aligned with an ideological pact of the time (Carlos Lacerda's antipathy toward *Deus e o diabo* doesn't alter the picture significantly, in my view). This developmentalist pact consisted of attacking the poverty of a marginalized peasantry and its cause, the *latifúndios*, but avoiding contemporary topics that might mobilize a bourgeoisie that, despite its national and nationalistic pretensions, steered away from complicated issues related to the proletariat and grassroots organization. This is probably one of the reasons why the hegemonic films of the Cinema Novo in 1963–64 were so overwhelmingly rural and avoided urban settings. The many workers' movements of those years, which arose in multiple industrial hubs, went unnoticed.

In his work with those very peasant masses, Leon Hirszman toed the developmentalist line but adopted a posture that set *Maioria absoluta* apart from the films mentioned above. Within the confines of the pact between the Communist Party and João Goulart's administration, he presents a defenseless, apathetic mass of peasants, with the exception of a few individual voices (the remarkable "it's a downright disgrace" monologue), and an irresponsible elite.[1] *Maioria absoluta* fights for literacy, a path to voting rights for peasants, and calls for government and the well-off to accept the responsibility for their plight. The final words ("The film ends here. Out there, your life, like the lives of these men, goes on") are a call to action, spoken over a shot of peasants walking down a road and away into the distance—an image not so different from the ending of *Vidas secas*.

Cabra marcado para morrer is framed in a completely different way. It does not envision a utopian humanism, nor does it appeal to government. The peasants are not apathetic, but organized; they form the Peasants' Leagues and face down the farming structure and landowning powers—all of which led to the assassination of João Pedro. This vision is clearly as distant from the humanistic approach as it is from Hirszman's.

If *Cabra marcado para morrer* had been finished, we would frame the history of the cinema from 1963–64 differently; it would have been a counterpoint, balancing out the political and ideological posture of the films from the same period.

It would also be an answer to another key parameter in the ideological and cinematographic framework of the period: consciousness-raising. The understanding was that consciousness precedes action. The masses were, in the language of the period, "alienated"; hence the need to raise their awareness (this task taken on by leaders and socially "engaged" artists) so that, once aware, they might become politically active. This thesis, which was widely disseminated at the time—of consciousness as necessary for action and necessarily prior to it, and hence of action as the consequence of consciousness—fit neatly into the humanist-developmentalist pact. Indeed, it allowed for a heavy focus on consciousness-raising, not action. From this angle, we can understand how the films of Glauber Rocha, Nelson Pereira dos Santos, and Ruy Guerra, as well as Leon Hirszman's, do not take on the issue of action; rather, they put it off. It's no coincidence that in *Deus e o diabo*, Glauber films not the "great war in the backlands" but rather the events that would precede it.

Now, from what we can glean from Coutinho's interrupted film, *Cabra marcado para morrer* would not have been a consciousness-raising film (in the accepted sense), nor did it postpone action. He set out to film the action and film his characters in action. We can intuit—and I don't believe that I'm overstepping my bounds in saying so—that in this film, action does not rest on consciousness-raising to prepare the ground for action, and that action itself builds consciousness. If *Cabra marcado para morrer* had been finished, perhaps it might have helped provide a more critical understanding of the conscious/consciousness-raising/action equation.

And Eduardo Coutinho himself might have played a different role during that time, if . . .

Note

1. Editors' note: Hirszman's short film examines the experiences of illiteracy, poverty, hunger, and lack of political rights that plagued the "absolute majority" of Brazilians at the time of its filming in 1964. The documentary juxtaposes middle-class residents in southeastern cities with people living in the rural Northeast. This notable "it's a downright disgrace" monologue appears near the end of the film as a rural laborer emphatically explains, "Father of seven kids, living off the land, or by going to the co-op, a farmer has to buy a kilo of flour for lunch. It's agony, it's a downright disgrace. It's a downright disgrace. It's a disgrace, it's agony. Now all the peasants, this world of land, I'm going to buy a kilo of flour. A kilo of flour is what city people have to buy, because they're workers and don't plant, but the peasant out here? Who does this? It's the landowner, who privatizes the land, puts it in his hands, and doesn't let the peasant plant."

21

Jogo de cena

JEAN-CLAUDE BERNARDET,
TRANSLATED BY FLORA THOMSON-DEVEAUX

Editors' note: This piece initially appeared as entries on Bernardet's blog between January 14, 2008, and June 24, 2010. Ohata edited the excerpts according to chronological order for inclusion near the end of the 'Routes and Detours of a Filmmaker" section. The text includes the dates and the titles as published on the blog. The posts provide insight into Bernardet's reactions to initial viewings of Jogo de cena *and* Moscou, *which Carlos Alberto Mattos categorizes as part of Coutinho's experimental phase. The informality and immediacy of blogging allow Bernardet to meditate upon the idea of performance and the relationship between person and character as considers the relevance of these films within Coutinho's career and, more generally, Brazilian and world cinemas.*

1) *Jogo de cena* blows away the entirety of interview-based cinema, including Eduardo Coutinho's latest films. This film reveals an extraordinary courage in its willingness to question the director's own work. 2) The cut before the repetition of "So I stopped focusing so much on my marriage" is frankly historic. 3) *Jogo de cena* has a tragic aspect to it. Around the middle of the film, or a bit past it, a woman tells her story. But I just heard the same story told a few minutes ago. Who told it? Which face? There comes a point when discourse is disconnected from speaking bodies. It begins to exist on its own Discourse speaking itself. The speakers are merely the hosts of the speech. *Jogo de cena* questions the being, at least as a being

that expresses its subjectivity with words and tears. 4) What does this mean for those who believed that the words of interviewees in Coutinho's films were the expression of their subjectivity? 5) The well-known actresses work as an anchor sunk in reality. We know that they are performing. But what if there are actresses whose faces aren't so familiar to us? And what are the actresses performing? Another person, or their own personal experience playing another person—hence themselves? 6) *Santiago* and *Jogo de cena* are proof that philosophical essays are possible in cinema, not as monologues illustrated with images, but by making use of and testing the limits of the resources of cinematographic language.

The Documentary Boom (July 31, 2009)

The documentary boom, which has lasted for around two decades now, is a new wave of naturalism. We might reference films like *Wilson Simonal* or *Loki*, among a generous array. Their artifices and conventions are becoming evident: the interview format, for example. And the *Ulysses* of documentary film has already exploded. Its title: *Jogo de cena*. It hasn't left many survivors.

I believe that we need to understand the scope of *Jogo de cena*. It is not an important, transformative film for Brazilian documentary cinema, it is a 7.0 on the Richter scale for documentary cinema in general, or, to be more specific, documentary based on speech. *Jogo de cena* is a transformative explosion of a magnitude caused, in the past, by the films of Eistenstein or Godard. We might say that *Jogo de cena* heralds the end of a cycle of cinema begun by Jean Rouch half a century ago, with *Moi, un noir*.

Can we move past *Jogo de cena*? Yes, but how?

Moscou (August 6, 2009)

I agree wholeheartedly with a comment by Eduardo Escorel (*piauí* 35, August 3, 2009) about Eduardo Coutinho's latest film: *Moscou* is a catastrophe and an impasse.

[. . .]

As for the impasse, I believe that it should be understood from an angle apart from Coutinho's career or his filmography: he has made remarkable films, and, unfortunately, this latest one isn't quite so good. I believe that the impasse isn't Coutinho's alone; it is collective. *Jogo de cena* casts doubt (with exceptional courage) on all of Coutinho's films since *Santo forte*. *Jogo de cena* casts doubt on all documentary films based on speech as the discourse of subjectivity and on accounts of life stories. It casts doubt on the relationship between the speaking body and the speech of subjectivity (who produces it? what does it speak of?). It casts doubt on the relationship between speech and subjectivity.

After watching *Jogo de cena*, I spoke and felt the strangeness of it (and this is true): Who is speaking? Me? Me who? The film destabilizes the idea of the subject. Either I'm seeing things, or *Jogo de cena* is tragically radical. This problem isn't Coutinho's. It's shared by all those who feel impacted by that tragically radical swerve.

Films I took part in, shot before *Jogo de cena*, now strike me as childish. I'm currently working on a documentary that involves the discourse of subjectivity and accounts of life stories, and I simply can't get into it. *Jogo de cena* has gone too far.

Escorel's words—"Coutinho is the great absence in *Moscou*"—are quite beautiful and extraordinarily precise. Coutinho could not "be" present because the subject is destabilized. When will we be present again?

I fantasized that, in order to break the impasse that *Jogo de cena* has put us in, Coutinho could/should sit down in front of a camera, in the foreground, and remain silent indefinitely.

Moscou 2 (August 12, 2009)

I watched *Moscou* again. A profoundly melancholic film.

[. . .]

The biggest problem with *Moscou* may be the phantasms that stand between it and us. *Jogo de cena* is certainly there, a film so radical and definitive that it is a point of no return. And another phantasm seems to cast its shadow over *Moscou: The Seagull*.

Perhaps we should try to change our tack and follow the path indicated by Carlos Mattos: why has Coutinho left his place as the interviewer, interlocutor, the filmmaker sitting behind the camera? As I see it (for now), there's no great mystery: this interlocutor-filmmaker sitting behind the camera not only doesn't make any more sense, it's not even a possibility after *Jogo de cena*, which ultimately dissolved the subject-interviewee and thus the subject-interviewer. In *Moscou*, the subject behind the camera is dissolved, doubly so, I might say: it affects not only Coutinho, but also Enrique Diaz (however much the shrinking of the theater director's role may be explained by the dynamic of workshops).

There is another path we might follow, and this one I don't understand. Coutinho ceasing to be the subject who provokes and receives the speech of another—I believe that this is the logical, inexorable consequence of *Jogo de cena*, and this I can intuit. Coutinho ceasing to be a filmmaker who moves around—that I don't understand. Why has he shut himself up in a single space? Why is there no light in this chosen space? Why go from *O fim e o princípio*, a film of movement and luminosity (the opening sequence of *Peões* also makes me think of movement and luminosity) to a closed-off, dark space? What is he looking for?

Eduardo Coutinho & Sophie Calle—2 (August 13, 2009)

It was while writing about Sophie Calle (Coutinho & Sophie Calle, August 3, 2009) that, for the first time, I thought of *Jogo de cena* as a centripetal film.

This allowed me to approach the film from a new angle. Its identity/opposition between film and exhibition has left its mark on how we understand the trajectory of Coutinho's work.

In *Jogo de cena*, all of the women invited to speak converge, moving through a narrow passage (the staircase) to the point where they will meet the filmmaker, sit down, and speak. This is a novelty in the structure of Coutinho's films.

Up to that point, Coutinho had gone to meet the people he would interview, whether that meant the favela in *Santo forte* or the endless apartments of the Edifício Master.

If we turn to *Cabra marcado para morrer*, we see that it is essentially a film in movement. Coutinho returns to the region where he began filming the first *Cabra*, in 1964. He goes out in search of people who took part in the film and finds a few. The information he gathers leads him to Elizabeth Teixeira, and from there he sets out in search of her children, who have scattered across Brazil. From a spatial point of view, the second *Cabra* is a film without a center. Coutinho is not a center, he is an agent whose constant movement connects the fragments of a shattered history.

I will not draw conclusions from this or assign it significance. I'll simply observe that, from *Cabra marcado para morrer* to *Jogo de cena*, Coutinho shifted from an acentric model (not "eccentric," but rather lacking a center), based on movement, to a powerfully centric model.

Eduardo Coutinho & Luiz Ruffato (February 26, 2010)

I read *Estive em Lisboa e lembrei de você*, by Luiz Ruffato. [. . .] What is the operation proposed by *Estive em Lisboa*? The author takes ownership of the narrative of a person telling a story from their own life. But in this novel, both the story and the appropriation are fictional, simulated. LR is doing in literature what Eduardo Coutinho has done in his most recent films (*Edifício Master*, etc.): the audiovisual appropriation of the narratives of people encouraged to tell stories from their lives. Which Coutinho took to such disturbing (not to say tragic) lengths in *Jogo de cena*: the story is displaced from the subject who experienced it to become the basis for the interpretive work of an actor. One further displacement, and we might imagine that having experienced the event in question is not indispensable for the text to hold its own, or for the actor to work convincingly. The text must simply be coherent, plausible, and compelling. This is where LR comes in. The Coutinho of these films and the Ruffato of this novel belong to the same aesthetic and social universe. Both belong to the era of the reality show, or the "reality sphere" or "nebulous reality," or "reality as a show," or "reality is a show," or "the show is reality." That which manifests itself in cinema as documentary and in literature as the "appetite for reality in the contemporary publishing market" (to quote Vilma Costa). And not just for reality, but also for simulacra.

Coutinho & Paul Ricoeur

Currently prevalent strains of philosophy and psychology have moved away from substantialist and essentialist theories of the ego. The ego is not a substance, an identity stowed away in the depths of one's being, put into play by the path taken by one's life and life story. The ego tends to be seen as a production, in constant construction. More than that: it is that production. The conception of the ego as a never-ending dynamic would lead to its dissolution; hence, that construction is also made up of gestures of closing and stabilization that help to fix the meaning of life.

The gesture of stabilization is an integral part of the gesture of production. Major authors (such as Paul Ricoeur, with his *Soi-Même Comme un Autre* and *Temps et Récit*, and Jean-Claude Kaufmann, with *L'invention de soi, Une Théorie de l'identité*) ascribe to narrative a fundamental role in the dynamic of the production of oneself and establishing the meaning of life. Seen from this angle, identity is the story that each of us tells ourselves.

Paul Ricoeur brooks no argument: individual identity is constructed through narrative. The process of the construction of identity is a narrative process. The ego rests on the dialogue between lived experience and the account of it. And Kaufmann adds: between lived experience and the account of it, we are often at a loss to say which is the real driver, and which holds sway.

Well, it seems that *Jogo de cena* takes an ironic jab at the narration cast as a fundamental part of the process of building identity, since that very account can move through mouths and bodies that did not experience what they are recounting.

Jogo de cena 2 (August 26, 2011)

In her book *El espacio biográfico*, Leonor Arfuch recalls that the "interview," which appears in the press in the second half of the nineteenth century, goes in the opposite direction from autobiography. The latter moves from the private, or even the intimate, toward the public. The interview, meanwhile, originates in the public sphere: the journalist seeks to unearth the private, in search of information. Then the journalist publishes the words they have gathered (and reworked). Interview-based cinema follows essentially the same model, whether dealing with the authorized words of a specialist, autobiographical testimony, or that of a witness.

In multiple of Coutinho's works, this gesture is represented concretely. We see the filmmaker and his team moving toward the interviewee, as in *Cabra marcado para morrer* and other films. The interviewer seeks out the interviewee.

This gesture is modified in *Jogo de cena*: the interviewees come into the interviewer's space. It's plain to see: the movement on the part of these people who will speak is the product of a prior agreement. There has been a selection, and only those selected will reach the discursive space. Here, the movement represented visually is the opposite from that of his earlier films (as has been amply commented). The selection in *Jogo de cena* follows a different logic.

In *Edifício Master*, the apartment building offered a finite world of potential interviewees, who were subjected to a selection process in multiple stages. All signs seem to indicate that this selection was done personally. Someone from the team would invite a resident to be interviewed for the film. The person would be free to accept or refuse, give a "yes" or a "no," and be able to negotiate that "yes" (restricting topics of conversation, duration, day, time, etc.). A negotiation that will take place between the "invitee" and the representative from the team.

In *Jogo de cena*, the gesture between filmmaker and potential interviewee exists. But—and this is the first key differential—it is not personal, and it draws on a practically boundless universe of people. If we are to believe the film, the gesture consists of this, a classified ad in a newspaper: "Invitation/ If you are a woman over age 18, living in Rio de Janeiro, have stories to tell, and would like to take part in a screen test for a documentary, contact us. Call us starting April 17, 10 a.m. to 6 p.m., at . . . /Limited spots."

The first stage is addressed to an anonymous group. What happens next? On the team's end, nothing. All they can do is wait for phone calls. On the other end, people will have to call in and abandon anonymity. In this phone call, I see one of the great contributions that the film proposes. What changes?

The reader of the ad (which is practically an open call), initially a blank for the person who places the ad, only becomes an individual when she takes the decision to reply. This model requires a decision-making process that is incomparably more determined and voluntary than simply saying "yes" when invited face to face, verbally, to give an interview. One must identify with the proposal, want to have one's "stories" made public, and, what's more, having presented oneself as an individual, one also runs the risk of not making the cut.

The level of initiative required by this model makes me think that *Jogo de cena* opens up an "autobiographical space." The space manifests itself in *Edifício Master*, in which people tell stories from their lives. But the sort of personal decision called for by *Jogo de cena* is so much greater that it crosses a border into the space in which a subject takes the initiative to make their life story public. The "autobiographical desire" must be manifested more intensely, with no direct contact with the person proposing the interaction. The difference no longer lies in which stories are told or how they are recounted, nor even in the fact that they are drawn from life, but in the intensity and the nature of the decision to be taken when entering the process that has been proposed.

IMPORTANT note: these comments reflect exclusively on interview-based cinema as practiced in Brazil, and do not speak to the multiple forms in which autobiographical space and desire manifest themselves on television and online.

Another observation: I undertook the experiment of answering an ad like that in *Jogo de cena*, for the play *Nãotemnemnome*.
[With Cláudia Mesquita and Ilana Feldman.]

Notes [2013]

When I first saw the cut that introduces Andréa Beltrão in the film, I had a physical reaction. And I physically saw a life story slip, unruffled, from the body of one woman to the body of another. The story is indifferent to the body pronouncing it; it has become autonomous. This is the matter: the *narrative-autonomy-of-the-life-story*. Now, a few questions: when did I formulate this expression? Either the very moment when I reacted to the cut (unlikely, since it was a sensory reaction), or a bit later but still during the screening (not impossible), or after the screening; and if it was afterwards, then it was right afterwards, as I left the theater. But this doesn't answer the essential question for what I like to refer to as film-essays, cinematographic essays that don't verbally address the topics they're working with. That is to say, they use cinematographic language alone to refer viewers to the concepts at hand. But is that possible? Philosophers would say no, that philosophy is only the written word. Even so, *Jogo de cena* pulls off the feat: the film is a powerful reflection on the construction of subjectivity, subjectivity not as essence but as production, the transformation of lived experience into narratives and the process by which those narratives become autonomous, henceforth expressing only an illusion of subjectivity (as accounts, not as utterances). So far, so good. My concern has to do with what really happened, to wit: do I understand the film this way because of the film and its constructive principles? Alternatively, I may be interacting with another phenomenon entirely: a reading, however unruly, of *Time and Narrative*, by Paul Ricoeur, or *The Invention of the Self*, by Jean-Claude Kaufmann, may have prepared me to project onto the film concepts used by these authors or activated by the act of reading (I'm using the term "concept" in a flexible sense, which I believe is healthy) (and this is slightly different from the fact that every viewer sees the film from his or her own cultural background).

I don't believe that I can come up with a definitive answer. The only thing I am certain of is that I didn't think about those books during the screening, but that doesn't mean much. The doubt remains, and it speaks to our relationship to the film. And don't all reflections lead us to relationships?

While I watched Alain Resnais' *You Ain't Seen Nothin' Yet*, the memory of *Jogo de cena* surfaced multiple times, powerfully so. Context: old actors and actresses are watching the video of a new staging of a play that they performed when they were young, several of them having played the same character.

The spectacle unleashes memories. The characters of Orpheus and Eurydice, once performed, manifest themselves like ghosts, running through the bodies which hosted them once upon a time.

There is a magnificent cut (at around the 33-minute mark) which makes the character of Eurydice move from the body of one actress to the body of another. The actresses' gestures link up: the first is leaning back and the second straightens herself as if to continue the first woman's movement. And there is—and this is essential to the moment—an absolutely rhythmic continuity to the dialogue. This cut belongs to the same family as the cut in *Jogo de cena* (at approximately 7 minutes and 8 seconds) which introduces Andréa Beltrão. In Coutinho's film the two shots are framed similarly, with the woman placed on the right-hand side of the screen, the first wearing dark clothes and the second a light-colored sweater. The actress continues the story that the first woman had been telling, adding a "so" to connect her words to the last sentence spoken in the previous shot. That "so," just like the way the second actress in Resnais's film straightens up, is a little jolt that gives us the physical sensation of the discourse moving from one body to another. These two cuts create a powerful affinity between the two films. What these people are saying in front of the camera is nothing new. They have told it a thousand times, to themselves and to others. Parts of the narrative have crystallized, while others have shifted over time, repetition after repetition. Bit by bit, the connections to lived experience have worn thin, and bit by bit, these narratives have been taken on as the faithful memory of our lives. These are what I call narrative fossils. This is what these people say before the camera, with all of the power of victimization, self-justification, guilt, regret, as well as joys and victories, all of it helping to consolidate the fossils. Coutinho knows that.

What is new here is the utterance. It may belong to the person who lived it, or to a narrator, we can't tell the difference. But there's certainly something more that we'll never know, and which is unique to the women who took up the invitation in the ad and were selected, apart from the actresses: what led that person to the set? Overwhelming loneliness, a form of exhibitionism, a desire to relieve pain through socializing or to get something off their chest through the spectacle, the hope that some estranged person involved in their story may see the film and feel regret, or get the message: see me, beautiful as can be, here in a film? What is there beyond *Jogo de cena*? The lived experience that does not become a part of the stories.

Contributors

Jens Andermann is professor of Spanish and Portuguese at New York University and an editor of the *Journal of Latin American Cultural Studies*. His most recent book is *Entranced Earth: Art, Extractivism, and the End of Landscape* (2023).

Natalia Brizuela is professor of Spanish and Portuguese and film and media and the Class of 1930 Chair of the Center for Latin American Studies at the University of California, Berkeley. She is the author of *Fotografia e império. Paisagens para um Brasil moderno* (2012) and the coauthor, with Jodi Roberts, of *The Matter of Photography in the Americas* (2018).

Ashley Brock is assistant professor of Spanish and Portuguese at the University of Pennsylvania. She is the author of *Dwelling in Fiction: Poetics of Place and the Experimental Novel in Latin America* (2023).

Krista Brune is associate professor of Portuguese and Spanish and director of the Global and International Studies program at the Pennsylvania State University. She is the author of *Creative Transformations: Travels and Translations of Brazil in the Americas* (2020).

Bruno Carvalho is professor of Romance languages and literatures and African and African American Studies and codirector of the Harvard Mellon Urban Initiative at Harvard University. He is the author of *Porous City: A Cultural History of Rio de Janeiro* (2013).

Nilo Fernando Couret is associate professor of Spanish at the University of Michigan. He is the author of *Mock Classicism: Latin American Film Comedy, 1930–1960* (2018).

Gustavo Procopio Furtado is associate professor of Romance Studies and codirector of the Amazon Humanities Lab at Duke University. He is the author of *Documentary Filmmaking in Contemporary Brazil: Cinematic Archives of the Present* (2019).

Luz Horne is professor of literature at the Universidad de San Andrés, Buenos Aires. Her most recent book is *Futuros menores: Filosofías del tiempo y arquitecturas del mundo en Brasil* (2021).

Adriana Johnson is associate professor of comparative literature at the University of California, Irvine. She is the author of *Sentencing Canudos: Subalternity in the Backlands of Brazil* (2010).

Brenno Kenji Kaneyasu is a visual artist, writer, and educator. He received a PhD in Hispanic languages and literatures from the University of California, Berkeley, and was formerly an assistant professor of Spanish and Portuguese at the University of Southern California.

Vinicius Navarro is associate professor of visual and media arts at Emerson College. He is the coeditor, with Juan Carlos Rodríguez, of *New Documentaries in Latin America* (2014) and coauthor, with Louise Spence, of *Crafting Truth: Documentary Form and Meaning* (2011).

Rielle Navitski is associate professor in the department of theater and film studies at the University of Georgia. Her most recent book is *Transatlantic Cinephilia: Between Latin America and France, 1945–1965* (2023).

Fernando Pérez Villalón is an academic and director of the doctoral program in media studies at the Universidad Alberto Hurtado, Santiago de Chile. He is the author of *Variaciones* (2021) and *La imagen inquieta: Juan Downey and Raúl Ruiz en contrapunto* (2016).

Flora Thomson-DeVeaux is a translator, writer, and research director at Rádio Novelo in Rio de Janeiro. She received her PhD in Portuguese and Brazilian studies from Brown University. Her most recent translations are *The Apprentice Tourist* by Mário de Andrade and *The Posthumous Memoirs of Brás Cubas* by Machado de Assis.

Index

O ABC da Greve (film), 78
Abertura (television program), 137
Absolute Majority. See *Maioria absoluta*
Absorption and Theatricality (Fried), 193n1
abstraction, voice relation to, 39
accountability, narrative, 118
Acosta, Abraham, 253
acting, 185
  in representation, 178
action, 352
Adamic language, 252
adaptations, of literary works, 286–287
adolescents, interviews with, 155–156
aesthetic
  in *O fio da memória*, 99
  of violence, 41–42, 91
  of voice, 1, 210
aesthetics of hunger
  in *Boca de lixo*, 112
  of Cinema Novo, 92, 135
  Rocha and, 9–10, 91
affective responses, to music, 211–212, *212*, 213
Agamben, Giorgio, 223–224
  on metaphysics, 249
Aguilar, Gonzalo, 216n3
Alessandra, in *Edifício Master*, 250, *250*
Aleta, in *Jogo de cena*, 189–190, 192
aletheia, 192, 195n10

allegory, 60nn26–28
  in ethnography, 55–56
  The Seventh Seal as, 308
Allen, Alice, 21
Amado, Jorge, 286
Amar, verbo intransitivo (Andrade, M. se), 286
ambient sound, 205–206
analogy, 254–255
Anastácia, 326–327
ANCINE. *See* National Agency of Film
Andermann, Jens, 40, 43
Andrade, João Batista de, 78, 137, 140, 141, 142, 345
Andrade, Mário de, 286
Andrade, Oswald de, 286
Angústia (Ramos), 191
anthropology
  of cleanliness, 32
  savage, 3, 101, 158, 160, 245
apparatus (*dispositivo*), 197
  subject affected by, 205
  video in, 217n10
appearance
  in *Babilônia 2000*, 248
  characters and, 255
  in performance, 249, 251
  truth in, 250
apprentissage, 50
Araújo, Mauro Luciano Souza de, 38, 56

366 | Index

archival documentary, 271
archival material, 272, *273*, 281n9
   in *As canções*, 276
   songs as, 274
archive, 14
   Cabra marcado para morrer as, 76–77
   cinema as, 78
   documentary relation to, 67
   film relation to, 74, 82
   preservation of, 75
   temporality in, 66
Arfuch, Leonor, 358
"Art and Objecthood" (Fried), 193n1
Asfalto selvagem (Rodrigues), 286
Assis, Francisco de, 216n8
Athanasiou, Athena, 113, 115
   on dispossession, 121
Ato Institucional 5, 136
attunement, 280
audibility, 2–3
audience, 102
   documentary relation to, 90
   of *Globo Repórter*, 140, 148
   of performance, 179
   spectacle relation to, 346
   of theater, 194n3
   trust with, 184–185
audiovisual counterpoint, 203
Augusto, José, 209
authenticity, 206
   in documentary, 59n15, 275
   performance relation to, 120
   in representation, 2, 46, 47, 264
   in self-portrait, 59n14
   in sertão, 55–56
   in testimony, 117
author-centered reflexivity, 73
   mise-en-scène and, 69
   participant-centered reflexivity compared to, 70
authority
   in Brazilian television, 165, 168

   documentary, 264, 265, 280
   narrative, 24, 33n3
authorship
   of *Últimas conversas*, 243
   in *Um dia na vida*, 169–170
   voice and, 197–198, 200
autobiographical space, 359
Avellar, José Carlos, 6–7, 14–15, 317–318
   on film, 113
   as RioFilme director, 100
axiographics, 25
Azoulay, Ariella, 27

Babilônia 2000 (documentary), 22, 31, 217n14, 249
   characters in, 247–248
   favela in, 105
   interviews in, 29–30, 181
   music in, 209–210
   voice-over in, 108n20
Barnouw, Erik, 12
Barren Lives. See *Vidas secas*
Barreto, Bruno, 286
Barros, Luís de, 299
Barros, Nelson Lins e, 216n8
Barthes, Roland, 199, 217n9
Bazin, André, 66, 161
Beckett, Samuel, 178
Being and Time (Heidegger), 195n10
belief, fiction and, 189
Beltrão, Andréa, 116–117, 186, 275, 360, 361
Benjamin, Walter, 60nn26–28, 128, 215, 349
   on language, 199, 251, 252
Bennett, Jane, 33n1
Bentes, Ivana, 92
Béranger, Jean, 309
Berg, Jordana, 12, 100, 101, 156
   Últimas conversas completed by, 238, 243, 266

Berger, John, 163–164
Bergman, Ingmar, 287–288, 307–309, 310–311
　mise-en-scène of, 313
Berlant, Lauren, 252
　on intimacy, 253
Bernardet, Jean-Claude, 10, 14–15, 20, 77, 317, 319–320
　on *Cabra marcado para morrer*, 107n13
　Cineastas e imagens do povo of, 233
　on interviews, 12
　on *Jogo de cena*, 115, 130n3
Bezerra, Cláudio, 80, 84n16, 90
Bezerra, Theodorico, 33n3, 94, 138, 145–146, 147
Black God, White Devil. See *Deus e o diabo na terra do sol*
Black Orpheus (film), 209
Blimp Filmes, 140
Boca de lixo (documentary), 21, 25, 33n2, 97, *127*, *208*
　aesthetics of hunger in, 112
　Cabra marcado para morrer compared to, 28
　camera in, 339
　CECIP as producer of, 99
　Cícera in, 124–125
　conversation in, 337, 338
　Corcovado in, *112*
　dispossession in, 127
　image in, 26–27, 28, 71–72, 100, 104, 115, 120, 122, *123*, 126, 128–129, *337*
　interviews in, 29–30, 181
　Jogo de cena compared to, 120
　mise-en-film in, 73
　music in, 207, 208, 209, 217n11
　participant-centered reflexivity in, 70–71, 72
　place in, 31
　representation in, 121–122, 123–124, 335–336
　São Gonçalo landfill in, 111
　self-reflexivity in, 22–23
　voice in, 318
body, 76, 159
　speech relation to, 125
　voice relation to, 211, 214–215
Bolsonaro, Jair, 105
Borges's Pierre Menard, 170, 180
bossa nova, 213, 216n5
Bourdieu, Pierre, 193n2
Braga, Ana Maria, 175n1
Branco, Castelo, 330
Brazil, 29, 106n1. *See also* northeastern Brazil
　cinema in, 107n8, 291, 305n1, 319, 328, 333–334
　democracy in, 8, 38, 74–75, 96
　film in, 89
　landscape in, 105
　Mexico relation to, 301
　music in, 213
　neocolonialism in, 43
　the people (o povo) in, 9–10
　political cinema in, 264
　religion in, 100–101
　The Seventh Seal screened in, 307
　slavery in, 99, 318, 326–328, 330
　telecommunications infrastructure in, 136
　television in, 5, 94
Brazilian Communist Party, 106n4, 136–137
Brazilian military dictatorship, 5, 93
　Cabra marcado para morrer affected by, 271
　CPC ended by, 37
　Globo Repórter relation to, 136–137, 149, 291–292
Brazilian television, 162–163, 164
　authority in, 168

368 | Index

Brazilian television *(continued)*
   Cuban television compared to, 166–167
   subject in, 165–166
Breno, in *Últimas conversas*, 247
Brown, Jeckie, 187, 194n7
Bruna, in *Últimas conversas*, 250, 251
Buarque, Chico, 185
"Building, Dwelling, Thinking" (Heidegger), 259n1
Buñuel, Luís, 287, 295, 298
Burton, Julianne, 319
Butler, Judith, 113, 115, 118, 121
Buzina do Chacrinha (television program), 139

Cabra marcado para morrer (*Twenty Years Later*) (documentary), 56, 95–96, 180, 279–280, *323*
   action in, 352
   archival material in, 272, *273*, 274, 281n9
   as archive, 76–77
   audience of, 102
   Bernardet on, 107n13
   Boca de lixo compared to, 28
   Brazilian military dictatorship effect on, 271
   "Canção do subdesenvolvido" in, 203–204
   chance and, 321, 322
   chronology of, 341–342
   Cícero in, 80, 81, *81*
   conversation in, 337
   death in, 256, 257
   ending of, 342–343
   ethics in, 52
   fragmentation in, 345, 346–347
   in Galiléia, 48–49, 74
   image in, 75–76
   interviews in, 5–6, 38–39, 325–326
   Mariano in, 50, 51
   Memórias do cárcere compared to, 349
   military coup interruption of, 74, 91, 142
   movement in, 356
   Peões compared to, 79
   script for, 286
   self-reflexivity in, 50
   sertanejos in, 54
   sound in, 201–204, 344
   structure of, 350
   Teixeira, E., in, 3, *97*, 103, 344–345
   voice-of-God narration in, 10
   voice-over in, 37, 47, 49, 201–202, 203–204, 317
Cabral, Pedro Álvares, 45
Calle, Sophie, 356
camera, 4
   in axiographics, 25
   in *Boca de lixo*, 339
   characters relation to, 131n6
   in documentary, 290
   in *O fim e o princípio*, 23–24
   in *Jogo de cena*, 192–193
   the people relation to, 335–336
   the real relation to, 290
   reality relation to, 340
   reflexivity of, 1
   subjectivity of, 264
   as violence, 70–71
camera effect, 265
Camus, Marcel, 209
"Canção do subdesenvolvido," 37, 203–204
As canções (*The Songs*) (documentary), 28, 274
   affective responses in, *212*
   archival material in, 276
   Moscou compared to, 278
   music in, 207, 210–212
   performance in, 277
capitalism, 281n2
Capturing Reality (documentary), 232

Cardiff, Jack, 298
Carlos, Roberto, 207
cartography, 230
"Casa da Flor," 330, 334, 335–336
Casals, Pablo, 296
Cavarero, Adriana, 7–8, 211, 216n4, 218n16
Ceccon, Claudius, 96
CECIP. *See* Centro de Criação de Imagem Popular
censorship, 94
    of Ato Institucional 5, 136
    of *Buzina do Chacrinha*, 139
    of *Globo Repórter*, 292
    visual language and, 141
Centro de Criação de Imagem Popular (CECIP), 25, 90, 96
    Boca de lixo produced by, 99
    popular voices and, 97
    Santo forte produced by, 100
Centro Popular de Cultura (CPC), 5, 89, 90, 317
    Brazilian Communist Party relation to, 106n4, 136–137
    Brazilian military dictatorship ending, 37
    Cabra marcado para morrer relation to, 322
    Cinco vezes favela of, 92, 142, 345
    Lyra and, 216n5, 216n8
    marginalized peoples relation to, 103
    military coup effect on, 93
    Violão da rua of, 99
centro-sul, 21
Certeau, Michel de, 22, 155, 159, 169–170
Céu, Maria do, 31, 32
Chanan, Michael, 90, 264, 281n2
chance, 268
    Cabra marcado para morrer and, 321, 322
    reality relation to, 294

change, listening for, 101
Chapelin, Sérgio, 138, 146, 150n5
Chaplin, Charlie, 287, 295–296, 299n1
characters (*personagens*), 67, 98, 202, 243–244, 245
    appearance and, 255
    in *Babilônia 2000*, 247–248
    camera relation to, 131n6
    conversation with, 197
    in *O fim e o princípio*, 237
    intimacy with, 253
    language of, 246–247
    listening to, 90
    representation of, 254
    singularity of, 255
    spectators relation to, 200, 258–259
    in *Últimas conversas*, 238–241
Chekhov, Anton, 82, 277–278
Cheuiche, Jacques, 231, 242n9
Cheyenne Autumn (film), 298
Chion, Michel, 199, 216n6
Chronique d'un été (documentary), 69–70, 90, 228
chronology, 232
    of *Cabra marcado para morrer*, 341–342
    in *Um dia na vida*, 160–161
chronos, *kairos* compared to, 265, 266
Cícera, in *Boca de lixo*, 124–125
Cícero, 80, 81, *81*
Cinco vezes favela (*Five Times Favela*) (documentary), 92, 142, 345
Cineastas e imagens do povo (Bernardet), 233, 319
cinema, 158
    as archive, 74, 78
    in Brazil, 107n8, 291, 305n1, 319, 328, 333–334
    copyright in, 174
    of duration, 95, 101
    ethics of, 280
    as language, 310

cinema *(continued)*
    in Mexico, 287, 301–302, 304–305
    of the present, 264–265
    as record, 68
    reflexivity in, 83
    television compared to, 162, 169
    temporality in, 66
    Third, 91
Cinema du Réel film festival, 289
Cinema Novo, 350–351
    aesthetics of hunger of, 92, 135
    ideology of, 38
    interviews in, 9
    others in, 8–9
    the people (*o povo*) in, 10
    poverty in, 47, 53
    production modes of, 91
    revolutionary politics of, 54
    sertanejos in, 44
    sertão in, 39–41
    television relation to, 137
"cinema of conversation," 8, 65, 89
    dialogue in, 67–68
    at *Globo Repórter*, 145
    in *Santa Marta*, 98
    in *Santo forte*, 6, 101
    in *Theodorico, o imperador do sertão*, 95
    utterances in, 7
    voice in, 21
"cinema of listening," 4, 8, 65
cinéma vérité, 90, 91, 228, 255, 256
    paradox in, 193
    in *Seis dias de Ouricuri*, 138
Cinemateca do Museu de Arte Moderna do Rio de Janeiro, 148
cinematic conversation, ethics of, 73
Clark, Walter, 139
cleanliness, anthropology of, 32
Clifford, James, 55–56, 60n28
close-ups, in *O fim e o princípio*, 44
Colla, Carlos, 207

collaborative reflexivity, 73
collectivity, 54, *121*
colonialism, 37
commodities, on television, 163–164
communication, 173–174, 216n4
Os condenados (film), 286
confessor, 198
Confraria do Garoto, 326
Conselheiro, Antônio, 41, 58n9
consumption, as production, 170
contemplation, 254
contingency, 47, 56, 66
conversation, 228. *See also* "cinema of conversation"
    in *Boca de lixo*, 337, 338
    in *Cabra marcado para morrer*, 337
    with characters, 197
    cinematic, 73
    in *O fim e o princípio*, 231
    in interviews, 263
    interviews compared to, 230
    language in, 65
    listening in, 98
    with subject, 226
    trust relation to, 71
Copacabana beach, 22, 33n2
copyright, 171–172, 174
Corcovado, 111, *112*
cordel folk songs, 42
coronelismo, 146, 150n6
corporeality
    in image, 76
    of voice, 108n20
cosmetics, of hunger, 92
Costa, Armando, 286
countersignature, 27, 30–31
A Countess from Hong Kong (film), 295, 296
Coutinho, Eduardo, 51, 267. *See also specific topics*
Coutinho.doc, Apartamento 608 (documentary), 84n18

CPC. *See* Centro Popular de Cultura
Crary, Jonathan, 160
crew, reflexivity of, 1
Cries and Whispers (film), 311, 312–313
crisis, of place, 28–29, 33
criticism, by Bernardet, 319–320
critique, of representation, 33
Cuban Revolution, 41
Cuban television, Brazilian television compared to, 166–167
Cukor, George, 297
culture industry, spectacle in, 173–174
Cunha, Euclides da, 58n7, 58n9
curiosity, 280

Da-Rin, Silvio, 107n13
Dahl, Gustavo, 140
daily life, in Rio de Janeiro, 14
Daniela, in *Edifício Master*, 249–250
Day of Black Consciousness, 329
death, 239–240, 256–257, 258
  in *The Seventh Seal*, 311–312
Deleuze, Gilles, 230
democracy, 49, 57n3
  in Brazil, 8, 38, 74–75, 96
  representation in, 9
Depetris-Chauvin, Irene, 212
depth, 254
Derrida, Jacques, 26–27, 195n9
Deus e o diabo na terra do sol (*Black God, White Devil*) (film), 10, 40, 58n8, 350–351, 352
  diegetic space of, 41–42
  mythical language in, 91
dialogue, 77
  in "cinema of conversation," 67–68
  language relation to, 293
  with subject, 272
Dias, Ferreira, 47, 108n20
Diaz, Enrique, 355–356
Didi-Huberman, Georges, 114, 128

diegetic sound, 65, 126
  in *Boca de lixo*, 126
diegetic space
  of *Deus e o diabo na terra do sol*, 41–42
  in *Edifício Master*, 28, 32
  as landscape, 23
digital video, in *Peões*, 102
The Discreet Charm of the Bourgeoisie (film), 298
dispositivo. *See* apparatus
dispossession
  in *Boca de lixo*, 127
  collectivity relation to, 121
  in *Jogo de cena*, 118
Dispossession (Athanasiou and Butler), 113
Djalma, in *Peões*, 79, 80, *80*
Djanira, in *Babilônia 2000*, 247
Doane, Mary Ann, 66–67
documentary
  archival, 271
  archive relation to, 67
  audience relation to, 90
  authenticity in, 59n15, 275
  camera in, 290
  enjambment in, 236
  ethics of, 60n23, 241n4, 279
  ethnography compared to, 4
  fictional film compared to, 225, 237
  gaze in, 285, 289–290
  interviews in, 12–13
  participatory, 228
  performative, 281n3
  of personhood, 25
  place in, 21
  poetry compared to, 223–224
  popular voices in, 94
  the real in, 144, 145, 285, 291
  reality relation to, 91–92
  reflexive, 278, 281n13
  representation in, 115, 227, 231–232

documentary *(continued)*
   scripts in, 230
   self-reflexivity in, 256
   on television, 293
   truth in, 244
   voice in, 1–3
documentary authority, 264, 265, 280
Documentary (Barnouw), 12
Dolar, Mladen, 39, 210, 218n15
Dona Flor e seus dois maridos (film), 286
Douglas, Mary, 32
Dove, Patrick, 57
drama, 198
dreams, 207, 331, 332
Drew, Robert, 139
Drew Associates, 139
drought, 5, 19, 94, 138, 143–144, 145
Dubois, Phillipe, 67, 69, 73
Duda, 75
Dumont, Santos, 333
duplicity, 188, 189, 192
duration, 66, 149, 161
   cinema of, 95, 101
   kairos and, 266, 268
   language and, 156
   of long shots, 58n10
   in television, 167, 169

É Tudo Verdade film festival, 149
Ebert, Roger, 229, 234
Echeverría, Rodolfo, 302, 304, 305
"The Echo of the Subject" (Lacoue-Labarthe), 214
ecology, 24, 29, 30–31, 32, 33n1
   in *Boca de lixo*, 25–28
   landscape and, 21
Edifício Master (documentary), 3, 15, 29, 82, 232, *250*
   audience of, 102
   conversation in, 228
   Coutinho.doc, Apartamento 608 and, 84n18
   Daniela in, 249–250
   diegetic space in, 28, 32
   interviews in, 181, 358–359
   landscape in, 32–33
   power relations in, 234–235
   Roberto in, 104, *104*, 105, 234–235
   social environment in, 31–32
editing, parallel, 103
Eduardo Coutinho, 7 de outubro (documentary), 65–66, 245
Eduardo Coutinho (Ohata), 285
ego, as production, 357–358
Eisenstein, Sergei, 203
Eldorado (film), 297
Eles não usam black-tie (film), 348
Embrafilme agency, 150n4
Embratel, 136
The End and the Beginning. See *O fim e o princípio*
"The End of the Poem" (Agamben), 223
endings, 225, 232
   of *Cabra marcado para morrer*, 342–343
   of *O fim e o princípio*, 236–237
   in *Últimas conversas*, 241
English language, 217n14
   in Brazilian television, 165
Engraçadinha depois dos trinta (film), 286
enjambment, 223–224, 225, 236
Entreatos (film), 84n12
enunciative moments, 170–171
environmental topics, 140
epistemological purity, 193n2
Escorel, Eduardo, 22, 277, 278, 346
   Lição de amor directed by, 286
   on *Moscou*, 354, 355
El espacio biográfico (Arfuch), 358
"um espírito militante" (a militant spirit), 39
Esposito, Roberto, 32
Estaphanie, in *Últimas conversas*, 239

"Estética da fome" (manifesto), 40, 112.
    See also aesthetics of hunger
Estive em Lisboa e lembrei de você
    (Ruffato), 357
ethics, 14
    in Cabra marcado para morrer, 52
    of cinema, 280
    of cinematic conversation, 73
    of documentary, 60n23, 241n4, 279
    of filmmaking, 144, 145
    kairos relation to, 266, 278–279
    of listening, 89, 199
    others and, 264
    of representation, 90
ethnography, 60n22
    allegory in, 55–56
    documentary compared to, 4
    postcolonial, 54
Euripides, 185
experimentation, at Globo Repórter,
    140–141
Exu, uma tragédia sertaneja (Exu, a
    Backlands Tragedy) (documentary),
    140, 145

Fabian, Johannes, 40
falas. See utterances
A falecida (film), 286
Farias, Roberto, 150n4
farm labor movement, 57n3
Fátima, in Babilônia 2000, 210, 217n14
    "Me and Bobby McGee" sung by,
        209, 248–249
Faustão (film), 39, 286
favela, 100–101
    in Babilônia 2000, 105
    cinema and, 107n8
    in Edifício Master, 31
    in Rio de Janeiro, 6, 92
    of Santa Marta, 98
Feldman, Ilana, Jogo de cena analysis of,
    115

feminism, 281n2
fiction, 118, 119, 191–192
    belief and, 189
    logic in, 190
"fiction of knowledge," 22
fictional film, 223–224, 236
    documentary compared to, 225,
        237
Figueiredo (President), 76
Filho, Oduvaldo Vianna, 317, 322
film, 217n10, 258
    archive relation to, 74, 82
    copyright and, 172
    reality in, 66
    reversal, 141
    self-reflexivity in, 53–54
    speech in, 11
    of the unfilmable, 113
    video compared to, 7, 72, 100
film criticism, 287
film festivals, 102
    Cinema du Réel, 289
    É Tudo Verdade, 149
    Mostra Internacional de Cinema em
        São Paul, 157
filmmaking, 89
    ethics of, 144, 145
O fim e o princípio (The End and the
    Beginning) (documentary), 21,
    33n3, 56, 235, 356
    audience of, 102
    camera in, 23–24
    conversation in, 231
    ecology in, 25–26
    ending of, 236–237
    interviews in, 44, 53, 181
    kairos in, 269–270
    Leocádio in, 45–46, 46, 251–253
    music in, 206
    reflexivity in, 82
    sertanejos in, 52–53, 54
    sertão in, 39, 56–57, 92, 105

O fim e o princípio (*The End and the Beginning*) (continued)
   Vernon, Florida compared to, 232–233
   voice-over in, 48
O fio da memória (documentary), 98, 326–327, 333
   music in, 206
   narration in, 328–331, 332
   voice-over in, 99, 317
first-person films, 83n5
Five Times Favela. See *Cinco vezes favela*
Flaherty, Robert, 23
FLM Magazine, 242n8
flow, of time, 75
Fonda, Jane, 298
Fontes, Paulo, 185
Ford, John, 297–298
Formagini, Beth, 84n18
Foster, Hal, 192
Foucault, Michel, 181–182, 233
Fox, Dan, 259n4
Fraga, Guti, 185
fragmentation
   in *Cabra marcado para morrer*, 345, 346–347
   in *O fio da memória*, 326, 328, 330–331, 332–333
França, José de, 330, 333
Frankfurt School, 166, 173–174
Frenzy (film), 297
Freud, Sigmund, 128
Fried, Michael, 193n1, 194n3
Fundação de Artes do Estado do Rio de Janeiro (FUNARJ), 98
Furtado, Filipe, 175n1
Furtado, Gustavo, 272
Os fuzis (*The Guns*) (film), 19, 348

Galiléia, 48–49, 74
Gama, Sonia, 140
garbage, 129n2, 330
   in *Boca de lixo*, 26–28
   as metaphor, 128–129
   the people compared to, 114
Garota de Ipanema (film), 286
Gates of Heaven (documentary), 226, 228–229, 232, 234
   conversation in, 231
   interviews in, 242n8
gaze
   in documentary, 285, 289–290
   unresolved, 124, 131n7
Geisel, Ernesto, 137
general intellect, 157, 173
gentrification, 32
Geraldo, in *Peões*, 108n24, *236*
gestures, 293
Getino, Octavio, 106n5
Gil, Gilberto, 223
Gilberto, João, 213
Giving an Account of Oneself (Butler), 118
Globo Repórter, 4, 39, 60n21, 89, 90, 95
   audience of, 140, 148
   Brazilian military dictatorship relation to, 136–137, 149, 291–292
   Chapelin as narrator for, 146, 150n5
   "cinema of conversation" at, 145
   experimentation at, 140–141
   Soares as director of, 93–94
   standard of quality of, 135, 291–292
   Time-Life Corporation relation to, 139
Globo-Shell Especial, 139, 140
Globo television network, 135. See also *Globo Repórter*
Gödel, Kurt, 193n2
Goethe, 177
Goffman, Erving, 208
Gonçalves, Milton, 99, 318, 329
Gonzaga, Ademar, 299

Gorgias, of Leontini, 268
Gota d"água (play), 185–186
Goulart, João, 136, 321, 330
government incentives, for Videofilmes, 102
The Grammar of the Multitude (Virno), 155
Grande, Volta, 299
Greek Sophists, 268
Greve (film), 78
Grierson, John, 11
Grupo Galpão, 274
Guarnieri, Gianfrancesco, 348
Guattari, Félix, 21, 24, 32, 33n1, 230
Guerra, Ruy, 348
  Os fuzis of, 19
Guitar Hero, 175n1
Gullar, Ferreira, 14–15, 202, 318
  in *O fio da memória*, 99, 329
  poetry of, 322
  voice-over by, 317
The Gunfighter of Serra Talhada. See *O pistoleiro de Serra Talhada*
The Guns. See *Os fuzis*

Hamburger, Esther, 33n3, 101
Hamlet (play), 178, 179
Haraway, Donna, 240
Hawks, Edward, 297, 299n2
Heffes, Gisela, 129n2, 131n6
Heidegger, Martin, 31–32, 195n10, 244, 247, 248
  "Building, Dwelling, Thinking" of, 259n1
  on death, 258
  on life, 257
  on metaphysics, 249
Heisenberg, Werner, 193n2
Henrique, in *Edifício Master*, 82–83
heterogenesis, 32
hierarchy, 165, 179

Hirszman, Leon, 78, 345, 348, 352n1
  Maioria absoluta of, 10, 12, 351
Hitchcock, Alfred, 297
Hollywood, 40, 304
O homem que comprou o mundo (*The Man Who Bought the World*) (film), 142
O homem que virou suco (film), 345
Horne, Luz, 14, 129n2, 318, 320
horror, representation of, 113–114
Housing Problems (film), 11
humanism, 4
hunger
  aesthetics of, 9–10, 91, 92, 112, 135
  cosmetics of, 92

identity, 357–358
  in language, 251
  in music, 207
  in performance, 208–209
  of Teixeira, E., 346–347
  in testimony, 198
  in voice, 199
ideology
  of Cinema Novo, 38
  progressive, 41
  radical, 42
  revolutionary, 90
image
  in *Boca de lixo*, 26–27, 28, 71–72, 100, 104, 115, 120, 122, *123*, 126, 128–129, 337
  in *Cabra marcado para morrer*, 75–76, 203
  corporeality in, 76
  in *Jogo de cena*, 115
  literature relation to, 129n2
  materiality of, 127
  mise-en-film of, 75, 79, 82
  pensive, 124
  politics relation to, 112, 113–114

image *(continued)*
  as record, 67
  in *Seis dias de Ouricuri*, 142–143
  in television, 169–170
  in *Theodorico, o imperador do sertão*, 147
Imagining Indians (film), 70
imperialism, 37
improvisation, 174, 201, 290
Incompleteness Theorem, 193n2
Indigenous people, Vídeo nas Aldeias group and, 70
infancy, of language, 249
Ingold, Tim, 31, 32–33
Instituto Moreira Salles, 13
Instituto Nacional do Cinema, 301
intellect, general, 157, 173
intellectuals, 135, 149n1
International Film Festival, in Rio de Janeiro, 102
interpretation, 192
interviews, 4
  with adolescents, 155–156
  in *Babilônia 2000*, 29–30
  in *Boca de lixo*, 29–30, 181
  in *Cabra marcado para morrer*, 5–6, 38–39, 325–326
  in Cinema Novo, 9
  conversation compared to, 230
  conversation in, 263
  in documentary, 12–13
  in *Edifício Master*, 358–359
  in *O fim e o princípio*, 44, 53
  in *Gates of Heaven*, 242n8
  of João Mariano, in *Cabra marcado para morrer*, 50–51, 52, 204–205, 344
  in *Jogo de cena*, 83
  listening in, 5
  logic of, 233–234
  long shots in, 332
  of Nader, 251, 252
  with others, 180–181
  savage anthropology in, 245
  of Teixeira, E., 346, 349
  voice in, 8
intimacy, 252, 253
Introduction to Documentary (Nichols), 227–228
The Invention of the Self (Kaufmann), 360
ISER. *See* Superior Institute for the Study of Religion
Itaoca landfill, in São Gonçalo, 26–27, 70, 99, 111, 338

James, Henry, 287
Jameson, Frederic, 60n27
Jardim Gramacho landfill, 72
Jobim, Tom, 286
O jogo da dívida (documentary), 97
Jogo de cena (*Playing*) (documentary), 28, 32, 93, 129, 170, 326
  affective responses in, 212
  archival material in, 274
  audience of, 102
  Bernardet on, 115, 130n3
  Boca de lixo compared to, 120, 125, 126, 127
  Brown, Jeckie, in, 187
  camera in, 192–193
  dispossession in, 118, 121
  duplicity in, 188
  Estive em Lisboa e lembrei de você compared to, 357
  identity in, 208–209, 358
  image in, 115
  interviews in, 83, 358, 359
  mise-en-scène in, 182–184, 210, 288
  names in, 192
  reenactment in, 275–276
  representation in, 118–119, 178, 183, 190–191
  Sheyla in, 184, 185–186, 188, 194n7

sound in, 189
speech in, 82, 354, 355
subjectivity in, 353–354, 350
theater in, 181–182
trust in, 189
University of California, Berkeley screening of, 177
utterances in, 361–362
women in, 116–117, 194n4
John Paul II (Pope), 100
Johnson, Randal, 318
Jornal do Brasil, 93, 142, 286, 317
Jornal Nacional (news program), 136
Ju, Fátima, 326–327

Kahana, Jonathan, 264–265
kairos, 265–266
  attunement and, 280
  ethics relation to, 278–279
  in *O fim e o princípio*, 269–270
  in *Moscou*, 276, 277
  in *Peões*, 271
  speech and, 268
Kaputt (Malaparte), 75, 343, 347
Kaufmann, Jean-Claude, 360
A King in New York (film), 296
Klein, Bonnie, 228
Kracauer, Siegfried, 66, 75
Krauss, Rosalind, 73
Kubitschek, Juscelino, 40–41, 247

Labelle, Brandon, 211
labor market, in neoliberalism, 79
Lacan, Jacques, 118
Lacoue-Labarthe, Philippe, 214
Lagerlöff, Selma, 309
Land in Anguish. See *Terra em transe*
landfills
  Itaoca, in São Gonçalo, 26–27, 70, 99, 111, 338
  Jardim Gramacho, 72
  marginalized peoples in, 113

landscape
  in Brazil, 105
  diegetic space as, 23
  ecology and, 21
  in *Edifício Master*, 32–33
language, 44, 199, 228
  Adamic, 252
  censorship of, 292
  of characters, 246–247
  cinema as, 310
  in conversation, 65
  dialogue relation to, 293
  duration and, 156
  identity in, 251
  infancy of, 249
  intimacy in, 253
  of Leocádio, 45–46
  life relation to, 257
  of marginalized peoples, 105
  in music, 217n14
  mythical, 91
  overproduction of, 168, 174
  poverty of, 42–43
  pretension in, 251
  score for, 172–173
  in songs, 213–214, 217n14
  spontaneity of, 108n20
  subjectivity relation to, 115
  visual, 141
Last Conversations. See *Últimas conversas*
Lefebvre, Martin, 21
Lei Rouanet, 101–102
Leite, Paulo Moreira, 146
Lemos, Tite de, 202
Leocádio, in *O fim e o princípio*, 45–46, 46, 251–253
Lévinas, Emmanuel, 216n4
Liar Paradox, 190
Lição de amor (film), 286
life, language relation to, 257
Ligas Camponesas, 286
Lima, Vênecio A. de, 136

Lima Júnior, Walter, 137, 140, 141, 142
Limelight (film), 296
Linha de montagem (film), 78
Lins, Consuelo, 22, 30, 44, 81, 92, 199
  on *Boca de lixo*, 111
  on cinema of the present, 264
  on *Edifício Master*, 232, 235
  on Fátima, in *Babilônia 2000*, 217n14, 248–249
  on image, 100
  on interviews, 234
  on language, 108n20, 251, 252
  as researcher, 101
  on *Santa Marta*, 98
  on self-fabulation, 54
  Últimas conversas analysis of, 155–156, 243, 245–246, 257
listening. *See specific topics*
literary works, adaptations of, 286–287
Literaturas reales (Horne), 129n2
literature, image relation to, 129n2
logic
  in fiction, 190
  of interviews, 233–234
  theater and, 183
long shots, 350
  duration of, 58n10
  in interviews, 332
long takes, 12, 292
  in *Seis dias de Ouricuri*, 94, 95, 143–144, 145
  temporality in, 65
Luiza, in *Últimas conversas*, 240–241
"Lula." *See* Silva, Luiz Inácio "Lula" da
Lyotard, Jean-François, 33
Lyra, Carlos, 37, 201
  "Canção do subdesenvolvido" of, 203–204
  CPC and, 216n5, 216n8

MacDougall, David, 237

Maciel, Luiz Carlos, 141
Maciel, Manuel Deodoro, 329
Magaldi, João Carlos, 139
Maia, Guilherme, 216n6
Maioria absoluta (*Absolute Majority*) (film), 10, 12, 351
Malaparte, Curzio, 75, 343
Malmö Municipal Theater, 310
Man, Paul de, 60nn26–28
The Man Who Bought the World. *See O homem que comprou o mundo*
Marcabru, Pierre, 312–313
Marcorelles, Louis, 302
marginalized peoples
  CPC relation to, 103
  in landfills, 113
  language of, 105
  poverty of, 351
Mariano, João, *51*, 325–326
  interview of, 50–51, 52, 204–205, 344
Martins, Carlos Estevam, 106n4
Masayesva, Victor, Jr., 70
Massey, Doreen, 25
material poverty, 43–44
materiality, of image, 127
Mattos, Carlos Alberto, 96, 353
Mauro, Humberto, 299
"Me and Bobby McGee," 209, 248–249
Medea (play), 185
media networks, 105
Mekas, Jonas, 83n5
Memórias do cárcere (film), 345, 348–349
memory, songs relation to, 213
Mesquita, Cláudia, 30, 44, 78, 252
metal workers' movement, 57n3
Metalworkers. *See Peões*
metaphor, 128–129
metaphysics, 249, 253, 254
Mexico, 287, 301–302, 303, 304–305

The Mighty Spirit. See *Santo forte*
a militant spirit ("um espírito militante"), 39
military coup
  Cabra marcado para morrer
    interrupted by, 74, 91, 142, 322
  CPC affected by, 93
Minh-Ha, Trinh T., 2, 3, 60n22
miracle, of speech, 66, 68, 84n18
mise-en-abyme, 72, 80, 81
  in *Cabra marcado para morrer*, 343
  in *Hamlet*, 179
mise-en-film, 67
  in *Boca de lixo*, 71–72, 73
  of image, 75, 79, 82
  participant-centered reflexivity and, 68–70
  in *Peões*, 74, 79
mise-en-scène, 67, 80, 310
  in archival documentary, 271
  author-centered reflexivity and, 69
  of Bergman, 313
  in *As canções*, 210
  of Cukor, 297
  duplicity in, 189
  in *Hamlet*, 179
  in *Jogo de cena*, 182–184, 193, 288
  of *Moscou*, 82
Moi, un noir (documentary), 24, 354
Moisés, Chico de, 53, 237
Moore, Michael, 226, 230, 241
Moraes, Vinícius de, 286
moral philosophy, 118
Moreira, Cid, 138, 143
Moreno, Mario, 303
Morin, Edgar, 69, 90, 228
Morris, Errol, 14, 224, 228–229, 230–231, 232, 242n8
  Coutinho compared to, 226–227
Moscou (*Moscow*) (documentary), 28, 257–258, 274, 354–355
  As canções compared to, 273

kairos in, 276, 277
mise-en-scène of, 82
Mostra Internacional de Cinema em São Paulo, 157
movement, 356
movie theaters, 171
Muniz, Vic, 84n10
music, 197, 296
  affective responses to, 211–212, *212*, 213
  in *Babilônia 2000*, 209–210
  in *Boca de lixo*, 207, 208, 209, 217n11
  in *Cabra marcado para morrer*, 201–202
  in *As canções*, 210–212
  identity in, 207
  language in, 217n14
  in *Santa Marta*, 206, 217n11
  self relation to, 214
  on television, 167
música sertaneja, 27, 217n13
"My Way," 82–83, 232
mythical language, 91

Nader, Carlos, 65–66, 245, 251, 252, 257
names, 184, 192
narcissism, video and, 73
narration, 290–291
  in *O fio da memória*, 328–331, 332
  voice-of-God, 10, 19–20, 138
narrative accountability, 118
narrative authority, 24, 33n3
narrative strategies, 235
narrators, 99
National Agency of Film (ANCINE), 102
National Film Bank, of Mexico, 302, 303
National Students' Union (UNE), 322
neocolonialism, in Brazil, 43

neofascism, 32
neoliberalism, 32, 79, 281n2
neorealism, 304
New Latin American Cinema, 106n5
New Testament, 308
New York Times (newspaper), 102
Nichols, Bill, 2, 25, 281n3
   Introduction to Documentary of, 227–228
   on reflexive documentary, 281n13
   on reflexivity, 68–69
Nixon, Richard, 298
normality, 198
northeastern Brazil, 140
   drought in, 5, 19, 138
   popular culture in, 45, 293–294
   poverty in, 39, 350, 352n1
Nós do Morro, 185
Not a Love Story (documentary), 228
Novaes, Washington, 147–148
nuevo cine, 304, 305

"O olhar no documentário. Carta-depoimento para Paulo Paranguá" (Coutinho), 285
objectification, 244
   of women, 162, 163, 166
observation, in theory, 193n2
"Ocupação Eduardo Coutinho" exhibit, 13
Ohata, Milton, 285, 286
Opinião pública (documentary), 346
opinions, 198
   in *Últimas conversas*, 245–246
oral culture, 293–294
Os romeiros do Pedro Cicero (documentary), sertão in, 39
Os sertões (Cunha), 58n7, 58n9
otherness, 59n15
   in theater, 181–182
others, 4, 101, 279
   in Cinema Novo, 8–9
   ethics and, 264
   interviews with, 180–181
   singularity of, 159
Ouricuri, 94, 143–144, 145. *See also* northeastern Brazil
overproduction, of language, 168, 174

Page, Joanna, 278
Palavras (Words) (documentary). See *Últimas conversas*
panoramic shots, in *Boca de lixo*, 22
para-filmic encounters, 7
paradox, 250
   in *cinéma vérité*, 193
   of language, 252
   liar, 190
Paraíba, 23, 44–45
parallel editing, 103
Paranaguá, Paulo, 289
Paris, 304–305
participant-centered reflexivity, 73, 84n10
   in *Boca de lixo*, 70–71, 72
   mise-en-film and, 68–70
participatory documentary, 228
Pasolini, Pier Paolo, 128, 247
passion, in songs, 212
Pecadora (film), 303
Pelmex, 302–303
pensive image, 124
Peões (Metalworkers) (documentary), 23, 77–78, 80, *80*, 229, 235
   archival material in, 272, *273*, 274, 281n9
   conversation in, 231
   digital video in, 102
   Geraldo in, 108n24, *236*
   kairos in, 271
   mise-en-film in, 74, 79
the people (*o povo*), 8
   in Brazil, 9–10
   camera relation to, 335–336
   garbage compared to, 114
   speech of, 78–79

Pêra, Marília, 130n5
performance
    appearance in, 249, 251
    audience of, 179
    authenticity relation to, 120
    in *As canções*, 210, 276, 277
    identity in, 208–209
    in *Jogo de cena*, 116–117, 129, 189
    reflexivity in, 82–83
    representation in, 177–178
    score in, 172–173
    of self, 199–200
    on television, 174
performative documentary, 281n3
Pernambuco. *See* northeastern Brazil
person (*pessoa*), 98
persona, in theater, 194n9
A personagem no documentário de Eduardo Coutinho (Bezerra, C.), 84n16
personagens. *See* characters
personhood
    in "cinema of conversation," 21
    documentary of, 25
Petrobras, 102
The Phantom Carriage (film), 309
phenomenology, 244
philosophy, moral, 118
photography, 27, 73
    in *Boca de lixo*, 100
Piaget, Jean, 32
Pierce, C. S., 84n15
pirated material, 175n1
    in *Um dia na vida*, 157–158
O pistoleiro de Serra Talhada (*The Gunfighter of Serra Talhada*) (documentary), 4, 140
place
    in *Boca de lixo*, 31
    crisis of, 28–29, 33
    in documentary, 21
"Plan of National Development," 40
plastic surgery, 163

Plato, 193n2
Playing. *See Jogo de cena*
poaching, 170–171
poetry, 223–224, 247
    of Gullar, 322
political cinema, 38, 43, 264
political modernism, 256, 258
political radicalization, of sertão, 40
politics
    image relation to, 112, 113–114
    transformation and, 255–256
The Politics of Documentary (Chanan), 90
Pons, María Antonieta, 303
Ponti, Carla, 296
Pontifícia Universidade Católica (PUC), 148, 160–161
popular cinema, 10
popular culture, in northeastern Brazil, 45, 293–294
popular voices
    CECIP and, 97
    in documentary, 94
Portugal, 333
postcolonial ethnography, 54
poverty, 40, 330
    in *Boca de lixo*, 125
    in Cinema Novo, 47, 53
    image of, 113
    of language, 42–43
    of marginalized peoples, 351
    in northeastern Brazil, 39, 350, 352n1
    of *sertanejos*, 44
o povo. *See* the people
O povo canta (album), 216n8
power relations, in *Edifício Master*, 234–235
The Practice of Everyday Life (de Certeau), 155, 159
presence
    in representation, 178
    in theater, 179
present, cinema of the, 264–265

preservation, of archive, 75
pretension, 251, 259n4
Primary (documentary), 139
Prince Valiant (Foster), 192
producers, Salles, J., as, 101, 102
production
   Cinema Novo modes of, 91
   of documentary, 1–2
   ego as, 357–358
   of *Globo Repórter*, 291
   of television, 168, 169–170
progressive ideology, 41
prose, 223–224
Protestantism, 309
PT. *See* Workers' Party
PUC. *See* Pontifícia Universidade Católica
Puritanism, 309

A queda (film), 348
Queen of the Centenary of Abolition, 326–327

radical ideology, 42
Rafaela, in *Últimas conversas*, 251
Ramos, Graciliano, 42, 191, 345
Rancière, Jacques, 114, 124, 128
Rangan, Pooja, on audibility, 2–3
the real, 48, 93, 116, 253–254, 275, 346
   camera relation to, 290
   contingency of, 56, 66
   in documentary, 144, 145, 285, 291
   language and, 91, 249
   subject and, 266
   transformation of, 47, 60n28
reality, 15
   camera relation to, 340
   chance relation to, 294
   documentary relation to, 91–92
   in dreams, 207
   in film, 66

record
   cinema as, 68
   image as, 67
recycling, 129n2
Rede Globo, 185, 186
redemption, 343–344
reenactment, 195n9
   in *Jogo de cena*, 275–276
   in representation, 178
reflexive documentary, 278, 281n13
reflexivity, 254. *See also* self-reflexivity
   in cinema, 83
   collaborative, 73
   in documentary, 1–2, 3
   in *O fim e o princípio*, 82
   participant-centered, 68–70, 71, 72, 84n10
   in performance, 82–83
   of political modernism, 256
Regarding the Pain of Others (Sontag), 113–114
Reik, Theodor, 214
relativity, 193n2
religion
   in Brazil, 100–101
   music in, 207
   on television, 164–165, 217n12
repetition, 347
reported speech, 247
representation, 25, 180
   authenticity in, 2, 46, 47, 264
   in *Boca de lixo*, 121–122, 123–124, 335–336
   of characters, 254
   critique of, 38
   in democracy, 9
   in documentary, 115, 227, 231–232
   ethics of, 90
   of horror, 113–114
   in *Jogo de cena*, 118–119, 183, 190–191, 193
   in performance, 177–178

of *sertanejos*, 54
truth relation to, 204
Republic (Plato), 193n2
Rescala, Tim, 217n11
Resnais, Alain, 361
The Return of Navajo Boy (film), 70
revelations, 199–200, 259
reversal film, 141
Revista Cinemais, 180
revolutionary ideology, 90
revolutionary politics, of Cinema Novo, 54
"Rhetoric of the Image" (Barthes), 217n9
Rickert, Thomas, 279–280
Ricoeur, Paul, 81, 357–358, 360
Ridenti, Marcelo, 93
de los Río, Valeria, 129n2
Rio de Janeiro
   Cinemateca do Museu de Arte Moderna do, 148
   daily life in, 14
   favela in, 6, 92
   International Film Festival in, 102
   Teatro Glauce Rocha in, 183
Rio Lobo (film), 297
RioFilme, 100, 102, 317
The Road to Glory (film), 297
Roberto, in *Edifício Master*, 104, 104, 105, 234–235
Rocha, Glauber, 8
   Abertura hosted by, 137
   aesthetics of hunger and, 9–10, 91, 135
   aesthetics of violence and, 41–42
   Coutinho compared to, 285
   "Estética da fome" of, 40, 112
Rodrigues, Nelson, 286
Roque, Chico, 207
Rosa, in *O fim e o princípio*, 252–253
Rosa, Noel, 213
Rossini, Rogério, 201, 202, 216nn5–6

Rouch, Jean, 24, 69, 90, 228, 354
Rousseff, Dilma, 105
Ruby, Jay, 69
Ruffato, Luiz, 357
rural communities. *See* sertão
Russell, Catherine, 53–54, 55, 59n15
   on ethnography, 60n28

Sacramento, Igor, 93, 145
Salles, João Moreira, 5, 47, 71, 81, 84n12
   on *Boca de lixo*, 123
   As canções produced by, 276
   on *Jogo de cena*, 186
   on narrative strategies, 235
   as producer, 101, 102
   Últimas conversas completed by, 238, 243, 266
Salles, Walter, 103
samba, 213
Santa Marta—Duas semanas no morro (documentary), 28–29, 97–98
   music in, 206, 217n11
Santo forte (*The Mighty Spirit*) (documentary), 90, 280n1, 326
   CECIP as producer of, 100
   "cinema of conversation" in, 6, 101
   interviews in, 181
   music in, 207
   RioFilme funding of, 317
   voice-over in, 108n20
Santos, Edson, 144
Santos, Gabriel Joaquim dos, 99, 329, 331
   on Brazil, 333
   "Casa da Flor" of, 330, 334, 335–336
Santos, Nelson Pereira dos, 19, 40, 42, 345
São Paulo, 149, 157
São Paulo, sinfonia da metrópole (*São Paulo, A Metropolitan Symphony*, 1929) (documentary), 12

São Rafael, 77
Sape, 48
Sartre, Jean-Paul, 69
savage anthropology, 3, 101, 158
   in interviews, 245
   in *Um dia na vida*, 160
Sayad, Cecilia, 47, 52, 53, 58n10, 108n20, 169
   on Coutinho, 263
   on *Santo forte*, 280n1
   on *Últimas conversas*, 243
scapeland, 33
Schwarz, Roberto, 136
score, in performance, 172–173
Scott, James, 174
scripts, 290
   for *Cabra marcado para morrer*, 49, 286, 346
   in documentary, 230
   voice relation to, 11
Seis dias de Ouricuri (*Six Days in Ouricuri*) (documentary), 4, 142, *144*, 148, 149
   long takes in, 94, 95, 143–144, 145
   voice in, 5
   voice-of-God narration in, 19–20, 138
self
   music relation to, 214
   performance of, 199–200
self-fabulation, 54
self-portrait, 59n14
self-reflexivity, 37, 46, 47–48, 56, 57n2
   in *Boca de lixo*, 22–23
   in *Cabra marcado para morrer*, 50
   in documentary, 256
   in film, 53–54
   in *Theodorico, o imperador do sertão*, 146
sertanejos, 39, 41, 57
   in *O fim e o princípio*, 52–53, 54
   poverty of, 44
   representation of, 54
   in *Vidas secas*, 42–43
   violence and, 42
sertão, 42
   authenticity in, 55–56
   cinema and, 107n8
   in Cinema Novo, 39–41
   Conselheiro in, 58n9
   in *O fim e o princípio*, 39, 56–57, 92, 105
7 Women (film), 298
The Seventh Seal (film), 287–288, 309–310
   as allegory, 308
   Brazil screening of, 307
   death in, 311–312
   structure of, 313
Sevilla, Niñón, 303
Shakespeare, William, 179
Shell oil company, 139
Sheyla, Mary, 184, 185–186, 188, 194n7
Shoeshine (film), 298–299
de Sica, Vittorio, 295, 296, 298–299
"Signature, Event, Context" (Derrida), 195n9
silence
   of Mariano, 325–326
   television relation to, 167, 292
   in *Últimas conversas*, 240
Silva, Luiz Inácio "Lula" da, 9, 77, 84n12
   Peões relation to, 23, 272
Silva, Marianna Duccini Junqueira da, 48
Silveira, Breno, 71
Silverman, Kaja, 244, 254–255
   on language, 253
singularity
   of characters, 255
   of others, 159
Six Days in Ouricuri. See *Seis dias de Ouricuri*
Sjöström, Victor, 307, 309

slavery, in Brazil, 99, 318, 326–328, 330. See also *O fio da memória*
Smiles of a Summer Night (film), 308, 312
Smith, John E., 268
Soares, Paulo Gil, 93–94, 137, 140, 141
Sobreviventes da Galiléia (documentary), 80, *81*
social critique, voice-over as, 137, 138
The Social Documentary in Latin America (Burton), 319
social environment
  in *Edifício Master*, 31–32
  at Jardim Gramacho landfill, 72
social labor, 172–173
social relations, 164
  speech in, 246
Solanas, Fernando, 106n5
songs, 209, 211
  as archival material, 274
  language in, 213–214, 217n14
  passion in, 212
The Songs. See *As canções*
"Sonho por sonho," 207, 208
Sontag, Susan, 113–114
sound, 197
  in *Cabra marcado para morrer*, 201–204, 344
  diegetic, 65, 126
  in *Jogo de cena*, 189
  in *Seis dias de Ouricuri*, 142–143
  on television, 167
  in *Theodorico, o imperador do sertão*, 145, 147
  vococentric, 199, 205–206
Soviet Russia, documentary in, 90
space, 256, 259n1
  autobiographical, 359
  in *Cabra marcado para morrer*, 202
spectacle
  audience relation to, 346

  in *Cabra marcado para morrer*, 343, 344, 345, 347
  in culture industry, 173–174
spectators, characters relation to, 200, 258–259
speech, 2, 159
  body relation to, 125
  in film, 11
  in *Jogo de cena*, 82, 354, 355
  kairos and, 268
  miracle of, 66, 68, 84n18
  of the people, 78–79
  reported, 247
  in social relations, 246
  songs relation to, 213–214
  subjectivity relation to, 355
  utterances as, 6–7
Spitz, Jeff, 70
Spivak, Gayatri, 253
spontaneity, 57
  of language, 108n20
Stam, Robert, 318
standard, of quality, of *Globo Repórter*, 135, 291–292
Standard Propaganda agency, 139
stereotypes, 198
Stevens, George, 297
Strindberg, August, 307, 309
structure, 290
  of *Cabra marcado para morrer*, 350
  of *The Seventh Seal*, 313
subject, 268
  apparatus effect on, 205
  in Brazilian television, 165–166
  conversation with, 226
  Coutinho as, 355–356
  dialogue with, 272
  dispossession of, 118, 120
  the real and, 266
  in television, 162
  in theater, 179
subjectivity, 214, 215
  of camera, 264

subjectivity *(continued)*
  in *Jogo de cena*, 353–354, 360
  language relation to, 115
  in song, 209
  speech relation to, 355
subtraction, 30
Superior Institute for the Study of Religion (ISER), 96
Survival of the Fireflies (Didi-Huberman), 128

Tapajós, Renato, 78, 93
taskscape, 31
Tayna, in *Últimas conversas*, 246–247
Teatro Glauce Rocha, 183, 275
Teixeira, Elizabeth, 74, 279, 322, 341
  in *Cabra marcado para morrer*, 3, 48, 49, 50, 52, 76, 95–96, *97*, 103, 344–345
  identity of, 346–347
  interview of, 346, 349
  in São Rafael, 77
  script relation to, 286
  testimony of, 201
Teixeira, João Pedro, 6, 48, 49, 50, 77, 92. See also *Cabra marcado para morrer*
telecommunications infrastructure, 136, 143
television, 162, 340. See also Brazilian television; *Um dia na vida*
  cinema compared to, 169
  Cinema Novo relation to, 137
  commodities on, 163–164
  documentary on, 293
  language on, 174
  performance on, 174
  production of, 168, 169–170
  religion on, 164–165, 217n12
  silence in, 292
  temporality of, 160, 167

temporality, 259
  in archive, 66
  in *Cabra marcado para morrer*, 202, 203
  in long takes, 65
  of television, 160, 167
  of video, 72
Terra em transe (*Land in Anguish*) (film), 10
  mythical language in, 91
testimony, 77, 216n3
  authenticity in, 117
  identity in, 198
  of Mariano, 205
  of Teixeira, E., 201
theater, 183
  audience of, 194n3
  Bergman relation to, 310–311
  otherness in, 181–182
  persona in, 194n9
  presence in, 179
Theodorico, o imperador do sertão (*Theodorico, the Sertão Emperor*) (documentary), 4, *147*, 148, 149
  long takes in, 94–95
  narrative authority in, 33n3
  voice-over in, 138, 145–146, 147
Theodoro, Thiago, 239–240, 257
theory
  observation in, 193n2
  theater and, 183
therapist, 198
Third Cinema, 91
"Third-World Literature in the Era of Multinational Capitalism" (Jameson), 60n27
Thomson-DeVeaux, Flora, 242n7
A Thousand Plateaus (Deleuze and Guattari), 230
The Three Sisters (play). See *Moscou*
Tibino, Nicolò, 224

time, 75. See also *kairos*
Time and Narrative (Ricoeur), 360
Time-Life Corporation, 139
Tom and Jerry (television program), 163
Torres, Fernanda, 119, 178, 189, 192
  representation of, 190–191
Tower of Babel, 45
Tramaning (play), 310–311
Transcultural Cinema (MacDougall), 237
transformation
  politics and, 255–256
  of the real, 47, 60n28
transnational corporations, 139
trust
  with audience, 184–185
  conversation relation to, 71
  duplicity effect on, 188
  in *Jogo de cena*, 189
truth
  in appearance, 250
  in *cinéma vérité*, 228
  in documentary, 244
  metaphysics and, 254
  representation relation to, 204
  in *Últimas conversas*, 250, 251
Tuan, Yi-Fu, 30
Turin, Victor, 23
Turrent, Tomás Perez, 303, 304, 305
Twenty Years Later. See *Cabra marcado para morrer*

Últimas conversas (*Last Conversations*) (documentary), 1, 12, 60n25, 155–156, 201, 246
  authorship of, 243
  characters in, 238–241
  Coutinho in, 266–267, 267, 268
  curiosity in, 280
  death in, 256–257, 258
  kairos in, 270
  opinions in, 245–246
  reported speech in, 247
  truth in, 250, 251
  Um dia na vida compared to, 174
Um dia na vida (documentary), 7, 175n1
  authorship in, 169–170
  chronology in, 160–161
  enunciative moments in, 170–171
  Lins analysis of, 155–156
  objectification of women in, 162, 163
  pirated material in, 157–158
  Últimas conversas compared to, 174
Uncertainty Principle, 193n2
underdevelopment, 37, 44–45, 203–204
  poverty and, 43, 53
  in sertão, 40–41
UNE. See National Students' Union
unfilmable, film of the, 113
Union of Film Production Workers, of Mexico, 302, 303–304
Universidad Autónoma de México's Centro Universitario de Estudios Cinematográficos, 305
Universidade Federal do Rio Grande do Norte, 148
Universidade Federal Fluminense, 148
unresolved gaze, 124, 131n7
urban cleansing, 32
utterances (*falas*), 361–362
  as speech, 6–7

Vargas, Getúlio, 330–331
Vargas, Pedro, 303
Veloso, Caetano, 223, 233
Vernon, Florida (documentary), 226, 229, 230–231
  conversation in, 228
  O fim e o princípio compared to, 232–233
Verón, Eliseo, 169
Vertov, Dziga, 90, 228

Viana, Zelito, 286
Vidas secas (*Barren Lives*) (film), 10, 19, 40, 58n8
   diegetic space of, 41
   long shots in, 350
   sertanejos in, 42–43
video
   in apparatus, 217n10
   digital, 102
   film compared to, 7, 72, 100
   first-person films on, 83n5
   narcissism and, 73
Vídeo nas Aldeias group, Indigenous people and, 70
Videofilmes, 89, 90, 101, 103, 317–318
   government incentives for, 102
A vingança dos doze (film), 286
Violão da rua (imprint), 99
violence, 53
   aesthetic of, 41–42, 91
   camera as, 70–71
   of representation, 121–122
   on television, 164
Virgínio, João, 77
Virgínio, José, 342–343, 347
Virno, Paolo, 155, 159, 172, 173–174
visual language, censorship and, 141
vococentric sound, 199, 205–206
voice, 218nn15–16
   abstraction relation to, 39
   aesthetic of, 1, 210
   authorship and, 197–198, 200
   in *Boca de lixo*, 318
   body relation to, 211, 214–215
   in "cinema of conversation," 21
   in communication, 216n4
   corporeality of, 108n20
   in documentary, 1–3
   identity in, 199
   in interviews, 8
   listening relation to, 3, 4, 7–8
   popular, 94, 97
   scripts relation to, 11
   in *Seis dias de Ouricuri*, 5
The Voice in Cinema (Chion), 199
"The Voice of Documentary" (Nichols), 2
voice-of-God narration
   in *Cabra marcado para morrer*, 10
   in *Seis dias de Ouricuri*, 19–20, 138
voice-over, 317
   in *Cabra marcado para morrer*, 37, 47, 49, 201–202, 203–204
   in *Deus e o diabo na terra do sol*, 42
   in *O fim e o princípio*, 48
   in *O fio da memória*, 99
   in *Peões*, 23
   in *Santo forte*, 108n20
   in *Seis dias de Ouricuri*, 143
   as social critique, 137, 138
   in *Theodorico, o imperador do sertão*, 145–146, 147
Volta redonda—Memorial da Greve (documentary), 28–29

Waiting for Godot (play), 178
Warburg, Aby, 128
Wayne, Mike, 91
Weber, Samuel, 193n2
Wells, Sarah, 257–258
westerns, 297
White, Eric Charles, 268
Wild Strawberries (film), 308, 311, 312
Winston, Brian, 59n15
women
   in *Jogo de cena*, 116–117, 194n4
   objectification of, 162, 163, 166
Words (documentary). See *Últimas conversas*
work-to-rule strike, 174
Workers' Party (Partido dos Trabalhadores) (PT), 9
working class, intellectuals relation to, 149n1

written word, 285–286
Wyler, William, 297

Xavier, Ismail, 184, 281n4, 348
　on camera effect, 265
　on interviews, 253

You Ain't Seen Nothin' Yet (film), 361
YouTube, 103

Zélia, 78
Zivin, Erin Graff, 60n27
Zumbi dos Palmares, 329

www.ingramcontent.com/pod-product-compliance
Lightning Source LLC
Chambersburg PA
CBHW031412230426
43668CB00007B/290